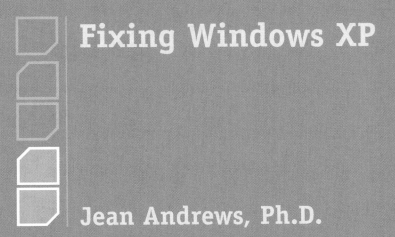

Fixing Windows XP

Jean Andrews, Ph.D.

THOMSON

COURSE TECHNOLOGY

Australia • Canada • Mexico • Singapore • Spain • United Kingdom • United States

Fixing Windows XP is published by Thomson Course Technology.

Executive Editor:
Steve Helba

Acquisitions Editor:
Nick Lombardi

Senior Product Manager:
Michelle Ruelos Cannistraci

Developmental Editor:
John Bosco

Marketing Manager:
Guy Baskaran

Editorial Assistant:
Jessica Reed

Manufacturing Coordinator:
Justin Palmeiro

Content Project Manager:
Kelly Robinson

Quality Assurance:
Serge Palladino, Christian Kunciw

Copy Editor:
Chris Smith

Proofreader:
Harry Johnson

Indexer:
Rich Carlson

Internal Design:
Betsy Young

Compositor:
Integra, Inc.

Brief Contents

Table of Contents

Introduction

Fixing Windows XP was written to help make your life easier and more fun! Like it or not, in our present society we're all, to one degree or another, dependent on computers. And life has enough frustrations without a broken computer being one of them. After having studied this book, think how wonderful life can be the next time you're faced with a broken computer and you can confidently say, "Hey, I know what caused that problem, and I know how to fix it!" Well, that's the goal of this book—to put that power in your hands. I've written this book for those computer users who want to take charge of their own computer problems. Consider this book your ultimate take-charge tool!

When I first came up with the idea for this book, I made several trips to the shelves of computer bookstores to compare the idea to what was already written. Browsing through the offerings, I found books at two extremes. There were books written on how to use Windows XP and books written for Windows XP support technicians and developers. However, I didn't find a single book that hit in between these two extremes of expertise and lack thereof. This book targets the reader in the middle: You're beyond the how-to-use-the-OS level, and yet not really interested in the extremely technical intricacies of the OS. You just want to know how to fix the darn thing when it breaks! Well, you found your book! This book expects you to know how to use Windows XP, but doesn't assume any technical expertise beyond that. And, yes, using this book, you *will* learn how to fix the darn thing when it breaks.

FEATURES

To make the book function well for the individual reader as well as in the classroom, you'll find these features:

- ◢ **Learning Objectives and Focus Problems:** Every chapter opens with a list of learning objectives and a Focus Problem that set the stage for the goals and content of the chapter.
- ◢ **Step-by-Step Instructions:** Detailed information on installation, maintenance, optimizing system performance, and troubleshooting are included throughout the book.
- ◢ **Art Program:** A wide array of photos, drawings, and screen shots support the text, displaying in detail the exact hardware and software features you will need to understand, fix, and maintain Windows XP.

- ◢ **Notes:** Note icons highlight additional helpful information related to the subject being discussed.

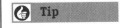

- ◢ **Caution Icons:** These icons highlight critical safety information. Follow these instructions carefully to protect the PC and its data and also for your own safety.
- ◢ **Tip Icons:** These icons highlight additional insights and tips to remember.

▲ **End-of-Chapter Material:** Each chapter closes with the following features, which reinforce the material covered in the chapter and provide real-world, hands-on testing of the chapter's skill set.

- **Chapter Summary:** This bulleted list of concise statements summarizes all the major points of the chapter.

- **Key Terms:** The new, important terms introduced in the chapter are defined at the end of the chapter. The definitions of all terms are also included at the end of the book in a full-length glossary.

- **Reviewing the Basics:** A comprehensive set of review questions at the end of each chapter check your understanding of fundamental concepts.

- **Thinking Critically:** These sections present you with scenarios that require you to use both real-world common sense and the concepts you've learned in the chapter to solve problems or answer questions.

- **Hands-On Projects:** Several in-depth, hands-on projects are included at the end of each chapter, designed to ensure that you not only understand the material, but can apply what you've learned.

- **Real Problems, Real Solutions:** These projects give you valuable practice in applying the knowledge you've gained in the chapter to real-world situations, often using your own computer or one belonging to someone you know.

INSTRUCTOR RESOURCES

The following supplemental materials are available when this book is used in a classroom setting. All of the supplements available with this book are provided to the instructor on a single CD-ROM.

Electronic Instructor's Manual: The Instructor's Manual that accompanies this textbook includes additional instructional material to assist in class preparation, including suggestions for classroom activities, discussion topics, and additional projects.

Solutions: Answers to all end-of-chapter material, including the Review Questions, and where applicable, Hands-On Projects, are provided

ExamView®: This textbook is accompanied by ExamView, a powerful testing software package that allows instructors to create and administer printed, computer (LAN-based), and Internet exams. ExamView includes hundreds of questions that correspond to the topics covered in this text, enabling students to generate detailed study guides that include page references for further review. The computer-based and Internet testing components allow students to take exams at their computers, and also save the instructor time by grading each exam automatically.

PowerPoint® presentations: This book comes with Microsoft PowerPoint slides for each chapter. These are included as a teaching aid for classroom presentation, to make available to students on the network, for chapter review, or to be printed for classroom distribution. Instructors, please feel at liberty to add your own slides for additional topics you introduce to the class.

Figure files: All of the figures in the book are reproduced on the Instructor Resources CD, in bit-mapped format. Similar to the PowerPoint presentations, these are included as a teaching aid for classroom presentation, to make available to students for review, or to be printed for classroom distribution.

ORGANIZATION

This book is organized to address the most common Windows XP Professional and Windows XP Home Edition problems. I call them Focus Problems, and you'll see them mentioned at the beginning of each chapter that tackles each problem. Here are the Focus Problems and the chapters that show you exactly what to do to solve each problem.

> **⅜ Focus Problem**
>
> "My Windows XP system is really slow and I need a quick fix!"

- ◢ Chapter 1: "My Windows XP system is really slow and I need a quick fix!"
- ◢ Chapter 2: "My Windows XP startup is sluggish and gives me strange error messages."
- ◢ Chapter 3: "I'm under attack! Nasty software has attacked my system. How do I clean up the mess?"
- ◢ Chapter 4: "I need better security for my Windows XP computer or small network."
- ◢ Chapter 5: "I need to connect to a wireless or wired network. I want to set up my own network."
- ◢ Chapter 6: "My applications or devices give errors, won't work, won't install, or won't uninstall."
- ◢ Chapter 7: "Windows won't start up! I have data in there somewhere!"
- ◢ Chapter 8: "I think I might need to upgrade my computer."

In the chapters, I've tried to stick to the bottom-line information of how to fix the problem at hand. But if you'd really like to know a bit more of what happens under the hood, check out Appendix D, "How Windows XP Works."

ACKNOWLEDGMENTS

When the idea for this book was being kicked around at Thomson Learning, Steve Helba, the Executive Editor, said this to me that made my heart jump with joy: "I want this book to be Jean Andrews unleashed! Write like you want to write, use as many pages as you want to use, and have fun with it!" Well, Steve, I did just that! Thank you! And, yes, it *was* fun.

Many thanks to Kelly Robinson, Nick Lombardi, Michelle Ruelos Cannistraci, and Steve Helba at Thomson Learning. Thank you, John Bosco, the Developmental Editor, for your careful attention to every detail of the book. To you goes the credit of the idea of organizing the book around the top eight Windows XP problems. Thank you, Chris Smith, our excellent copy editor who lowered her shields a bit in the name of author style. And thank you, Serge Palladino, for checking and rechecking each technical detail of the book. And thank you, Wally Beck of Gainesville College, who came up with some super ideas about the book's organization and content. The following reviewers all provided invaluable insights and showed a genuine interest in the book's success: Thank you to Todd Verge, Nova Scotia Community College; Don Stroup, Ivy Tech Community College; Gus Chang, Heald College; and Paul Bartoszewicz, K-Bar Computer Consulting. Thank you to Joy Dark who was here with me making this book happen. I'm very grateful.

This book is dedicated to the covenant of God with man on earth.

- Jean Andrews, Ph.D.

WANT TO WRITE THE AUTHOR?

If you'd like to give any feedback about the book or suggest what might be included in future books, please feel free to email Jean Andrews at jean.andrews@buystory.com.

PHOTO CREDITS

Unless otherwise stated in the photo credits table, all photographs were made by my daughter, Joy Dark.

PHOTO CREDITS TABLE

Figure	Caption	Request
4-22	This Quantum Travan 40 tape drive holds up to 40 GB of data. It comes with backup software, data cartridge, USB 2.0 cable, power supply, power cord, and documentation.	Courtesy of Quantum Corp.
4-23	This external DVD drive by Plextor can use a FireWire or Hi-Speed USB connection and supports several speeds and read/write standards, including 4X DVD+R, 2.4X DVD+R/RW, 12X DVD-ROM, 16X CD-R write, 10X CD-RW rewrite, and 40X CD read	Courtesy of Plextor Corp.
4-24	This Crossfire external hard drive holds 160 GB and uses a FireWire or High Speed USB connection	Courtesy of SmartDisk Corporation
5-69	This wireless access point by D-Link supports 802.11b/g	Courtesy of D-Link Corporation
6-2	A diagnostic card displays BIOS error codes at startup	Courtesy of Microsystems Development, www.postcodemaster.com
8-11	This FireWire adapter card provides two FireWire 800 ports and one FireWire 400 port and uses a PCI expansion slot	Courtesy of ADS Technology
8-12	Use this USB device to watch TV on your desktop or notebook computer and capture video and stills (WinTV-USB from Hauppauge)	Courtesy of Hauppauge Computer Works, Inc.
8-13	The AVerTV video capture and TV tuner card by AVerMedia uses a PCI slot and works alongside a regular video card	Courtesy of AVerMedia Technologies, Inc. USA
8-24a	2.66" 200-pin SO-DIMM contains DDR2 SDRAM	Courtesy of Kingston Technology Company
8-24b	2.66" 200-pin SO-DIMM contains DDR SDRAM	Courtesy of Crucial Technology
8-24c	2.66" 144-pin SO-DIMM contains SDRAM. One notch is slightly offset from the center of the module.	Courtesy of Crucial Technology
8-24d	160-pin SO-RIMM contains Rambus memory and has two notches	Courtesy of High Connection Density, Inc.

Windows XP Quick Fixes

Personal computers using the Windows operating system have become just about the most valuable tools on our desktops today, making our work easier and more efficient, giving us a way to stay in touch with friends and family around the world, providing fun and games, and creating easy access to global information. It's great! But when things go wrong, many times the results are frustration, insane attempts at fixing the problem, and just plain helplessness. If you've ever experienced this frustration, then this book is for you.

In the book, I'm assuming that you're a knowledgeable Windows XP user, able to install and use applications, and that you're comfortable with common Windows tools such as Windows Explorer. I'm also assuming that you're new to Windows troubleshooting. And finally, I'm assuming you plan to use these skills not only to fix your own Windows XP problems, but also to help users other than yourself. Based on this last assumption, where it's appropriate, I've given some suggestions on how to relate to users and especially how to protect their data as you work.

One of the most common Windows XP problems creeps up on us over time as we install and uninstall software and use our computers for all sorts of things—Windows just gets tired and slow. Most often, this problem is caused by poor maintenance. You'll learn how to make Windows young again using some simple and easy-to-use Windows XP tools. Next, you'll learn how to *keep* it young using some necessary routine maintenance tasks. I consider the fixes in this chapter to be Windows XP quick fixes. If the problem is complex, we apply a patch so we can move on. For example, if a device or program is giving problems, we're going to just disable it. In later chapters, we'll deal with how to fix underlying problems.

But that's just the beginning. Next, you'll learn how to approach a Windows problem, how to set your priorities, and how to plan your fix. In remaining chapters, we'll dig deeper into more complex problems with more complex solutions. By the end of this book, you can be a technically savvy Windows XP fixer-upper, confident and capable of dealing with the nastiest Windows XP problems.

⊰⊱ Focus Problem

"My Windows XP system is really slow and I need a quick fix!"

HOW TO MAKE WINDOWS YOUNG AGAIN

When you first purchased that new computer, Windows XP loaded quickly, software installed with no errors, and the system worked like a breeze. But now, after a few months or even years, you've noticed startup is slow and gives funny error messages or boxes pop up out of nowhere. Then, when you're using your system, it just doesn't seem as fast as it once was and strange things often happen that you can't explain. Most people don't take the time to do the routine and necessary maintenance tasks on their systems that would keep them in top-notch condition, so one of the most common Windows XP complaints you'll hear is, "My Windows XP system is just slow and sluggish. I'd love to see it working as fast as the day I bought it."

The problem of a slow and sluggish Windows XP system is pretty open-ended and probably has more than one cause. Most likely, to solve the problem, you'll find yourself doing a lot of different things that, together, take you to a clean and young Windows system. In other words, there's no magic bullet, but rather many little things for you to do. A Windows system can be slow and sluggish because of these reasons:

▲ Too many applications are running in the foreground or background. A program running in the background is called a service. Windows provides many services, and services can also be installed when you install an application, a device driver, utility software, or a virus. A device driver is software that tells the OS exactly how to communicate with a hardware device.

▲ Device drivers might be corrupted or outdated or the hardware device might have gone bad. Both problems can slow down performance.

▲ Viruses, adware, worms, and other malicious software might be pulling the system down.

▲ The hard drive does not have enough free space to work. Windows needs a certain amount of free hard drive space to use for temporary files. Microsoft says you need at least 318 MB of free hard drive space for normal operations, 15 percent free space to defrag the drive, and 1.8 GB of free space to install Windows XP Service Pack 2. That's a lot of free space!

▲ The hard drive might be fragmented, which can slow down Windows performance.

▲ You might not have enough available RAM or your memory settings might not be correct. A heavily used Windows XP computer probably needs as much as 512 MB of RAM.

▲ In general, the system might not be robust enough to handle Windows XP. Microsoft recommends you have at least a Pentium II 300 MHz and 128 MB RAM. But experience says you need much more power than this for XP not to bog down.

✎ Notes

Appendix D, How Windows Works, is for the reader who really wants to understand this stuff. But it's relegated to the end of the book to keep it politely out of the way of those readers who don't have the time or patience for more in-depth study—they just want the bottom-line fix and they want it *now*. So if you're the type of reader who really wants the inside scoop on how Windows works, check out Appendix D. You'll find a very interesting discussion on how Windows uses a service or device driver, both key terms mentioned in this section.

To begin solving the problem of a slow and sluggish system, you need to examine the system just to get a lay of the land and decide what to do first.

DO A QUICK PHYSICAL

Ever run into the emergency room with a bad cut and a bloody towel in your hand? The problem and its fix might be obvious to you, but something will happen first in that emergency room before anyone fixes your bleeding cut. You'll get a quick physical. Nothing fancy, but enough so that your general physical condition is established before the real work begins.

It's the same with PC problems. Don't jump in with your fix until you give that PC a quick physical. The idea is that you need to know about the PC's general health so you can be ready for any potential gotchas just around the corner as you work. Based on your quick examination of the system, you might decide to change the order in which you would do something so that you can address the most pressing problem first. You also need to know about any serious underlying problems that might mean additional, more intensive solutions are necessary.

Here are the things to do to examine the system so you can get a general idea of what's going on:

- ◢ *Get a pad and pen.* You'll need it to take notes as you go.
- ◢ *Begin with a hard boot.* Several users who didn't log off and left applications open might be the cause of a sluggish system. A reboot cleans up the mess. Notice the time the boot takes from the time you press the power-on button until the Windows desktop is fully loaded and the hourglass on the mouse pointer stops. If you want to get serious about this, use a stopwatch and note the seconds required for startup. Also write down any error messages you see and anything else that looks abnormal.
- ◢ *Did you receive hardware errors during the boot?* If you did receive an error message and the device is essential, you might have to solve the hardware problem before you can deal with the Windows XP problem. However, if the device is nonessential, go into Device Manager and disable it for now. Get Windows in good shape, and then you can return to Device Manager to deal with the hardware problem. To disable a device using Device Manager, click **Start**, click **Run**, type **devmgmt.msc** in the Run dialog box, and press **Enter**. Yes, I know there are other ways to get to Device Manager, but typing the command is faster if you memorize it. Right-click the device and click **Disable** from the shortcut menu (see Figure 1-1).
- ◢ *What processor and RAM are installed?* You can quickly get this information from the System Information window or System Properties window. For System Properties, right-click **My Computer** and select **Properties** from the shortcut menu. For example, for the system in Figure 1-2, a 1.5 GHz Pentium 4 processor is installed with 256 MB of RAM. Not exactly a screaming system, but for normal Windows XP use, it should do.
- ◢ *What Windows XP service packs are installed?* On the screen shown in Figure 1-2, you can see that Service Pack 1 is installed. Microsoft has released two service packs for Windows XP. Make yourself a note that you need to download and install Service Pack 2 before you're done with this system.

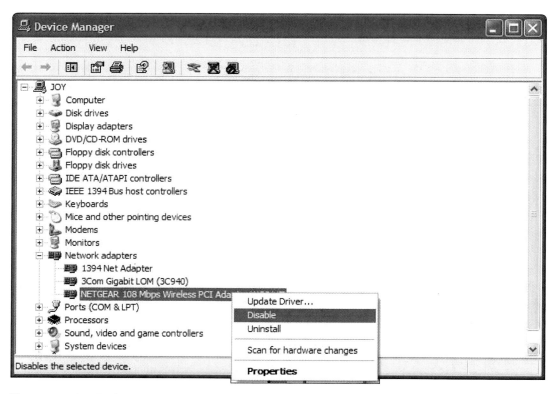

Figure 1-1 Use Device Manager to disable a device

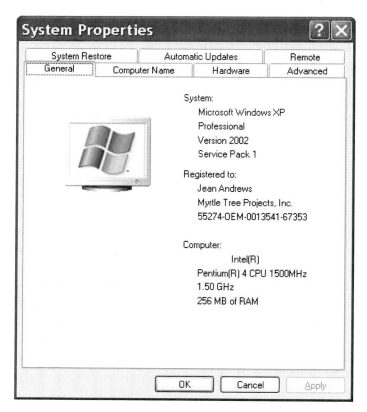

Figure 1-2 The System Properties window gives information about the hardware and currently installed OS

▲ *How is Windows Update configured?* While you have the System Properties window up, click the **Automatic Updates** tab. Note in Figure 1-3 that this system is set so that updates are not automatically installed. For sure, you'll need to manually download and install all updates on this computer, and then ask the user for permission to set updating to automatic. (The only reason you would not set updating to automatic is if the user has a slow Internet connection that is only connected when he is working on the PC, and he doesn't want to be bothered with downloading updates as he works.)

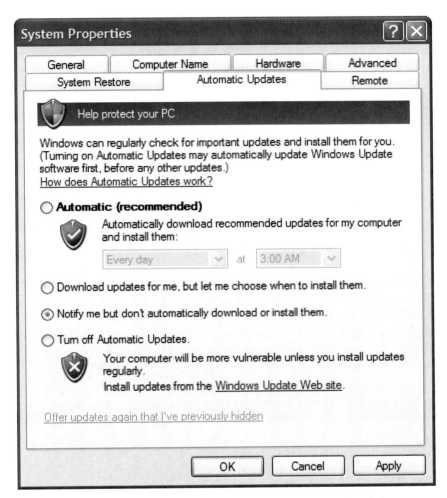

Figure 1-3   Use the Automatic Updates tab of the System Properties window to note how Windows updates are set to be installed

▲ *How much free hard drive space do you have?* Open Windows Explorer and look at the volume on which Windows is installed, most likely drive C. Look at the amount of free space on the drive. For example, free space on drive C in Figure 1-4 is only 346 MB. Yikes! No wonder the user is complaining of a slow system. Microsoft says Windows XP needs 318 MB of free hard drive space, but experience says it needs at least 1 GB of free space. As you can see in the figure, the size of the volume is only 4 GB. Are we dealing with a 4 GB hard drive or multiple partitions? To know for sure, turn to Disk Management.

▲ *What size is the hard drive?* To view the size of a hard drive and how it is partitioned, use Windows Disk Management. In Control Panel, open the Administrative Tools applet and double-click the **Computer Management** icon.

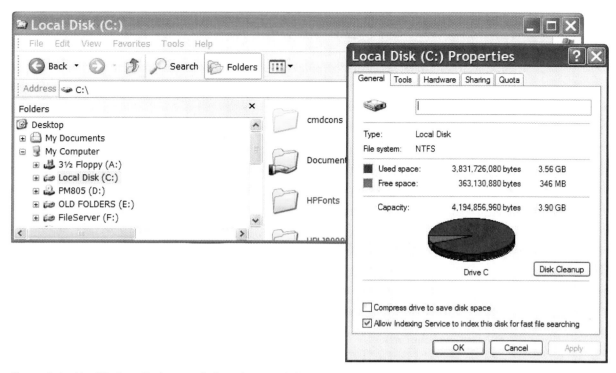

Figure 1-4   Use Windows Explorer to find out how much free space is on drive C

In the Computer Management window, click **Disk Management**. (Or you can type **diskmgmt.msc** in the Run dialog box and press **Enter**.) Figure 1-5 shows a funky arrangement for a hard drive of a system in serious need of maintenance. The hard drive has been partitioned into three volumes: C, E, and F. Windows is installed on drive C. Drives E and F are used for data and backups from another computer on the peer-to-peer network.

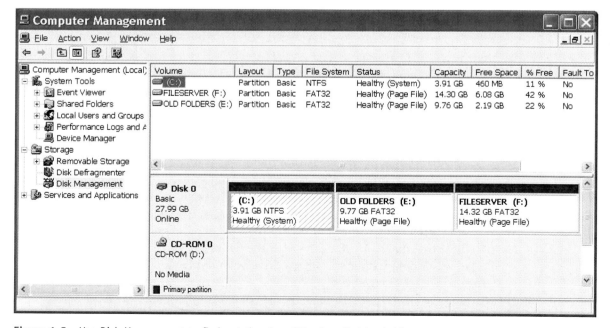

Figure 1-5   Use Disk Management to find out the size of the installed hard drive

Make a note to discuss with the user how to better partition the drive so Windows has some room to grow. However, unless you have access to Partition Magic or some similar third-party tool, to repartition means you're going to have to start over with the Windows installation. Ugh!

◢ *What's showing in the system tray?* Icons in the system tray represent some, but not all, of the background processes that are currently running. To take a look at these icons, first you need to expand the system tray because Windows XP won't normally show you everything hiding there. To do that, click the **left-pointing arrow** to the left of the system tray (see Figure 1-6). If you're not familiar with an icon you see in the system tray, use your mouse to hover over it to help identify it.

Click the left-pointing arrow to expand the system tray

Figure 1-6 Expand the system tray to see all the icons

You can also try right-clicking the icon to get a shortcut menu which might tell you about the service the icon represents. Another alternative is to double-click the icon to open a window. Take note of any icons that represent processes you might not need. For example, in Figure 1-7, the system tray is pretty full. It has an AOL Instant Messenger icon as well as one for MSN Messenger. It's possible that the user doesn't use both or is not even aware that both are taking up resources. Make a note to find out whether the user uses AOL Instant Messenger, MSN Messenger, or both. If necessary, you can remove the unused one later.

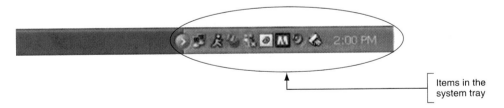

Items in the system tray

Figure 1-7 The system tray shows icons that represent running background processes

◢ *What applications are open?* Use Task Manager (Taskman.exe) to see what applications are running. To open Task Manager, right-click a blank area of the taskbar and select **Task Manager** from the shortcut menu. When the Task Manager window opens, click the **Applications** tab, if necessary. Note any applications that are open. Because you haven't opened any yourself, they had to be opened during startup. Make note of them so you can find out if the user really wants the system set this way. Opening applications at startup might mean they stay open even when the user doesn't really need or want them. In an ideal world, at this point, there should be no running applications, as shown in Figure 1-8.

Figure 1-8 The Applications tab of Task Manager shows no running applications

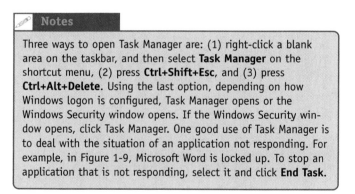

Notes

Three ways to open Task Manager are: (1) right-click a blank area on the taskbar, and then select **Task Manager** on the shortcut menu, (2) press **Ctrl+Shift+Esc**, and (3) press **Ctrl+Alt+Delete**. Using the last option, depending on how Windows logon is configured, Task Manager opens or the Windows Security window opens. If the Windows Security window opens, click Task Manager. One good use of Task Manager is to deal with the situation of an application not responding. For example, in Figure 1-9, Microsoft Word is locked up. To stop an application that is not responding, select it and click **End Task**.

◢ *What services are running?* Now we're getting down to the inside scoop of what's really happening in this system. Click the **Processes** tab. As you read Chapters 2 and 3, you'll learn a lot about what you should and should not see in this window. Especially significant are the processes running under the user's account, which indicate they're not required system processes. For example, check out the window in Figure 1-10, which has a ton of processes running under the user (Jean Andrews). Most of these are nonessential Windows processes, yet they all were launched at startup. To *really* clean up the system, you'll need to get to the bottom of these processes—what are they, how are they started, and are they needed? If they're not needed, how do you remove them? By the time you have this system running in top-notch shape, this window should show only a few processes running under the current user. However, in this chapter, we're going to take a shortcut and simply disable all

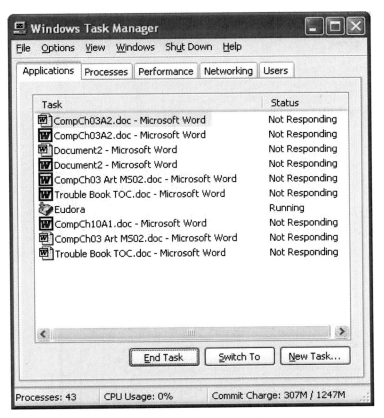

Figure 1-9 Use Task Manager to stop a program that is not responding

processes that are started when Windows is loaded and that are not part of the required Windows components. Then, in the next chapter, you'll learn to pick from the running processes the ones to keep and the ones to throw out.

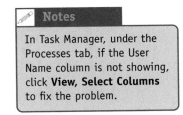

Notes

In Task Manager, under the Processes tab, if the User Name column is not showing, click **View, Select Columns** to fix the problem.

As you worked through the tasks of examining the system using System Properties, Windows Explorer, and Task Manager, you had a chance to see just how slow the system is. You also have seen which problems appear to be worse than others. As you read in the next section how to clean up Windows, you might want to change the order of things to do so that you address the worst problem first.

FIVE STEPS TO MAKING WINDOWS YOUNG AGAIN

Now that you have a general idea about what you're up against, you're ready to clean things up. Here's what to do and the order in which I would do these things for a system that needs a general cleanup and doesn't have a major problem that stands out above the rest.

1. Reduce the startup process to bare bones by running the System Configuration Utility (Msconfig.exe).

2. Clean up the hard drive, deleting unwanted files, defragmenting the hard drive, and scanning it for errors.

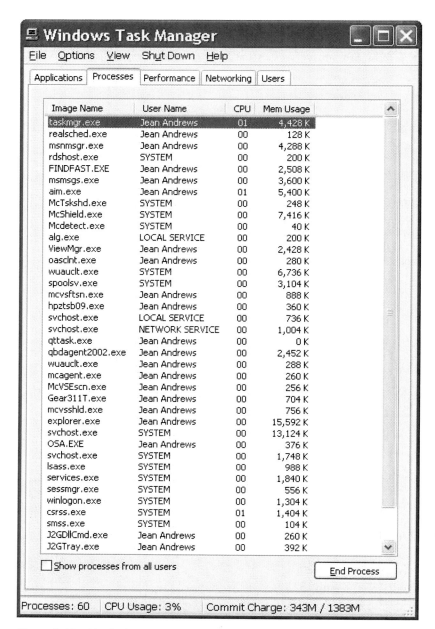

Figure 1-10 Use Task Manager to view processes running in the background

3. Use the Add or Remove Programs applet in Control Panel to uninstall any applications or utilities that are no longer needed.

4. Run antivirus software to scan the system for viruses, and run anti-adware and/or anti-spyware software.

5. Download and install Windows XP updates, patches, and service packs.

Now let's look at how to do all this in detail. If you run into errors as you work, know that the next chapters cover how to handle more drastic Windows XP problems and errors other than a slow and sluggish system.

REDUCE STARTUP TO ESSENTIALS

In the next chapter, you'll learn about the many different ways programs and services can get launched at startup. You'll also learn how to figure out how these processes got set up to launch in the first place and how to remove the ones you don't want at this root level. But for now, we're going to take a quick-and-dirty approach and just stop them all! The tool we'll use is the System Configuration Utility, more commonly called Msconfig after the program name, Msconfig.exe. Msconfig works in a similar way to Windows Safe Mode; it reduces the startup process to essentials, but it's not intended to be a permanent solution to a problem. The idea is to use it to stop all nonessential processes and services from launching at startup. If the problem goes away, then you can add them back one at a time until the problem reappears. It's a great Windows troubleshooting tool, but should not be considered a permanent solution to a problem.

Here's how to use Msconfig:

1. To launch Msconfig, type **msconfig** in the Run dialog box and press **Enter**. The System Configuration Utility window opens. Click the **Startup** tab, as shown in Figure 1-11.

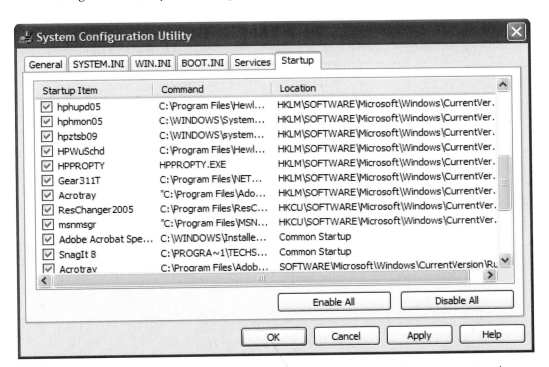

Figure 1-11 Use the System Configuration Utility (Msconfig) to temporarily disable a startup task

2. To disable all nonessential startup tasks, click **Disable All**.

3. Now click the **Services** tab (see Figure 1-12). Notice that this tab also has a Disable All button. If you use that button, you'll disable all nonessential Windows services as well as third-party services such as virus scan programs. Use it only for the most difficult Windows problems, because you'll disable some services that you might really want, such as Windows Task Scheduler, Print Spooler, Automatic Updates, and the System Restore Service.

4. To view only those services put there by third-party software, check **Hide All Microsoft Services**. If you have antivirus software running in the background (and

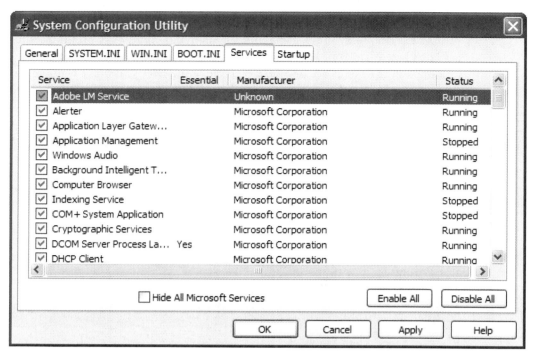

Figure 1-12   View and control services launched at startup

you should), you'll see that listed as well as any service launched at startup and put there by installed software. Uncheck all services that you don't recognize or know you don't want. Later, you'll need to investigate each service you don't recognize to decide if you really need it or not.

5. Click **Apply** to apply your changes. Now click the **General** tab and you should see Selective Startup selected, as shown in Figure 1-13. Msconfig is now set to control

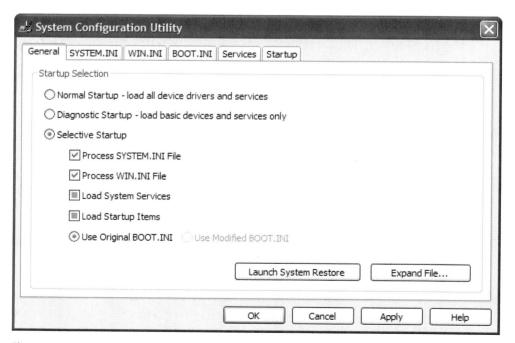

Figure 1-13   Msconfig is set to control the Windows startup process

the startup process. If you suspect some legacy devices or services are controlled using the legacy System.ini or Win.ini files, you also need to uncheck these items and click Apply. Click **Close** to close the Msconfig window.

6. After you apply a fix, reboot before you complicate matters with fixes on top of fixes. So let's reboot and observe what happens.

7. When Windows starts up, you'll see the window in Figure 1-14 that says Msconfig has controlled the startup process. Remember, using Msconfig is only recommended as a temporary fix, and this window reminds us of that.

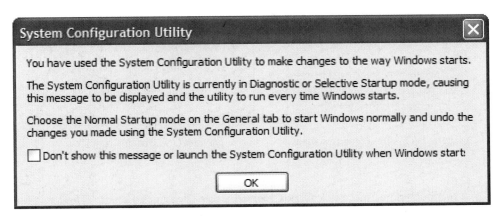

Figure 1-14 The System Configuration Utility informs you it is controlling the startup process

Watch for error messages during the boot that indicate we've created a problem with our fix! After the boot, if you can no longer use that nifty little utility that came with your digital camera, you need to find out which service or program you stopped that you need for that utility. Go back to the Msconfig tool and enable that one service and reboot. In the next chapter, you'll learn all about the Windows startup programs and services, and how to research services and programs you don't recognize and permanently remove the ones you don't want. At that point, you will no longer need Msconfig and can return it to normal startup mode.

CLEAN UP THE HARD DRIVE

The next step in cleaning up a slow and sluggish system is to clean up the hard drive. To do that, we'll use three Windows XP maintenance tools for hard drives to delete temporary files, defrag the drive, and scan it for errors.

Disk Cleanup

Temporary or unneeded files accumulate on a hard drive for a variety of reasons. For instance, an installation program might not clean up after itself after it finishes installing an application, and cached Web pages can take up a lot of disk space if you don't have the Internet settings correct. In addition, don't forget about the Recycle Bin; deleted files sit there taking up space until you empty the Recycle Bin.

Microsoft says that Windows XP needs at least 318 MB of free hard drive space for normal operation, and the Defrag utility needs at least 15 percent of the hard drive to be free before it can completely defrag a drive. So it's important to occasionally delete unneeded files. Disk Cleanup is a convenient way to delete temporary files on a hard drive. To access Disk Cleanup, right-click the drive in Windows Explorer, and select **Properties** from the shortcut menu. The Disk Properties window appears, as shown in Figure 1-15.

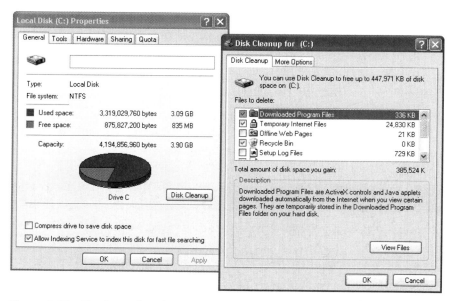

Figure 1-15 The Properties window for a drive provides Disk Cleanup, a quick and easy way to delete temporary files on a hard drive

On the General tab, click **Disk Cleanup**. Disk Cleanup calculates how much space can be freed and then displays the Disk Cleanup window, also shown in Figure 1-15. From this window, you can select nonessential files to delete in order to save drive space.

Windows Disk Defragmenter and Defrag

Another problem that might slow down your hard drive is fragmentation. Fragmentation happens over time as Windows writes files, deletes files, and writes new files to your drive. Files end up in fragmented segments all over the drive. Then, when Windows reads a fragmented file, the drive must work hard to move its read-write head all over the drive to retrieve the file. Also, if a file becomes corrupted, data recovery utilities are less likely to be able to find all the pieces to the file if the file is fragmented rather than written on the drive in one location. For these reasons, you should defragment your hard drive at a minimum of every six months, and ideally every month, as part of a good maintenance plan.

Depending on how fragmented the drive and how large the drive, defragging it can take less than an hour to all night. Therefore, it's best to start the defrag utility when you aren't going to be using your PC for a while. Close all open applications and then launch the Windows XP defragmenter using one of these methods:

▲ Click **Start**, point to **All Programs**, point to **Accessories**, and then point to **System Tools**. Click **Disk Defragmenter**. From the Disk Defragmenter window (see Figure 1-16), you can select a drive and defragment it.

▲ To use the Defrag command (**Defrag.exe**) at a command prompt, enter **defrag X:**, where X: is the drive you want to defrag. If you enter the command in a command prompt window, the window looks like the one in Figure 1-17, which shows an analysis before and after defragmenting.

Generally, defragmenting a hard drive should be done when the hard drive is healthy; that is, it should be done as part of routine maintenance. If you get an error message when attempting to defrag, try the utilities discussed next to repair the hard drive and then try to defrag again.

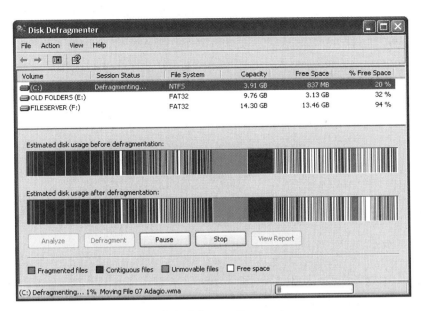

Figure 1-16 Windows XP as it is defragmenting a volume

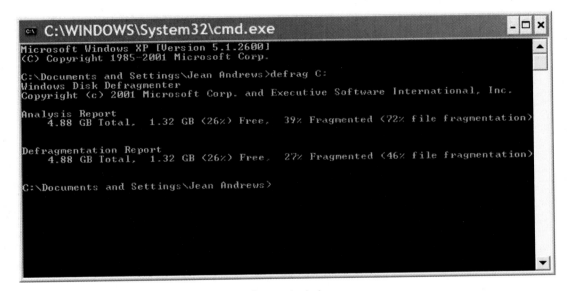

Figure 1-17 Windows XP defrag in a command prompt window

Windows XP Error Checking and Chkdsk

Next, to make sure the drive is healthy, you need to search for and repair file system errors, using the Windows Chkdsk utility. Using Windows Explorer, Chkdsk is called Error Checking. As with defragging, error checking and repair can take a long time depending on the size of the drive and how many files are present. To launch the utility, use one of two methods:

▲ Using Explorer or My Computer, right-click the drive, and select **Properties** from the shortcut menu. Click the **Tools** tab, as shown in Figure 1-18, and then click **Check Now**. The Check Disk dialog box appears, also shown in Figure 1-18. Check the **Automatically fix file system errors** and **Scan for and attempt recovery of bad sectors** check boxes, and then click **Start**. For the utility to correct errors on the drive, it needs exclusive use of all files on the drive, which Windows calls a locked drive. If files are open, a dialog box appears telling you about the problem and asking your permission to scan the drive the next time Windows starts. Reboot the system and let her rip.

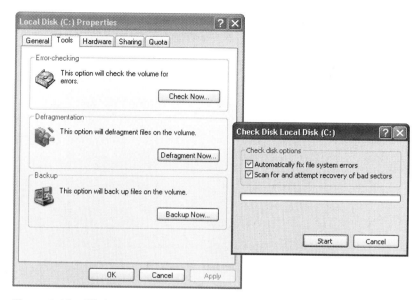

Figure 1-18   Windows XP repairs hard drive errors under the drive's Properties window using Windows Explorer

▲ At a command prompt, to use Chkdsk to check for and fix file system errors and to search out bad sectors and recover the data from them if possible, enter this command:

```
chkdsk c:/r
```

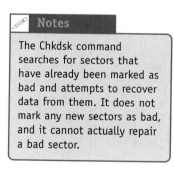

Notes

The Chkdsk command searches for sectors that have already been marked as bad and attempts to recover data from them. It does not mark any new sectors as bad, and it cannot actually repair a bad sector.

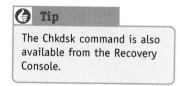

Tip

The Chkdsk command is also available from the Recovery Console.

Before you move on to the next step in cleaning up an old and tired Windows XP installation, reboot the system and verify all is well. If the drive was heavily fragmented with errors and unneeded files, you should now see a marked improvement in performance.

Free Up Additional Hard Drive Space

Use Windows Explorer to find out how much free space is on the drive. If you still don't have the minimum required, move on to the next section where you'll look for and remove any unwanted software. If removing software doesn't free up enough space, you can consider the following to get some additional space:

▲ Move some data to other drives or devices. Most of us enjoy our digital cameras and we tend to keep a lot of photos on a hard drive. Gather them all up and burn them to a couple of CDs.
▲ If a volume is formatted using the NTFS file system, you can compress folders on the drive to save space. Right-click the folder and click **Properties** from the shortcut menu. Click **Advanced** and then click **Compress contents to save disk space,** as shown in Figure 1-19. Click **OK.**

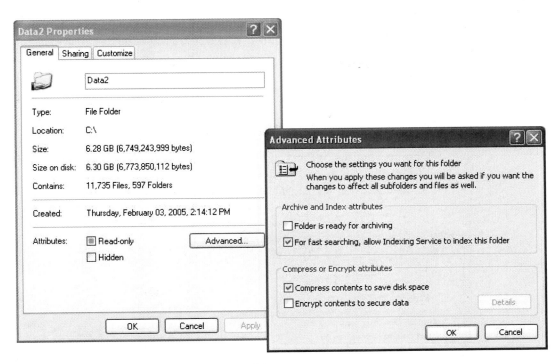

Figure 1-19 Compress folders or files to save disk space

▲ Consider installing a second hard drive to be used for the data and applications software. How to install a second hard drive is covered in Chapter 8.

▲ Does the drive have more than one partition? If so, you can move some data or applications to another partition. To move applications from one partition or hard drive to another, you'll first have to uninstall the application. Most applications install their program files in the C:\Program Files folder, but during installation, they suggest this location and give you the opportunity to change it. You can then point to a different drive or partition in the system to hold the application.

▲ If the Windows partition is too small and the hard drive has the additional space, you can enlarge the Windows partition. There are two ways to accomplish this. The first method is to completely repartition the hard drive. You'll lose everything written on the drive and you'll have to install the OS and all software again. The second method is to use third-party software to resize the partitions on the drive. If you decide to use this method, use reliable software such as Partition Magic by Symantec (*www.symantec.com*) or Partition Manager by Acronis (*www.acronis.com*). Using one of these products, you can resize your partitions without disturbing Windows, data, or applications installed on the drive.

▲ Windows uses a file, Pagefile.sys, in the same way it uses memory. This file is called virtual memory and is used to enhance the amount of RAM in a system. Normally, the file

> **Notes**
>
> If your hard drive partition is formatted using the FAT32 file system, you can convert the partition to NTFS. For large drives, NTFS is more efficient and converting might improve performance. NTFS also offers better security and file and folder compression. For two Microsoft Knowledge Base articles on converting from FAT to NTFS, go to *support.Microsoft.com* and search on articles 314097 and 156560.

is a hidden file stored in the root directory of drive C. To save space on drive C, you can move Pagefile.sys to another partition on the same hard drive or to a different hard drive. Don't move it to a different hard drive unless you know the other hard drive is at least as fast as this drive. (How to make that determination is covered in Chapter 8.) Also, make sure the new volume has plenty of free space to hold the file—at least three times the amount of installed RAM. To change the location of Pagefile.sys, right-click **My Computer** and click **Properties**. On the System Properties window, click the **Advanced** tab, and then, under the Performance group, click **Settings**. The Performance Options window opens. Click the **Advanced** tab (see Figure 1-20). Click **Change**. The Virtual Memory window opens. From the list of drives showing in the window, select the new location for Pagefile.sys and click **OK**. Close all windows.

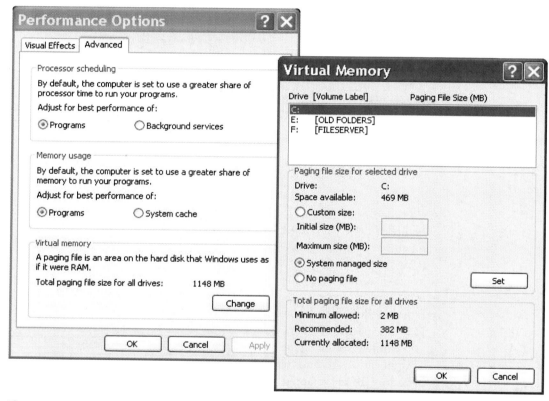

Figure 1-20   Move the virtual memory file to a new drive or volume

Here are some things you can do to save space on your primary Windows partition that is normally used by Internet Explorer:

▲ To reduce the amount of space Internet Explorer is allowed to use to cache files: In Internet Explorer, click **Tools, Internet Options**. The Internet Options window opens (see Figure 1-21). On the General tab, click **Settings**. In the Settings dialog box, change the amount of disk space to use. You can reduce the size to as low as 50 MB.

▲ If you have some room on a second partition, you can move the Internet Explorer cache folder to that partition. Normally, this folder is C:\Documents and Settings*username*\Local Settings\Temporary Internet Files. To move it somewhere else, on the General tab of the Internet Options window, click **Settings**. In the Settings dialog box, click **Move Folder**.

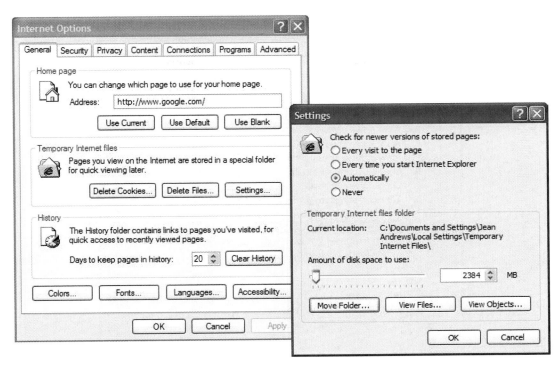

Figure 1-21   Use the Internet Options window to move the IE cache folder

◢ You can also set IE so the cache folder is emptied each time you close the browser. To do that, on the Internet Options window, click the **Advanced** tab (see Figure 1-22). Scroll down to the Security section, check **Empty Temporary Internet Files folder when browser is closed** and click **Apply**. This setting is also good to use when you're using a public computer and want to make sure you don't leave tracks about your private surfing habits.

REMOVE UNWANTED SOFTWARE

The next step in our quick-fix list of making Windows young again is to uninstall any unwanted software. To do that, open Control Panel, and then open the Add or Remove Programs applet. In Figure 1-23, notice the far-right column where you can see how much hard drive space the application is taking up. Also, consider that at startup an application might start a service or program that is taking up system resources.

For example, look at the Kodak EasyShare software in Figure 1-23. My daughter installed that on my PC when she was visiting and wanted to download her photos to my PC. It's responsible for several startup services on my system, takes up 42 MB of hard drive space, and I never use it! It's gotta go! You'll find similar situations on most PCs that have been used for a while.

If you see software listed that you don't recognize, enter the title in a Google search. Don't remove software unless you know you won't need it later.

To remove the software, click **Remove** and follow the directions onscreen. During the uninstall process, a message might appear in the Remove Shared File dialog box asking permission to delete a shared file, which is a file usually kept in the \Windows\system32 folder that is used by more than one application. Don't allow Windows to delete the file if another application is using it. If you choose not to delete a shared file, click **No** in the Remove Shared File dialog box.

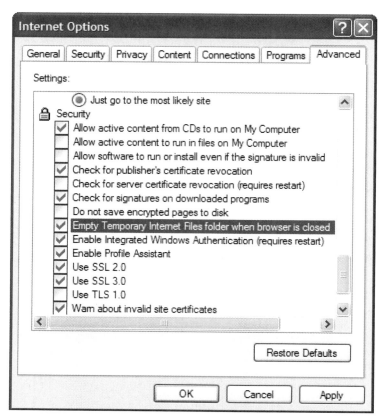

Figure 1-22 Set Internet Explorer not to keep a cache after the browser is closed

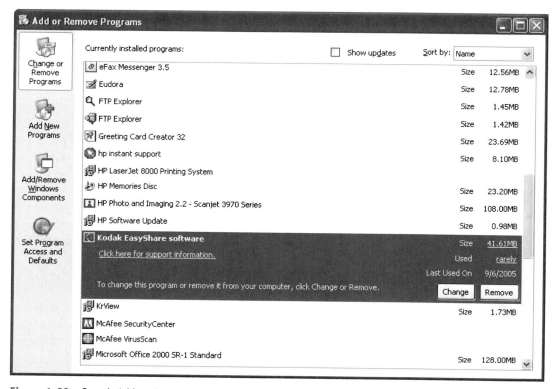

Figure 1-23 Search Add or Remove Programs list for software you can remove

Well-behaved software like Kodak EasyShare will uninstall with no problems, but this is not always the case with many shareware and freeware applications and utilities. In fact, it's my opinion that many software producers purposely make their uninstall routines buggy so you have to keep the darn things. Also, when you attempt to remove stubborn software, it can do strange things to your system such as pulling down your Windows Firewall. If an application or utility refuses to uninstall or gives errors when uninstalling, you might have to manually delete the program files and edit the registry to remove entries pertaining to the program. (I know you're probably tired of hearing me say something will be covered in later chapters, but we can't do *everything* in Chapter 1.) Removing buggy software is covered in Chapter 2.

Something else you can do to speed up Windows is to uninstall device drivers you no longer use and update older device drivers with newer versions. To uninstall a device you no longer need, open **Device Manager**, right-click the device, and select **Uninstall** from the shortcut menu. How to update device drivers is covered in Chapter 6.

SCAN THE SYSTEM FOR VIRUSES, ADWARE, AND SPYWARE

The next step in cleaning up a system is to scan it for viruses, adware, and spyware. First scan for viruses, and then scan for adware and spyware.

Scan the System for Viruses

For a list of antivirus software products recommended by Microsoft, go to the link *www.microsoft.com/security/partners/antivirus.asp*. Table 1-1 lists a few of these products.

Antivirus Software	Web Site
AVG Anti-Virus by Grisoft	*www.grisoft.com*
F-Secure Antivirus by F-Secure Corp.	*www.f-secure.com*
eSafe by Aladdin Knowledge Systems, Ltd.	*www.esafe.com*
F-Prot by FRISK Software International	*www.f-prot.com*
McAfee VirusScan by McAfee Associates, Inc.	*www.mcafee.com*
NeaTSuite by Trend Micro (for networks)	*www.trendmicro.com*
Norman by Norman Data Defense Systems, Inc. (complicated to use, but highly effective)	*www.norman.com*
Norton AntiVirus by Symantec, Inc.	*www.symantec.com*
PC-cillin by Trend Micro (for home use)	*www.trendmicro.com*

Table 1-1   Antivirus software and information

Here's how to use antivirus software:

1. If you already have antivirus software installed, connect to the Internet, open the antivirus software main window, and execute the command to download any needed updates and virus definitions. For example, Figure 1-24 shows the main window for McAfee VirusScan. To update the software, click **updates** in the upper-right corner. Viruses are released every day and your antivirus software is only as current as its latest update.

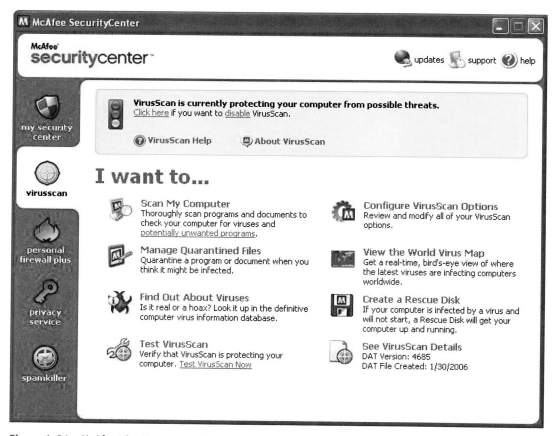

Figure 1-24   McAfee VirusScan main window

2. If you don't have antivirus software installed, you need it! Buy the software online or on CD and install it. When you're installing it, most likely the software will also scan for viruses as part of the installation process.

3. Run the antivirus software on the entire hard drive. Be sure to set it to check all folders and all types of files. If it finds a virus, run it again to make sure nothing new crops up.

4. Now set the antivirus software to run in the background of your system to keep it virus free. If it has the option, set it to scan e-mail before the e-mail or attachments are opened.

5. If it offers the option, set the software to automatically keep updates current. For example, when you click the **updates** link in Figure 1-24, the window in Figure 1-25 appears, telling you the status of how the software is set for updating. Click **Configure** to change those settings. Notice in Figure 1-25 that the software is set to download and install updates without your involvement.

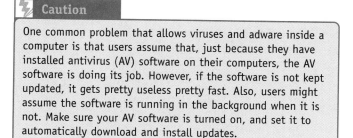

Caution

One common problem that allows viruses and adware inside a computer is that users assume that, just because they have installed antivirus (AV) software on their computers, the AV software is doing its job. However, if the software is not kept updated, it gets pretty useless pretty fast. Also, users might assume the software is running in the background when it is not. Make sure your AV software is turned on, and set it to automatically download and install updates.

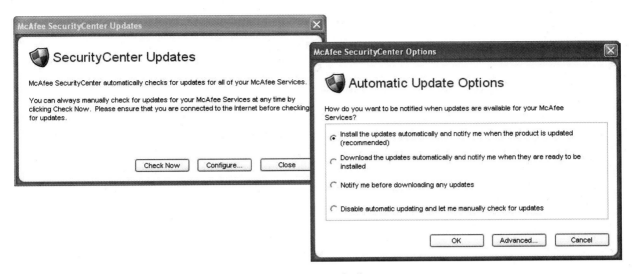

Figure 1-25   Set your antivirus software to stay updated automatically

Scan for Adware and Spyware

The distinction between adware and spyware is slight. Sometimes a malicious software program is displaying pop-up ads and also spying on you. Even though most popular AV software can find and remove adware and spyware, I've learned that to locate the most adware and spyware, you need software designed specifically for the job.

There are tons of adware- and spyware-removal products available on the Web, but I recommend the three listed here.

> **Notes**
>
> If you have problems updating or running the antivirus software, try booting into Safe Mode and running the software from there. Safe Mode loads Windows with a rather plain, vanilla-flavored configuration, which might eliminate a problem that keeps the software from running. To get to Safe Mode, reboot and hold down the **F8** key while Windows is loading. The Windows Advanced Options Menu appears, as shown in Figure 1-26. Select **Safe Mode with Networking** and press **Enter**.

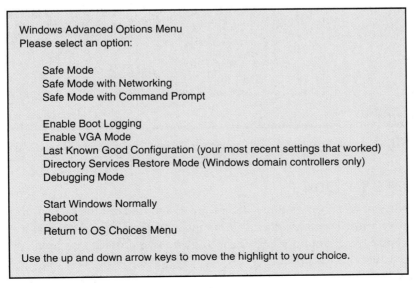

Figure 1-26   Windows XP Advanced Options menu

They all can catch adware, spyware, cookies, browser hijackers, dialers, keyloggers, and Trojans. All these types of nasty software are explained in Chapter 3, but for now, all you need to know is you don't want them. To get rid of them, download and install one or two of these products:

- Ad-Aware by Lavasoft (*www.lavasoft.com*) is one of the most popular and successful adware- and spyware-removal products. It can be downloaded without support for free.
- Spybot Search and Destroy by PepiMK Software (*www.pepimk.com*). This product does an excellent job of removing malicious software.
- Windows Defender by Microsoft (*www.microsoft.com*) is an up-and-coming product that, even in its current beta stage, does a great job removing malicious software. (During its first beta release, this product was named Antispyware.)

If you have scanned your system with AV software and then scanned using one of these products, but you still have a problem, download and run one more of these products. In Figure 1-27, you can see Ad-Aware scanning the registry. After the scan is complete, you decide what to keep or throw out. It finds tracking cookies, so you might decide to keep these. You can download Ad-Aware for free, but if you buy the software, it includes the option to run it in the background so it can block software before it gets in your system.

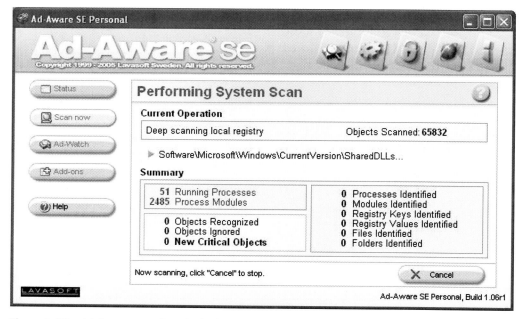

Figure 1-27 Ad-Aware scans for ads, keyloggers, Trojans, dialers, browser hijackers, and other malware

UPDATE WINDOWS

The Microsoft Web site offers patches, fixes, and updates for known problems and has an extensive knowledge base documenting problems and their solutions. It's important to keep these updates current on your system to fix known problems and plug up security holes to keep viruses and worms out.

If you don't have an Internet connection, you can download Windows updates to another computer and then transfer them to the computer you are working on. Also, you can order a CD from Microsoft for Windows XP Service Pack 2, which contains improved security features (among other things).

How to Install Updates

To launch Windows Update, connect to the Internet and then click **Start,** point to **All Programs,** and click **Windows Update.** Or you can access Windows Update by going to the Microsoft site *windowsupdate.microsoft.com.* When you get to the site, click **Express Install (Recommended)** to begin the update process.

The Windows Update process uses ActiveX controls to scan your system, find your device drivers and system files, and compare these files to the ones on the Windows Update server. If you do not already have Active Setup and the ActiveX controls installed on your computer, a prompt to install them appears when you access the site. After Windows Update scans your system and locates update packages and new versions of drivers and system files, it offers you the option of selecting files for download. Click **Download and Install Now,** and the window in Figure 1-28 appears so you can watch the progress.

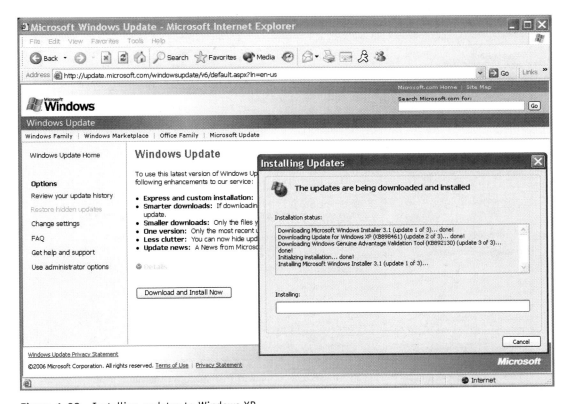

Figure 1-28   Installing updates to Windows XP

If the PC hasn't been updated in a while, Windows selects the updates in the order you can receive them and will not necessarily list all the updates you need on the first pass.

Notes

If you think you might later want to uninstall a critical update or service pack, select the option to Save uninstall information. Later, to uninstall the fix, again execute the downloaded file. When given the option, select "Uninstall a previously installed service pack."

After you have installed the updates listed, go back and start again until Windows Update tells you there is nothing left to update. It might take two or more passes to get the PC entirely up to date.

Windows XP Service Pack 2 (SP2)

So far, Microsoft has released two major service packs for Windows XP. The latest is Service Pack 2. Service Pack 2 offers some really great benefits, including Windows Firewall and Internet Explorer Pop-up Blocker. As you work your way through the Windows Update process, when the system is ready to receive Service Pack 2, you'll see it listed as the only update to download and install. It will take some time and a reboot to complete the process of installing Service Pack 2. You'll need at least 1.8 GB of free space on the drive for the installation. Alas, Figure 1-29 shows what will happen if the hard drive doesn't have enough free space for the SP2 installation.

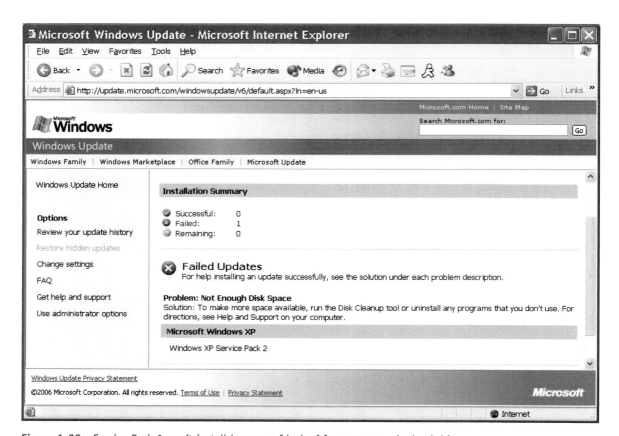

Figure 1-29   Service Pack 2 won't install because of lack of free space on the hard drive

Automatic Updates

After you've gotten Windows XP current with all its updates, set the system so that it will stay current. To do that, click **Start**, right-click **My Computer**, and click **Properties**. In the System Properties window, click the **Automatic Updates** tab (see Figure 1-30).

You'll want to make these automatic update settings according to how the PC connects to the Internet and user habits. For an always-up broadband connection (such as cable modem or DSL), select **Automatic (recommended)** and choose to automatically download and install updates every day. If the PC doesn't have an always-up Internet connection (such as dial-up), you might want to select **Notify me but don't automatically download or install them.**

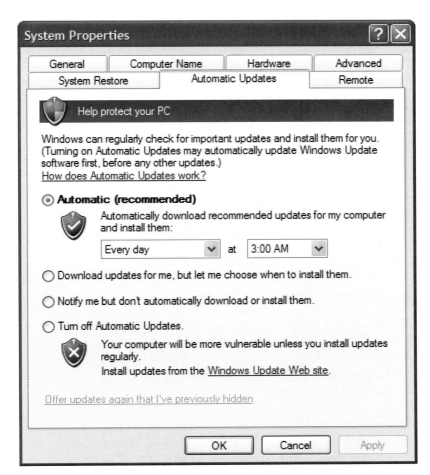

Figure 1-30 Set Automatic Updates for automatic and daily updating

This option works better if a user doesn't want to be bothered with a long and involved download when the PC first connects to the ISP using a slow dial-up connection. Discuss the options with the user. Make sure the user understands that if the update process is not fully automated, he or she needs to take the time to do the updates at least once a week.

ONE LAST CHECK

By now, the system should be clean and purring. Reboot and check for errors. Take another look at Task Manager and verify that it looks clean. Remember, you used Msconfig to control the startup process, and this is just a temporary fix until you can get to the root of all those processes bogging down startup. If you still see problems or performance hasn't improved, here are some more things you can do or try:

- ◢ Windows might have corrupted system files, which calls for a more drastic measure. Try using System File Check (Sfc.exe) to scan the installation for corrupted or missing system files. Use the command **sfc /scannow** to immediately scan all **system files** to make sure they're not corrupted. Or you can use **sfc /scanonce** to scan the system at the next reboot. The process requires you to provide the Windows XP setup CD. How to repair a corrupted Windows installation is covered in Chapter 7.

◢ Consider a hardware upgrade. You might need to upgrade memory or the processor, or you might consider a second hard drive. How to upgrade memory and install a second hard drive are covered in Chapter 8.

Windows should now be running faster and smoother. And now you're ready to set Windows so it is better protected to stay fit and clean.

> 🖉 **Notes**
>
> If you're responsible for several PCs in a small office or home office, you might find it difficult to keep track of which setup CD belongs to which system. I keep a brown manila envelope for each PC in my office. In the envelope are all the setup CDs for hardware and the OS on that one system and also any user manuals. It also contains a list of any changes I've made to the system, such as changes to CMOS setup.

KEEPING WINDOWS FIT

Now that Windows is all cleaned up, you'll want to keep it that way. And, if you're helping someone else clean up his or her computer, be sure to teach this user what to do to keep Windows fit and how to make good backups of important data. The best troubleshooting practice is to prevent the problem from happening to begin with. Here are a few tips to practice yourself and to teach other users:

◢ Keep good backups of data and protect the computer from mischief. How to schedule automated backups is covered in Chapter 4. Most Windows problems are caused by user error or malicious attacks that could have been prevented if proper protective measures had been taken.

◢ Keep Windows updates current. Set Windows Update to Automatic so you don't have to remember to perform the updates.

◢ Know and practice defensive measures when using the Internet. Make sure each network or Internet connection has Windows Firewall enabled. Configure AV software to continually run in the background and automatically download and install updates.

◢ Clean up your hard drive on a regular basis.

◢ Be a responsible Web surfer and e-mail and chat room user. Don't expose the system by downloading and installing freeware from untrustworthy sites. Don't open an e-mail attachment unless you trust the sender and have scanned it for viruses. Other ways to protect your privacy, your computer, and your identity are covered in Chapters 4 and 5.

◢ To protect your hardware, don't smoke around your computer; don't jar or move the computer case while the PC is on; protect your CDs and DVDs, and use a surge protector and adequate grounding.

◢ Consider installing a startup and registry monitor such as WinPatrol by BillP Studios (*www.winpatrol.com*). A little black Scotty dog woofs when the registry is about to be invaded or startup services added. Then an alert window appears and you can approve or stop the change (see Figure 1-31).

◢ When working with other users, ask permission to configure Windows and AV software so that the firewall is up and updates are kept current. Teach users how to back up data, how to clean up the hard drive, how to protect hardware, and how to use the Internet responsibly. Encourage users to not "tinker" with Windows unless they know what they're doing. For users that tend to use the Internet without restraint, ask permission to install a startup and registry monitor, such as WinPatrol.

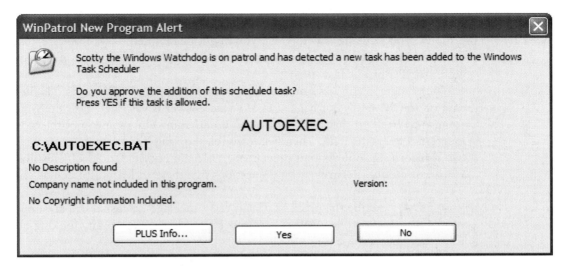

Figure 1-31 WinPatrol alerting the user a task is about to be added to the Task Scheduler

WHAT TO EXPECT FROM THE REST OF THIS BOOK

In this chapter, you've seen how to solve a common Windows XP problem, which is mostly caused by poor maintenance. In the chapter, as we solved the problem of a sluggish Windows system, you've also seen what must happen to keep Windows fit. In the rest of the book, we'll generally take this same approach of seeing how to fix a problem and also how to keep it from coming back. Let's take a look at how to approach a Windows problem in general, and then we'll look at the list of problems covered in this book.

HOW TO APPROACH A WINDOWS PROBLEM

Generally, when trying to fix a Windows problem (or any problem, for that matter), the process begins by asking questions and finding answers. Based on the answers, take appropriate action and then evaluate the result. And, if you really want to be an expert troubleshooter, take some notes about what you learned so you can better remember it when dealing with future computer problems. See Figure 1-32.

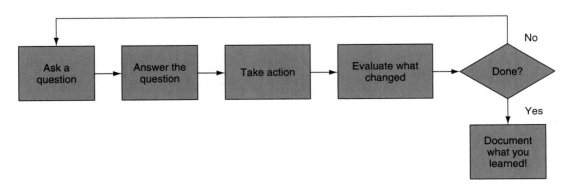

Figure 1-32 Learn to be an effective problem solver

ASK YOURSELF OR THE USER SOME QUESTIONS

If the PC you're fixing is your own, you might be tempted to skip this step. But don't. Step back and ask yourself the same questions you would ask other users if they came to you with their PC problem.

When facing a Windows problem, the very first thing to find out is, "Is there valuable data on the PC that's not backed up?" If the answer is yes, then absolutely, positively do all you can to back up that data before you do anything else. Sometimes the most valuable thing on a PC is the data. Then begin troubleshooting by isolating the problem into one of two categories: problems that prevent the PC from booting and problems that occur after a successful boot. Begin by asking questions like these to learn as much as you can:

- ◢ Please describe the problem. What error messages, unusual displays, or failures did you see? (Possible answer: I see this blue screen with a funny looking message on it that makes no sense to me.)
- ◢ When did the problem start? (Possible answer: When I first booted after loading this neat little screen saver I downloaded from the Web.)
- ◢ What was the situation when the problem occurred? (Possible answers: I was trying to start up my PC. I was opening a document in MS Word. I was researching a project on the Internet.)
- ◢ What programs or software were you using? (Possible answer: I was using Internet Explorer.)
- ◢ Did you move your computer system recently? (Possible answer: Well, yes. Yesterday I moved the computer case from one side of my desk to the other. By the way, if someone told me that, my next question would be: Did you power down the system before you did that? If they answered no, I'd begin by suspecting a crashed hard drive.)
- ◢ Has there been a recent thunderstorm or electrical problem? (Possible answer: Yes, last night. Then when I tried to turn on my PC this morning, nothing happened.)
- ◢ Have you made any hardware, software, or configuration changes? (Possible answer: No, but I think my sister might have.)
- ◢ Has someone else used your computer recently? (Possible answer: Sure, my son uses it all the time.)
- ◢ Is there some valuable data on your system that is not backed up that I should know about before I start working on the problem? (Possible answer: Yes! Yes! My term paper! It's not backed up! You gotta get me that!)
- ◢ Can you show me exactly how to reproduce the problem? (Possible answer: Yes, let me show you what to do.) Remember that many problems stem from user error. As the user shows you how to reproduce the problem, watch what the user is doing and ask questions.

Based on the answers to your questions, you're ready to set your priorities and address the problem. At the top of your priority list should be to protect any important data that is not backed up.

PROTECT THE DATA

If valuable data is at stake, don't do anything to jeopardize it. Back it up as soon as possible. If you must take a risk with the data, let it be the user's decision to do so, not yours. Here are some examples of the urgency of protecting the data and what you might do to protect it:

- ◢ Mary's only copy of her term paper is on the hard drive, and Windows is giving strange errors when she opens Internet Explorer. Before you do anything to solve the

IE problem, copy her term paper to a flash drive or a floppy disk and hand it to her for safekeeping. She can now relax while you work.

▲ Zack is responsible for a huge database that is not currently backed up. And Windows is giving an error and refusing to boot. You believe the only way to solve the Windows problem is to reinstall the OS. Before you do that, remove the hard drive from the system, install it as a second hard drive in another PC, and copy the database to the primary hard drive in the working system. Then move the hard drive back to the original PC and begin working on the Windows boot problem. In Chapter 8, you'll learn how to move a hard drive to another system in order to recover the data.

▲ Isaac tells you the only important data on his desktop computer's hard drive is his e-mail, the e-mail attachments, and his e-mail address book. He uses Eudora as his e-mail software, which is configured to store all that information in the C:\Email folder. Before you begin upgrading his OS from Windows 98 to Windows XP, copy the contents of the C:\Email folder to Isaac's notebook computer. Install Eudora on the notebook and have Isaac verify that he can access all the e-mail there. Now you're free to upgrade his desktop OS. You'll learn more about backing up and recovering e-mail data in Chapter 4. In Chapter 5, you'll learn how to connect two computers to copy data from one to the other using a super-simple network.

After the data is safe, you can begin troubleshooting the problem. At this point, you might not want the user watching, especially if you're new at this and someone watching might make you nervous. You can say to the user something like, "Okay, now I just need to work on the problem. I'll let you know if I need something or have more questions."

TIPS WHEN PROBLEM SOLVING

Following the steps the user showed you earlier, reproduce the problem as you carefully observe what happens. Here are some useful tips:

▲ Keep a pad and pencil handy as you work. Take notes as you work so you can backtrack if need be, and so you can keep track of what you've already tried or not tried. Once you fix the problem, you'll also have a valuable document to take into the next troubleshooting situation.

▲ Start troubleshooting with a reboot. Many problems go away with a reboot. However, if the problem still exists, you know your starting point. The exception to this rule is when a user points out a problem currently displayed onscreen that he or she doesn't know how to reproduce. When a problem comes and goes at odd times (called an intermittent problem) and you see it displayed, take the time to investigate as much as you can about the current situation before you reboot.

▲ As you attempt to solve the problem, first reproduce the problem and learn what you can as you go. Start at the beginning. Watch everything carefully: error messages, lights, and so forth. Take notes. Be a careful observer.

▲ Does the problem occur during the boot? If the problem occurs during the boot, is it hardware or software related? Does the problem occur with hardware before the OS load begins? Is the problem related to loading the OS?

▲ If the problem occurs after the boot, is it related to hardware or software? Has the hardware or application ever worked?

▲ Simplify and isolate the problem. For example, if you have a problem with an application, close all other applications.

▲ As you try one thing after another, reboot between fixes. You might have solved the problem with your fix, or you might have created a new problem. At the least, each reboot gives you a fresh perspective on what's going on. Also, for external devices such as printers or routers, turn them off and then back on to begin fresh.

◢ Use the Internet for research. You'll see many examples in this book of how the Internet can be useful when problem solving. Search the Web site of the device or software manufacturer, open a chat session with the site's technical support staff, or use a search engine such as *www.google.com* to research an error message or symptom. For just about any PC problem, someone somewhere has had the same problem. It can be particularly useful to Google specific text from error messages, which often goes directly to the problem. For example, if an error message appears and includes a reference to the program "badpc.exe", simply searching for "badpc.exe" on Google may bring up numerous pages that identify this file as a known malicious program. Also, newsgroups can be very helpful in researching problems.

◢ Don't stop until you know you're done. If you think the problem is fixed, test the fix and the system. Make sure all is working before you stop. Then have the user verify the problem is solved.

TOOLS OF THE TRADE

In this book, we're going to use all kinds of resources. You'll learn to use some Windows utilities and some third-party utilities, and you'll also learn how to research a problem using the Internet and other sources. Here's a summary of these tools and resources:

◢ Perhaps the most powerful and useful tool for solving problems with Windows is the Internet. Appendix A lists resources on the Web. The most important is the Microsoft support site (*support.microsoft.com*). This site is extremely useful in finding information on software and hardware problems and solutions. Windows updates are also available from the site.

◢ Windows XP comes with many utility tools. In this chapter, you already learned about Task Manager, System Configuration (Msconfig), Device Manager, Disk Management, Safe Mode, and System File Checker. In later chapters, you'll learn to use many other Windows utility tools such as the Recovery Console and the Registry Editor.

◢ A third-party utility is software *not* written by Microsoft that you can download from the Web and install on your system to help get behind the scenes in Windows and to solve problems. Many third-party utilities are shareware (download and try before you buy) or freeware (download for free or with a donation). You'll learn to use several third-party utilities in this book; most of them can be downloaded for free. This software is generally divided into two categories:

  ◢ Software that runs in the background to defend and protect. Examples are Norton Antivirus by Symantec (*www.symantec.com*) and Ad-Aware by Lavasoft (*www.lavasoft.com*); both are discussed in this chapter.

  ◢ Software used by a technician to examine a system and manually fix a problem. Examples are Process Explorer by Sysinternals (*www.sysinternals.com*) and Win Tasks by Uniblue (*www.liutilities.com*). Process Explorer can be used to track processes running on your PC and gives more information than does Task Manager. Win Tasks provides a more detailed view of processes than either Task Manager or Process Explorer and allows an administrator to precisely manage them.

Use this book as your most valuable Windows troubleshooting tool. In the book, you'll learn step-by-step strategies to solve the most difficult and most common Windows problems. As you follow these steps, you're going to learn an awful lot about how

Windows works and how to get inside its guts to fix it. With this knowledge comes power. You can take what you've learned and apply it to other Windows problems and build on it to learn even more about how Windows works and how to fix it.

TOP EIGHT WINDOWS PROBLEMS

In this and the remaining chapters, we'll take each problem one at a time, give you the insights and understanding you need about the problem, and step you through the process of fixing the problem. It's going to be fun! So here are the top eight complaints you'll hear when supporting Windows:

1. My Windows system is sluggish and slow.

2. When I start up Windows, it's slow and clunky, and I see strange messages.

3. I'm under attack! Nasty software has attacked my system!

4. I need better security for my computer or small network, but I don't know how to get it.

5. I can't connect using wireless or wired networks.

6. I think I might need to upgrade my system.

7. My applications or devices give errors, won't work, won't install, or won't uninstall.

8. Windows won't start up at all. I have data in there somewhere!

Let the fun begin!

>> CHAPTER SUMMARY

▲ A sluggish Windows system is most likely caused by poor maintenance resulting in too many applications and services loading at startup, too little free hard drive space, a fragmented hard drive, or not enough memory or powerful enough processor.

▲ Before you start trying to fix a Windows problem, take a few minutes to examine the system so you know what essential hardware is present, how much free space on the hard drive is available, and what programs and processes are running.

▲ Clean up a sluggish Windows system by first using the System Configuration Utility (Msconfig) to stop all nonessential and non-Windows processes from loading at startup. Later you'll need to allow those to start that you really want.

▲ Clean up the hard drive by deleting unwanted files, defragging the hard drive, and scanning it for errors.

▲ To clean up the system, remove any unwanted software, scan it for viruses and other malicious software, and download and install Windows updates, patches, and fixes.

▲ Routine maintenance of a system includes keeping Windows current with updates and patches, using a firewall and antivirus software, and using good judgment when using the Internet or tinkering with Windows settings.

▲ When solving a Windows problem, interview the user and protect any important data not backed up.

▲ Classify a computer problem as being one that either occurs during the boot or after the Windows desktop is loaded.

◢ Key troubleshooting tools include the Internet for research, Windows tools, third-party tools, and this book.

>> KEY TERMS

device driver   A program stored on the hard drive that tells the computer how to communicate with a hardware device such as a printer or modem (for more explanation, see Appendix D).

freeware   Software you can download for free or with a donation.

service   A program running in the background that provides support to Windows, an application, or a device (for more explanation, see Appendix D).

shareware   Software you can download and try before you buy.

third-party utility   Software not written by Microsoft that you can download from the Web and install on your system to help solve a Windows problem.

>> REVIEWING THE BASICS

1. A PC problem can be divided into what two main categories?

2. What Windows utility do you use to find out how a hard drive is partitioned?

3. What Windows utility can easily let you see how much free space is available on drive C?

4. When someone asks you for help solving a Windows problem, what is the first thing you should do?

5. Why is it important to keep notes as you solve a Windows problem?

6. Name two third-party utilities that can track processes running in the background on your PC and give more information than does Task Manager.

7. What Windows tool can you use to see which processor is installed and how much RAM is installed?

8. What Windows tool lets you quickly see which service packs have been applied to Windows?

9. Why would a user *not* want to turn on Automatic Updates for Windows?

10. How much hard drive free space does Microsoft say Windows XP must have for normal operation?

11. What are three things you can do to clean up a hard drive?

12. What Windows utility can give a list of open applications?

13. Using Task Manager, which tab gives a list of running services, programs, and background processes?

14. In Task Manager, if you see a process you don't recognize, what is one way you can find information about it?

15. When trying to run antivirus software, if you get errors, what can you do to solve the problem(s)?

>> THINKING CRITICALLY

1. You are helping a user who is suddenly having trouble printing. Select the steps you should take in attempting to solve this problem, and list them in the appropriate order:

   ◢ Allow the user to back up his or her data.
   ◢ Reboot the system.
   ◢ Have the user demonstrate how he or she is trying to print.
   ◢ Interview the user about how the problem started.
   ◢ Close out unnecessary applications.

2. Why might Windows updates still be necessary even if your computer is not connected to the Internet? How could you get these updates without an Internet connection?
3. You have a system with a 1 GHz Pentium 4 processor, 128 MB of RAM, and a 6 GB hard drive. Which upgrade (processor, RAM, or hard drive) would most benefit your system and what, if anything, does this depend on?

>> HANDS-ON PROJECTS

PROJECT 1-1: Investigating Running Processes

Open Task Manager and click the **Processes** tab to view the processes running under your current user's account and write down each of them. Next, use the Internet to research each of these processes and determine what they do and what (if any) applications they are associated with.

PROJECT 1-2: Checking for Spyware

Go to *www.lavasoft.com* and download the latest version of Ad-Aware. Once it is installed, use it to remove any spyware that has infected your PC.

PROJECT 1-3: Cleaning Up Your Hard Drive

Open **My Computer** and right-click your hard drive. On the shortcut menu, click **Properties** and then click **Disk Cleanup** in the properties window. In the Disk Cleanup window, select all the check boxes except Compress Old Files and click **OK**.

PROJECT 1-4: Running System File Checker

Open the command prompt by using the **cmd** command in the Run dialog box. Type **sfc /scannow** to scan your system for corrupted or missing system files. Note that you might be asked to insert your Windows XP installation CD.

>> REAL PROBLEMS, REAL SOLUTIONS

REAL PROBLEM 1-1: Examining a Windows XP Computer

Following directions given in the chapter, start with a fresh boot, and then answer the following questions intended to give you a quick survey of the condition of a Windows XP computer and determine its maintenance needs:

1. What processor is installed?

2. How much RAM is installed?

3. What Windows XP service packs are installed?

4. What is the size of the hard drive? How much free space is on the primary drive partition (drive C)? What file system is this partition using (NTFS or FAT32)?

5. Are there any installed devices that don't appear to be running or that have a problem?

6. What applications or processes are currently running that appear as though they might not be necessary or might be malicious?

7. List some quick fixes presented in this chapter that might improve performance. List them in the order that you would do them.

REAL PROBLEM 1-2: Cleaning Up a Sluggish Windows XP System

Using all the tools and techniques presented in this chapter, clean up a sluggish Windows XP system. Take notes as you go, showing what you checked before you started to solve the problems, what you did to solve the problems, and what the results were of your efforts. What questions did you have along the way? Bring these questions to class for discussion.

CHAPTER 2

Making Windows XP Boot Like New

In Chapter 1, you saw how to clean up a slow and sluggish Windows XP system. For the most part, we fixed the problems using routine maintenance tools such as Defrag and Chkdsk. If a problem wasn't easy to solve, we simply applied a quick patch and moved on. For example, if we saw a strange service running in the background, we just stopped it—we didn't take the time to get at the underlying problem of how the service got there to begin with and remove it at its root. In this chapter, we go for the roots.

This chapter is organized as a how-to chapter to make your work as easy as possible. First, you'll learn about some quick-and-dirty solutions to startup problems that might clean things up easily for you. Then you'll learn about the most common ways to clean up the startup process. These methods are presented to you in the order you should use them. Next, we'll dig a little deeper into some more complex solutions that you'll only need to use in the most difficult of situations. Last, as always in this book after the problem is solved, you'll learn how to keep the problem from coming back— you'll learn about some things you can do to keep the startup process clean as a whistle.

 **Focus Problem**

"My Windows XP startup is sluggish and gives me strange error messages."

QUICK FIXES FOR DRASTIC STARTUP PROBLEMS

Sometimes you have to put out a fire or two before you can begin solving an underlying problem. This section is about some things you can do if you have an immediate Windows XP startup problem that you need to deal with first. If your Windows XP startup is generally just slow and is not giving errors, you can skip this section and move on to the next, "Clean Up Startup." However, if you've got an error message staring you in the face or a device is not working that you need before you can move on, try these quick-and-dirty solutions presented next. If your problem is still not solved, then you need to move on to Chapter 7, "Resurrecting the Dead." That chapter pulls out the big guns to solve the really nasty startup problems that prevent a system from booting.

The tools covered in this section are the Last Known Good Configuration, Safe Mode, System Restore, and the System Configuration Utility. Let's get started with the first one, which you can try if Windows XP won't boot to the Windows desktop.

LAST KNOWN GOOD CONFIGURATION

If Windows XP will not boot to the Windows desktop, you can try to use the Last Known Good Configuration on the Advanced Options menu. Windows XP considers the startup to be a good startup just after a user logs onto the system. At that time, it saves the configuration it used for that startup in a place in the registry and calls this information the Last Known Good Configuration, which most technicians simply call the Last Known Good. If you are having a problem starting up Windows, you can have Windows revert back to the Last Known Good. Here's what to do:

1. While Windows is loading, hold down the **F8** key. The Windows Advanced Options Menu shown in Figure 2-1 appears.

2. On the menu, highlight **Last Known Good Configuration (your most recent settings that worked)** and press **Enter**.

The system reboots and the Last Known Good is applied.

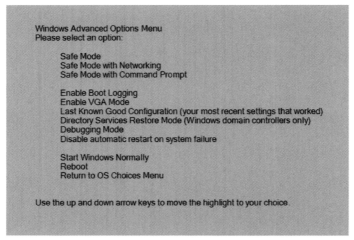

Figure 2-1 Windows XP Advanced Options Menu

This method will solve your startup problem if certain things are true:

▲ The Last Known Good is taken immediately after a user logs on. If you've logged on several times after the problem started, you've probably overwritten the Last Known Good that was good, if you know what I mean. Therefore, it's important to try the Last Known Good early, after the problem has first started.

▲ The Last Known Good is good only for solving a problem caused by an error in the Windows XP configuration, such as when you just installed a bad device driver or other program that has corrupted the registry.

If applying the Last Known Good doesn't solve your problem, then try Safe Mode.

SAFE MODE ON THE ADVANCED OPTIONS MENU

If you think you know what the problem is that prevented Windows from starting normally (such as newly installed software being corrupted), then you can fix the problem (such as uninstalling that software). However, if you don't know the source of

> **Notes**
>
> When you start Windows XP in Safe Mode, it uses only the core device drivers needed to operate essential hardware devices and does not load installed applications or third-party services. In other words, Windows loads using a bare-bones configuration. Figure 2-2 shows what the Windows desktop looks like in Safe Mode. Notice Safe Mode written in all four corners of the screen. Also, notice in the figure the Task Manager processes list is shown. No processes are listed except the essential Windows processes.

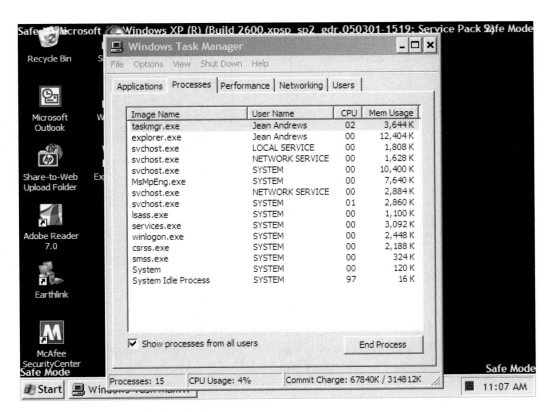

Figure 2-2 Windows XP in Safe Mode

your problem, start Windows XP in Safe Mode. To do that, press **F8** while Windows is loading to display the Windows Advanced Options Menu. Then select **Safe Mode with Networking**. When you see a logon screen, log on using an administrator account. After the Windows XP Safe Mode desktop appears, do the following to solve the problem:

◢ Use up-to-date antivirus software to scan for viruses. If you find a virus, clean it and reboot to see if the problem is solved.

◢ You can also scan the hard drive for errors. To do that, open Explorer and right-click logical **drive C**. Select **Properties** from the shortcut menu. The drive Properties box appears. Select the **Tools** tab (see Figure 2-3). Click **Check Now** to scan for bad sectors.

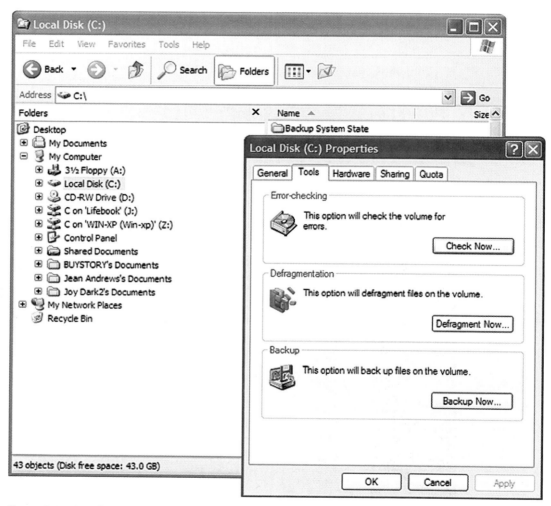

Figure 2-3   Scan logical drive C for errors

◢ You should also verify the drive has some free space—at least 318 MB, which Windows needs to work with. If there's not enough hard drive space, empty the Recycle Bin and temporary folders and whatever else you must do to give Windows some free hard drive space for its working temporary files.

◢ If you know of some setting or software installation that you suspect to be the source of the problem, make these changes to the Windows configuration and then try a reboot. For example, you might need to disable a device or remove software you just installed.

◢ If System Restore has been configured to create restore points, use System Restore to bring the system back to a restore point. Reboot after this change. The next section explains how to use System Restore.

◢ If you still have the problem and you have a current backup of the system state, use Ntbackup to restore the system state. How to use Ntbackup to save and restore the system state is covered later in this chapter.

Here are some tips when trying to use Safe Mode:

◢ Before you try Safe Mode, first try Safe Mode with Networking. If that doesn't work, try Safe Mode. And if that doesn't work, try Safe Mode with Command Prompt.

◢ Safe Mode won't help you if core Windows components are corrupted, including the Ntoskrnl.exe and Hal.dll programs.

◢ If your system is infected with really nasty viruses, boot into Safe Mode and run antivirus software from there, rather than from the regular Windows desktop. This helps because in Safe Mode the viruses might not be allowed to load, which means they are less likely to be able to attack your antivirus software. Also, if you don't have antivirus software installed on your system, installing it in Safe Mode might mean you have a better chance of success.

◢ When you first boot into Safe Mode, before the Windows desktop is loaded, a dialog box appears (see Figure 2-4). You can choose between continuing to Safe Mode or

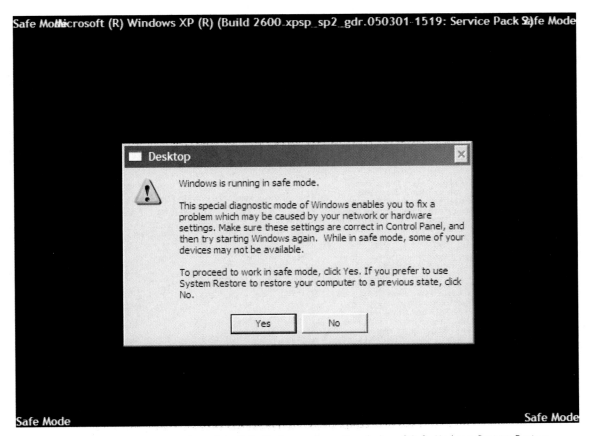

Figure 2-4 When you attempt to boot into Safe Mode, you have the choice of Safe Mode or System Restore

using System Restore. If you click No, Windows XP takes you directly to System Restore rather than to Safe Mode.

SYSTEM RESTORE

Ever wish you could backtrack to a previous point in time when things were nice? That's what System Restore can do for you—well, sometimes. System Restore restores the system to its condition at the time a snapshot was taken of the system settings and configuration. These snapshots are called restore points. If System Restore is turned on, Windows automatically creates a restore point before you install new software or hardware or make other changes to the system. You can also manually create a restore point at any time.

If you restore the system to a previous restore point, user data on the hard drive will not be altered, but you can affect installed software and hardware, user settings, and OS configuration settings.

USING A PREVIOUS RESTORE POINT

To restore the system configuration to an earlier time, you can start System Restore using one of these methods:

◢ As discussed in the last section, when you boot into Safe Mode, the startup process asks if you want to go to the Safe Mode desktop or directly to System Restore. If you choose to go to System Restore, the window in Figure 2-5 appears to begin the system restoration process. If you go directly to the Safe Mode desktop, you can still launch System Restore using the next method.

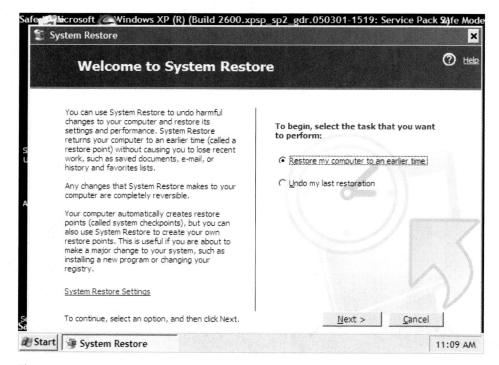

Figure 2-5 You can launch System Restore from Safe Mode

From the Windows desktop, click **Start**, point to **All Programs**, point to **Accessories**, point to **System Tools**, and then click System Restore. The System Restore window opens, as shown in Figure 2-6. The difference between this screen shot and the one in Figure 2-5 is that one was taken in Safe Mode and the other was taken when Windows started normally.

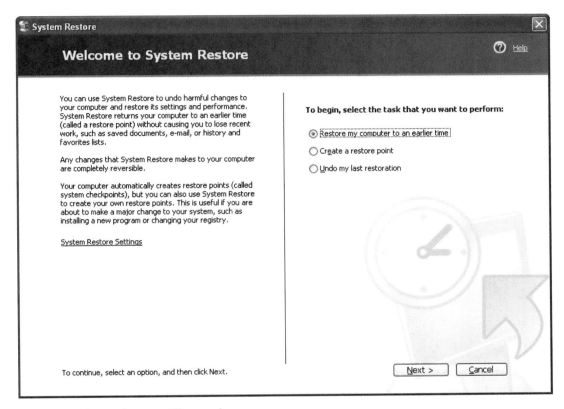

Figure 2-6 System Restore utility opening screen

To restore to a previous restore point, click **Restore my computer to an earlier time** in the System Restore window and click **Next**. On the next screen, shown in Figure 2-7, select a restore point. Select a point as close to the present as you can so that as few changes to the system as possible are lost. The system will require a reboot for the changes to take effect. Data files are not affected, but any installation or configuration changes made after the restore point are lost. If the changes don't work, you can use System Restore to try a new restore point or to undo your changes.

POINTS TO REMEMBER ABOUT SYSTEM RESTORE

System Restore is a great tool to try to fix a device that is not working, restore Windows settings that are giving problems, or solve problems with applications. It's a super-duper tool in some situations, but it has its limitations. Keep these points in mind:

Using System Restore to restore the system to a previous restore point requires that you at least are able to boot normally or boot into Safe Mode. If you can't boot into Safe Mode, System Restore is useless.

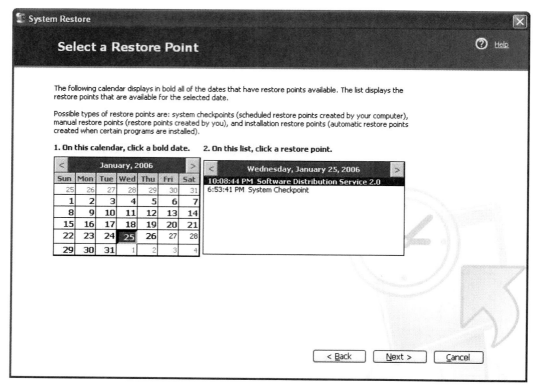

Figure 2-7   Select a restore point

▲ System Restore only works to recover from errors if the registry is somewhat intact, because restore points replace certain keys in the registry but cannot completely rebuild a totally corrupted registry.

▲ The restore process cannot help you recover from a virus or worm infection unless the infection is launched at startup.

▲ System Restore might create a new problem. I've discovered that whenever I use a restore point, my antivirus software gets all out of whack and sometimes even needs reinstalling. So use restore points sparingly.

▲ Before using System Restore to undo a change, if the change was made to a hardware device, first try Driver Rollback so that as few changes as possible to the system are lost. Driver Rollback is covered in Chapter 6.

▲ System Restore won't help you if you don't have restore points to use. Normally, Windows creates restore points without your knowledge. How to make sure System Restore is set to do that and how to create your own restore points are covered later in the chapter.

SYSTEM CONFIGURATION UTILITY (MSCONFIG)

Recall from Chapter 1 that we used the System Configuration Utility (Msconfig.exe) to disable many processes that normally would load at startup. Although we used it there to temporarily control an out-of-control startup, it should not be considered a permanent fix. Once you've identified the process that is causing the problem, use other tools to permanently remove it from the startup process.

To use Msconfig, enter **msconfig.exe** in the Run dialog box. The window in Figure 2-8 opens.

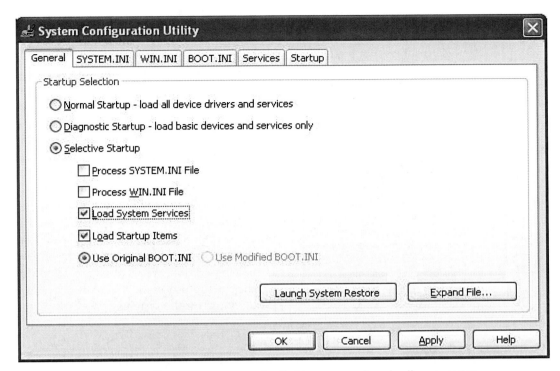

Figure 2-8 Use the Msconfig utility to temporarily disable processes from loading at startup

On the General tab, you can decide to start Windows XP as a normal startup or a diagnostic startup with basic devices and services only. Or you can decide to use a selective startup where you control which services and programs to launch.

Notice in Figure 2-8 the three tabs, System.ini, Win.ini, and Boot.ini. Using these tabs, you can edit the contents of these three initialization files. Most likely you won't find much reason to do this because System.ini and Win.ini are only used to manage 16-bit drivers and applications. Boot.ini is also probably best left unchanged, unless you want to change the Windows boot parameters, which include which OS will boot (when two OSs are installed) or to which hard drive the system looks to find an OS.

The two more important tabs used to temporarily control the Windows startup process are the Services tab and the Startup tab. The Services tab contains a list of services automatically launched at startup, and the

> **Notes**
>
> To roll back the system to a Windows XP restore point using Windows XP requires that you can boot from the hard drive. However, there are other options using third-party utility software. For example, ERD Commander 2003 by Winternals (*www.winternals.com*) is an operating system that can be loaded from CD. Boot from the ERD Commander 2003 CD, which loads a GUI interface that looks like Windows XP. Using this Winternals desktop, you can access the registry, event logs, and Disk Management Console and reset a forgotten administrator password. You can also roll back the Windows XP system to a restore point.

> **Notes**
>
> Msconfig only reports what it is programmed to look for when listing startup programs and services. It looks only in certain registry keys and startup folders, and sometimes a startup process is not reported by Msconfig. Later in the chapter, you'll learn about some third-party tools that search in more locations than does Msconfig and that give a better report of startup processes.

Startup tab contains a list of programs started by entries in the registry or in startup folders. You learned to use these two tabs in the last chapter.

To troubleshoot a startup problem: you can check the items you want to start and uncheck the ones you want to temporarily disable; apply your changes; close the utility; and reboot your system. If this solves your problem, go back to Msconfig and enable one service at a time until the problem reappears. You've then discovered the service that is your problem. You'll need to investigate this service. If you don't recognize it, try entering its name in an Internet search engine such as *www.google.com* for information about the service. To permanently stop a service, you can use the Services console, which you'll learn to use later in the chapter.

> **Notes**
>
> If you suspect a Windows system service is causing the problem, you can use MSconfig to disable the service. If this works, then replace the service file with a fresh copy from the Windows setup CD.

If you're following along at your computer while you're reading this chapter, before you move on to the next section, open the Msconfig window of your computer and verify that Normal Startup is selected on the General tab. In the next section, we want to use Task Manager to examine the startup processes when all processes have been turned loose on the system.

CLEAN UP STARTUP

In the previous section, you learned how to deal with pressing problems that need a quick fix. In this section, you'll learn step-by-step procedures to clean up the Windows startup process. The idea is to start at the highest and easiest level of tools and methods to use to affect the startup process. If that doesn't do the job, we must dig deeper using more technical tools and work behind the scenes to manage startup. Another goal is to strike at the root of the tree rather than its branches. In other words, we want to not just kill a process or block it from loading at startup, but rather we want to altogether remove the unwanted application or driver, or at least change its startup parameters.

The first step is to perform a cold boot to start Windows XP. If you have a stopwatch handy or a watch with a second hand, time the seconds required to get to the Windows desktop when all hourglass icons have disappeared and Windows is ready to use. Also note the items in your system tray and windows that appear when you start up. All these things will be our measuring stick to show the progress we're making as we work. (Another measuring stick will be the resources available to provide an optimized Windows environment, but optimizing resources is left to Chapter 8.)

In this section, I'm assuming you can start Windows with no errors. If you are having trouble loading Windows, it's best to address the error first rather than use the tools described here to do a general cleanup.

VIEWING PROCESSES WITH TASK MANAGER

In this section, we'll use Task Manager to take a good look at what's running on a system before we begin the cleanup. Recall that one way you can open Task Manager is to right-click the taskbar and select Task Manager from the shortcut menu. The Task Manager window opens, as shown in Figure 2-9. The Applications tab shows the list of currently opened applications. Sometimes the Applications tab shows only the name of the application, but not the program filename associated with it. To get that information, right-click the application in the Applications tab and select **Go To Process** from the shortcut menu. This takes you to the correct process on the Processes tab of Task Manager.

2

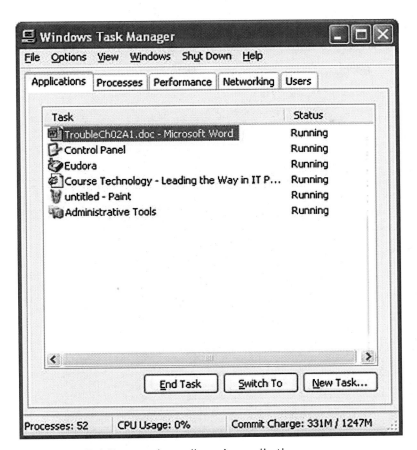

Figure 2-9 Task Manager shows all running applications

To see a list of processes currently running, click the **Processes** tab (see Figure 2-10). The Processes tab normally lists all processes running in user mode in Windows XP.

User mode is one of two modes in which OS programs and other programs can run. User mode has less access to hardware than the other mode, kernel mode. Applications normally run in user mode and device drivers normally run in kernel mode. Windows XP programs can run in either mode depending on how the program is used by the OS. A virus or worm can run in either mode. Sometimes a malicious process shows up in Task Manager and sometimes it does not. One reason it does not show up is because it's running in kernel mode.

Looking back at Figure 2-10, you can see a process is registered as running under a user name or user account. Most core Windows processes running in user mode run under the Local System account, which is sometimes displayed as the System account. Other processes run under the current user (Jean Andrews), Local Service, or Network Service account. Both the Local Service and Network Service accounts have lower privileges than the System account. Services that run under the System, Local Service, or Network Service accounts can't display a dialog box onscreen or interact with the user. To do that, the service must be running under a user account.

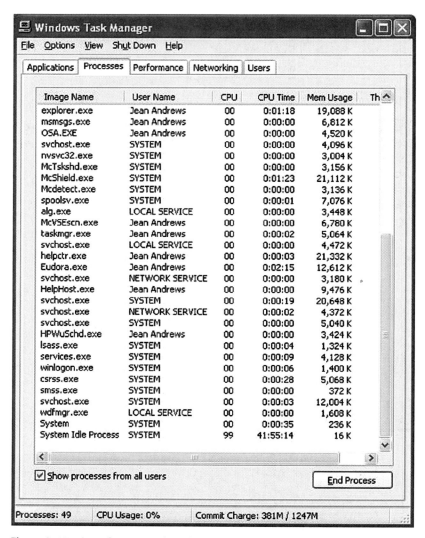

Figure 2-10 A service runs under a System, Local Service, Network Service, or user account

CORE WINDOWS PROCESSES

Figure 2-11 shows the Processes tab of Task Manager for a new installation of Windows XP, before any changes are made or applications are installed.

As a good Windows troubleshooter, you should be familiar with all the processes showing in Figure 2-11, the path to each program file, which in most cases is C:\Windows\system32, and the account under which the process normally runs. Consider this list your starting point for learning to recognize legitimate Windows processes. Here is the list of processes, their purposes, and paths, including some processes not shown in Figure 2-11 that can be automatically launched depending on Windows settings:

▲ *Taskmgr.exe.* This is the Task Manager utility itself. The program file is stored in C:\Windows\system32.
▲ *Msmsgs.exe.* MSN Messenger, a chat application located in C:\Program Files\MSN Messenger. This process is not a core Windows process and can be easily removed if you don't use MSN Messenger.

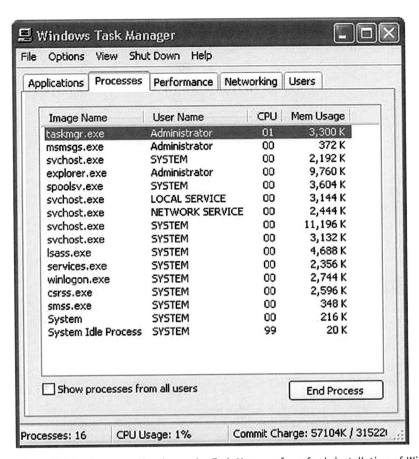

Figure 2-11 Processes showing under Task Manager for a fresh installation of Windows XP

▲ *Svchost.exe.* This process manages each process that is executed by a DLL. One instance of Svchost runs for each process it manages. The program file is stored in C:\Windows\system32. To see a list of services managed by Svchost, enter this command in a command-prompt window: **tasklist/SVC**. (Note that the Tasklist command is not available with Windows XP Home Edition.)

▲ *Explorer.exe.* The Windows graphical shell that manages the desktop, Start menu, taskbar, and file system. The program file is stored in C:\Windows.

▲ *Spoolsv.exe.* Handles Windows print spooling and is stored in C:\Windows\system32. Stopping and starting this process can sometimes solve a print spooling problem.

▲ *Lsass.exe.* Manages local security and login policies. The program file is stored in C:\Windows\system32.

▲ *Services.exe.* Starts and stops services. This program file is stored in C:\Windows\system32.

▲ *Winlogon.exe.* Manages login and logout events. The program file is stored in C:\Windows\system32.

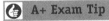 **A+ Exam Tip**

A **DLL** is a program file that contains a collection of subroutines used by other programs. See Appendix D, "How Windows XP Works," for more information.

A+ Exam Tip

When your Windows desktop is locked up, you can sometimes solve the problem by using Task Manager to stop and start Explorer.exe. For more information about how the desktop works, see Appendix D, "How Windows XP Works."

- ◢ *Csrss.exe.* Client/server runtime server subsystem; manages many commands in Windows that use graphics. The program file is stored in C:\Windows\system32.
- ◢ *Smss.exe.* Windows sessions manager; essential Windows process and is stored in C:\Windows\system32
- ◢ *Internat.exe.* Displays an icon in the system tray that can be used to switch from English to another language when supplemental language support is enabled using the Regional and Language Options applet in Control Panel
- ◢ *Mstask.exe.* The task scheduler that runs tasks at scheduled times
- ◢ *Winmgmt.exe.* 50A core Windows component that starts the first time a client process requests to connect to the system
- ◢ *System.* Windows system counter that shows up as a process, but has no program file associated with it
- ◢ *System Idle Process.* Appears in the Task Manager to show how CPU usage is allotted. It is not associated with a program file.

> **Notes**
>
> In this book, we use the most likely path to the Windows System Root folder: C:\Windows. However, your system might have a different System Root folder, such as E:\Winnt. In this case, you'll need to substitute your specific System Root folder in the command line or path.

THE REAL THING AND THE COUNTERFEIT

Do you know how bank tellers are trained to spot counterfeit money? Interestingly enough, they're not normally given special instructions on how to spot a counterfeit. Rather, they spend hours and hours handling the real thing. Then when a counterfeit passes by, they recognize it. In this book, you're going to see a lot of screen shots of Task Manager processes. After some practice, you'll be able to spot a true Windows process and a counterfeit one. You'll also learn how to investigate processes you don't recognize.

For example, sometimes a virus will disguise itself as Svchost.exe. You can recognize it as a counterfeit process if it's not running under System, Local Service, or Network Service. If you spot an Svchost.exe process running under a user name, suspect a rat. Also, if you notice the Svchost.exe program file is located somewhere other than C:\Windows\system32, this most likely means it's a counterfeit version put there to make trouble. And how do you know the path to a program file? One way is to use the Services console, which is discussed later in the chapter. Another way is to use third-party utilities similar to, but better than, Task Manager. A couple of these are discussed later in the chapter.

INVESTIGATING AN UNKNOWN PROCESS

When trying to identify a process that shows in Task Manager, your very best tool to investigate the process is the Internet. There are several good online databases of processes, and many times a Google search turns up excellent information. Beware, however! Much information on the Web is written by people who are just guessing about what they are saying, and some of the information is put there to purposefully deceive. Check things out carefully, and learn which sites you can rely on. This section looks at some of these trustworthy sites and how to use them.

The most reliable site to use when researching processes is the Microsoft support site (*support.microsoft.com*). A search on a process name, an error message, a description of a process or problem with a process, or other related information can turn up a Knowledge Base article with the information you need. For example, in Figure 2-12, you can see the results of searching for information on the service Svchost.exe. Article 314056, "A description of Svchost.exe in Windows XP" is excellent.

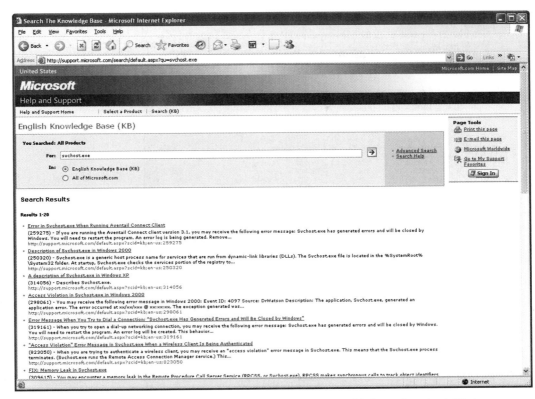

Figure 2-12 The Microsoft Knowledge Base is an excellent source of information about Windows processes

However, Microsoft doesn't normally maintain information about processes other than its own, so for that you must go elsewhere. Suppose for example, when you look at the Processes tab under Task Manager, you see the list shown in Figure 2-13. You see a process you don't recognize, dfsvc.exe. Your search on the Web turns up a hit on the McAfee Security Web site identifying the process as a worm (see Figure 2-14). This McAfee site is a trustworthy site, so you can safely conclude you have an infected system. Knowing this fact helps you set your priorities when cleaning up the system—begin by ending the process and running antivirus software. (How to end a process is coming up.) Then reboot and make sure the worm has been cleaned up. For a highly infected system, you can first boot into Safe Mode and then run your AV software, so that worms and viruses are less likely to be loaded.

Some other useful sites that can be trusted to give you information about unknown processes are:

- Answers That Work at *www.answersthatwork.com*
- Jim Foley, The Elder Geek at *www.theeldergeek.com*
- Process Library by Jelsoft Enterprises, Ltd. at *www.processlibrary.com*
- Uniblue at *www.liutilities.com*
- All the antivirus software sites listed in Chapter 1 in Table 1-1

HOW TO END A PROCESS

As you clean up startup, you might need to close an application or service. To close an application, normally you would use the menus within the application or click the Close button in the upper-right corner of the window in which the application is running. To close a service, under normal conditions, you would use the Services console, which is discussed later in the chapter. However, if a process (application or service) is not responding or is giving errors, these normal methods might not work. To end a process that is not responding, first try to use Task Manager.

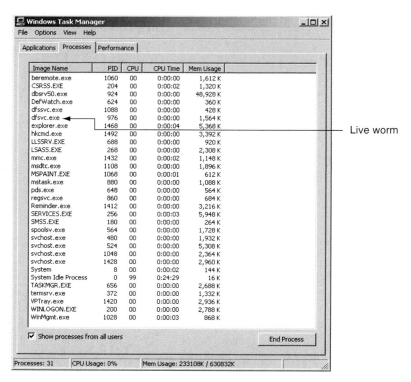

Figure 2-13 The Processes tab of Task Manager uncovers a live worm

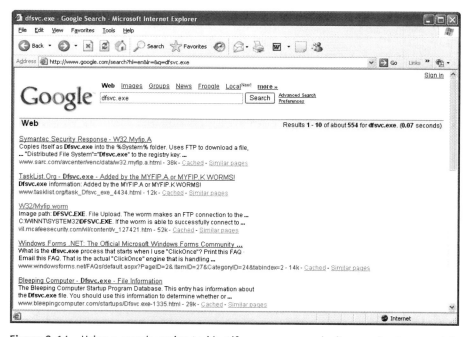

Figure 2-14 Using a search engine to identify processes you don't recognize turns up information about a worm

Here is what you can do to end a process that is giving you trouble:

- Using Task Manager, to end a program that is not responding to the system, click the **Applications** tab, select the program (called a task in the window), and click **End Task**. This action is the same as if you had used a menu option on the application's window to close the application. If the problem with the application is not too drastic, you might have the opportunity to close data files that are open.
- Sometimes the application is so locked up, clicking End Task will not close the application. In this case, click the **Processes** tab, select the application, and click **End Process**. This action is more drastic than End Task, because it closes the process immediately without giving you the opportunity to close open data files.
- If clicking End Process does not work, the application might be locked up as it waits for your response to a dialog box displayed onscreen. Close the dialog box and then click End Process.
- Sometimes when you try to end a service, you get an error message that access is denied and the process does not end. In this case, you might not have the right permissions. Try closing a service when you are logged in as an administrator.
- For Windows XP Home Edition, if Task Manager cannot end a process, try using the Tskill command. For example, in a Command Prompt window, to end the process Mcagent.exe use this command (don't include the file extension in the command line): **tskill mcagent.**
- For Windows XP Professional, if Task Manager cannot end a process, you can use the Tskill command or the more powerful Taskkill command. As you can see in Figure 2-15, first use the Tasklist command to get a list of processes. Then use the PID (process ID) to identify the process in the Taskkill command line. For example, to kill the process Spoolsv.exe (the print spooler), use this command: **taskkill /f /pid:1148**. Notice in Figure 2-15 that the /f parameter to forcefully kill the process is required for this particular process. Be careful using this command; it is so powerful that you can end critical system processes that will cause the system to shut down.

DO A GENERAL CLEANUP

It might seem pretty mundane, but the first things you need to do to begin the actual cleaning of Windows startup are the obvious routine maintenance tasks. Begin by doing these things:

- As always, if valuable data is not backed up, back it up before you do anything else. Don't risk the data without the user's permission.
- If you suspect a virus is present that might be affecting the startup, boot into Safe Mode and run antivirus software. You learned how to do that in Chapter 1.
- If you see an error message, respond to it. If you've made a change to the system, such as installing software or hardware, assume the installation is the guilty party until it's proven innocent.
- If you have just installed a new application or utility program, go to the Add or Remove Programs applet in Control Panel and uninstall the software. Reboot the system. If the problem goes away, then try reinstalling the software. If the problem comes back, go to the software manufacturer's Web site and download and install any updates or fixes.

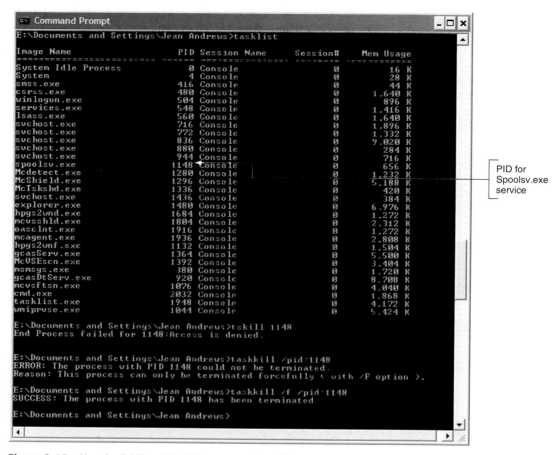

Figure 2-15 Use the Tskill and Taskkill commands to kill a process

⊿ If you have just installed a new hardware device, use Device Manager to disable the device. If the problem doesn't go away, then uninstall the device. If this solves the problem, then try to find updated device drivers for the device. Search the Microsoft Web site for known problems with the device or search the device manufacturer Web site. Try updating the device drivers.

⊿ If you have just updated a device driver, the update might be causing the problem. Open Device Manager and use Driver Rollback to restore the old drivers. If an error message appears that makes you think the problem is related to the device, disable it in Device Manager or uninstall it.

⊿ Using the Add or Remove Programs applet in Control Panel, remove any unwanted software. Be sure to stop the software first. If necessary, you can use Task Manager to end a process and then uninstall it.

⊿ Clean up the hard drive, deleting unwanted files and using Defrag and Chkdsk, as you learned to do in Chapter 1. If the system is slow while trying to do this, boot into Safe Mode and do these maintenance tasks from there.

> **Notes**
>
> Appendix B lists all the entry points discussed in this chapter that Windows looks to for programs and services to load at startup. Appendix B is intended to be a handy future reference.

All these steps are pretty obvious things to do to generally clean up the startup process. Now let's turn our attention to looking for startup tasks that are bogging down startup.

STARTUP FOLDERS

Certain folders are designated as startup folders for all user accounts or a particular user account. Scripts, programs, or shortcuts to programs can be placed in these startup folders by the user, by an administrator, or by a program without the user's knowledge. For example, Figure 2-16 shows a startup folder with all kinds of services placed there by Windows and other software.

Figure 2-16 This startup folder holds several unneeded services that appear in the system tray and take up system resources

To clean up startup, look in each startup folder mentioned in this section. If you find a program or shortcut there that you don't think you want, unless you know it's malicious, move it to a different folder rather than deleting it. Later, if you like, you can return it to the startup folder, or you can start the program manually from the new folder.

CURRENT USER STARTUP FOLDER

A program file or a shortcut to it can be placed in this folder:

C:\Documents and Settings*username*\Start Menu\Programs\Startup

Each time this particular user logs on, the program is launched. The user who owns the folder and users with administrator privileges can place programs or shortcuts in this folder.

> **Notes**
>
> To keep programs kept in startup folders from executing as you start Windows, hold down the Shift key just after you enter your account name and password on the Windows logon screen. Keep holding down the **Shift** key until the desktop is fully loaded and the hourglass has disappeared. To permanently disable a startup item, remove it from its startup folder.

ALL USERS STARTUP FOLDER

Someone with administrator privileges can place a program file or shortcut in this folder so that the startup event applies to all users:

◢ C:\Documents and Settings\All Users\Start Menu\Programs\Startup

The program starts up when any user logs on.

UPGRADE FROM WINDOWS NT

If Windows XP has been installed as an upgrade from Windows NT, the C:\Windows\Profiles folder will exist. Programs and shortcuts to programs might be in these folders:

▲ C:\Windows\Profiles\All Users\Start Menu\Programs\Startup
▲ C:\Windows\Profiles*username*\Start Menu\Programs\Startup

After you check these four folders for startup processes you don't want, you can then move on to the next thing to check: the Scheduled Task folder.

SCHEDULED TASK FOLDER

Windows offers a Task Scheduler that can be set to launch a task or program at a future time, including at startup. When tasks are scheduled, a file is stored in the C:\Windows\Tasks folder. For example, in Figure 2-17, the one scheduled task is named Calculator. When you right-click the task and select Properties from the shortcut menu, you can see the task is scheduled to start at startup. This means each time a user logs onto the system, the Windows Calculator application is started.

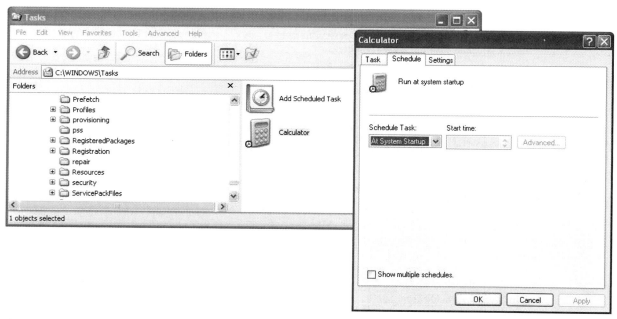

Figure 2-17 The Tasks folder can contain tasks that launch at startup

The easiest way to view a list of scheduled tasks is to open the Scheduled Tasks applet in Control Panel. When the Scheduled Tasks folder appears, click **View, Details**, to see the details of a task, as shown in Figure 2-18 where two tasks are scheduled. One task was placed there automatically when a Hewlett-Packard printer was installed, and another was placed there by an administrator. Tasks can be scheduled to run when users log on, when Windows launches, or at a particular time of day, week, or month. Tasks can be scheduled to run one time or many times. Tasks can be applications, services, or other background processes, and tasks can be scheduled to download e-mail or open Internet Explorer and download a Web page. Tasks can also consist of batch programs or Windows scripting. Using the Scheduled Tasks window, you can add, delete, or

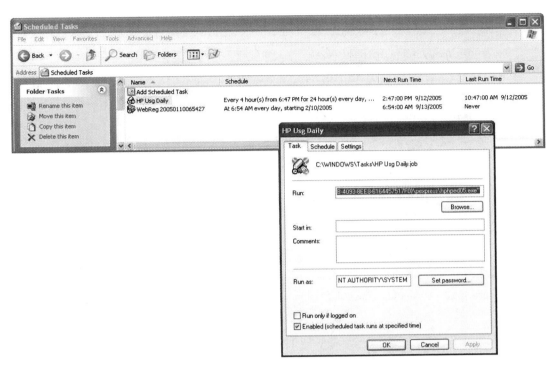

Figure 2-18 The Scheduled Tasks applet can be used to schedule a task at Windows startup

change a task, and you can also use the command Schtasks at the command line to do the same things. (The Schtasks command is not included in Windows XP Home Edition.)

The Scheduled Task process generates a log of activity. The log file is C:\Windows\SchedLgU.Txt and is shown in Figure 2-19. You can easily view the log file by clicking **Advanced, View Log**, in the Scheduled Tasks window. Entries are placed in the file immediately after the last entry and cycle through the fixed-length file (that is, older entries are removed to make way for more recent entries). To find the most recent entry, using Notepad, search for the word "recent," as seen in Figure 2-19.

All this information is helpful when researching scheduled tasks to unravel the mystery of processes or activities that fail or bog down a system. In cleaning up startup, delete any scheduled tasks you don't want, and you're ready to move on to the next step, which is to check for legacy startup programs.

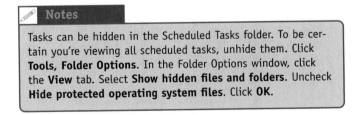

Notes

Tasks can be hidden in the Scheduled Tasks folder. To be certain you're viewing all scheduled tasks, unhide them. Click **Tools, Folder Options**. In the Folder Options window, click the **View** tab. Select **Show hidden files and folders**. Uncheck **Hide protected operating system files**. Click **OK**.

LEGACY SYSTEM FILES USED FOR STARTUP

Four legacy system files used to control the startup process under DOS, Windows 3.x, and Windows 9x/Me are Autoexec.bat, Config.sys, System.ini, and Win.ini. System.ini and Win.ini are located in the C:\Windows folder, and Windows XP executes commands and settings in these files to create an environment to support legacy hardware and software. Under DOS and Windows 9x, Autoexec.bat and Config.sys were stored in the root directory and were used to load device drivers and software settings. Windows XP executes neither Autoexec.bat nor Config.sys. Therefore, you only need to be concerned with entries in System.ini and Win.ini.

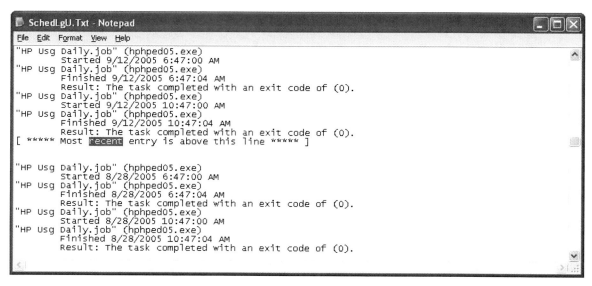

Figure 2-19   View a log of activities of scheduled tasks

The easiest way to check these files is to use MSconfig. You can also use Notepad to check the files. Right-click the filename and select **Open** from the shortcut menu. The file opens in Notepad, as shown in Figure 2-20. In the files, know that a semicolon at the beginning of a line means the line is a comment line and is not executed. For Win.ini, look for entries in the Load= and Run= lines of this text file. Normally, if System.ini and Win.ini are not used by your system to support legacy devices and software, these two lines won't even exist in Win.ini. If you find program names in the Load= or Run= lines and you don't have legacy devices installed, suspect a problem.

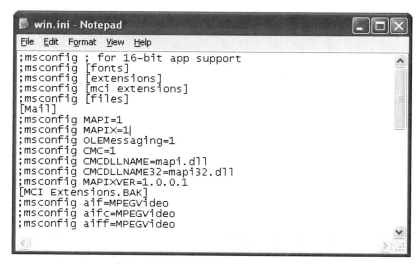

Figure 2-20   A harmless and unused Win.ini file

SERVICES

Recall that a service is a program that runs in the background to support other programs. Services are managed by the Services console (Services.msc). Use the Services console to see what services have been set to automatically start when Windows loads. To launch the

Services console, type **Services.msc** in the Run dialog box and press **Enter**. The Services window opens, as shown in Figure 2-21.

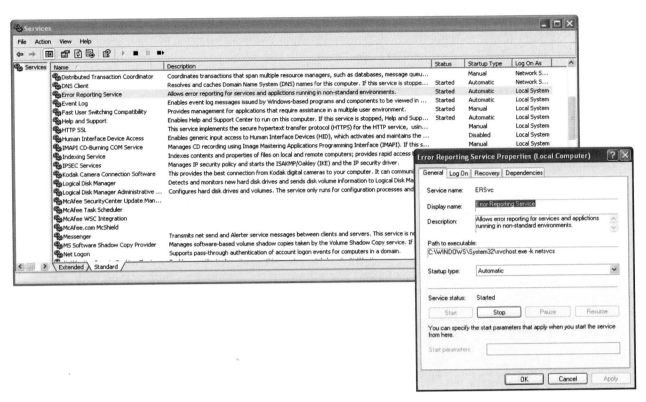

Figure 2-21 The Services console is used to start, stop, and schedule services

To learn more about a service, right-click it and select **Properties** from the shortcut menu. In the resulting Properties window, also shown in Figure 2-21 for one selected service, you can see the name of the program file and its path. From this window, you can start and stop the service and change the startup type. Choices for the startup type are Automatic (automatically launched at startup), Manual (can be started after Windows is launched by a user or by another program), or Disabled (cannot be started). You can also start and stop a service by right-clicking the service in the Services console window and selecting the appropriate action on the shortcut menu.

If you are having trouble with a service, you can sometimes solve the problem by pausing or stopping the service and then resuming or starting it. For example, suppose a print job is stuck in the print spooling window. Pausing and resuming, or stopping and starting the Print Spooler might solve the problem. Beware, however, that when you stop a service, other services that this service needs to work are also stopped. This can result in some service being stopped that another service is also dependent on. To see a list of services that a service depends on, in the service's Properties window, click the **Dependencies** tab.

When investigating a service, try using a good search engine on the Web to search for the

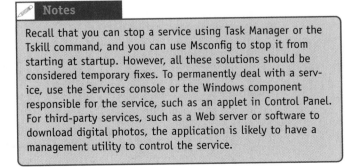

Notes

Recall that you can stop a service using Task Manager or the Tskill command, and you can use Msconfig to stop it from starting at startup. However, all these solutions should be considered temporary fixes. To permanently deal with a service, use the Services console or the Windows component responsible for the service, such as an applet in Control Panel. For third-party services, such as a Web server or software to download digital photos, the application is likely to have a management utility to control the service.

name of the service or the name of the program file that launches the service. Either can give you information you need to snoop out unwanted services. If you're not sure you want to keep a certain service, use Msconfig to temporarily disable it at the next boot so you can see what happens.

When you permanently disable a service using the Services console or some other tool, don't forget to reboot to make sure everything works before moving on to the next tool to use in cleaning up startup: Group Policy.

GROUP POLICY

When using Windows XP Professional, an administrator can use the Group Policy console (Gpedit.msc) to manage many computers on a network, limiting the way users can use Windows and applications and control Windows settings and features. (Windows XP Home Edition does not have the Group Policy console.) Group Policy can also be used to manage a single stand-alone computer and can be used to launch programs at startup. Group Policy works by making entries in the registry, applying scripts to the Windows startup, shutdown, and logon processes, and affecting security settings. To access the Group Policy console, enter **gpedit.msc** in the Run dialog box. Notice in the Group Policy window (see Figure 2-22) that there are two main groups of policies: Computer Configuration and User Configuration. There is some overlap in policies between these two groups. When this happens, Computer Configuration takes precedence. Group Policy also takes precedence over any settings you make using Windows menus.

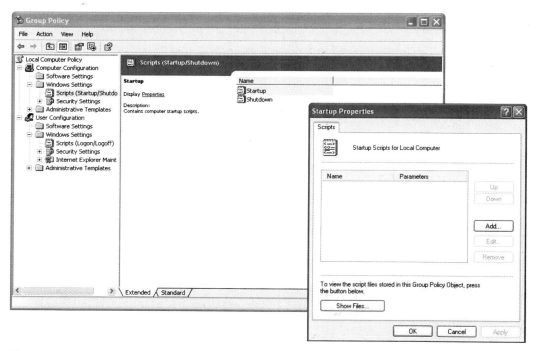

Figure 2-22   Using the Group Policy console, you can control many Windows events and settings, including the startup process

Also in Figure 2-22, you can see four ways a script can be launched using Group Policy: at startup, shutdown, when a user logs on, or when a user logs off. Because a script can launch a program, Group Policy can be used to launch a program. These scripts are stored in one of these four folders:

- ◢ C:\WINDOWS\System32\GroupPolicy\Machine\Scripts\Startup
- ◢ C:\WINDOWS\System32\GroupPolicy\Machine\Scripts\Shutdown

▲ C:\WINDOWS\System32\GroupPolicy\User\Scripts\Logon
▲ C:\WINDOWS\System32\GroupPolicy\User\Scripts\Logoff

To see what Group Policies are currently applied, you can use the Windows XP Help and Support Center. Click **Start, Help and Support**. On the right side of the window, click **Use Tools to view your computer information and diagnose problems**. In the left pane, click **Advanced System Information**. Next, click **View Group Policy settings applied**. Information is first collected and then the window in Figure 2-23 appears.

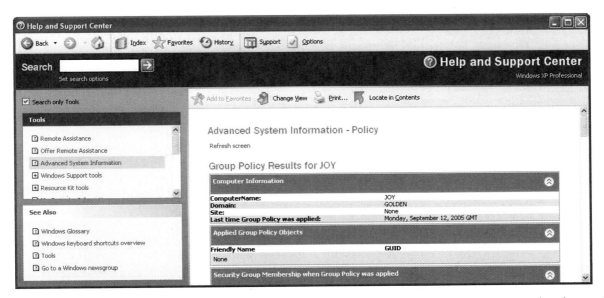

Figure 2-23   Use the Help and Support Center to view Group Policies currently applied to your system and environment

To add or remove a Group Policy that is executed at startup, open the Group Policy console (Gpedit.msc) and do the following:

1. In the Group Policy window, under either Computer Configuration or User Configuration, open **Administrative Templates**, open **System**, and then open **Logon** (see Figure 2-24).

2. In the right pane, double-click **Run these programs at user logon**, which opens the properties window shown in Figure 2-24. Select **Enabled** and then click **Show**. The Show Contents dialog box opens, also shown in Figure 2-24.

3. To add a script or executable program to the list of items to run at logon, click **Add**. In the figure, Microsoft Word has been added so that it will launch at logon. To remove an item from the list, select it and click **Remove**. Click **OK** to close the dialog box and **Apply** to apply the changes. Click **OK** to close the Properties window.

When someone makes one of the above changes using Group Policy, an entry is made in the registry. When you want to reverse a Group Policy setting, it is best to not do it by editing the registry, for a couple of reasons. First, editing the registry is dangerous, because it is so easy to make mistakes and any change is immediately applied. Second, Group Policy might undo your changes because Group Policy stores its settings in a remote place in the registry and routinely refreshes settings to keys that apply the policies.

After making a change to Group Policies, be sure to reboot before moving on to the next step in cleaning up the startup process: uninstalling unused fonts.

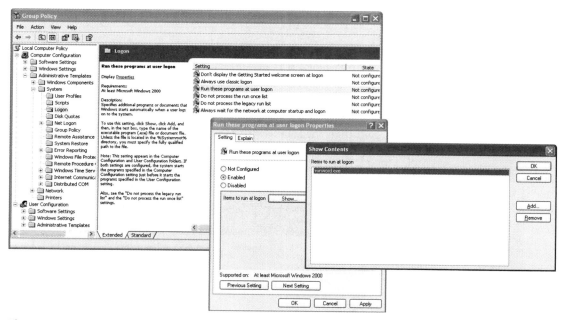

Figure 2-24 Use Group Policy to launch a program or script at logon

UNINSTALL UNUSED FONTS

One more thing you can do to clean up the startup process is uninstall fonts that you don't use. When Windows XP is installed, it comes with a group of fonts that can be used for the Windows desktop and in a variety of other places. Some applications install additional fonts and you can purchase and manually install other fonts. All installed fonts are loaded at startup, so if a system has had many new fonts installed, these can slow down startup.

Windows XP keeps installed fonts in files in the C:\Windows\Fonts folder. See Figure 2-25. To install or uninstall a font is to simply move it in or out of this folder.

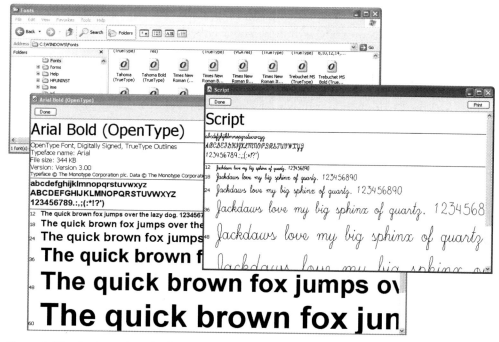

Figure 2-25 Fonts are kept in the C:\Windows\Fonts folder

When Windows starts up for the first time after the Fonts folder has been changed, it rebuilds the fonts table, which means the first reboot after a font change is slowed down.

Check the C:\Windows\Fonts folder. If you see more than 260 files in this folder, new fonts have been installed. You can try moving some files to a different folder to reduce the number of fonts loading at startup. Actually, you can move all the files out of this folder and Windows will still work because it doesn't keep the one system font here. But then, your documents will look pretty plain. If you change the Fonts folder, don't forget it'll take the second reboot before you should notice any improvement in startup.

Unless you have some unusually difficult problems to solve, your Windows XP startup should now be smooth and fast. However, you might have to dig deeper into some more complex issues. That's the subject of the next section.

DIGGING DEEPER INTO STARTUP PROCESSES

In this section, you'll learn to search the registry and remove startup tasks left there by software that has been uninstalled incorrectly or by malicious software. You'll also learn how to remove software that won't politely uninstall when you use the Add or Remove Programs applet. Then you'll learn to use some really cool third-party utilities that give more information than Windows is willing to cough up.

EDITING THE REGISTRY

As you have seen, many actions, such as Group Policy changes or installing application software, can result in changes to the registry. These changes can create new keys, add new values to existing keys, and change existing values. For really difficult problems, you might need to edit or remove a registry key. This section looks at how the registry is organized, which keys might hold entries causing problems, and how to back up and edit the registry.

HOW THE REGISTRY IS ORGANIZED

The most important Windows component that holds information for Windows is the registry. The registry is a database designed with a tree-like structure (called a hierarchical database) that contains configuration information for Windows, users, software applications, and installed hardware devices. During startup, Windows builds the registry in memory and keeps it there until Windows shuts down. During startup, after the registry is built, Windows reads from it to obtain information to complete the startup process. After Windows is loaded, it continually reads from many of the subkeys in the registry.

Windows builds the registry from the current hardware configuration and from information it takes from these files:

- ◢ Five files stored in the C:\Windows\System32\config folder. These files are called hives, and they are named the Sam, Security, Software, System, and Default hives.
- ◢ The file C:\Documents and Settings*username*\Local Settings\Application Data\Microsoft\Windows\Usrclass.dat.
- ◢ The file C:\Documents and Settings*username*\Ntuser.dat

After the registry is built in memory, it is organized into five tree-like structures. Each of the five segments is called a key. Each key can have subkeys, and subkeys can have more subkeys and can be assigned one or more values.

Here are the five keys and their purposes:

▲ *HKEY_CURRENT_USER (HKCU)*—This key contains configuration information for the current user of the computer. This includes the location of the user's files and folders, desktop configuration settings, and applications.

▲ *HKEY_USERS (HKU)*—This key stores information for every user that has ever used the computer. If the user logs on again, his or her personal settings are retrieved and copied to the HKEY_CURRENT_USER key.

▲ *HKEY_LOCAL_MACHINE (HKLM)*—This key contains configuration information for all software, hardware, and security settings installed on a computer. Information stored in this key is applied to every computer user.

▲ *HKEY_CLASSES_ROOT (HKCR)*—This key stores information that determines which application is opened when the user double-clicks a file. This process relies on the file's extension to determine which program to load. For example, this registry key might hold the information to cause MS Word to open when a user double-clicks a file with a .doc file extension.

▲ *HKEY_CURRENT_CONFIG (HKCC)*—This key contains Plug and Play information about the hardware configuration that is used by the computer at startup. Information that identifies each hardware device installed in a PC is kept in this area.

 Tip

For a better explanation of how the registry is organized, how it is built, and how Windows uses it, see Appendix D, "How Windows XP Works".

BEFORE YOU EDIT THE REGISTRY, BACK IT UP!

As you investigate startup problems and see a registry entry that needs changing, remember from Chapter 1 that it is important to use caution when editing the registry. If possible, make the change from the Windows tool that is responsible for the key—for example, by using Group Policy or Add/Remove Programs in Control Panel. If that doesn't work and you must edit the registry, always back up the registry before attempting to edit it. Changes made to the registry are implemented immediately. There is no undo feature in the registry editor, and no opportunity to change your mind once the edit is made.

There are basically two ways to back up the registry: the safest way is to back up the entire system state and the registry; alternatively, you can back up only those keys in the registry that you expect to change.

Back Up the System State and Registry

The **system state** is all the Windows system files necessary to load Windows XP. Follow these steps to back up the system state, which includes backing up the registry:

1. Click **Start**, point to **All Programs**, point to **Accessories**, point to **System Tools**, and then click **Backup**. Depending on how Windows is configured, the Backup or Restore Wizard launches or the Backup Utility window appears, as shown in Figure 2-26. If the wizard launches, click **Advanced Mode** to display the Backup Utility window shown in Figure 2-26.

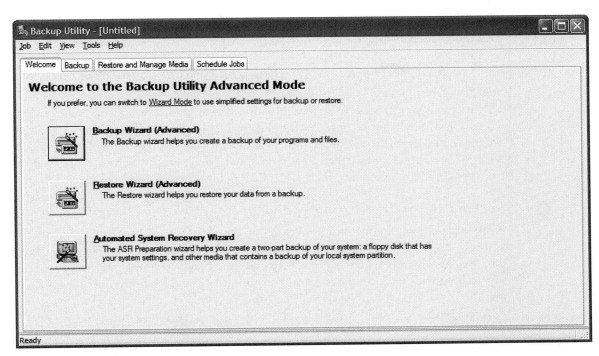

Figure 2-26 The Windows Backup Utility in advanced mode

2. Click the **Backup** tab and check the box next to System State (see Figure 2-27).

3. Click **Browse** to open the Save As window and select the location on your computer or the network to save the system state data. Click **Save** to close the window.

4. To begin the backup, click **Start Backup**. When the process is completed, close the Backup Utility.

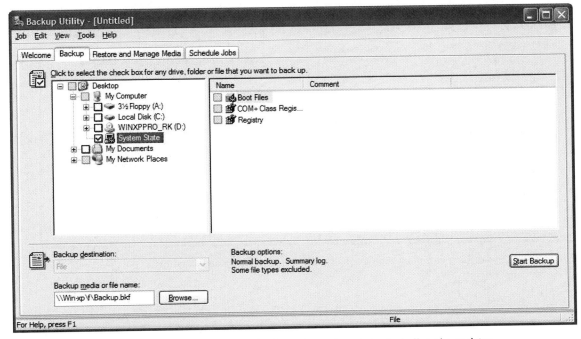

Figure 2-27 Use the Windows Backup Utility to back up the system state, including the registry

When Windows backs up the system state, it puts a copy of the registry files in the C:\Windows\repair folder.

How to Restore the Registry Using the System State Backup

You can use the files saved by the System State backup in the event you need to restore the registry after making changes. To restore the entire system state, which includes the registry, open the Backup Utility window (refer back to Figure 2-26) and select **Restore Wizard (Advanced)**. To just restore the registry, make a copy of all the files in the C:\Windows\System32\config folder to another folder and then copy the Default, Sam, Security, Software, and System files from the C:\Windows\Repair folder to the C:\Windows\System32\config folder.

Backing Up and Restoring Individual Keys in the Registry

A less time-consuming method of backing up the registry is to back up a particular key that you plan to edit. However, know that if the registry gets corrupted, having a backup of only a particular key most likely will not help you much when trying a recovery. Also, don't use this technique to back up the entire registry or an entire tree within the registry. Use this method to back up a subkey and all the subkeys within it.

To back up a key along with its subkeys in the registry, follow these steps:

1. Open the registry editor. To do that, click **Start**, click **Run**, type **regedit** in the Run dialog box, and press **Enter**. Figure 2-28 shows the registry editor with the five main keys and several subkeys listed. Click the **+** (plus sign) to see subkeys. When you select a subkey, such as KeyboardClass in the figure, the names of the values in that subkey are displayed in the right pane along with the data assigned to each value.

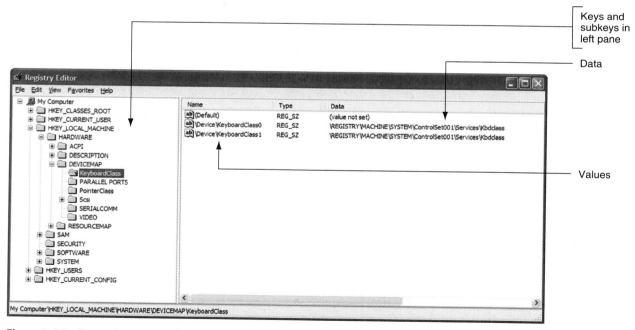

Figure 2-28 The registry editor showing the five main keys, subkeys, values, and data

2. Suppose we want to back up the registry key that contains a list of installed software, which is HKLM\Software\Microsoft\Windows\CurrentVersion\Uninstall. (HKLM stands for HKEY_LOCAL_MACHINE.) We first click the appropriate plus signs to

navigate to the key. Next, right-click the key and select **Export** on the shortcut menu, as shown in Figure 2-29. The Export Registry File dialog box appears.

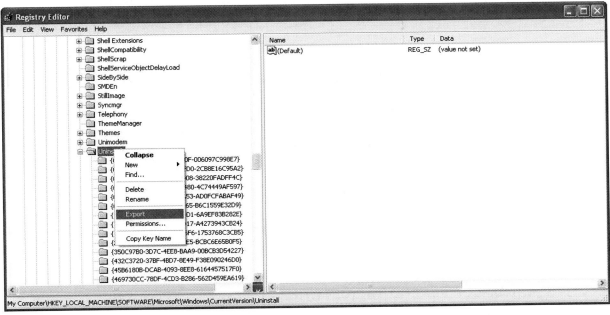

Figure 2-29 Using the Windows XP registry editor, you can back up a key and its subkeys with the Export command

3. Select the location to save the export file and name the file. A convenient place to store an export file while you edit the registry is the desktop. Click **Save** when done. The file saved will have a .reg file extension.

4. You can now edit the key. Later, if you need to undo your changes, exit the registry editor and double-click the saved export file. The key and its subkeys saved in the export file will be restored. After you're done with an export file, delete it.

EDITING THE REGISTRY

When you make a change in the Control Panel, Device Manager, or many other places in Windows XP, the registry is modified automatically. This is the only way most users will ever change the registry. However, on rare occasions, you might need to edit the registry manually.

Before you edit the registry, you should use one of the two backup methods just discussed so that you can restore it if something goes wrong. To edit the registry, open the registry editor and locate and select the key in the left pane of the registry editor, which will display the values stored in this key in the right pane. To edit, rename, or delete a value, right-click it and select the appropriate option from the shortcut menu. For example, in Figure 2-30, I'm ready to delete the value SMSERIAL and its data. Changes are immediately applied to the registry and there is no undo feature. Notice in Figure 2-30 that the selected key is displayed in the status bar at the bottom of the editor window. If the status bar is missing, click **View** on the menu bar and make sure **Status Bar** is checked. To search the registry for keys, values, and data, click **Edit** on the menu bar and then click **Find**.

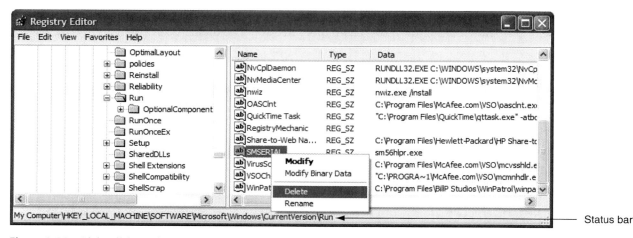

Figure 2-30 Right-click a value to modify, delete, or rename it

Now let's look at a situation where it is appropriate to edit the registry to remove unwanted software entries.

MANUALLY REMOVING SOFTWARE

Just about every uninstall routine I've ever known, including some I've written myself, leaves behind some files or registry entries here and there in a Windows system. Even Microsoft, in the Knowledge Base Article 254250, lists more than 100 files, folders, and registry keys left behind when Microsoft Office 97 uninstalls itself! The article shows you how to manually delete each one! When you install and uninstall software, most likely the end result is going to be more files and folders and a larger registry than you had before you installed the software.

> **Notes**
>
> Before uninstalling software, make sure it's not running in the background. Antivirus software can't be uninstalled if it's still running. You can use Task Manager to end all processes related to the software. Then remove the software.

In this section, we focus on getting rid of software that refuses to uninstall itself or gives errors when uninstalling. In these cases, you can manually uninstall a program. Doing so often causes problems later, so use the methods discussed in this section only as a last resort after the Add or Remove Programs applet has failed.

UNINSTALL ROUTINE

Some programs have an uninstall routine which is installed in the All Programs menu when the software is first installed. For example, in Figure 2-31 you can see Uninstall WinPatrol as an option for this software installation. Click this option and follow the directions onscreen to uninstall the software.

Next, verify the software is no longer listed in the Add or Remove Programs window. If the software is still listed in the window, you can select it and then click **Remove**. Windows will tell you the software has already been uninstalled and ask if you want it removed from the list. When you say okay, the software will be removed from the list. If you get an error, you can edit the registry to manually remove the software from the list. How to do that is covered in the next sections.

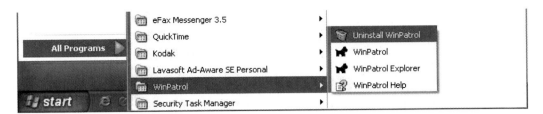

Figure 2-31 Some applications have an uninstall utility included with the software

DELETE PROGRAM FILES

If neither Add or Remove Programs nor an uninstall routine work, as a last resort, you can manually delete the program files and registry entries used by the software you want to uninstall. In our example, we'll use the WinPatrol software by BillP Studios. Follow these steps:

1. Most likely, the program files are stored in the C:\Program Files folder on the hard drive (see Figure 2-32). Using Windows Explorer, look for a folder in the Program Files folder that contains the software. In Figure 2-32, you can see the WinPatrol software under the BillP Studios folder. Keep in mind, however, that you might not find the program files you're looking for in the C:\Program Files folder because when you install software, the software installation program normally asks you where to install the software. Therefore, the program files might be anywhere, and you might need to search a bit to find them.

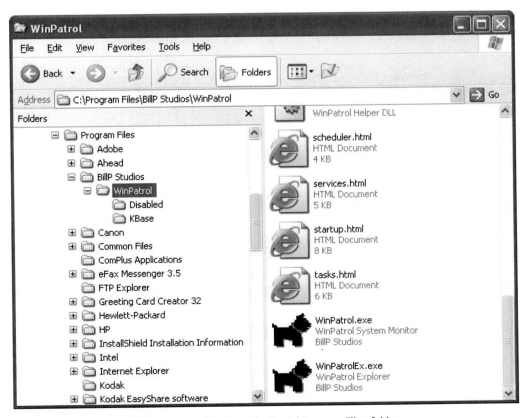

Figure 2-32 Program folders are usually stored in the C:\Program Files folder

2. Delete the WinPatrol folder and all its contents. You can also delete the BillP Studios folder.

DELETE REGISTRY ENTRIES

Editing the registry can be dangerous, so do this with caution! Do the following to delete registry entries for a program that cause it to be listed as installed software in the Add or Remove Programs window:

1. Click **Start**, click **Run**, and then type **regedit** in the Run dialog box. Click **OK** to open the registry editor.

2. Locate this key, which contains the entries that comprise the list of installed software in the Add or Remove Programs window: HKEY_LOCAL_MACHINE\Software\Microsoft\Windows\CurrentVersion\Uninstall

3. Back up the Uninstall key to the Windows desktop so that you can backtrack if necessary. To do that, right-click the Uninstall key and select **Export** from the shortcut menu (refer to Figure 2-29).

4. In the Export Registry File dialog box, select the **Desktop**. Enter the filename as **Save Uninstall Key**, and click **Save**. You should see a new icon on your desktop named Save Uninstall Key.reg.

5. The Uninstall key is a daunting list of all the programs installed on your PC. When you expand the key, you'll see a long list of subkeys in the left pane, which have meaningless names that won't help you find the program you're looking for. Select the first subkey in the Uninstall key and watch its values and data display in the right pane (see Figure 2-33). Step down through each key, watching the details in the right pane until you find the program you want to delete.

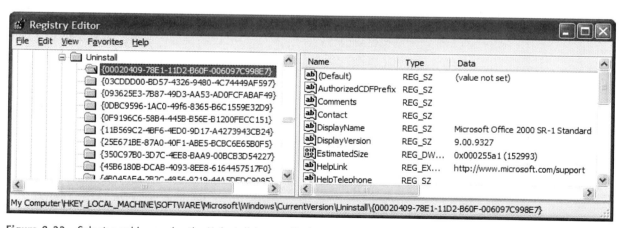

Figure 2-33   Select a subkey under the Uninstall key to display its values and data in the right pane

6. To delete the key, right-click the key and select **Delete** from the shortcut menu (see Figure 2-34). When the Confirm Key Delete dialog box appears asking you to confirm the deletion, click **Yes**. Be sure to search through all the keys in this list because the software might have more than one key. Delete them all and exit the registry editor.

7. Open the Add or Remove Programs window and verify that the list of installed software is correct and the software you are uninstalling is no longer listed.

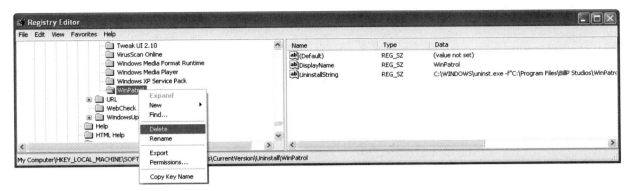

Figure 2-34 Delete the registry key that lists the software in the Add or Remove Programs window

8. If the list of installed software is not correct, to undo your change to the registry, double-click the **Save Uninstall Key.reg** icon on your desktop to restore the Uninstall key.

9. If the list in the Add or Remove Programs window is correct, clean up after yourself by deleting the Save Uninstall Key.reg icon and file on your desktop. Right-click the icon and select **Delete** from the shortcut menu.

REGISTRY KEYS THAT AFFECT STARTUP AND LOGON EVENTS

You have just seen how you can manually edit the registry to remove the entries that identify software as installed software. Listed in this section are some registry keys where startup processes can be located. As one step in cleaning up startup, you can search through these registry keys for processes left there by uninstalled or corrupted software that might be giving startup problems.

As you read through this list of registry keys to search, know that the list is not exhaustive. With experience, you'll learn the registry is an ever-changing landscape of keys and values.

Registry keys that affect the startup and logon events are listed below. Your registry might or might not have all these keys. As you search the registry for entries in these keys, don't forget to first back up the registry. Because you'll be searching all over the registry and not just in one particular place, it's a good idea to back up the system state as your registry backup method so that the entire registry will be backed up.

These keys cause an entry to run once and only once at startup:

- ◢ HKCU\Software\Microsoft\Windows\CurrentVersion\RunOnce
- ◢ HKCU\Software\Microsoft\Windows\CurrentVersion\RunOnceEx
- ◢ HKLM\Software\Microsoft\Windows\CurrentVersion\RunOnce
- ◢ HKLM\Software\Microsoft\Windows\CurrentVersion\RunOnceEx

Figure 2-35 shows what you might see when you view the first key in the list above, the RunOnce key for the current user. The entry in this key was put there when I uninstalled some software and the uninstall routine asked permission to restart Windows. I said no, so now this key has an entry that will cause the final task of the uninstall routine to run once the next time I reboot. After that, the key should be empty, displaying "value not set."

Check each key in the list above and move on to the next list.

Group Policy places entries in these keys to affect startup:

- ◢ HKCU\Software\Microsoft\Windows\CurrentVersion\Policies\Explorer\Run
- ◢ HKLM\Software\Microsoft\Windows\CurrentVersion\Policies\Explorer\Run

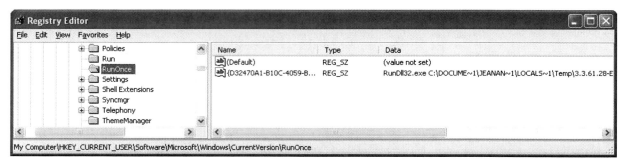

Figure 2-35 The RunOnce key has one entry that will complete when the current user reboots

Figure 2-36 shows the first key with a really bad entry. Pludpm.exe is a virus.

Windows loads many DLL programs from the following key, which is sometimes used by malicious software. Entries in this key are normal, so don't delete one unless you know it's causing a problem:

▲ HKLM\Software\Microsoft\Windows\CurrentVersion\ShellServiceObjectDelayLoad

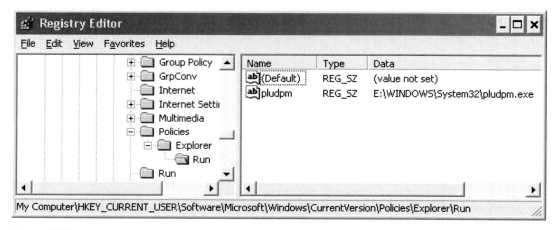

Figure 2-36 An example of what can be found when searching for unwanted startup processes

Windows XP Tweak UI places entries in the following keys to affect the login process. The first key executes a program, Userinit.exe, that performs logon scripts and applies Group Policies and other user settings, including network drive mapping.

▲ HKLM\Software\Microsoft\Windows NT\CurrentVersion\Winlogon\Userinit
▲ HKLM\Software\Microsoft\Windows NT\CurrentVersion\Winlogon\Shell

---

Notes

Tweak UI is a group of small programs called Power Toys written by Microsoft and available on the Microsoft Web site at *www.microsoft.com/windowsxp/pro/downloads/powertoys.asp*. Using these Power Toys, you can make many minor and not-so-minor changes to the Windows environment, including changing the applets displayed in Control Panel, mouse-hovering actions, and what applications are displayed when you click the New option in a folder's shortcut menu.

Figure 2-37 shows these registry values with three executable programs showing: Explorer.exe (the shell), Logonui.exe (Tweak UI), and Userinit.exe. Look for other programs replacing these three legitimate programs.

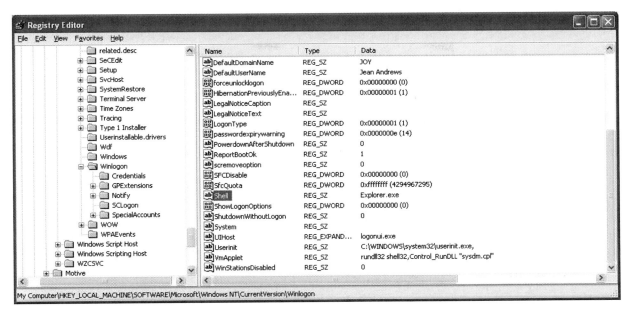

Figure 2-37 The Winlogon key contains several values that affect startup

Entries in the keys listed next apply to all users and hold legitimate startup entries. Don't delete an entry unless you suspect it to be bad:

- HKCU\Software\Microsoft\Windows NT\CurrentVersion\Windows
- HKCU\Software\Microsoft\Windows NT\CurrentVersion\Windows\Run
- HKLM\Software\Microsoft\Windows\CurrentVersion\Run
- HKCU\Software\Microsoft\Windows\CurrentVersion\Run

This key and its subkeys contain entries that pertain to background services that are sometimes launched at startup:

- HKLM\System\CurrentControlSet\Control\Services

The following key contains a value named BootExecute, which is normally set to autochk. It causes the system to run a type of Chkdsk program to check for hard drive integrity when it was previously shut down improperly. Sometimes another program adds itself to this value, causing a problem. For more information about this situation, see the Microsoft Knowledge Base article 151376, "How to Disable Autochk If It Stops Responding During Reboot" at *support.microsoft.com*.

- HKLM\System\CurrentControlSet\Control\Session Manager

Here is an assorted list of registry keys that have all been known to cause various problems at startup. Remember, before you delete a program entry from one of these keys, research the program filename so that you won't accidentally delete something you want to keep:

- HKCU\Software\Microsoft\Command
- HKCU\Software\Microsoft\Command Processor\AutoRun
- HKCU\Software\Microsoft\Windows\CurrentVersion\RunOnce\Setup

⊿ HKCU\Software\Microsoft\Windows NT\CurrentVersion\Windows\load
⊿ HKLM\Software\Microsoft\Windows NT\CurrentVersion\Windows\AppInit_DLLs
⊿ HKLM\Software\Microsoft\Windows NT\CurrentVersion\Winlogon\System
⊿ HKLM\Software\Microsoft\Windows NT\CurrentVersion\Winlogon\Us
⊿ HKCR\batfile\shell\open\command
⊿ HKCR\comfile\shell\open\command
⊿ HKCR\exefile\shell\open\command
⊿ HKCR\htafile\shell\open\command
⊿ HKCR\piffile\shell\open\command
⊿ HKCR\scrfile\shell\open\command

THIRD-PARTY TOOLS

If you have a problem with software loading at startup and you can't find how the software is loaded using the tools and methods discussed so far in this chapter, you can use the tools in this section to take the investigation to a totally new level.

So far in this book, we've used only Windows tools to examine a system and fix it. But there are some great third-party tools that show you more about processes, services, and the guts of Windows than Windows allows you to see. Here's the list of tools we're going to look at in this section:

⊿ Process Manager by Sysinternals and WinTask Pro by Uniblue give you more information about a process than does Task Manager.
⊿ Autoruns by Sysinternals and Startup Control Panel by Mike Lin can help with startup problems better than Msconfig.

Now let's briefly look at all four of these products. You might enjoy downloading them and giving them a try. Then, when you need to pull out the big guns to investigate an elusive problem, you'll be ready.

PROCESS MANAGER BY SYSINTERNALS

One of my favorite Web sites to find excellent Windows utility shareware and freeware is Sysinternals (*www.sysinternals.com*). Process Explorer works like Task Manager, but takes us to another level of information. If you go to the Web site, download the utility for free, and run it, the window in Figure 2-38 appears.

In Figure 2-38, we are using the mouse to hover over the process KodakCCS.exe, which is causing the path to the process filename to be displayed. This file is part of a digital camera driver software. Also notice in the figure the lower pane, which contains a list of open handles for KodakCCS.exe. A handle is a relationship between a process and a resource it has called into action. An open handle is a relationship that has not yet completed. A handle includes a relationship the process has with a registry key, and these keys are listed in the lower pane.

If you click the toggle button labeled in Figure 2-39, you can switch the lower pane to display DLLs showing in the figure. These files are all the DLLs that the process has loaded. As you can see, Process Explorer gives much information about a process and is a useful tool for software developers when writing and troubleshooting problems with their software, installation routines, and software conflicts. You can use the tool to smoke out processes, DLLs, and registry keys that elude Task Manager.

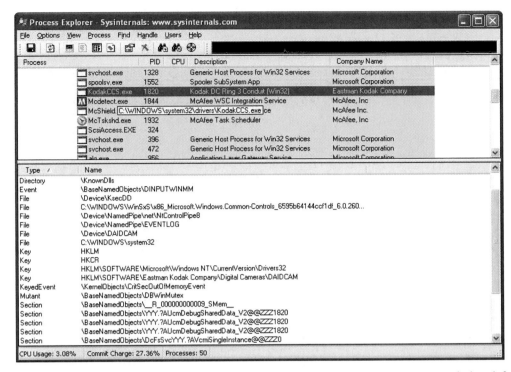

Figure 2-38 Process Explorer color codes child-parent relationships among processes and gives information about processes, including related DLLs

Click this button to display lower pane

Click this button to toggle between handles and DLLs displayed for a selected process

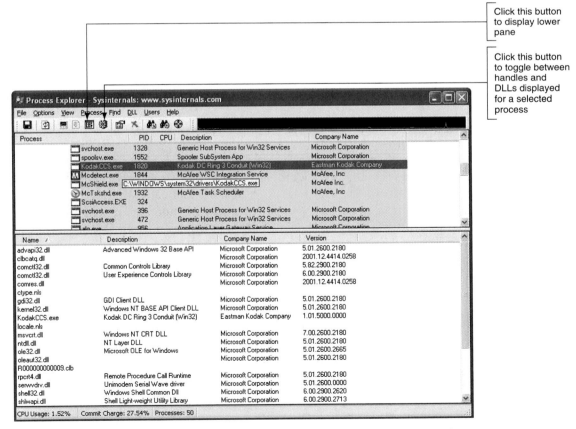

Figure 2-39 Process Explorer in DLL mode displays a list of DLLs loaded by the selected process

WINTASKS PRO BY UNIBLUE

WinTasks Pro by Uniblue (*www.liutilities.com*) is available for purchase as a download from the Web site or in a boxed retail version. Because it is not free, we expect it to provide more information than Process Explorer provides. It displays information about running processes and allows you to temporarily or permanently stop and start them. After downloading the software, installing it, and executing it, the window in Figure 2-40 appears. If you select a process and click the Process Lib button, a window appears with information from the online database maintained by Uniblue, which is shown in the figure for the Kodak digital camera driver software we examined earlier.

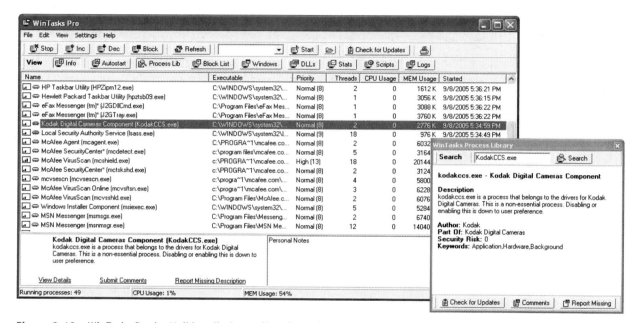

Figure 2-40   WinTasks Pro by Uniblue displays a list of running processes and online information about a selected process

Because it provides easy access to the online database, WinTasks Pro is a useful utility if you spend a lot of time researching unknown processes. Using it, you can block, stop and start, and remove a process from the list of processes executed at startup, including editing their registry entries. It can also measure memory and CPU usage.

WinTasks Pro is especially powerful when troubleshooting an application's DLL calls. Select the process and click the DLLs button to display a list of DLLs. This list includes all the DLLs that the process can reference and use. This is a little different from the list of DLLs provided by Process Explorer, which lists only the DLLs the process is currently using. Using WinTasks Pro, you can also log information about when and what DLLs are opened and closed, which software developers find very useful when troubleshooting software conflicts and installation problems. Consider WinTasks Pro an excellent tool if you are responsible for supporting Windows software in depth. If you are simply troubleshooting occasional problems with Windows, Process Explorer will probably do the job and it's free.

AUTORUNS BY SYSINTERNALS

Autoruns by Sysinternals (*www.sysinternals.com*) finds startup and login programs that Msconfig and other third-party programs don't find. Also, Autoruns gives more information about a program than does Msconfig.

To download and use Autoruns, go to the Sysinternals Web site and download the Autoruns zip file. When you run the program, the Autoruns window appears, as shown in Figure 2-41.

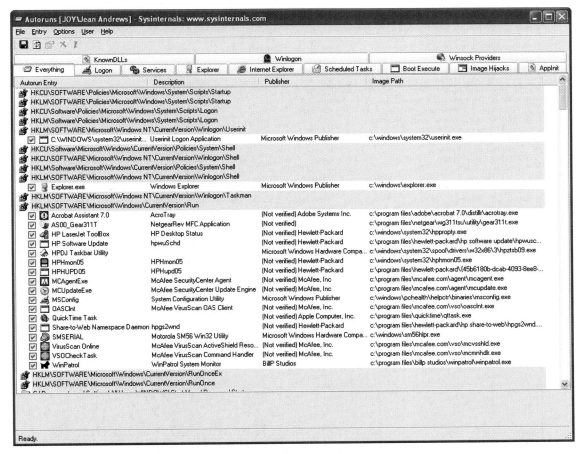

Figure 2-41 Use Autoruns by Sysinternals to display and manage startup and login items

Looking at the Autoruns window, the first thing you notice is the number of entry points Autoruns tracks compared to Msconfig. Autoruns version 8.13 shown in Figure 2-41 is tracking more than 40 registry keys that can launch processes at startup, compared to the four registry keys tracked by Msconfig. (New versions of Autoruns are released as Sysinternals discovers more entry points to track.) Also notice in Figure 2-41 that Autoruns gives more information about a running process than does Msconfig, and, by using the several tabs on this window, you can view information about programs launched while using Windows. This makes it a useful tool when tracking activities while using your browser or other applications.

Autoruns is also useful when searching for the way a listed item was started. Double-click an item and one of two things will happen: Regedit will launch and search for the registry key that was responsible for launching the item or Explorer will launch and locate the program file responsible for launching the item. Either way, you are conveniently taken to the root of a possible problem.

When you click Options on the menu bar, check Hide Signed Microsoft Entries, and then click the Refresh button near the top of the window, Autoruns refreshes the list to only show items installed on your system by third-party software, making it easier for you to locate a potential problem (see Figure 2-42).

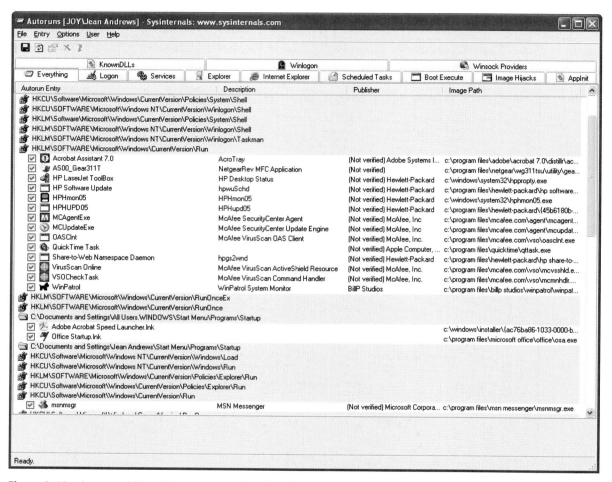

Figure 2-42   Autoruns hides all items except those installed by third-party software

To cause an item to not launch at startup or login, uncheck it on the left side of the screen. You can also save Autoruns information to a text file so that you can keep a record of a current state. To do that, click File, click Save As, and enter a path and filename to save the text data. All in all, Autoruns gives better and more complete information than does Msconfig and takes up very little hard drive space or system resources to run.

STARTUP CONTROL PANEL BY MIKE LIN

Another third-party product is Startup Control Panel by Mike Lin, which gives a very user-friendly presentation. Follow these directions to download and use the software:

1. Go to Mike Lin's Web site and download Startup Control Panel at this URL: *www.mlin.net/StartupCPL.shtml*.

2. Extract the zipped file and double-click it to install the applet. Open Control Panel and look for a new applet named Startup. Double-click the Startup icon. The Startup Control Panel window appears. Figure 2-43 shows the Startup Control Panel window with the HKLM / Run tab selected.

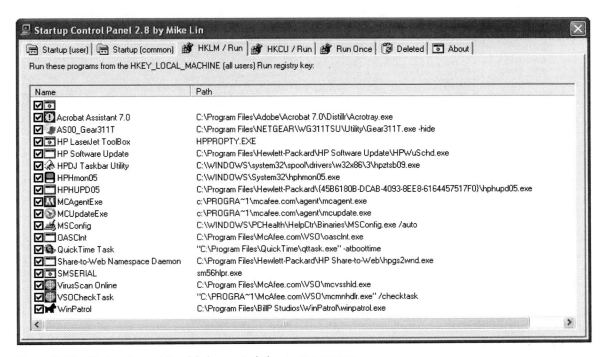

Figure 2-43 Startup Control Panel helps control the startup process

3. Tabs on the Startup Control Panel window are organized so you can more easily determine the source of a program than does Msconfig. To disable a program from launching at startup, uncheck it.

MICROSOFT BOOTVIS FOR WINDOWS XP

Microsoft no longer supports a nifty little tool called BootVis, but you can download it for free from some Web sites and use it to possibly speed up the Windows XP startup process. BootVis is normally used to evaluate startup performance problems for developers and, officially, Microsoft advises that it is not meant to be used as a startup optimization tool. However, because it initiates some optimization processes that Windows XP might not normally do, many users see a performance increase after using it.

Use a Web search engine to find BootVis, download it from a reliable Web site, and install it on your PC. Then time in seconds your Windows startup before and after running BootVis. To have it optimize your startup, launch BootVis and choose **Optimize System** on the **Trace** menu (see Figure 2-44). The system will need a couple of reboots to see the performance increase. For my system, it shaved about 40 seconds off the boot process.

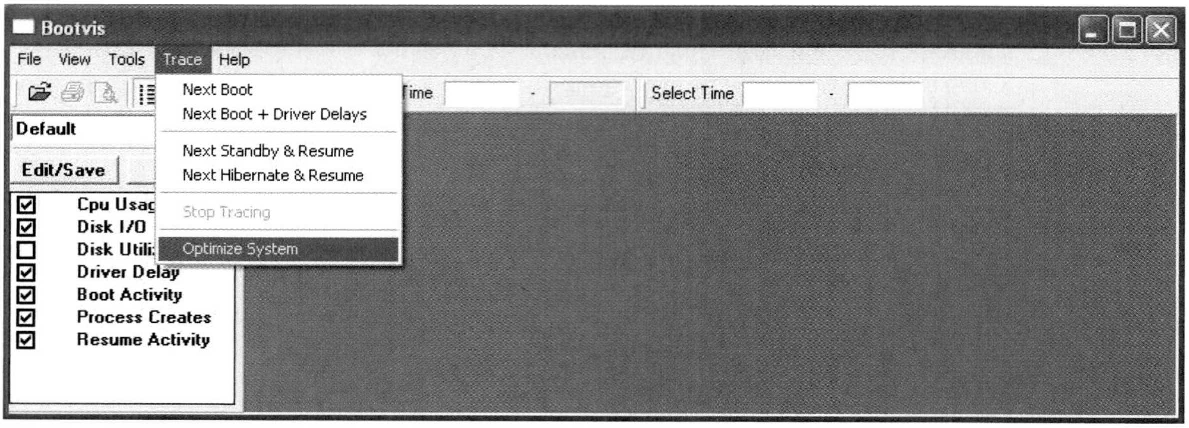

Figure 2-44 Use the BootVis utility from Microsoft to improve startup performance

KEEP XP STARTUP CLEAN AND PREPARE FOR DISASTER

After you have Windows startup squeaky clean, I know you want to keep it that way. In this section, you'll learn about things you can do to protect startup and to prepare in advance for problems.

BACK UP THE SYSTEM STATE

Earlier in the chapter, you learned how to back up the system state, which backs up all the Windows XP system files needed for a successful startup, including the registry files. It's an excellent idea to make this a routine task that you do whenever you make any major changes to your system, such as when you install new software or hardware. Later, if a problem occurs, you might be able to use System Restore to recover from the problem, but having the entire system state backed up assures you that you'll have an even better chance of recovering the system. Know, however, that you can't restore the system state from backup unless you can boot into the Windows desktop. In Chapter 7, you'll learn some other ways to back up the system that can help you with catastrophic failures.

MAKE SURE SYSTEM RESTORE IS TURNED ON AND USE IT

System Restore is normally turned on by Windows XP, and snapshots of the system (restore points) are taken at regular intervals and just before you install software or hardware. However, to make sure System Restore has not been turned off, right-click **My Computer** and select **Properties**. In the System Properties box, click the System Restore tab (see Figure 2-45). Make sure **Turn off System Restore** is not checked. From this window, you can also control how much hard drive space is available to keep restore points. Here is some useful information about how and when restore points are made:

- ◢ Restore points are normally kept in the folder C:\System Volume Information, which is not accessible to the user. Restore points are taken at least every 24 hours, and can use up to 12 percent of disk space.
- ◢ Just after a Windows installation, if Windows determines that free hard drive space is less than 200 MB, System Restore is suspended until 200 MB of free space becomes available.

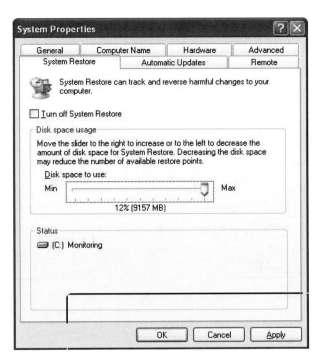

Figure 2-45 Make sure System Restore is turned on

◢ During normal operation, when hard drive free space drops to below 80 MB, System Restore gives up some of its data storage area and fewer restore points are kept. If free drive space drops below 50 MB, System Restore is suspended until 200 MB becomes available. When disk space drops to the 80 or 50 MB levels, warning messages are displayed, such as, "You are running out of disk space on Local Drive C:".

You can create a restore point anytime you want, which can be handy if you're about ready to tinker with some Windows settings and want an easy way to back out of your change. To manually create a restore point:

1. Click **Start**, point to **All Programs**, point to **Accessories**, point to **System Tools**, and then click System Restore. The System Restore window appears.

2. Select **Create a restore point**, and then click **Next**.

3. Type a description of the restore point, such as "Just before I updated the video driver." The system automatically assigns the current date and time to the restore point.

4. Click **Create** and then **Close**. The restore point is saved.

MONITOR THE STARTUP PROCESS

Once you've got the startup process the way you want it, you can use several third-party tools to monitor any changes to it. A good one is WinPatrol by BillP Studios (*www.winpatrol.com*), discussed earlier in this chapter. Download and install the free program to run in the background to monitor all sorts of things, including changes to the registry, startup processes, Internet Explorer settings, and system files. In Figure 2-46, you can see how WinPatrol alerted me when it detected McAfee VirusScan software was placing an entry in the registry to launch at startup to update the antivirus software. WinPatrol displays a little black Scotty dog in the system tray to indicate it's running in the background guarding your system.

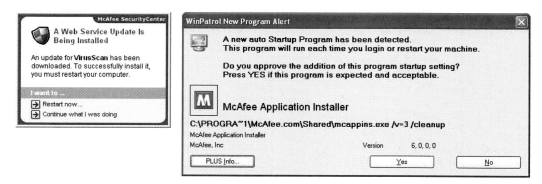

Figure 2-46 WinPatrol by BillP Studios alerts you when the startup process has been altered

MONITOR THE REGISTRY

Registry entries can be changed when you make changes to the Windows environment, install or uninstall software or hardware, or change hardware or software settings. Sometimes malicious software can be caught if you monitor these changes to the registry. A good tool to do that is Regmon by Sysinternals (*www.sysinternals.com*). To use it, go to the Sysinternals Web site at *www.sysinternals.com*, locate and download the free Regmon utility, and open it. The Regmon window appears, as shown in Figure 2-47.

Regmon logs all activity to the registry, including reading and writing keys and values. You can use the File, Save As option to save a log of events showing registry activity.

Regmon is a useful tool for software developers trying to tweak when and how an application accesses the registry. I like to use it when installing software. I can turn it on just before I install the software. After the software is installed, I can get a report of all the registry entries created or changed by the software.

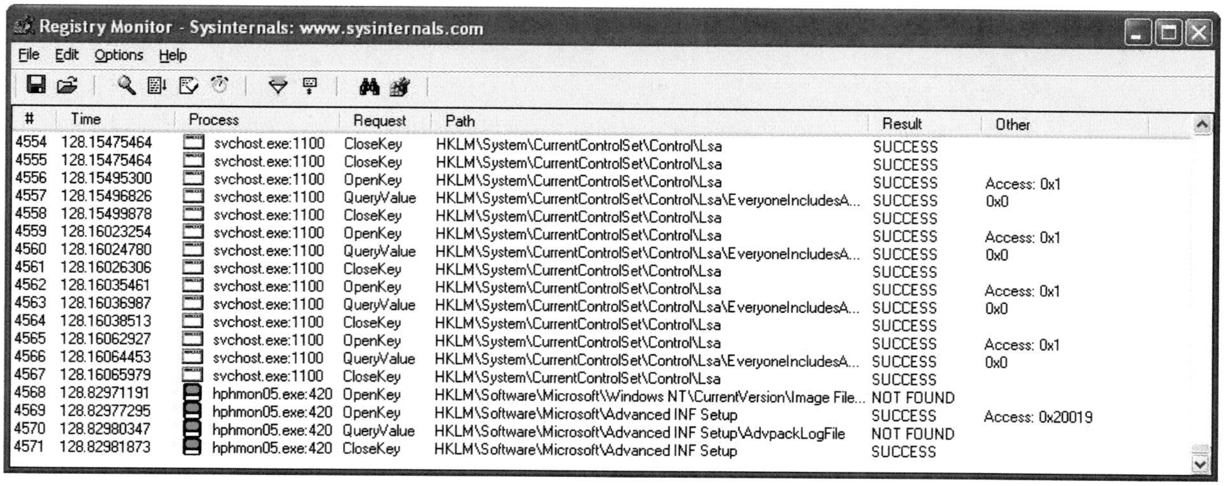

Figure 2-47 Use the Regmon utility by Sysinternals to monitor changes made to the registry

>> CHAPTER SUMMARY

◢ When you're having trouble starting Windows XP, use the Last Known Good Configuration on the Windows XP Advanced Options menu to return the configuration to its settings at the last successful boot.

◢ Windows XP Safe Mode boots with a minimum of drivers and options installed and can be used to troubleshoot a failed boot or to run antivirus software when viruses are launched during a normal startup.

◢ Using System Restore, you can return the system settings to a point in time when a snapshot of the system was taken.

◢ The System Configuration Utility (Msconfig) can be used to limit startup processes and services so that you can troubleshoot a problem with Windows startup.

◢ Task Manager is a Windows tool to monitor, start, and stop programs running in Windows. To effectively support Windows, a technician needs to be familiar with each process that Task Manager finds when it is first launched after starting Windows.

◢ The Internet is a powerful tool to use when identifying unknown processes running on your system.

◢ When cleaning up a slow or error-prone startup, address any error messages before you begin a general cleanup.

◢ Services, scripts, and other programs can be launched when Windows starts up or a user logs on.

◢ Windows looks for items to launch in startup folders, entries in system files, and registry entries.

◢ Three folders used to contain startup programs and shortcuts are the All Users startup folder, the Current User startup folder, and the Scheduled Task folder.

◢ Legacy system files that can contain legacy startup entries still supported by Windows XP are System.ini and Win.ini.

◢ A service can be launched at startup by making an entry using the Services console, which causes an entry to be put into the registry. The Services console is the tool to use to manage Windows and some third-party services. Other third-party applications provide utilities to manage their services.

◢ Group Policy can affect startup or logon, launching scripts that can contain programs to run. Group Policy is managed using the Group Policy console, gpedit.msc. Scripts are stored in the GroupPolicy folder under \Windows\system32.

◢ Too many loaded fonts can slow down startup. Fonts are installed in the C:\Windows\Fonts folder.

◢ Some programs have an uninstall routine that can be executed to uninstall the software rather than using the Add/Remove Programs applet.

◢ As a last resort, an application can be manually deleted by deleting its folder in the C:\Program Files folder and deleting its entries in the registry that identify it as installed software.

◢ To back up the entire registry, use the Backup tool to back up the system state. A copy of registry files is placed in C:\Windows\repair.

▲ To back up an individual key and its subkeys, use the Export command in the registry editor.

▲ Many registry keys exist that can affect the startup process. When searching out obscure locations for startup entries, all these keys need to be searched.

▲ Tweak UI is a group of Power Toys written by Microsoft to affect the Windows environment. The software can be downloaded for free from the Microsoft Web site.

▲ Third-party software can be used to monitor many Windows events and affect those events, making it easier to support Windows. Some examples are Regmon, WinPatrol, Autoruns, and Process Explorer.

▲ To monitor the startup process so items are not added without your knowledge, WinPatrol or some other third-party tool can be used.

>> KEY TERMS

DLL (dynamic link library)   A group or library of programs packaged into a single program file that can be called on by a Windows application. A DLL file can have a .dll, .fon, .ocx, .drv, .nls, .evt, or .exe file extension.

handle   A relationship between a process and a resource it has called into action.

kernel mode   The Windows privileged processing mode that has access to hardware components.

open handle   A handle that is still in progress.

restore point   A snapshot of the Windows XP system state, usually made before installation of new hardware or applications. *Also see* System Restore.

System Restore   A Windows XP utility that is used to create a restore point and then restore the system to a restore point.

user mode   In Windows XP, a processing mode that provides an interface between an application and the OS, and only has access to hardware resources through the code running in kernel mode

>> REVIEWING THE BASICS

1. What applet in Control Panel can be used to schedule a task to run at startup?

2. If a program is frozen and refuses to continue, what Windows tool should you first use to attempt to stop the process?

3. What is the complete path to the folder that contains startup items that are launched when the current user logs on?

4. What is the complete path to the folder that contains startup items that are launched when all users log on?

5. Tasks scheduled by the Scheduled Tasks applet are placed in what folder?

6. What is the name of the executable program file used to manage services, called the Services console?

7. What are the two main groups of policies managed by the Group Policy console?

8. What is the name of the executable program file used to manage group policies, called the Group Policy console?

9. If the user has made a change to a Windows setting and Group Policy has made a different change, which value will be applied, the one made by the user, or Group Policy?

10. At what four events can Group Policy launch a script?

11. What Windows tool can you use to see what group policies are currently applied?

12. Give an example of a registry key that causes a task to run only once at startup.

13. What is the purpose of the BootExecute value in the HKLM\System\CurrentControlSet\Control\Session Manager key?

14. When you back up the system state, where does Windows store a backup copy of the registry files?

15. What command in the Windows registry editor can be used to back up a key?

16. A file holding the backup copy of a registry key has what file extension?

17. What is the name of the executable program file used to launch Windows Explorer or the Windows desktop?

18. What is an example of a third-party utility that gives better information than Msconfig about the startup process?

19. What is the path and filename to the log of events created by Scheduled Tasks?

20. When one process calls another process, this relationship is called a _____.

21. Which applet in Control Panel is used to uninstall an application?

22. Which folder is most likely used to hold the program files for applications installed under Windows?

23. Which Windows tool should you use to temporarily disable a program from launching at startup?

24. What is the name of the executable program file used to manage Windows printer spooling?

25. Which registry key contains entries listed in the Add or Remove Programs window?

26. Which Windows registry subtree contains information about the currently logged-on user?

27. In Windows NT/2000/XP, a file that contains part of the Windows registry is called a(n) _____.

28. To which registry key does the HKEY_CURRENT_USER key point for information?

29. What is a restore point, and what is it used for?

30. What two files contain user settings that are read by the registry to build the registry subtree, HKEY_USERS?

>> THINKING CRITICALLY

1. When cleaning up the startup process, which of these should you do first?

   a. Run Msconfig to see what processes are started.

   b. Investigate an error message that is displayed when you start Windows.

   c. After you have launched several applications, use Task Manager to view a list of running tasks.

2. Using Autoruns, you discover an unwanted script is launched at startup. Of the items listed below, which ones would not be an appropriate solution to the problem?

   a. Look at the registry key that launched the script to help determine where in Windows the script was initiated.

   b. Use Autoruns to disable the script.

   c. Search Task Scheduler for the source of the script.

   d. Use Msconfig to disable the script.

   e. Search Group Policy for the source of the script.

>> HANDS-ON PROJECTS

PROJECT 2-1: Research Running Processes

Boot to the Windows desktop and then use Task Manager to get a list of all the running processes on your machine. Get a print screen of this list. Make a written list of each process running and write a one-sentence explanation of the process. Note that you most likely will need to use the Internet to research some of these processes.

Next, boot the system into Safe Mode and use Task Manager to list running processes. Which processes that were loaded normally are not loaded when the system is running in Safe Mode?

PROJECT 2-2: Edit and Restore the Registry

Practice editing and restoring the registry by doing the following:

1. Export the registry key HKEY_CURRENT_USER\Software\Microsoft\Windows\CurrentVersion\Explorer to an export file stored on the desktop.

2. To change the name of the Recycle Bin on the Windows XP desktop for the currently logged-on user, click the following subkey, which is the name of the Recycle Bin on the Windows desktop:

HKEY_CURRENT_USER\Software\Microsoft\Windows\CurrentVersion\Explorer\CLSID\645FF040-5081-101B-9F08-00AA002F954E

3. Double-click (**Default**) in the Name column in the right pane. The Edit String dialog box opens. The Value data text box in the dialog box should be empty. If a value is present, you selected the wrong value. Check your work and try again.

4. Enter a new name for the Recycle Bin. Click **OK**.

5. To see your change, right-click the desktop and select **Refresh** on the shortcut menu. The name of the Recycle Bin changes.

6. To restore the name to the default value, in the Registry Editor window, again double-click (**Default**) in the right pane. The Edit String dialog box opens. Delete your entry and click **OK**.

7. To verify the change is made, right-click the desktop and select **Refresh** on the shortcut menu. The Recycle Bin name should return to its default value

8. Delete the exported key you saved to your desktop.

From these directions, you can see that changes made to the registry take effect immediately. Therefore, take extra care when editing the registry. If you make a mistake and don't know how to correct a problem you create, then you can undo your changes by exiting the registry editor and double-clicking the exported key.

PROJECT 2-3:   Download and Install BootVis by Microsoft

Download, install, and launch BootVis by Microsoft. Verify that Boot Activity, CPU Usage, Disk I/O, Disk Utilization, and Process Creates are checked on the left side of the main window. On the Trace menu, choose to trace the next boot, and then reboot. Next, view the TRACE_BOOT log file. Answer these questions from the information provided by the trace:

1. How many seconds did the prefetching take for the boot?

2. How many seconds did it take to load the Windows shell?

3. How many seconds did it take to log on and load services?

4. Suggest three ways you might want to use this utility to solve startup problems.

PROJECT 2-4:   Investigating MSN Messenger

Using the startup tools and information in this chapter, describe how Windows automatically launches MSN Messenger at startup. How would a user disable it from loading at startup using the MSN Messenger window? How can it be disabled using a more technical approach? How did you arrive at your answer?

PROJECT 2-5:   Using System Restore

Create a restore point. Make a change to the display settings. Restore the system using System Restore. Are the changes still in effect? Why or why not?

>> REAL PROBLEMS, REAL SOLUTIONS

REAL PROBLEM 2-1:   Clean Up Startup

Using a computer that has a problem with a sluggish startup, apply the tools and procedures you learned in this chapter to clean up the startup process. Take detailed notes of what you did and the results.

CHAPTER 3

Removing Malicious Software

Malicious software, also called malware or a computer infestation, is any unwanted program that means you harm and is transmitted to your computer without your knowledge. The best-known malicious software is a virus, which is malicious software that can replicate itself by attaching itself to other programs. However, many types of malicious software have evolved over the past few years and there is considerable overlap in what they do, how they spread, and how to get rid of them.

In this chapter, you'll learn enough about how malware works to help you deal with it at a technical level. For the average user, the solution to cleaning up an infected system is to run antivirus software, and that is the first and most important step to solving the problem. However, in some situations, you'll need to dig a little deeper to root out some of the more difficult and stubborn malware problems. How to do all this is covered in this chapter.

After your system is clean, the next thing you want to do is to learn how to protect it from future problems. In the next chapter, we talk about all the many ways you can protect your home or small office computers and protect your notebook when traveling. Putting into place some solid security and knowing how to use that security are the ultimate solutions to protecting yourself.

 **Focus Problem**

"I'm under attack! Nasty software has attacked my system. How do I clean up the mess?"

WHAT ARE WE UP AGAINST?

In this section, we'll look at Windows XP symptoms that indicate you've got an infected system. Next, you'll learn about the different kinds of malware and how they work. Then I want to show you how I infected a computer so I'd have a good case study to use in the rest of this chapter where you'll learn to clean up the mess.

YOU'VE GOT MALWARE

Here are some warnings that suggest malicious software is at work:

- Pop-up ads plague you when surfing the Web.
- Generally, the system works much slower than it used to. Programs take longer than normal to load.
- The number and length of disk accesses seem excessive for simple tasks. The number of bad sectors on the hard drive continues to increase.
- The access lights on the hard drive and floppy drive turn on when there should be no activity on the devices. (However, sometimes Windows XP performs routine maintenance on the drive when the system has been inactive for a while.)
- Strange or bizarre error messages appear. Programs that once worked now give errors.
- Less memory than usual is available, or there is a noticeable reduction in disk space.
- Strange graphics appear on your computer monitor, or the computer makes strange noises.
- The system cannot recognize the CD-ROM drive, although it worked earlier.
- In Windows Explorer, filenames now have weird characters or their file sizes seem excessively large. Executable files have changed size or file extensions change without reason. Files mysteriously disappear or appear.
- Files constantly become corrupted.
- The OS begins to boot, but hangs before getting a Windows desktop.
- Your antivirus software displays one or more messages.
- You receive e-mail messages telling you that you have sent someone an infected message.
- Task Manager shows unfamiliar processes running.
- When you try to use your browser to access the Internet, strange things happen and you can't surf the Web. Your IE home page has changed and you see new toolbars you didn't ask for.
- A message appears that a downloaded document contains macros, or an application asks whether it should run macros in a document. (It is best to disable macros if you cannot verify that they are from a trusted source and that they are free of viruses or worms.)

 Notes

Malicious software is designed to do varying degrees of damage to data and software, although it does not damage PC hardware. However, when boot sector information is destroyed on a hard drive, the hard drive can appear to be physically damaged.

HERE'S THE NASTY LIST

You need to know your enemy! Different categories of malicious software are listed next and are described in a bit more detail in this section:

- A virus is a program that replicates by attaching itself to other programs. The infected program must be executed for a virus to run. The program might be an application, a macro in a document, a Windows XP system file, or one of the small programs at the beginning of the hard drive needed to boot the OS. (These programs are called the boot sector program and the master boot program.) The damage a virus does ranges from minor, such as displaying bugs crawling around on a screen, to major, such as erasing everything written on a hard drive. Figure 3-1 shows the results of a harmless virus that simply displays garbage on the screen. The best way to protect against viruses is to always run antivirus (AV) software in the background.

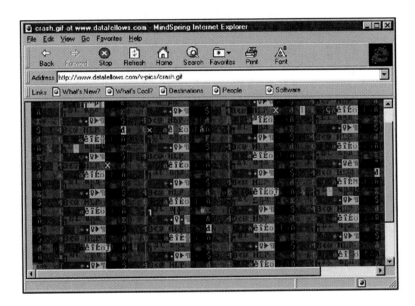

Figure 3-1 The crash virus appears to be destructive, making the screen show only garbage, but does no damage to hard drive data

- Adware produces all those unwanted pop-up ads. Adware is secretly installed on your computer when you download and install shareware or freeware, including screen savers, desktop wallpaper, music, cartoons, news, and weather alerts. Then it displays pop-up ads based on your browsing habits. Sometimes when you try to uninstall adware, it deletes whatever it was you downloaded that you really wanted to keep. And sometimes adware is also spying on you and collecting private information.
- Spam is junk e-mail that you don't want, didn't ask for, and which gets in your way.
- Spyware is software that installs itself on your computer to spy on you, and collects personal information about you that it transmits over the Internet to Web-hosting sites that intend to use your personal data for harm. Spyware comes to you by way of e-mail attachments, downloaded freeware or shareware, instant messaging programs, or when you click a link on a malicious Web site.
- A worm is a program that copies itself throughout a network or the Internet without a host program. A worm creates problems by overloading the network as it replicates. Worms cause damage by their presence rather than by performing a specific damaging act, as a virus does. A worm overloads memory or hard drive space by replicating

repeatedly. When a worm (for example, Sasser or W32.Sobig.F@mm) is loose on the Internet, it can cause damage such as sending mass e-mailings. The best way to protect against worms is to use antivirus software and a firewall.

▲ A browser hijacker, also called a home page hijacker, does mischief by changing your home page and other browser settings. Brower hijackers can set unwanted bookmarks, redirect your browser to a porn site when you key in a wrong URL, produce pop-up ads, and direct your browser to Web sites that offer pay-per-view pornography.

▲ A virus hoax or e-mail hoax is e-mail that does damage by tempting you to forward it to everyone in your e-mail address book with the intent of clogging up e-mail systems or tempting you to delete a critical Windows system file by convincing you the file is malicious. Also, some e-mail scam artists promise to send you money if you'll circulate their e-mail messages to thousands of people. I recently received one that was supposedly promising money from Microsoft for "testing" the strength of the Internet e-mail system. Beware! Always check Web sites that track virus hoaxes before pressing that Send button! Here are some good sites to help you debunk a virus hoax:

   ▲ *hoaxbusters.ciac.org* by Computer Incident Advisory Capability
   ▲ *www.hoaxkill.com* by Oxcart Software
   ▲ *www.snopes.com* by Urban Legends
   ▲ *www.viruslist.com* by Kaspersky Lab
   ▲ *www.vmyths.com* by Rhode Island Soft Systems, Inc.

▲ Phishing (sounds like "fishing") is a type of identity theft where the sender of an e-mail message scams you into responding with personal data about yourself. The scam artist baits you by asking you to verify personal data on your bank account, ISP account, credit card account, or something of that nature. Often you are tricked into clicking a link in the e-mail message, which takes you to an official-looking site complete with company or bank logos where you are asked to enter your user ID and password to enter the site.

▲ Scam artists use scam e-mail to lure you into their scheme. One scam e-mail I recently received was supposedly from the secretary of a Russian oil tycoon who was being held in jail with his millions of dollars of assets frozen. If I would respond to the e-mail and get involved, I was promised a 12% commission to help recover the funds.

▲ A dialer is software installed on your PC that disconnects your phone line from your ISP and dials up an expensive pay-per-minute phone number without your knowledge. The damage a dialer does is the expensive phone bill.

▲ A keylogger tracks all your keystrokes, including passwords, chat room sessions, e-mail messages, documents, online purchases, and anything else you type on your PC. All this text is logged to a text file and transmitted over the Internet without your knowledge. A keylogger is a type of spyware.

▲ A logic bomb is dormant code added to software and triggered at a predetermined time or by a predetermined event. For instance, an employee might put code in a program to destroy important files if his or her name is ever removed from the payroll file.

▲ A Trojan horse does not need a host program to work; rather, it substitutes itself for a legitimate program. In most cases, a user launches it thinking he or she is launching a legitimate program. Figure 3-2 shows a pop-up that appears when you're surfing the Web. Click OK and you've just introduced a Trojan into your system. A Trojan is likely to introduce one or more viruses into the system. These Trojans are called downloaders.

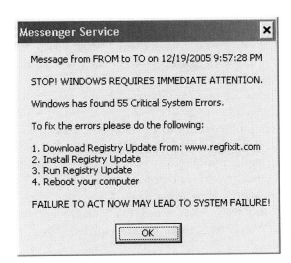

Figure 3-2   Clicking OK on a pop-up window might invite a Trojan into your system

◢ Last year, I got fooled with a Trojan when I got an e-mail message near the actual date of my birthday from someone named Emily, whom I thought I knew. Without thinking, I clicked the link in the e-mail message to "View my birthday card to you." Figure 3-3 shows what happened when I clicked.

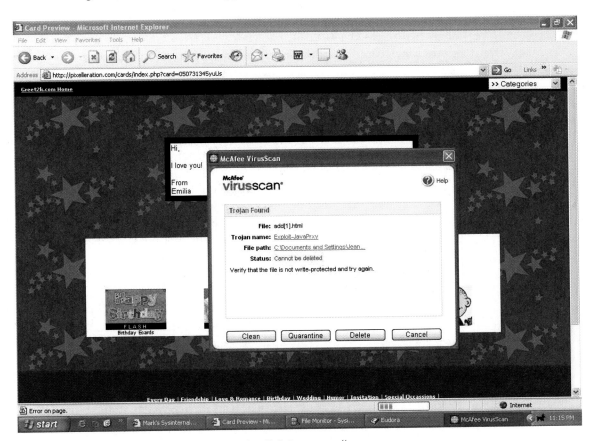

Figure 3-3   A Trojan can get in when you click a link in an e-mail message

In this part of the chapter, let's look at the different types of malicious software and how they work; then we'll look at best practices to avoid them. Lastly, we'll look at how to get rid of them once we're under attack.

HOW A VIRUS WORKS

A virus attacks your system and hides in several different ways. A boot sector virus hides in the boot sector program of a hard drive or floppy disk or in the master boot program in the very first sector of a hard drive called the master boot record (MBR). A file virus hides in an executable (.exe, .com, or .sys) program or in a word-processing document that contains a macro. A multipartite virus is a combination of a boot sector virus and a file virus and can hide in either. A macro is a small program contained in a document that can be automatically executed either when the document is first loaded or later by pressing a key combination. For example, a word-processing macro might automatically read the system date and copy it into a document when you open the document. Viruses that hide in macros of document files are called macro viruses. Macro viruses are the most common viruses spread by e-mail, hiding in macros of attached document files. A script virus is a virus that hides in a script, which might execute when you click a link on a Web page or in an HTML e-mail message, or when you attempt to open an e-mail attachment.

HOW MALWARE REPLICATES AND HIDES

A virus or other malware can use various techniques to load itself in memory and replicate itself. Also, malware attempts to hide from antivirus (AV) software by changing its distinguishing characteristics (its signature) and by attempting to mask its presence. Here are some techniques used by malware to start itself and prevent detection:

- ◢ A virus can search a hard drive for a file with an .exe extension and then create another file with the same filename but with a .com file extension. The virus then stores itself there. When the user launches the program, the OS first looks for the program name with the .com file extension. It then finds and executes the virus. The virus is loaded into memory and loads the program with the .exe extension. The user appears to have launched the desired program. The virus is then free to do damage or spread itself to other programs.
- ◢ Because AV software can detect a virus by noting the difference between a program's file size before the virus infects it and after the virus is present, the virus alters OS information to mask the size of the file in which it hides.
- ◢ The virus monitors when files are opened or closed. When it sees that the file in which it is hiding is about to be opened, it temporarily removes itself or substitutes a copy of the file that does not include the virus. The virus keeps a copy of this uninfected file on the hard drive just for this purpose. A virus that does this or changes the attributes of its host program is called a stealth virus.
- ◢ As a virus replicates, it changes its characteristics. This type of virus is called a polymorphic virus.
- ◢ Some viruses can continually transform themselves so they will not be detected by AV software that is looking for a particular characteristic. A virus that uses this technique is called an encrypting virus.
- ◢ The virus creates more than one process; each process is watching the other. If one process gets closed, it will be started up again by one of the other processes. (This method of preventing detection is also used by spyware.)
- ◢ Entries are often made in obscure places in the registry that allow the software to start when you start up Windows or launch Internet Explorer. (This method is used by several types of malware.)
- ◢ One type of malware, called a rootkit, loads itself before the OS boot is complete. Because it is already loaded when the AV software loads, it is sometimes overlooked by AV software. In addition, a rootkit hijacks internal Windows components so that it masks information Windows provides to user mode utilities such as

Task Manager, Explorer, the registry editor, and AV software—this helps it remain undetected.

EXPERIMENTING WITH A HONEYPOT

I've been using some very good methods to protect my network against malicious software for several years now. So much so, that I've almost forgotten what it feels like to be attacked by malicious software. Therefore, in preparing to write this chapter, I decided to set up a honeypot, a computer exposed to the Internet with the intent of attracting malicious software. Honeypots are often used by security professionals as traps to catch computer attackers, study their habits, and understand how to better improve network security. In this section, you'll first see how I set up the honeypot, how it was infected, and then what happened when I tried to clean the system using normal methods.

INFECTING MY HONEYPOT

Here's what I did to set up the honeypot:

1. I started with a clean partition (drive E) on my hard drive and installed Windows XP using a setup CD that did not have any service packs already applied. I did not install Service Pack 2. Neither did I install any antivirus software—just a straight Windows XP bare-bones installation. I then installed Microsoft Office and Acrobat Reader so I'd have some applications present.

2. I disconnected the PC from my network in order to protect my other computers.

3. I used a dial-up connection to my local ISP and did not enable a firewall. Naively, I figured it would be at least an hour or so before I saw any activity. Boy, was I wrong!

4. I was distracted from my honeypot for less than two minutes. When I turned back around to the honeypot—voila! I'd already attracted a bait window, which is shown in Figure 3-4. Rather than closing this window, I took the bait by clicking OK. The enemy had found an opening and the hordes began invading.

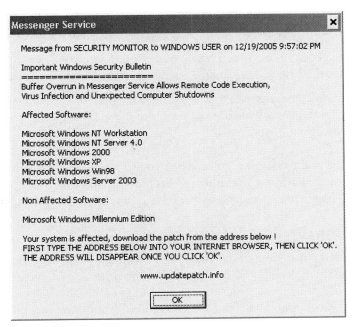

Figure 3-4   Bait window appears after a two-minute open connection to my ISP

5. Within fewer than 10 minutes, pop-up ads were on my screen, a Trojan spy software was at work, several viruses had embedded themselves in the registry, my taskbar had turned black, and the Start menu was not readable. Figure 3-5 shows what my desktop looked like.

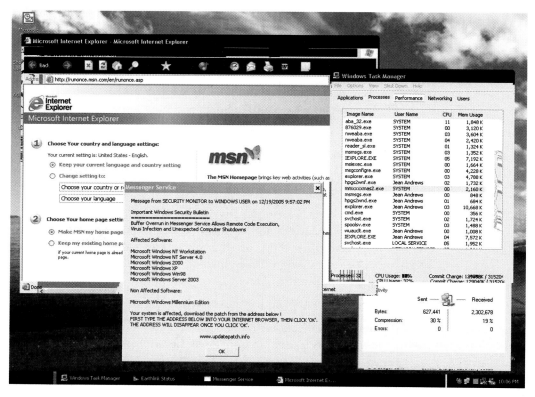

Figure 3-5   My infected desktop after 10 minutes

6. After about 20 minutes, over 7 MB of data had been downloaded to my PC without my permission, and the Windows Lsass.exe process announced it was having problems and was about to shut down the system. I tried to take one more screen shot and watched as the system shut down. I felt like I had pushed one of my soldiers over the compound wall and took pictures as the enemy mutilated and devoured him.

7. The system rebooted and a window popped up, as shown in Figure 3-6. I clicked OK and my browser opened, downloaded some stuff, and closed. I was no longer in control of my system.

Folks, the Internet is not a safe place to be when you're unprotected. It's infested with all kinds of varmints prowling around searching for open doors. On my system, I found Trojan downloaders, adware, spyware, viruses, a worm or two, and several browser hijackers.

WHAT DIDN'T WORK TO CLEAN MY SYSTEM

Next, I decided to use the normal methods most users would use to clean up an infected system so I could see what would work and what would not work. Here's what happened:

1. I rebooted the system and launched Msconfig. I disabled all non-Windows processes and services and rebooted again.

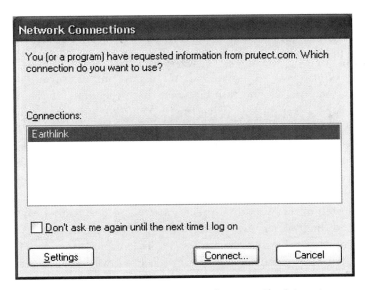

Figure 3-6 After a reboot, a process asks to use the Internet

2. After the desktop loaded, I opened Task Manager and took a screen shot, shown in Figure 3-7. You can see strange processes are running that Msconfig didn't catch. I searched the Web for information on the two suspicious processes shown in Figure 3-7, Dpm_32.exe and Pludpm.exe. My search turned up nothing.

3. I tried to stop the processes. But if you look closely at Figure 3-7, you can see two instances of Pludpm.exe. If I stopped one instance of this process, before I could stop

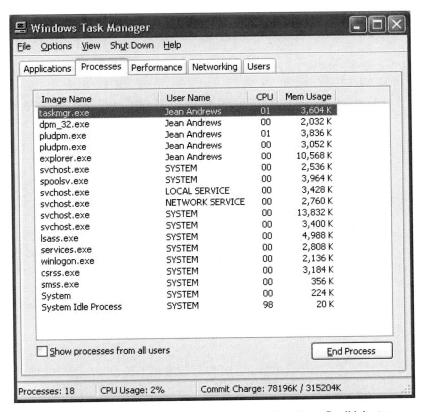

Figure 3-7 Task Manager shows processes running that Msconfig didn't stop

the other instance, a new Pludpm.exe process had started. Each instance was watching the other and restarting it if it was stopped. This method is often used by malware to keep itself running.

4. The next thing I did was try to download and install some antivirus software. I turned on Windows XP Internet Connection Firewall (that's the name of Windows Firewall before Service Pack 2 is installed). Then I used dialup to connect to my ISP and went to the McAfee Web site (*www.mcafee.com*) to get the software. When I tried to key in my password to my account there, I got an error message saying the password was invalid. I double-checked it on another computer, which gave me access to the McAfee site with no problem. A process on the honeypot was watching my browser and interfering. I noticed in Task Manager that several new processes launched, including Z00096.exe, stored in the Windows folder. I also noticed that my browser home page had changed and there was a mysterious toolbar present thanking me for choosing the Mirar pop-up blocker product. I also noticed the security settings for IE had been changed to customized settings, which pretty much allowed in anything.

5. I opened the Add or Remove Programs applet in Control Panel and discovered new software present called Command. When I tried to uninstall it, my browser opened and took me to this link: *command.adservs.com/uninstall.php*. I closed the browser.

6. Next I tried to remove the Mirar software. The browser again opened and took me to *remove.getmirar.com*.

I was now convinced that my system was so badly infected that normal measures of using AV software and uninstalling software were not going to help. So now I was ready to get really serious about cleaning up an infected system. That's the subject of the next section.

STEP-BY-STEP ATTACK PLAN

This section is a step-by-step attack plan to clean up an infected system. We'll first use AV software and anti-adware software to do a general cleanup. Then we'll dig deeper to use some more complex tools and methods to smoke out any lurking processes that eluded normal methods of de-infesting a system.

RUN AV SOFTWARE

A virus is often programmed to attempt to hide from antivirus (AV) software. It's also sometimes programmed to block downloading and installing the AV software if the software is not already installed. AV software can only detect viruses identical or similar to those it has been programmed to search for and recognize. AV software detects a known virus by looking for distinguishing characteristics called virus signatures, which is why AV software cannot detect a virus it does not know to look for. For all these reasons, it's important to have AV software installed, have it running in the background, and regularly download updates to it.

Table 3-1 lists popular antivirus software and Web sites that also provide information about viruses.

When selecting AV software, find out if it can:

▲ Automatically download new software upgrades and virus definitions from the Internet so that your software is continually aware of new viruses
▲ Automatically execute at startup
▲ Detect macros in a word-processing document as it is loaded by the word processor

Antivirus Software	Web Site
AVG Anti-Virus by Grisoft	www.grisoft.com
F-Secure Antivirus by F-Secure Corp.	www.f-secure.com
eSafe by Aladdin Knowledge Systems, Ltd.	www.esafe.com
F-Prot by FRISK Software International	www.f-prot.com
McAfee VirusScan by McAfee Associates, Inc.	www.mcafee.com
NeaTSuite by Trend Micro (for networks)	www.trendmicro.com
Norman by Norman Data Defense Systems, Inc. (complicated to use, but highly effective)	www.norman.com
Norton AntiVirus by Symantec, Inc.	www.symantec.com
PC-cillin by Trend Micro (for home use)	www.trendmicro.com

Table 3-1   Antivirus software and information

◢ Automatically monitor files being downloaded from the Internet, including e-mail attachments and attachments sent during a chat session, such as when using AOL Instant Messenger

◢ Send virus alerts to your e-mail address to inform you of a dangerous virus and the need to update your antivirus software

◢ Scan both automatically and manually for viruses

> **✎ Notes**
>
> It's handy to have AV software on CD, but recognize that this AV software won't have the latest updates and will need these updates downloaded from the Internet before it will catch new viruses.

Here are steps to use AV software on a highly infected system that does not already have AV software installed:

1. Purchase the AV software on CD (see Figure 3-8).

Figure 3-8   Having AV software on CD means you don't need Internet access to install the software

2. Disconnect from the Internet so you won't open yourself up for more mischief.

3. Boot into Safe Mode. To do that, press **F8** when Windows begins to load. The Windows XP Advanced Options menu appears. Choose **Safe Mode with Networking** and press **Enter**.

4. Insert the AV software CD. Most likely the AV main menu will be displayed automatically, as shown in Figure 3-9. Choose to install the software.

> **Notes**
>
> If viruses are launched even after you boot in Safe Mode and you cannot get the AV software to work, try searching for suspicious entries in the subkeys under HKLM\System\ CurrentControlSet\Control\ SafeBoot. Subkeys under this key control what is launched when you boot into Safe Mode. How to edit the registry is covered in Chapter 2.

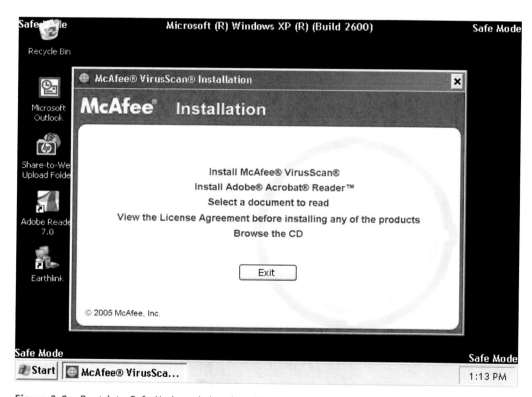

Figure 3-9   Boot into Safe Mode and then install the AV software

5. When given the opportunity, enter the information to register the AV software so that you will be allowed to download updates. At this point, you won't be connected to the Internet to complete the registration, but at least the software is poised to register you later when the connection works (see Figure 3-10).

6. During the installation, when given the opportunity, choose to scan the system for viruses (see Figure 3-11). Set the software to scan all drives and all types of files, and to look for all types of malware.

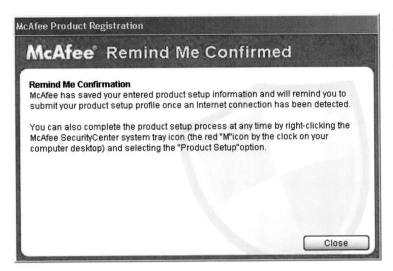

Figure 3-10   Choose to register your AV software so you can download updates

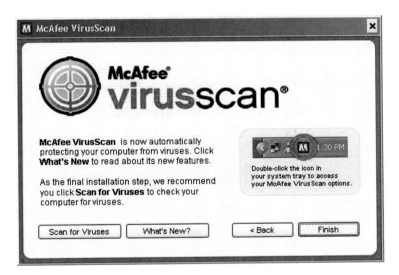

Figure 3-11   Choose to scan for viruses

7. Figure 3-12 shows the results of a McAfee scan that detected a bunch of adware, spyware, Trojans, and potentially unwanted programs (PUPs).

8. Sometimes AV software detects a program that you know you have downloaded and want to keep, but the AV software recognizes it as potentially harmful. This type of software is sometimes called grayware or a PUP (potentially unwanted program). When the AV software displays the list of detected files, unless you recognize something you want to keep, I suggest you tell the AV software to delete them all.

9. Reboot into Safe Mode with Networking, connect to the Internet, and allow your AV software to get any current updates from the AV software Web site. Figure 3-13 shows that happening for McAfee VirusScan software. If the software requests you reboot the system for the installation to complete, be sure to reboot into Safe Mode with Networking.

10. After the updating is finished, scan the system again. Most likely, some new malware will be discovered for you to delete. For example, when I cleaned up an infected

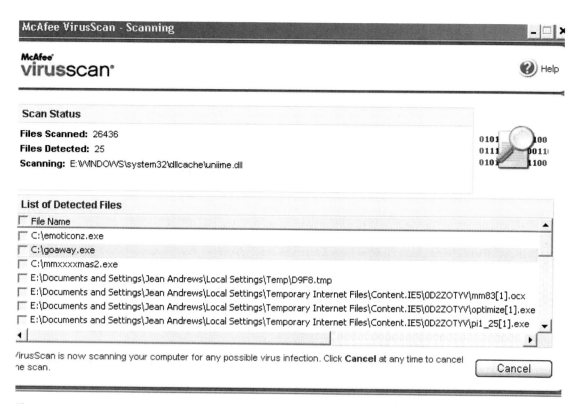

Figure 3-12   VirusScan detects unwanted programs

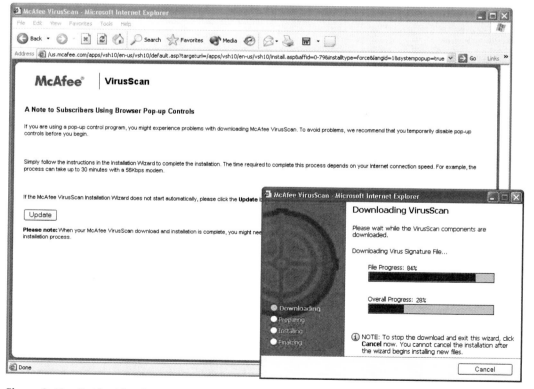

Figure 3-13   McAfee VirusScan receiving updates from the McAfee Web site

system using the McAfee CD version of the software, it found 34 viruses, Trojans, and adware. After all McAfee updates were applied, it found an additional 54 viruses, Trojans, adware, worms, and spyware. Keep repeating the scan until you get a clean scan. Reboot between scans and take notes of any program files the software is not able to delete.

11. Now it's time to see where you stand. If you use an always-up connection to the Internet, unplug your network cable. Reboot the system to the normal Windows XP desktop and check Task Manager. Do you see any weird processes, see pop-ups when you open your browser, or get strange messages like the one in Figure 3-14 asking permission to connect to the Internet? If so, you still have malware.

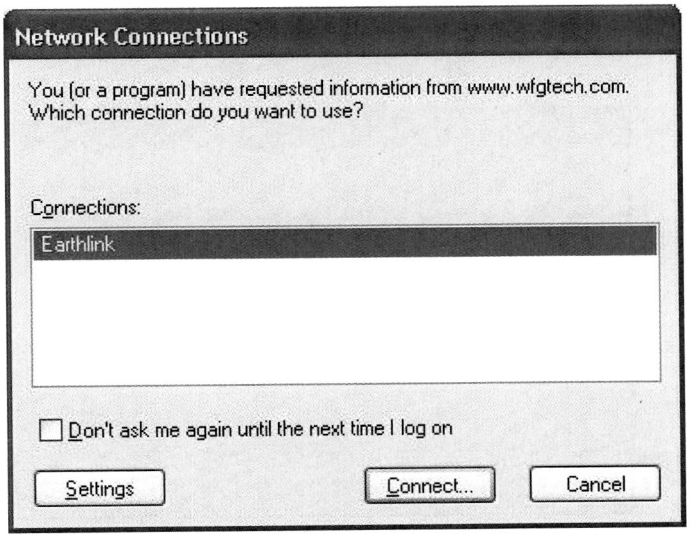

Figure 3-14 Evidence malware is still infecting the system

It might be more fun to begin manually removing each program yourself, but it's probably quicker and more thorough to use anti-adware software next. I suggest you resist the temptation to poke around looking for the malware and move on to the next step.

RUN ADWARE OR SPYWARE REMOVAL SOFTWARE

Almost all AV software products today also search for adware and spyware. However, software specifically dedicated to removing this type of malware generally does a better job of it than does AV software. The next step in the removal process is to use anti-adware or anti-spyware software.

The distinction between adware and spyware is slight, and sometimes a malicious software program is displaying pop-up ads and also spying on you. There are tons of removal software products available on the Web, but I recommend the three in the following list. They all can catch adware, spyware, cookies, browser hijackers, dialers, keyloggers, and Trojans.

- ◢ Ad-Aware by Lavasoft (*www.lavasoft.com*) is one of the most popular and successful adware and spyware removal products. It can be downloaded without support for free.
- ◢ Spybot Search and Destroy by PepiMK Software (*www.pepimk.com*) do an excellent job of removing malicious software.

◢ Windows Defender by Microsoft (*www.microsoft.com*) is an up-and-coming product that, even in its current beta stage, does a great job removing malware.

Figure 3-15 shows what Windows Defender discovered on one computer.

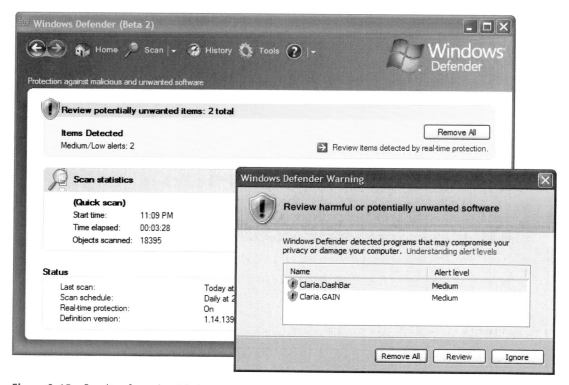

Figure 3-15 Results of running Windows Defender by Microsoft

To completely clean your system, you might have to run a removal product more than once or use several different products. For example, what Ad-Aware doesn't find, Windows Defender does, but what Windows Defender doesn't find, Ad-Aware finds. To be sure, run two products.

SEARCH OUT AND DESTROY WHAT'S LEFT

Next, you'll need to clean up anything the AV or anti-adware software left behind. Sometimes AV software tells you it is not able to delete a file or it deletes an infected file, but leaves behind an orphan entry in the registry or startup folders. If the AV software tells you it was not able to delete or clean a file, first check the AV software Web site for any instructions you might find to manually clean things up. In this section, you'll learn about general things you can do to clean up what might be left behind.

RESPOND TO ANY STARTUP ERRORS

On the first boot after AV software has found and removed malware, you might find some startup errors caused by incomplete removal of the malware. One example of such an error is shown in Figure 3-16. Somewhere in the system, the command to launch 0sis0ijw.dll is still working even though this DLL has been deleted.

3

Figure 3-16 Startup error indicates malware has not been completely removed

One way to find this orphan entry point is to use Msconfig. Figure 3-17 shows the Msconfig window showing us that the DLL is launched from a registry key.

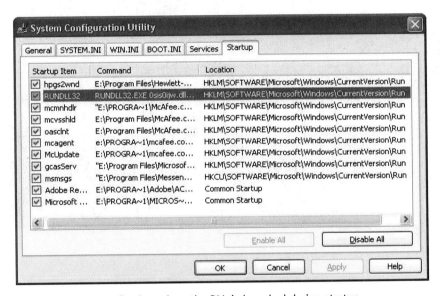

Figure 3-17 Msconfig shows how the DLL is launched during startup

The next step is to back up the registry and then use Regedit to find and delete the key (see Figure 3-18).

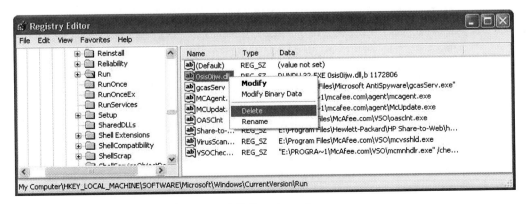

Figure 3-18 Delete orphan registry entry left there by malware

DELETE FILES

For each program file the AV software told you it could not delete, try to delete the program file yourself using Windows Explorer. For peace of mind, don't forget to empty the Recycle Bin when you're done. You might need to open a Command Prompt window and remove the hidden or system attributes on a file so that you can delete it. Figure 3-19 shows how this is done for the file C:\INT0094.exe. Table 3-2 explains each command used. If you are still not able to delete a file, open Task Manager and make sure the process is not running. A program file cannot be deleted if it is currently running.

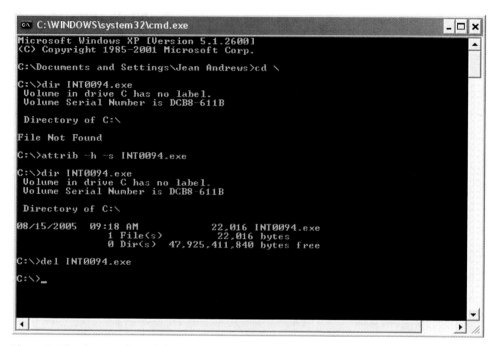

Figure 3-19 Commands to delete a hidden system file

Command	Explanation
cd \	Make the root directory of drive C the current directory
dir INT0094.exe	The file does not appear in the directory because it is hidden
attrib –h –s INT0094.exe	Remove the hidden and system attributes of the file
dir INT0094.exe	The Dir command now displays the file
del INT0094.exe	Delete the file

Table 3-2 Commands to delete a hidden system file

To get rid of other malware files, you might need to delete all Internet Explorer temporary Internet files. To do that, open the **Properties** window for drive C and click **Disk Cleanup** on the General tab. Then, from the Disk Cleanup window shown in Figure 3-20, make sure **Temporary Internet Files** is checked and click **OK**.

PURGE RESTORE POINTS

Some malware hides its program files in the data storage area of the Windows XP System Restore utility. Windows does not always allow AV software to look in this

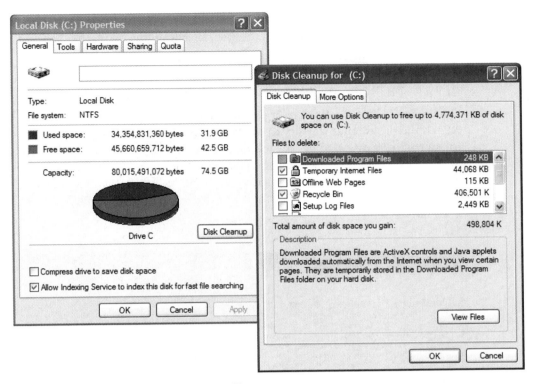

Figure 3-20   Delete all temporary Internet files

storage area when it is scanning for malware. To get rid of that malware, you must turn off System Restore, reboot your system, and turn System Restore back on. How to do that was covered in Chapter 2. Turning off System Restore causes the data storage area to be purged. You'll get rid of any malware there, but you'll also lose all your restore points.

If your AV software is running in the background and reports it has found a virus in the C:\System Volume Information_Restore folder, that means malware is in a System Restore point (see Figure 3-21). Unless you desperately need to keep a restore point you've

Figure 3-21   Malware found in a restore point

previously made, if you see a message similar to the one in Figure 3-21 or your AV software scan feature found lots of malware in other places on the drive, the best idea is to purge all restore points.

CLEAN THE REGISTRY

Sometimes AV software deletes a program file but does not delete the registry entries that launch the program at startup. In the last chapter, you learned how to search registry keys for startup processes. To get the job done more quickly, you can use Autoruns by Sysinternals to help you search for these registry entries. Figure 3-22 shows a screen shot where Autoruns is displaying a registry key used to launch the Pludpm.exe malware program. AV software had already found and deleted this program file, but it left the registry key untouched.

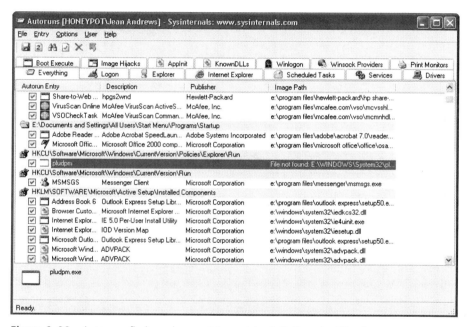

Figure 3-22 Autoruns finds orphan registry entries left there by AV software

Scan through the Autoruns window looking for suspicious entries. Research any entries that you think might be used by malware. To get rid of these keys, back up the registry and then use Regedit to delete unwanted keys.

ROOTKITS

A rootkit is a program that uses unusually complex methods to hide itself on a system, and many spyware and adware programs are also rootkits. The term rootkit applies to a kit or set of tools used originally on Unix computers. In Unix, the lowest and most powerful level of Unix accounts is called the root account; therefore, this kit of tools was intended to keep a program working at this root level without detection.

Rootkits can prevent Task Manager from displaying the running rootkit process, or may cause Task Manager to display a different name for this process. The program filename might not be displayed in Windows Explorer, the rootkit's registry keys might be hidden from the registry editor, or the registry editor might display wrong information. All this hiding is accomplished in one of two ways, depending on whether the rootkit is running in user mode or kernel mode (see Figure 3-23). A rootkit running in user mode intercepts the API calls between the time when the API retrieves the data and when it is displayed in a window. A rootkit running in kernel mode actually interferes with the Windows kernel and substitutes its own information in place of the raw data read by the Windows kernel.

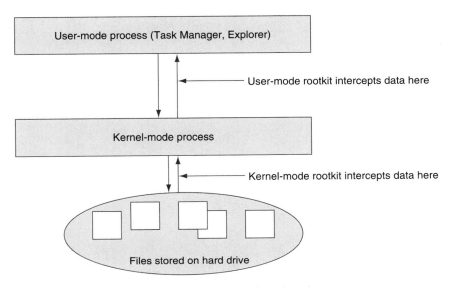

Figure 3-23 A rootkit can run in user mode or kernel mode

Because most AV software, to one degree or another, relies on Windows tools and components to work, the rootkit is not detected if the Windows tools themselves are infected. Rootkits are also programmed to hide from specific programs designed to find and remove them. Generally, anti-rootkit software works using these two methods:

> **Notes**
>
> An **API (application program interface)** is a Windows procedure that serves as the interface between a program running in user mode and the Windows kernel. When a program uses an API, the action is called an **API call**. For more explanation of an API and an API call, see Appendix D.

- ▲ The software looks for running processes that don't match up with the underlying program filename.
- ▲ The software compares files, registry entries, and processes provided by the OS to the lists it generates from the raw data. If the two lists differ, a rootkit is suspected.

Two good anti-rootkit programs are:

- ▲ Rootkit Revealer by Sysinternals (*www.sysinternals.com*)
- ▲ BackLight by F-Secure (*www.f-secure.com*)

After you have used other available methods to remove malware and you still believe you're not clean, you might want to download and run one of these products. Close all open applications and don't use the computer for any other task while the anti-rootkit software is running. If you change a file or the registry changes while the software is running, it might report a false positive—the list taken with the OS and without the OS might differ simply because you changed something between the times the two lists were taken. Figure 3-24 shows Rootkit Revealer scanning for rootkits.

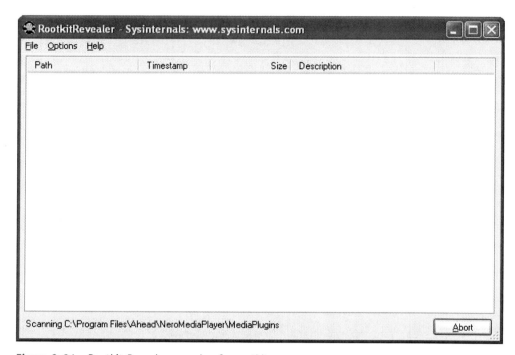

Figure 3-24   Rootkit Revealer scanning for rootkits

For best results when scanning for rootkits, run the anti-rootkit software from another computer so that the software is not dependent on the OS that might be infected. For example, you can share drive C on the network and then, from another computer on the network, run the anti-rootkit software and instruct it to scan drive C on the remote computer.

If the software detects a discrepancy that might indicate a rootkit is installed, you'll need to go to the Sysinternals or F-Secure Web site or do a general Web search to find information about the potential rootkit and instructions for removing it. Follow the instructions to manually remove the program and all its remnants. Sometimes the removal is so complicated, you might decide it makes more sense to just start over and reinstall Windows.

If you have tried all the techniques and products in this chapter and still have malware, I'm sorry to say the next suggestion I have to offer is to back up your data, completely erase your hard drive, reinstall Windows and all your applications, and then restore your data.

Once your system is clean, you'll certainly want to keep it that way. There's so much to say about protecting a computer from malware, I've devoted the entire next chapter to the subject.

>> CHAPTER SUMMARY

◢ Types of malicious software include viruses, Trojan horses, worms, adware, spyware, keyloggers, browser hijackers, dialers, and downloaders.

◢ The first defense against malicious software is antivirus software. If you cannot install and run AV software on an infected system, try installing and running the software in Safe Mode.

◢ Adware and spyware removal software sometimes finds malware that AV software does not find.

◢ AV software sometimes cannot delete a malware program and you must manually delete it.

◢ AV software might leave orphan registry entries behind that you can manually delete using the registry editor.

◢ Purging all restore points can rid the system of some malicious software.

◢ Rootkits can be detected by software designed for that purpose, and then the rootkits can be manually removed.

◢ Some systems become so highly infected, the only solution is reinstall Windows.

>> KEY TERMS

adware Software installed on a computer that produces pop-up ads using your browser; the ads are often based on your browsing habits.

API (application program interface) A predefined Windows procedure that allows a program to access hardware or other software.

API call A request made by software to the OS to use an API procedure to access hardware or other software.

boot sector virus A virus that hides in one or both of the small programs at the beginning of the hard drive used to initiate the boot of the operating system.

browser hijacker A malicious program that infects your Web browser and can change your home page or browser settings. It can also redirect your browser to unwanted sites, produce pop-up ads, and set unwanted bookmarks.

dialer Malicious software that can disconnect your phone line from your ISP and dial an expensive pay-per-minute phone number without your knowledge.

encrypting virus A type of virus that can continually transform itself so that it is not detected by AV software.

file virus A virus that hides in an executable (.exe, .com, or .sys) program or in a word-processing document that contains a macro.

honeypot A computer exposed to the Internet with the intent of attracting malicious software, and which is sometimes used by security professionals as traps to catch computer attackers, study their habits, and identify security weaknesses in protected networks.

infestation *See* malicious software.

keylogger A type of spyware that tracks your keystrokes, including passwords, chat room sessions, e-mail messages, documents, online purchases, and anything else you type on your PC. Text is logged to a text file and transmitted over the Internet without your knowledge.

logic bomb   A type of malicious software that is dormant code added to software and triggered at a predetermined time or by a predetermined event.

macro   A small sequence of commands, contained within a document, that can be automatically executed when the document is loaded, or executed later by using a predetermined keystroke.

macro virus   A virus that can hide in the macros of a document file.

malicious software   Any unwanted program that is transmitted to a computer without the user's knowledge and that is designed to do varying degrees of damage to data and software. Types of infestations include viruses, Trojan horses, worms, adware, spyware, keyloggers, browser hijackers, dialers, and downloaders. Also called malware or an infestation.

malware   *See* malicious software.

multipartite virus   A combination of a boot sector virus and a file virus. It can hide in either type of program.

phishing   Sending an e-mail message with the intent of getting the user to reveal private information that can be used for identify theft.

polymorphic virus   A type of virus that changes its distinguishing characteristics as it replicates itself. Mutating in this way makes it more difficult for AV software to recognize the presence of the virus.

rootkit   A type of malicious software that loads itself before the OS boot is complete and can hijack internal Windows components so that it masks information Windows provides to user-mode utilities such as Windows Explorer or Task Manager.

scam e-mail   E-mail sent by a scam artist intended to lure you into a scheme.

script virus   A type of virus that hides in a script which might execute when you click a link on a Web page or in an HTML e-mail message, or when you attempt to open an e-mail attachment.

spam   Junk e-mail you don't ask for, don't want, and which gets in your way.

spyware   Malicious software that installs itself on your computer to spy on you. It collects personal information about you that it transmits over the Internet to Web-hosting sites that intend to use your personal data for harm.

stealth virus   A virus that actively conceals itself by temporarily removing itself from an infected file that is about to be examined, and then hiding a copy of itself elsewhere on the drive.

Trojan horse   A type of malicious software that hides or disguises itself as a useful program, yet is designed to cause damage at a later time.

virus   A malicious program that often has an incubation period, is infectious, and is intended to cause damage. A virus program might destroy data and programs or damage a hard drive's boot sector.

virus hoax   E-mail that does damage by tempting you to forward it to everyone in your e-mail address book with the intent of clogging up e-mail systems or by persuading you to delete a critical Windows system file by convincing you the file is malicious.

virus signature   The distinguishing characteristics of malicious software that are used by AV software to identify a program as malicious.

worm   Malicious software designed to copy itself repeatedly to memory, on drive space, or on a network, until little memory or disk space remains.

>> REVIEWING THE BASICS

1. Define and explain the differences between viruses, worms, logic bombs, and Trojans.

2. Where can viruses hide?

3. What is the best way to protect a computer or network against worms?

4. What is the best way to determine if an e-mail message warning about a virus is a hoax?

5. Name three ways that a virus can hide from antivirus software.

6. Are boot sector viruses limited to hard drives? Explain.

7. What is the most likely way that a virus will get access to your computer?

8. List three products to remove malicious software that can deal with adware and spyware.

9. Why is it best to run AV software in Safe Mode?

10. What registry key keeps information about services that run when a computer is booted into Safe Mode?

11. What does AV software look for to determine that a program or a process is a virus?

12. What Windows tool can you use to solve a problem of an error message displayed at startup just after your AV software has removed malware?

13. What folder is used by Windows to hold System Restore restore points?

14. How can you delete all restore points and clean up the restore points data storage area?

15. What two methods does anti-rootkit software use to detect a rootkit?

16. Name two anti-rootkit products.

17. What is the major disadvantage of using an AV software installation CD to install the AV software to rid a system of viruses?

18. Why does having Windows display known file extensions help prevent a system from being infected with malware?

19. How does a rootkit running in user mode normally hide?

20. What is the difference between spyware and adware?

>> THINKING CRITICALLY

1. A virus has attacked your hard drive and now when you start up Windows, instead of seeing a Windows desktop, the system freezes and you see a "blue screen of death" (an error message on a blue background). You have extremely important document files on the drive that you cannot afford to lose. What do you do first?

    a. Try a data recovery service even though it is very expensive.

    b. Remove the hard drive from the computer case and install it in another computer.

    c. Try GetDataBack by Runtime Software (*www.runtime.org*) to recover the data.

    d. Use Windows utilities to attempt to fix the Windows boot problem.

    e. Run antivirus software to remove the virus.

2. Just after you reboot after running AV software, an error message is displayed that contains a reference to a strange DLL file that is missing. What do you do first?

   a. Run the AV software again.

   b. Run Msconfig and look for startup entries that are launching the DLL.

   c. Run Regedit and look for keys that refer to the DLL.

   d. Search the Internet for information about the DLL.

>> HANDS-ON PROJECTS

PROJECT 3-1:   Learning to Use Autoruns

Download Autoruns by Sysinternals (*www.sysinternals.com*) and run it on your PC. How many registry keys does Autoruns list that contain startup items on your PC? Compare the list of startup items to that generated by Msconfig. Describe any differences between the two lists.

PROJECT 3-2:   History of Rootkits

Rootkits became widely known when Sony included a rootkit with some of its audio CDs. The rootkit was intended to detect and prevent ripping or illegally copying the CDs. The rootkit was also written so it could not be detected or uninstalled by normal means. Use the Internet to research and answer these questions:

1. What are some of the audio CDs by Sony that contained the rootkit?

2. What are two software products that might be hidden on a Sony CD that contained the rootkit?

3. Describe Sony's response when consumers angrily protested the rootkit installation without their knowledge.

4. If you have used your computer to play a Sony audio CD that contained the rootkit, how can you best rid your computer of the rootkit?

PROJECT 3-3:   Using the Internet to Learn About Viruses

One source of information about viruses on the Web is F-Secure Corporation. Go to the Web site *www.f-secure.com/v-descs/*, shown in Figure 3-25, for information about viruses; the viruses are listed alphabetically with complete descriptions, including any known sources of the viruses. Print a description of three viruses from this Web site, with these characteristics:

◢ One virus that destroys data on a hard drive

◢ One harmless virus that only displays garbage on the screen

◢ One virus that hides in a boot sector

The site also lists information about the most recent viruses. Search the Web site at *www.f-secure.com*, list five recent viruses, and describe their payloads.

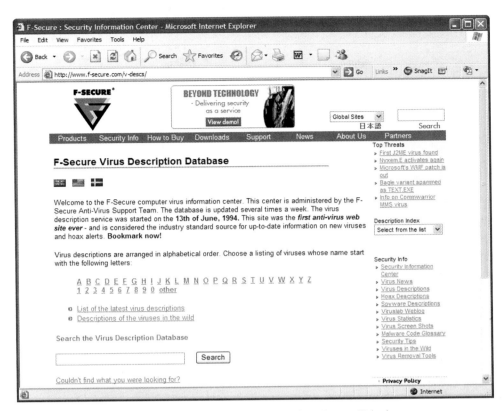

Figure 3-25 For comprehensive virus information, see the F-Secure Web site

---

PROJECT 3-4: Downloading the Latest Update of AV Software

If you own antivirus software, download the latest antivirus (AV) definition list from the Internet. For example, for Norton AntiVirus, follow these directions:

1. Go to the Symantec Downloads page: *www.symantec.com/downloads*.

2. Click **Virus Definitions and Security Updates** and then click **Download Virus Definitions**. Select your Norton AntiVirus product and operating system.

3. Follow the directions to download the latest update and signature list for the particular version of your AV software.

4. While online, see if the site offers information on virus hoaxes and create a list of hoaxes if it does.

>> REAL PROBLEMS, REAL SOLUTIONS

REAL PROBLEM 3-1: Cleaning Your System of Malware

Using the tools and techniques presented in this chapter, thoroughly clean your system of any malware. Take notes as you work and list any malware detected.

XP Pest Control

In the last chapter, you learned how to get rid of malware that has infected a system. In this chapter, you learn how to keep the stuff from getting inside in the first place. Securing your notebook or desktop computer is absolutely essential in today's world. The most common predators come in by way of the Internet, and so our focus is on protecting yourself from malware getting to you from that avenue. However, you also need to be able to secure a system from natural causes (such as your system being struck by lightning) and ill-intended hacking, stealing, and harassment, so these problems will also be discussed.

TOP TEN WAYS TO SECURE YOUR DESKTOP OR NOTEBOOK COMPUTER

In today's computing environment, we all need to know how to keep our shields up. This chapter focuses on the tools and methods you need to know to protect yourself. However, knowledge won't help much unless you use it. Be sure to apply what you're about to learn! Here are my top ten methods of securing a computer:

- Always use a personal firewall.
- Set AV software to run in the background and keep it current.
- Keep Windows updates current.
- Use alternate third-party client software and monitoring tools.
- Practice sensible Internet habits.
- Manage scripts and file extensions so malware can't trick you.
- Limit use of the administrator accounts.
- Physically protect your equipment.
- Secure your wired or wireless network.
- Keep good backups.

USE A PERSONAL FIREWALL

Never, ever connect your computer to an unprotected network without using a firewall. A firewall is software or hardware that prevents worms or hackers from getting into your system. A network is normally secured by a hardware firewall (a device that stands between the network and another network, including the Internet), and a single computer is normally secured by a software firewall (software installed on your computer that protects it from outsiders). A software firewall is a personal firewall, such as McAfee Personal Firewall, that protects a single computer.

Once while traveling, I used my Windows 2000 notebook to dial up my ISP before I remembered to turn on my McAfee firewall software. It was up no more than 10 minutes before I turned on the firewall, but in that time I received a nasty worm that infected my e-mail software. In that short time, it sent out dozens of e-mail messages to Navy military addresses.

Let's first look at how worms work and how a firewall stands up against them. Then, we'll look at some firewalls and how to use them.

HOW A WORM GETS INTO YOUR COMPUTER

Most worms come to your computer or network through the Internet. A computer communicates with other computers on the Internet by using identifying numbers called ports, which are similar to post office box numbers (see Figure 4-1).

When a computer is configured for network or Internet communication, it opens a series of port numbers to send and receive messages. One computer will say to the other, "I have a message for your port 25." If the receiving computer is not protected against worms, it will receive any message from any computer to any port it has opened for service. Worms on the Internet routinely perform "port scanning," meaning that they are constantly looking for open, unprotected ports through which they can invade a system. Once they are in the computer, they are free to download other software, move to other computers on the internal network, or produce mass e-mailings to bog down the network or Internet.

Table 4-1 lists some port numbers for several common services used on the Internet. For a complete listing of well-known and registered port number assignments, see the

Internet Assigned Numbers Authority (IANA) Web site at *www.iana.org/assignments/ port-numbers.*

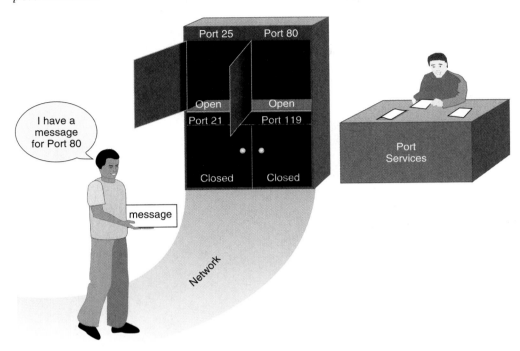

Figure 4-1 A computer receives communication over a network by way of ports that identify a communication service

Port	Protocol	Service	Description
20	FTP	FTP	File transfer data
21	FTP	FTP	File transfer control information
22	SSH	Secure Shell	Remote control to a networked computer
23	Telnet	Telnet	Telnet, an application used by Unix computers to control a computer remotely
25	SMTP	E-mail	Simple Mail Transfer Protocol; used by client to send e-mail
80	HTTP or HTTPS	Web browser	World Wide Web protocol
109	POP2	E-mail	Post Office Protocol, version 2; used by client to receive e-mail
110	POP3	E-mail	Post Office Protocol, version 3; used by client to receive e-mail
119	NNTP	News server	News servers
143	IMAP	E-mail	Internet Message Access Protocol, a newer protocol used by clients to receive e-mail
194	IRC	Chat	Internet Relay Chat Protocol

Table 4-1 Common TCP/IP port assignments for well-known services

HOW A FIREWALL WORKS

Recall that a firewall can be either a software firewall or a hardware firewall. A hardware firewall is a device that stands between a network and another network such as the Internet, or it can stand between a single computer and a network. The firewall filters or stops all port service requests that have not been initiated by computers inside the protected area. The device used most often for this purpose is a combo device like the one in Figure 4-2, and it is doing a lot more than just being a firewall. Using a device like this one is the best way to protect a small network, and in the next chapter you'll learn how to set one up and use it.

Figure 4-2 This combo device by Linksys is a firewall to protect a network, a router that allows computers on the network to share a broadband Internet connection, and a wireless access point for computers with wireless adapters

A software firewall is an application or OS utility installed on a single computer that protects that computer. A software firewall will not allow communication from another computer unless one of two things is true: (a) The computer being protected initiated the communicating and another computer is simply responding to the request; or (b) the firewall has been set to open a certain port (called port filtering). For example, if you want to allow chat sessions to be initiated by others, you would tell your firewall software to open port 194. Figure 4-3 illustrates a software firewall.

Software firewalls don't usually protect a computer as well as hardware firewalls, but you need to use a software firewall for two reasons: To protect your computer from worms that might be inside a network protected by a hardware firewall, and to protect your computer when a hardware firewall is not present. Software firewalls are particularly useful when you're traveling with a notebook computer or when you connect your computer at home directly to your ISP (Internet Service Provider).

Figure 4-3   A software firewall protecting a computer

HOW TO USE A SOFTWARE FIREWALL

Some examples of firewall software are ZoneAlarm (see Figure 4-4) by Zone Labs (*www.zonelabs.com*), Norton Personal Firewall by Symantec (*www.symantec.com*), Check Point Software by Check Point Software Technologies (*www.checkpoint.com*), McAfee Personal Firewall by McAfee (*www.mcafee.com*), Personal Firewall Pro by Sygate (*www.sygate.com*), and Windows XP Firewall. When evaluating firewall software, look for its ability to control traffic coming from both outside and inside the network. Sometimes you want to allow communication initiated by others, such as to play an online multiplayer game. Look for the software's ability to open a certain port that a game might use.

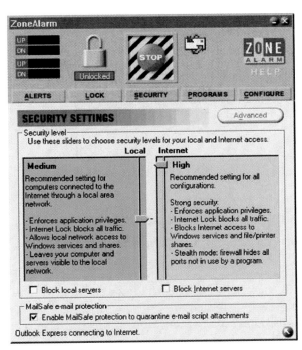

Figure 4-4   ZoneAlarm allows you to determine the amount of security the firewall provides

There's a problem with some software firewalls. They might do too good of a job protecting your computer and block communication that you really want to allow—such as when you've got shared folders on your computer and want to allow others on a local network to access these folders. For example, before Service Pack 2 for Windows XP was released, the firewall software for Windows XP was called Windows XP Internet Connection Firewall (ICF), and if this firewall were turned on, others on the LAN couldn't access resources on the PC. It was an all-or-nothing firewall. That's one more reason to be sure you have Windows XP Service Pack 2 installed.

You've already seen how to enable Windows Firewall, but now let's look at one feature you need to be aware of so that you can control when and how Windows Firewall filters requests to use a port service. Follow these steps:

1. To open the Windows Firewall window, right-click **My Network Places** and select **Properties**. The Network Connections window opens. Right-click your wired or wireless network connection icon and select **Properties** (see Figure 4-5). The connection properties window opens. Click the **Advanced** tab.

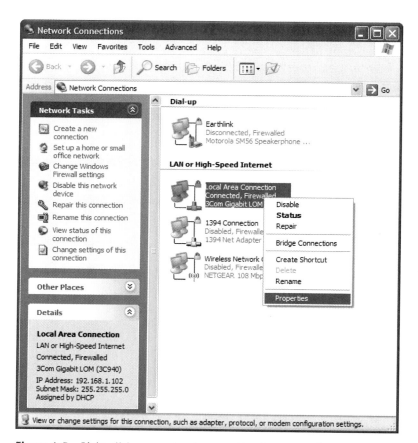

Figure 4-5   Right-click your network connection icon to configure the connection

2. Under Windows Firewall, click **Settings**. The Windows Firewall window opens (see Figure 4-6). Be sure the firewall is turned on.

   Notice the check box for *Don't allow exceptions*. If this box is checked, then you are fully protected from all outside activity you did not initiate. In other words, all your ports are closed. Check this box when you're traveling with your notebook, and

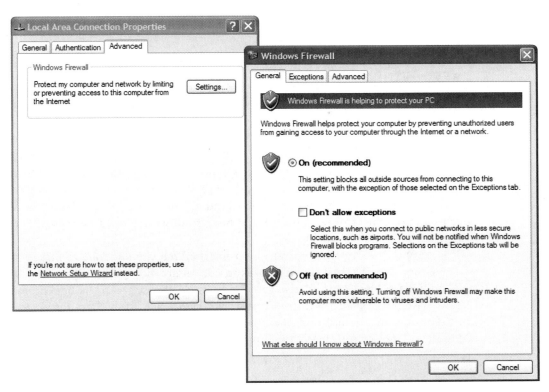

Figure 4-6 Windows Firewall window

make sure the box is checked *before* you connect to a public network. *To turn on this protection after you've connected might be too late.*

3. Are there times you might want to allow the firewall to let in exceptions? In other words, when might you want to open a port for another computer to send you a request for communication? If your computer is part of a local network that is protected from the Internet, others on the network might legitimately need to initiate communication with you. To open a port, uncheck **Don't allow exceptions**, click the **Exceptions** tab, and then select a program or service that is allowed in. Here are a couple of legitimate exceptions:

   ◢ You have shared files on your hard drive or a printer connected to your PC for others on the network to use. If so, make sure **File and Printer Sharing** is checked.
   ◢ You want to allow MSN Messenger chat sessions to be initiated by others. If so, check **MSN Messenger 6.2**.

4. After you have Windows Firewall configured the way you want it, click **OK** to close each window.

USE AV SOFTWARE

I know you're probably tired of reading this, but I'll say it one more time: install and run antivirus (AV) software and keep it current. Configure the AV software so that it automatically downloads updates to the software and runs in the background. To be effective, AV software must be kept current and must be turned on. Set the AV software to automatically scan e-mail attachments. You can find a list of AV software in the last chapter, so I won't repeat it here.

Because AV software does not always stop adware or spyware, it's also a good idea to run anti-adware software in the background.

KEEP WINDOWS UPDATES CURRENT

Although Unix, Linux, and the Apple Mac OS sometimes get viruses, Windows is plagued the most, by far, for two reasons. First, Windows is the most popular OS for desktop and notebook computers. Being the most popular also makes it the most targeted by authors of malware. Second, Windows is designed with highly integrated components and many user-level entry points into those components. Once a program has penetrated a Windows user-mode process, it is possible to infect more than one component. Security holes are being found all the time, and Microsoft is constantly releasing patches to keep up. But you have to download and install those patches before they'll help you.

Keep Windows updates current by using the Web site *windowsupdate.microsoft.com*. The easiest way to start the process is to click **Start**, point to **All Programs**, and click **Windows Update**. You can also set Windows XP to update in the background automatically without your involvement. To do that, right-click **My Computer**, select **Properties** on the shortcut menu, and then click the **Automatic Updates** tab. On this window, shown in Figure 4-7, select **Automatic (recommended)**.

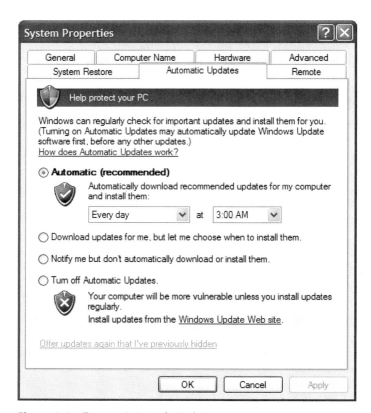

Figure 4-7   Turn on Automatic Updates

The only reason you would not want to keep this feature set to Automatic is if you don't use an always-up Internet connection and don't want to be bothered with the time spent downloading updates when you first connect to the Internet.

USE ALTERNATE CLIENT SOFTWARE AND MONITORING TOOLS

Using alternate client software, including browsers and e-mail clients, can give you an added layer of protection from malicious software that targets Microsoft's products. You can add even another layer of protection by installing third-party software to monitor any additions to your startup process. Both these security measures are discussed in this section.

BROWSER SOFTWARE

Internet Explorer gets attacked by malware more than any other browser product for these reasons:

▲ Internet Explorer is by far the most popular browser, and, therefore, writers of malware know they are more likely to get more hits than when they write malware for less popular browsers.

▲ Internet Explorer is written to more closely integrate with Windows components than other browsers. When malware penetrates IE, it can then get to other Windows components that are inherently tied to IE.

▲ IE is written to use ActiveX controls. An ActiveX control is a small program that can be downloaded by a Web site to your computer (sometimes without your knowledge). Microsoft invented ActiveX controls so that Web sites could use some nifty multimedia features. However, ActiveX controls allow Web pages to execute program code on your machine—and there's no way for you to know ahead of time whether that code is harmless or a malicious attack on your computer. For these reasons, you might consider using a different browser than IE. One excellent browser is Firefox by Mozilla (*www.mozilla.com*). It's free and easy to use. See Figure 4-8.

Figure 4-8   Firefox by Mozilla is not as vulnerable to malware as is Internet Explorer

If you do decide to stay with Internet Explorer, be sure to take advantage of its security features, which are described later in the chapter.

E-MAIL CLIENTS

Outlook and Outlook Express by Microsoft are probably the most popular e-mail clients. That means they're also the most often attacked. They also support ActiveX controls and are closely integrated with Windows components, making your system more vulnerable to malware. To help stay out of the line of fire, you can use alternate e-mail clients. Personally, I use Eudora by Qualcomm (*www.eudora.com*). Mozilla offers Thunderbird, which others have told me is also a great product.

> **Notes**
>
> You might want to also consider using an alternate e-mail address. When you have to give an e-mail address to companies that you suspect might sell your address to spammers, use a second e-mail address that you don't use for normal e-mailing.

MONITORING TOOLS

Remember from Chapter 2, you can install some third-party monitoring tools to monitor the startup processes and let you know when installation software attempts to add something to your startup routines. Three good products are Autoruns by Sysinternals (*www.sysinternals.com*), WinPatrol by BillP Studios (*www.winpatrol.com*), and Startup Control Panel by Mike Lin (*www.mlin.net*). You saw screen shots of these products in Chapter 2.

PRACTICE RESPONSIBLE INTERNET HABITS

In this section, we'll look at some best practices that, for the most part, simply equate to using good judgment when using the Internet to keep you out of harm's way. Here is a list of what I'll call the Ten Commandments for using the Internet:

1. *You shall not open e-mail attachments without scanning them for viruses first.* In fact, if you don't know the person who sent you the attachment, save yourself a lot of trouble and just delete it without opening it.

2. *You shall not click links inside e-mail messages.* Copy and paste the link to your browser address bar instead.

3. *You shall not forward an e-mail message warning without first checking to see if that warning is a hoax.* Save us all the time of having to delete the thing from our inbox.

4. *You shall always check out a Web site before you download anything from it.* Freeware isn't so free if you end up with an infected computer. Only download from trusted sites.

5. *You shall never give your private information to just any ol' Web site.* Use a search engine and search for information about a site before you trust it with your identity.

6. *You shall never trust an e-mail message asking you to verify your private data on a Web site with which you do business.* If you receive an e-mail that looks like it came from your bank, your PayPal account, or your utility company, don't click those links in that message. If you think it might be legitimate, open your browser, type in the link to the business's Web site, and check out the request.

7. *You shall always reboot a computer in a public place before you use it (that includes computers in school labs).* You never know who just used the thing and what they might have left there. Use a hard boot, not just a soft boot, to erase all memory-resident programs (including a memory-resident virus) from memory. Don't trust public computers with your private information.

8. *You shall never use the Internet without having your firewall turned on and your AV software working in the background.* For good measure, run anti-adware software, too.

9. *You shall never trust your valuable data to just one storage media.* Sooner or later, it will let you down. Always keep backups. How to make backups is covered later in the chapter.

10. *You shall never blindly trust your recovery routine.* It does no good to have backups, only to find out after a disaster that the backups don't work. Before disaster strikes, test your backups to make sure they're good and you know how to use them.

HOW TO DEBUNK AN E-MAIL HOAX

An e-mail hoax is itself a pest because it overloads network traffic when naïve users pass it on. Figure 4-9 shows an example of a virus hoax e-mail message I received.

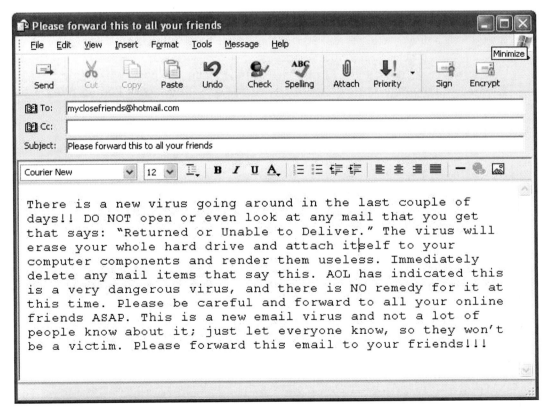

Figure 4-9 An example of a hoax e-mail message

Viruses grow more powerful every day, but this message is just absurd. It is unlikely that a virus can render computer components useless. No virus has been known to do actual physical damage to hardware, although viruses can make a PC useless by destroying programs or data, and a few viruses have been able to attack system BIOS code on the motherboard.

What's most important is not to be gullible and take the bait by forwarding the message to someone else. The potential damage a hoax like this can do is to overload an e-mail system with useless traffic, which is the real intent of the hoax. When I received this e-mail, over a hundred names were on the distribution list, sent by a friend who was innocently trying to help us all out.

Refer to Chapter 3 for a list of Web sites that specialize in debunking virus hoaxes.

WINDOWS AND IE SETTINGS

Several Windows and Internet Explorer settings can help you secure a computer from intruders on the Internet and from people who walk up to your computer with mischief in mind. These settings are discussed in this section.

INTERNET EXPLORER SECURITY SETTINGS

Be sure to take advantage of Internet Explorer's security features. Most of the features described in the following come with Internet Explorer version 6, which is installed with Windows XP Service Pack 2:

◢ Internet Explorer version 6 and later has a pop-up blocker. To control the Pop-up Blocker, open Internet Explorer, click **Tools,** and point to **Pop-up Blocker,** as shown in Figure 4-10. The first item in the menu in Figure 4-10 toggles between turning Pop-up Blocker on and off. To change settings, click **Pop-up Blocker Settings.** From the Pop-up Blocker Settings window that appears, you can create a list of Web sites that are allowed to present pop-ups and control how Pop-up Blocker informs you when it blocks a pop-up.

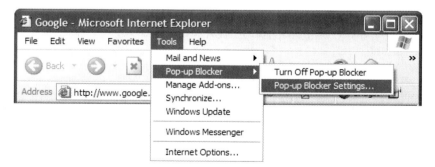

Figure 4-10   Internet Explorer Pop-up Blocker can be turned on or off and you can adjust its settings

Notes

If Pop-up Blocker is turned on, you might have a problem when you try to download something from a Web site. Sometimes the download routine tries to open a Security Warning window to start the download, and your pop-up blocker suppresses this window and causes an error. To solve the problem, you can temporarily turn off Pop-up Blocker before you begin the download or you can allow the Security Warning window to appear by clicking the pop-up block message and selecting **Download File**, as shown in Figure 4-11.

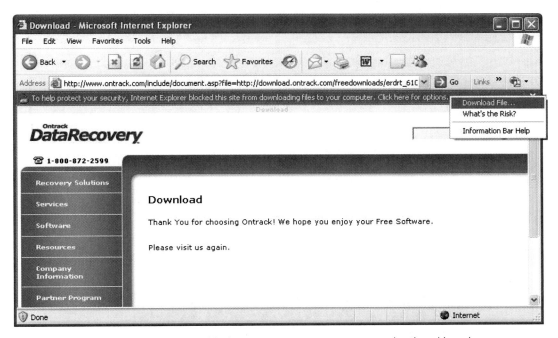

Figure 4-11 If your browser is set to block pop-ups, a message appears under the address bar of your browser

- Add-ons to Internet Explorer are also controlled from the Tools menu. To see a list of add-ons already installed, click **Tools**, and then click **Manage Add-ons**. The Manage Add-ons window opens (see Figure 4-12). You can toggle between a list of currently loaded add-ons and previously used add-ons. And you can update, disable, and enable add-ons. Also notice in the figure that you can see the DLL file that provides the add-on. To permanently get rid of an add-on, search for and delete that file.
- Internet Explorer offers several security options. To set them, click **Internet Options** on the Tools menu, and then click the **Security** tab (see Figure 4-13). Using the sliding bar on the left side of this window, you can choose the security level. The Medium level is about right for most computers. If you click the Custom Level button, you can see exactly what is being monitored and controlled by this security level and change what you want. These settings apply to ActiveX plug-ins, downloads, Java plug-ins, scripts, and other miscellaneous settings. Adware or spyware can make changes to these security settings without your knowledge. These settings are not password protected, so they will not help if you are trying to secure the browser from what other users of this computer can do.

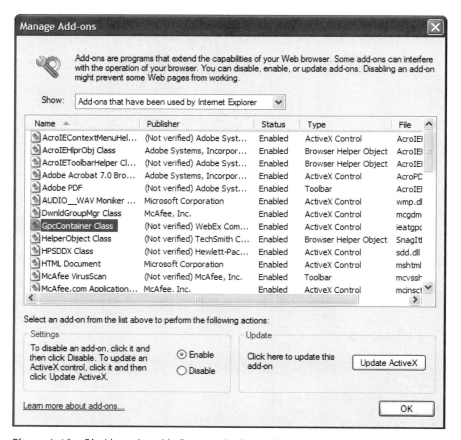

Figure 4-12 Disable and enable Internet Explorer add-ons

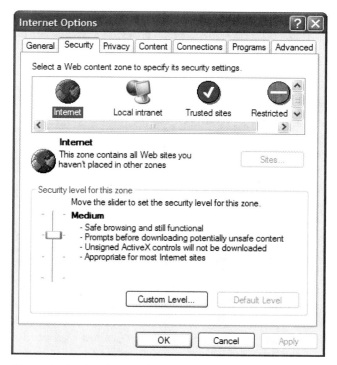

Figure 4-13 Set the security level of Internet Explorer using the Internet Options window

PROTECT AGAINST MALICIOUS E-MAIL SCRIPTS

One popular Trojan technique to spread a virus or worm is to put a malicious script in the body of an e-mail message or in an e-mail attachment. The e-mail is written with the intent of luring you to open the attachment or click a link in the e-mail text. For example, you receive spam in your e-mail, open it, and click the link "Remove me" to supposedly get removed from the spam list. However, by doing so, you spread a virus or worm, or install adware onto your PC.

To counteract this approach to spreading malicious software, let's take a look at how scripts work. Then we'll look at how you can protect yourself from malicious ones.

How Scripts Work

Scripts can be written in several scripting languages, such as VBScript or Jscript, and are executed in Windows using the Windows Scripting Host (WSH) utility, Wscript.exe. A script is stored in a file with a script file extension—the extension depends on the scripting language used to write the script. The scripting languages and file extensions that Windows recognizes by default are Jscript (.js file extension), Jscript Encoded (.jse), VBScript Encoded (.vbe), VBScript (.vbs), and Windows Script (.wsf). You can add other file extensions to this list.

The program that is used to handle a particular file type or file extension is determined by the Windows default settings. For instance, Windows knows how to handle a .txt file before any application is installed, because the program that is launched to open .txt files— Notepad (the executable is Notepad.exe)—is part of Windows.

On the other hand, file extensions that are not part of the Windows default settings can be added to the list of known file extensions when a new application is installed on a computer. For example, Windows will not know how to handle a .doc file until Microsoft Word has been installed. After Word is installed, when you double-click a .doc file, the Word executable, Winword.exe, is launched and then opens the document file.

How Scripts Are Spread

Now let's use all this information to help protect a system against malicious scripts. Many times a link that reads something like this one appears in an e-mail message from someone you don't know: "Click *www.symantec.com* to read about the latest virus attack." The link is not the URL to the Symantec Web site, but rather points to www.symantec.com.vbs, which is a script embedded in the e-mail message. When you click the link, the script with the .vbs file extension is executed by Wscript.exe and malicious software is spread to your computer.

Another malicious technique is to attach a file to an e-mail message. The filename is displayed, looking something like this: CoolPic.jpg. But because extensions of known file types are normally hidden, you are not aware that the real filename is CoolPic.jpg.vbs. When you click, thinking you're about to view a photo, you are executing a malicious script.

How to Help Protect Against Malicious Scripts

So how do you protect yourself? Here is what you can do:

- Set Windows so that script file extensions display by default. If that e-mail attachment had appeared as CoolPic.jpg.vbs, you probably would not have opened it.
- Set Windows to not execute scripts, but rather to open them in a Notepad window. Once you've examined a script, you can decide if you want to execute it.

Now let's see how to use both options. To display file extensions of scripts, do the following:

1. Using Windows Explorer or the Start menu, open **My Computer**. Click **Tools, Folder Options**. The Folder Options window appears. Click the **File Types** tab, as shown in Figure 4-14. Listed under *Registered file types* are all the file types that Windows knows how to handle.

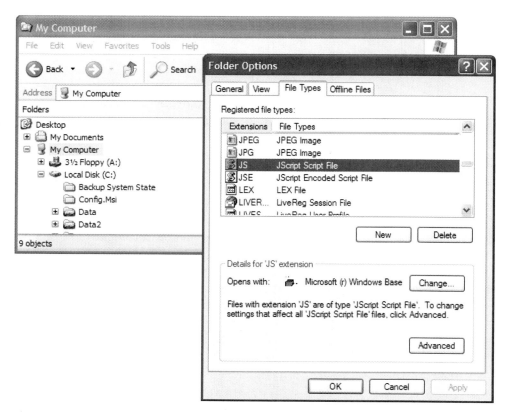

Figure 4-14 The File Types tab of the Folder Options window lists all file types that Windows recognizes

2. Select **JS** in the Extensions column and click **Advanced**. The Edit File Type window appears, as shown in Figure 4-15. Check the **Always show extension** check box. Click **OK**.

3. Do the same for the other script file types: JSE, VBE, VBS, and WSF. Click **Close** to close the Folder Options window.

A more drastic measure to protect yourself is to set Windows so that unknown scripts will not be executed. To do that, change the action that Windows takes each time you double-click a script file. Looking back at Figure 4-15, select **Edit** in the list of Actions (not the Edit button), click **Set Default**, and then click **OK**. The next time you double-click a script, it will be opened by Notepad for editing. Doing so will give you the opportunity to examine the script before it's executed. However, to actually execute the script, you have to manually use Wscript.exe to run it by entering this command at a command prompt (where *Myscript.vbs* is the name of the script):

```
Wscript.exe Myscript.vbs
```

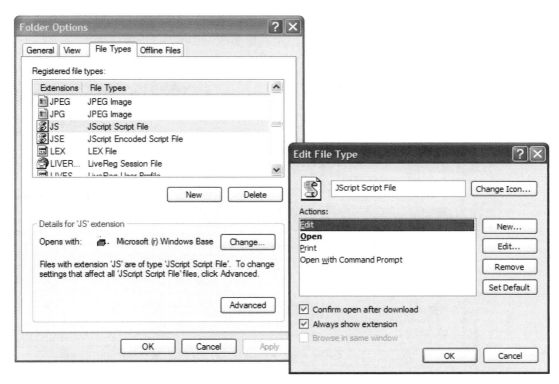

Figure 4-15 Use the Edit File Type window to change the way Windows displays and manages a file type

FOLDER AND FILE ENCRYPTION

Encryption puts data into code that must be translated before it can be accessed. Windows XP Professional encryption works only if you are using the NTFS file system on your hard drive partition. (Windows XP Home Edition does not provide encryption.) Encryption can be applied to either a folder or file. If a folder is marked for encryption, every file created in the folder or copied to the folder will be encrypted. At the file level, each file must be encrypted individually. Encrypting at the folder level is considered a best practice because it provides greater security: Any file placed in an encrypted folder is automatically encrypted so you don't have to remember to encrypt it. An encrypted file remains encrypted if you move it from an encrypted folder to an unencrypted folder on the same or another NTFS logical drive.

To encrypt a file or folder on an NTFS drive, do the following:

1. Right-click the folder or file you want to encrypt and select **Properties** from the shortcut menu. The Properties window for that file or folder opens (see Figure 4-16).

2. Click the **Advanced** button. The Advanced Attributes dialog box appears, also shown in Figure 4-16.

3. To encrypt the folder or file, check **Encrypt contents to secure data** and click **OK**. On the Properties window, click **Apply**. The dialog box shown in Figure 4-17 appears, asking you if you want the encryption to apply to subfolders. Make your choice and click **OK**.

If some other user who is not an administrator attempts to access the encrypted file or folder, a message "Access Denied" appears.

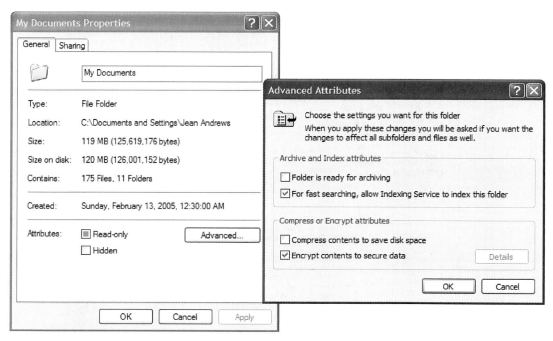

Figure 4-16   Encrypt a file or folder using the Properties window

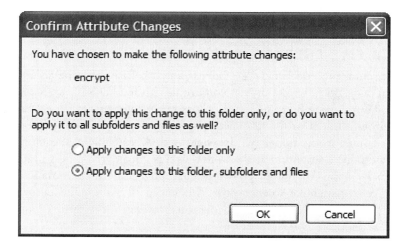

Figure 4-17   Encryption can apply to subfolders or just to one folder

HIDDEN SHARED FOLDERS

If you share folders on your computer with others on your local network, there is a way to hide those shared folders on the network so that other users can't see them. Only users who know the names of hidden shared folders can find and use them.

To hide a shared folder, use a dollar sign at the end of the folder name like this: C:\Private$. When you share the folder, it will not show up in My Network Places. A user on the network can access the folder by entering \\computername\Private$ in the Run dialog box. In Figure 4-18, the name of the computer is JOY.

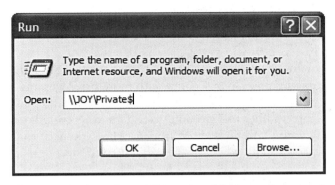

Figure 4-18 Accessing a hidden, shared folder on the network

USER GROUPS AND ADMINISTRATIVE PRIVILEGES

Another thing you can do to secure your computer is to limit the use of the more powerful user accounts. A user account defines a user to Windows and records information about the user, including the username, password used to access the account, groups that the account belongs to, and the rights and permissions assigned to the account. Permissions assigned to a user account control what the user can and cannot do in Windows. The privileges assigned to a user account largely depend on the user group the account is assigned to. We'll first look at how user groups work under Windows XP and how you can best use them to secure your computer, and then we'll look at how to create a user account.

UNDERSTANDING USER GROUPS

By default, Windows XP sets up different user groups that a user account can belong to. When a system administrator creates a new user account, he or she decides which group the account belongs to in order to control what that user can and cannot do.

Windows XP Home Edition provides two user groups, Administrators and Limited Users. Windows XP Professional offers these five default user groups:

- **Administrators,** who have access to all parts of the system, can install or uninstall devices and applications, and can perform all administrative tasks. When Windows XP is first installed, one user account is created in this group and the account is called the Administrator. During the installation of Windows XP, you can give this account a password. For security's sake, always use a password on the Administrator account. But don't forget it! It's a pain to recover from a forgotten Administrator password.
- **Backup Operators** can back up and restore any files on the system regardless of their access privileges to these files.
- **Power Users** can read from and write to parts of the system other than their own local drive, install applications, and perform limited administrative tasks.
- **Limited Users** (known as Users in Windows NT/2000) have read-write access only on their own folders, read-only access to most system folders, and no access to other users' data. They cannot install applications or carry out any administrative responsibilities.
- **Guests** use a workstation once or occasionally and have limited access to files and resources. A guest account has permission to shut down a computer. When Windows XP is first installed, one Guest account is created.

Just after you complete a Windows XP installation or you buy a new computer with the OS already installed, you have two accounts, the Administrator account and the Guest account.

You can't do much with the Guest account, so few people want to use it. Most of us find it convenient to log in each time as the Administrator, so we can install hardware and software and change any setting.

The problem is that a malware program might be at work while we're logged on and it will then most likely be running under our account with more privileges and the ability to do more damage than if we had been logged in under a less powerful account. For that reason, it's a good idea to create another user account to use for your everyday normal computer activities. Then only use the Administrator account when you need to do maintenance or installation chores that require the power of the Administrator account.

HOW TO CREATE A USER ACCOUNT

You must be logged in as an administrator to create a new user account. As an administrator, you can create a user account using the User Accounts applet in Control Panel. In addition, with Windows XP Professional, you can create a user account using the Computer Management console, in which case the account will automatically be added to the Limited group. If it is created using Control Panel, the new account will be a member of the Administrator group. When using Windows XP Professional, to create a local user account using Computer Management, follow these steps:

1. Log on to the computer as the administrator.

2. Click **Start** and then right-click **My Computer**. Select **Manage** on the shortcut menu. The Computer Management console window opens. (Note that you can also access Computer Management by way of the Administrative Tools applet in Control Panel.)

3. Expand **Local Users and Groups** by clicking the plus sign to its left. Right-click **Users** and then select **New User** on the shortcut menu. The New User window opens (see Figure 4-19). Enter the User name, enter the password twice, and check the boxes to decide how and when the password can be changed. You can also enter values for the Full name and Description to help identify the user. Click **Create**.

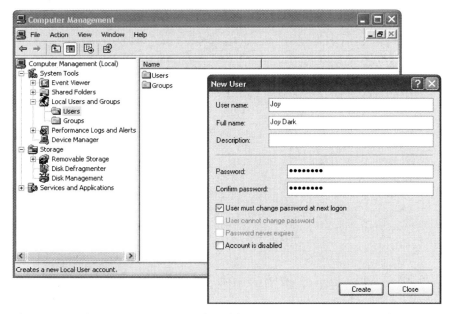

Figure 4-19 Create a user account using either Computer Management or the User Accounts applet in Control Panel

4. The account is created with the default type Limited, which means the account cannot create, delete, or change other accounts; make systemwide changes; or install software. If you want to give the account Administrator privileges, then open **Control Panel** and double-click the **User Accounts** applet.

5. The User Accounts window opens, listing all accounts. To make changes to an account, click **Change an account**, and then click the account you want to change.

6. In the next window, you can choose to change the name of the account, change the password, remove a password, change the picture icon associated with the account, change the account type, or delete the account. Click **Change the account type**.

7. In the next window, select **Computer administrator** and click **Change Account Type**. Click **Back** twice on the menu bar to return to the opening window.

When you set up a user account, the account can be put into the Administrator group or the Limited Group. However, if you want to put the account into another user group, you must use the Computer Management console. Do the following:

1. In the Computer Management window, under Local Users and Groups, double-click **Groups**. The list of groups appears in the right pane (see Figure 4-20).

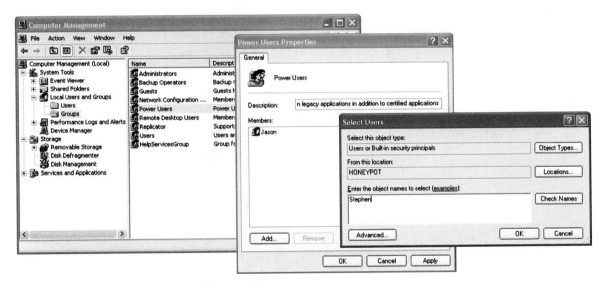

Figure 4-20   List of user groups on this computer

2. Right-click the group you want to assign a user to and select **Add to Group** from the shortcut menu. The group's Properties window appears. For example, in Figure 4-20, the Power Users Properties window is shown. Listed in this window are all users assigned to this group.

3. To add a new user to the group, click **Add**. The Select Users window opens. Enter the name of a user, click **OK**, and then click **Apply**.

MAKE A FORGOTTEN PASSWORD FLOPPY DISK

Sometimes a user forgets his or her password or the password is compromised. If this happens and you have Administrator privileges, you can access the account through Control Panel or the Computer Management Console and reset the user's password.

However, resetting a password under Windows XP causes the OS to lock out the user from using encrypted files or e-mail or from using Internet passwords stored on the computer. If you need to reset a password for a user who has encrypted data, first remove the encryption status on the folder or file before you reset the password.

If your computer has a floppy disk drive, each user, including the administrator, should create a forgotten password floppy disk, which can be used to log on if the user forgets his or her password. To create the disk, open the **User Accounts** applet in Control Panel, click your account, and select **Prevent a forgotten password** under Related Tasks in the left pane of this window. The Forgotten Password Wizard opens (see Figure 4-21). Follow the wizard to create the disk.

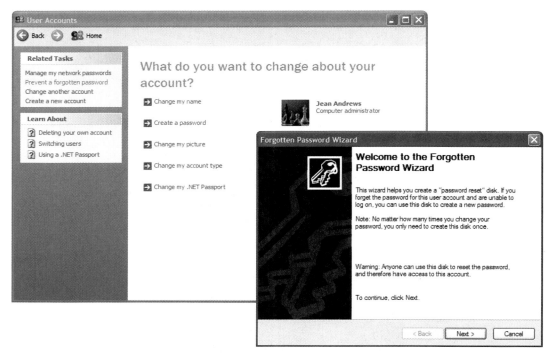

Figure 4-21   Create a forgotten password floppy disk

If a user enters a wrong password at logon, a message appears, giving the user the opportunity to use the forgotten password floppy disk to log on. Insert the disk and you can then enter a new password and log on. Encrypted files and e-mail are not affected.

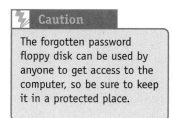

The forgotten password floppy disk can be used by anyone to get access to the computer, so be sure to keep it in a protected place.

A serious problem can arise if the administrator forgets the password to the Administrator account and a forgotten password disk has not been made. An administrator password is required when you boot into Safe Mode, use the Recovery Console (covered in Chapter 7), or perform many other critical tasks. If there's only one administrator account and this password is forgotten, you're in trouble!

Windows allows for no alternative in this situation other than reinstalling the OS. However, third-party utility software can sometimes help. For example, ERD Commander 2003 by Winternals (*www. winternals.com*) is a bootable operating system on CD that contains Locksmith, a utility that lets you reset a forgotten administrator password. You can boot the Windows XP system from the ERD Commander 2003 CD to launch a Windows-like desktop and use several recovery tools including the one to reset a forgotten administrator password.

PHYSICALLY PROTECT YOUR EQUIPMENT

It's only common sense, but worth mentioning anyway: There are some things you can do to physically protect your computer equipment. Here is my list of do's and don'ts. You can probably add your own tips to the list:

- ▲ *Don't move or jar your computer when it's turned on.* Before you move the computer case even a foot or so, power it down. Don't put the computer case under your desk where it might get bumped or kicked. Although modern hard drives are sealed and much less resistant to vibration than earlier models, it's still possible to crash a drive by banging into it while it's reading or writing data.

- ▲ *Don't smoke around your computer.* Tar from cigarettes can accumulate on fans, causing them to jam and the system to overheat. For older hard drives that are not adequately sealed, smoke particles can get inside and crash a drive.

- ▲ *Don't leave the PC turned off for weeks or months at a time.* Once my daughter left her PC turned off for an entire summer. At the beginning of the new school term, the PC would not boot. We discovered that the boot record at the beginning of the hard drive had become corrupted. PCs, like old cars, can give problems after long spans of inactivity.

- ▲ *High humidity can be dangerous for hard drives.* I once worked in a basement with PCs, and hard drives failed much too often. After we installed dehumidifiers, the hard drives became more reliable.

- ▲ *In CMOS setup, disable the ability to write to the boot sector of the hard drive.* This alone can keep boot viruses at bay. However, before you upgrade your OS, such as when you upgrade Windows XP to Windows Vista, be sure to enable writing to the boot sector, which the OS setup will want to do.

- ▲ *If your data is really private, keep it under lock and key.* You can use all kinds of security methods to encrypt, password protect, and hide data, but if it really is that important, one obvious thing you can do is store the data on a removable storage device such as a flash drive and, when you're not using the data, put the flash drive in a fireproof safe. And, of course, keep two copies. Sounds simple, but it works.

- ▲ *Keep magnets away from your computer.* Don't work inside the computer case with magnetized screwdrivers or set magnets on top of the computer case.

SECURE YOUR WIRED OR WIRELESS NETWORK

Unsecured networks are like leaving your front door open when you go to work in the morning or signing every check in your checkbook and then leaving it lying around in a coffee shop. Don't even think about it! If you're responsible for a home or small office network, take security seriously. Securing a wired or wireless network is covered in the next chapter. Read it with the intention of deciding on the best way to secure your network and then buy the equipment you need to do it. Most often, the device you'll want is a router that can be used to secure a wired network or provide a secured wireless network. Routers don't cost that much nowadays, and the investment is well worth it. However, after you buy it and set it up, be sure you implement what you'll learn in the next chapter to configure it for good security.

KEEP GOOD BACKUPS

Suppose the hard drive on your computer stopped working. It's totally dead and everything on it is lost. How would that affect you? What would be lost and what would that cost you in time, stress, and money? The time to prepare for disaster is before it happens. As a rule of thumb, if you can't get along without those data files, e-mail address lists, or e-mail attachments, back them up. How to make good backups is covered in the next section.

KEEPING GOOD BACKUPS

When it comes to computers, we all need a Plan B. You need to know how to back up data and how to use those backups when you need them. You also need to know how to back up the system files. And for really serious backer-uppers, you can even back up the entire hard drive, including the operating system, using a product like Norton Ghost. All these types of backups are covered in this section.

If you work for a large corporation, chances are the company has a data backup policy and backup media already in place. If that's the case, follow your IT department's instructions for keeping good backups. If you travel with a corporate notebook, you might need to get your notebook in sync with the corporate server on a regular basis, say daily. Syncing up your notebook is, in effect, backing up your data. Don't assume that your data is backed up, unless you've checked with your IT department for specific policies and procedures and you understand and use those procedures.

In this section, I'm assuming you don't have these backup methods available and you're responsible for your own backups.

BACKING UP DATA

For peace of mind and to be prepared for the worst-case scenario, we all need to keep data backed up. If you can't get along without it, back it up! As a general rule of thumb, back up your data for every eight to ten hours of data entry. That might mean you back up once a day, once a week, or once a month. In this section, we'll look at backup media, how to make backups, and how to restore your data from a backup.

BACKUP MEDIA

The most popular media for backing up data are tape drives, a second hard drive, and USB devices including flash memory, CDs, or DVDs. Tape drives are more difficult to use than other methods, but tapes are less expensive than other media if you have a ton of data to back up. Backing up to a second hard drive is the most convenient method, but for the best security, you need to keep the backed-up data off site, and that's not convenient when using a second hard drive. CDs and DVDs are good choices if you don't have too much data to back up. They're easy to use and easy to store in an off-site location. Flash memory is a great choice for small amounts of data.

Tape drives such as the one shown in Figure 4-22 currently have capacities of 20 to 800 GB compressed and come in several types and formats. Some tape drives can be installed inside the computer and others sit outside the computer case and use a USB or

Figure 4-22 This Quantum Travan 40 tape drive holds up to 40 GB of data. It comes with backup software, data cartridge, USB 2.0 cable, power supply, power cord, and documentation.

FireWire connector. When you buy a tape drive, consider the type of tapes it will use, because there are a bunch of them out there. When selecting a tape drive, use the Web to check out reviews of different tape drives and buy one that consistently gets good reviews.

If you don't have a CD or DVD burner on your computer, you might want to consider an external device such as the one shown in Figure 4-23. Unfortunately, several DVD technologies today are vying for the market, so be sure to match the blank DVDs to what the burner can use.

Figure 4-23　This external DVD drive by Plextor can use a FireWire or Hi-Speed USB connection and supports several speeds and read/write standards, including 4X DVD+R, 2.4X DVD+R/RW, 12X DVD-ROM, 16X CD-R write, 10X CD-RW rewrite, and 40X CD read

To back up to a second hard drive, you can use an external hard drive that connects to your computer by way of a FireWire or USB port (see Figure 4-24), a hard drive in another computer on your network, or a second drive installed inside your computer. And for really large backup needs, you can buy a group of hard drives housed in a case that connects to your network.

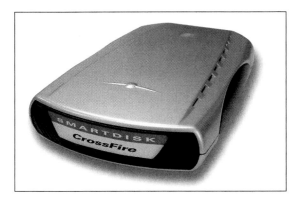

Figure 4-24 This Crossfire external hard drive holds 160 GB and uses a FireWire or Hi-Speed USB connection

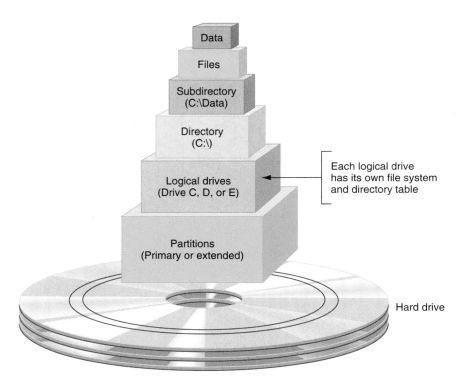

Figure 4-25 A hard drive is divided and organized at several levels

If you travel a lot, keeping good backups of data on your notebook computer might be a problem. Several Internet companies have solved this backup-on-the-go problem by providing remote backup services over the Internet. In a hotel room or other remote location, connect to the Internet and back up your data to a Web site's file server. If data is lost, you can easily recover it by connecting to the Internet and logging into your backup service Web site. If security is a concern, be sure you understand the security guarantees of the site. Two online backup services are @Backup (*www.backup.com*) and Remote Backup Systems (*www.remote-backup.com*).

HOW TO BACK UP DATA

Although Windows XP has a backup utility (Ntbackup.exe), you might want to invest in specialized backup software to make backups as efficient and effortless as possible. Many tape drives come with bundled backup software.

To perform a backup using Ntbackup.exe under Windows XP, follow these steps:

1. Click **Start**, point to **All Programs**, point to **Accessories**, point to **System Tools**, and then click **Backup**. The Backup Wizard appears. Click **Advanced Mode**.

2. The Backup utility opens. Click the **Backup** tab. Your screen should look like Figure 4-26. If you want to perform a backup immediately, check the drive and subfolders to back up.

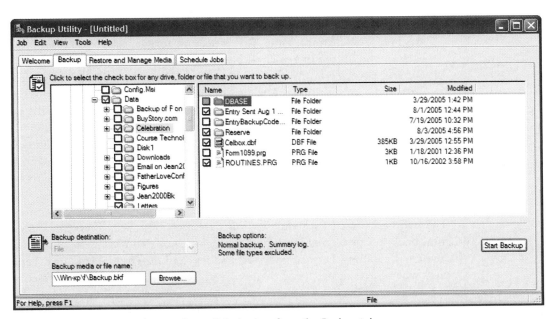

Figure 4-26 You can perform an immediate backup from the Backup tab

3. In the lower-left corner of the Backup Utility window, note the text box labeled Backup media or file name, which specifies where to back up to. To change this location, click the **Browse** button. The Save As dialog box appears. Navigate to the drive and path where you'd like to save the backup file and enter a name for the file. Click **Save**. The new path and name for the backup file appear in the text box.

4. Click the **Start Backup** button in the lower-right corner to perform the backup.

You can schedule a single backup to be done at a later time or repeated on a schedule until you terminate the schedule. When planning routinely scheduled backups, you have some options so that you don't have to back up everything at each backup. It's a lot less expensive and time-consuming to only back up what's changed since the last backup. Windows XP offers these options for scheduled backups:

▲ *Normal backup (also called a full backup)*. All files selected for backup are copied to the backup media. Each file is marked as backed up by clearing its archive attribute. Later, if you need to recover data, this full backup is all you need. (After the backup, if a file is changed, its archive attribute is turned on to indicate the file has changed since its last backup.)

▲ *Copy backup*. All files selected for backup are copied to the backup media, but files are not marked as backed up (meaning file archive attributes are not cleared). A Copy backup is useful if you want to make a backup apart from your regularly scheduled backups.

▲ *Incremental backup*. All files that have been created or changed since the last full backup are backed up, and all files are marked as backed up (meaning file archive attributes are cleared). Later, if you need to recover data, you'll need the last normal backup and all the incremental backups since this last normal backup.

▲ *Differential backup*. All files that have been created or changed since the last normal or incremental backup are backed up, and files are not marked as backed up. Later, if you need to recover data, you'll need the last normal backup and the last differential backup.

▲ *Daily backup*. All files that have been created or changed on this day are backed up. Files are not marked as backed up. Later, if you need to recover data, you'll need the last normal backup and all daily backups since this last normal backup.

The two best ways to schedule backups are a combination of normal backups and incremental backups, or a combination of normal backups and differential backups. When using incremental backups, because they are smaller than differential backups, you save time and money when backing up. On the other hand, recovering data is less time-consuming when using differential backups because you only need two backups to perform a full recovery (the last normal backup and the last differential backup.)

For a business with heavy data entry, suppose you decide you need to back up every night at 11:55. To implement this backup plan, you might decide to schedule two backups: A normal backup each Friday at 11:55 P.M., and a differential backup each Monday, Tuesday, Wednesday, and Thursday at 11:55 P.M. In a project at the end of this chapter, you'll learn how you can reuse tapes or other reusable storage media on a rotating basis for a backup plan similar to this one.

Notes

When making your backup plan, for extra protection, take into account that you might want to keep several generations of backups on hand. If you always overwrite the backup with a new backup, you only have one generation of backups. However, sometimes a file gets corrupted or accidentally deleted and you don't discover the problem for several weeks. If you don't keep several generations of backups, you will have no chance of recovering the data. On the other hand, if you back up weekly and keep the last 10 weeks of backups, you can go back and search through previous backups to recover the file.

To schedule a backup, do the following:

1. In the Backup Utilities window, begin by clicking the Schedule Jobs tab. Select a date on which you want to schedule a backup, and then click the Add Job button.

2. The Backup Wizard opens. On the first screen, click **Next**. Select **Back up selected files, drives, or network data**, and then click **Next**.

3. On the next screen, select the drives, folders, or files you want to back up, and then click **Next**.

4. Follow the steps through the wizard to choose where you want to save your backup, give a name to the backup, and select the type of backup (Normal, Copy, Incremental, Differential, or Daily).

5. Next, you must decide if you want to append the data to an existing backup or replace an existing backup. Your decision largely depends on how much space you have available for backups.

6. When asked if you want to perform the backup now or later, select **Later** and give the backup a name. Click the **Set Schedule** button.

7. The Schedule Job window appears, as shown on the right side of Figure 4-27. Schedule how often the backup is to occur, and then click **OK**. Notice in the figure, a backup is scheduled for each Monday, Tuesday, Wednesday, and Thursday at 11:55 P.M.

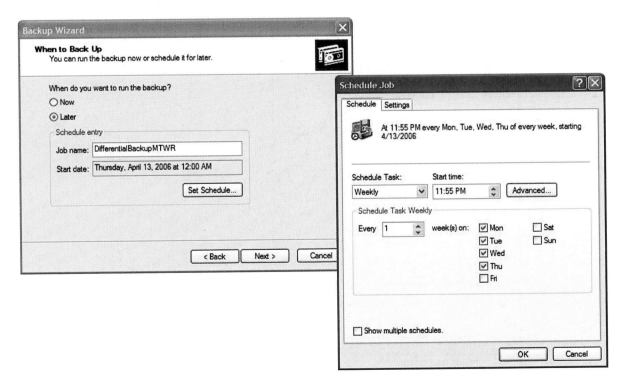

Figure 4-27 Schedule repeated backups

8. Click **Next** in the wizard, and follow the remaining instructions to complete the backup. At the end of the process, the wizard gives you an onscreen report summarizing information about the backup.

Besides the folders that contain your documents, spreadsheets, databases, and other data files, you also might want to back up these folders:

▲ *Your e-mail messages and address book*

   ▲ For Outlook and Outlook Express, back up this folder:

   C:\Documents and Settings*username*\\Local Settings\\Application Data\\Microsoft\\Outlook

   ▲ For Eudora by Qualcomm, you decide where to put your e-mail data when you install Eudora; or you can create a shortcut to Eudora on your desktop and change the location of the e-mail data folder in that shortcut. Either way, to see where Eudora is holding your e-mail data, right-click the Eudora shortcut and select **Properties** from the shortcut menu (see Figure 4-28). If you don't have a Eudora shortcut, and Eudora finds a Eudora.ini file in the folder in which Eudora is installed, it uses that folder for data. If no Eudora.ini file is present, Eudora looks for a Deudora.ini file and reads the [settings] entry to know where data is stored. See Figure 4-29. In this example, the data folder to back up is C:\Data\Email on Jean2000. Yours will be a different folder.

Figure 4-28   Look at the Eudora shortcut to know where your e-mail data is stored

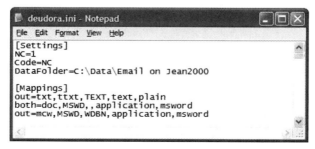

Figure 4-29   Look in the Deudora.ini file for the path to your Eudora e-mail data

4

◢ *Your Internet Explorer favorites list.* To back up your IE favorites list, back up this folder: C:\Documents and Settings*username*\Favorites.

RESTORING DATA FROM BACKUPS

To recover files, folders, or the entire drive from backup using the Windows XP Backup utility, click the **Restore and Manage Media** tab on the Backup Utility window, and then select the backup job to use for the restore. The Backup utility displays the folders and files that were backed up with this job. You can select the ones that you want to restore. When you restore from backup, you'll lose all the data you've entered in restored files since the backup, so be sure to use the most recent backup and then reenter the data that's missing.

Notes

By default, Windows XP Home Edition does not include the Backup utility. To install it manually, go to the \VALUEADD\ MSFT\NTBACKUP folder on your Windows XP setup CD and double-click **Ntbackup.msi**. The installation wizard will complete the installation.

BACKING UP SYSTEM FILES

You learned to back up the system state in Chapter 2, where we used Ntbackup.exe to back up the system state and registry before we edited the registry. You need to back up the system state after you have made major changes to the system, such as when you install a new hard drive or software application.

IMAGING A HARD DRIVE

If you are responsible for looking after several computers and you find yourself having to rebuild a corrupted hard drive more often than you'd like, you might want to consider disk imaging. With disk imaging, you back up the entire partition on the hard drive where Windows is installed. Then, if a problem arises, you can just whip out your image and quickly restore the entire partition. You must use third-party software to image a hard drive. Three products are Acronis True Image by Acronis (*www.acronis.com*), Paragon Drive Backup 7.0 by Paragon Software Group (*www.drive-backup.com*), and Norton Ghost by Symantec (*www.symantec.com*). (For excellent reviews of all three of these products, see the Web site *www.toptenreviews.com* by TopTenReviews, Inc.) Each of these products has its advantages and disadvantages, but Norton Ghost is probably the best known of the three, so we'll use it as our example of disk-imaging software.

USING NORTON GHOST TO IMAGE A DRIVE

Currently, when you purchase Norton Ghost, you get two CDs: Norton Ghost 2003 and Norton Ghost 10.0 (see Figure 4-30). Using Ghost, you can save the image to a second hard drive or to an external USB device, or you can burn the image to a CD or DVD. Later, if Windows is so corrupted you cannot boot to the Windows desktop, you can boot the system from a CD and restore the image. If you burn the Norton Ghost image to CD or DVD, Ghost can make the disc bootable. If you use compression on the image, you can back up about 10 GB of information onto a single DVD. This is more than enough room for an installation of XP with updates, drivers, and applications. However, if the image is too large for a single disc, Ghost will automatically span multiple discs.

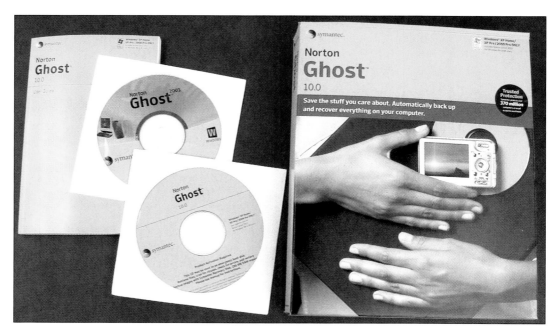

Figure 4-30   Use Norton Ghost to make an image of your Windows partition on your hard drive

To give you an idea of how Norton Ghost or another similar product can be used to image a system, let's look at the steps to create a backup image using Norton Ghost 2003. After the product is installed on a computer, here are the steps you would follow to image a drive:

1. Open **Norton Ghost**. The main screen opens, as shown in Figure 4-31.

2. Select **Ghost Basic** in the left pane, and then click **Backup**. On the next screen, click **Next** to launch the Backup Wizard.

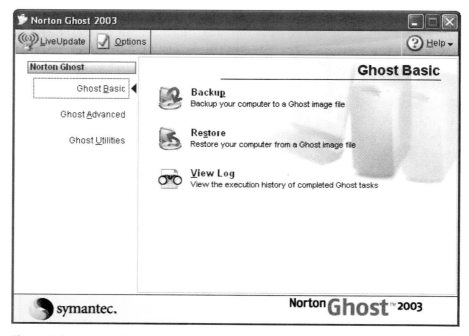

Figure 4-31   Norton Ghost main window

3. On the next screen, shown in Figure 4–32, you decide which drive to image and the media you will use for your image. Notice in the figure this computer has only a single drive, C, which is selected. To back up to another hard drive, click **File**. To back up to a CD or DVD, click **Recordable CD or DVD**. Then click **Next**.

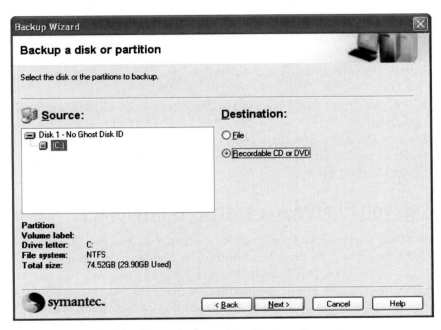

Figure 4-32   Select the drive to image and the image media

4. On the next screen, if you are saving the backup to a file, enter the filename, click the **Browse** button, and point to its location. Then click **Next** to move on to the next screen. After you complete the wizard, the last screen (see Figure 4-33) lets you know that the computer will reboot, and then Ghost.exe will launch to create the image.

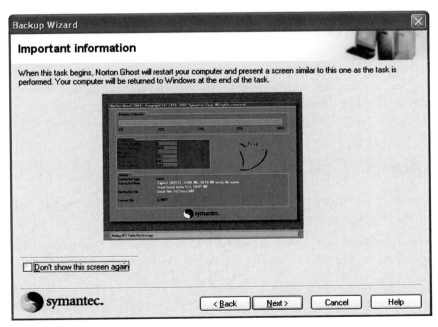

Figure 4-33   The Norton Ghost Wizard shows what your screen will look like after the reboot

After you have made your initial image of the drive, you can use Norton Ghost to make incremental backups of what's changed on the drive so that your image will be more current.

RESTORING A HARD DRIVE USING NORTON GHOST

Using an image previously made by Norton Ghost, you can recover individual files and folders from within Windows or, if the entire hard drive is corrupted, you can use the image to completely recover the hard drive, even if the Windows installation is in ruins. The Norton Ghost 10.0 CD is a bootable CD containing its own operating system. If you boot from this CD, some things you can do include the following:

- Browse files and folders in an image and recover individual files and folders saved in the image.
- Recover the entire hard drive from an image.
- Scan the hard drive for viruses before you restore to the image.
- Check the hard drive for bad sectors.

SLICING YOUR DRIVE FOR EASIER MAINTENANCE

When you buy a new desktop or notebook computer that already has Windows installed, most likely the entire hard drive is partitioned as a single partition named drive C, and that drive C can be really big. Look back at Figure 4-32; you can see the single drive on this computer, drive C, is 74.52 GB. If you use CDs that each hold about 700 MB to image this partition, you could need up to 100 CDs, depending on how full this drive is. That's just not practical! If you are responsible for partitioning a hard drive before you install Windows, you might want to consider breaking the drive into smaller, more manageable partitions. This hard drive is advertised as an 80 GB drive. Here is one way you could slice up that space into three partitions:

- Use 10 GB for Windows, device drivers, and maybe a few applications.
- Use 40 GB for data and other applications.
- Use 30 GB as a backup media for another hard drive on your network.

Of course, there are many other ways to slice the drive, but the point is you should decide how best to use the space and don't assume you have to have only a single partition. If you install Windows on a 10 GB partition, the partition will be small enough that you can easily image it and, if necessary, later restore that image. And, if the data is not stored on the same partition as Windows, restoring the Windows partition from an image won't disturb your data. How to create, format, and resize partitions is covered in Chapter 8.

>> CHAPTER SUMMARY

- A firewall is software or hardware that stands between your computer system and the Internet, protecting it against uninvited communication.

- A port is a number that is used to allow a program on another computer to communicate with your computer. A firewall closes all ports or only allows communication on selected ports.

- Hardware firewalls offer more protection than software firewalls, but software firewalls are useful when a hardware firewall is not present, such as when you are traveling with a notebook computer or you are on a local network and need protection from other computers on the network.

◢ For AV software or anti-adware software to be effective, it must be kept current and it must be always running in the background.

◢ Internet Explorer and Outlook or Outlook Express are most often targeted by malicious software. Using less popular clients such as Firefox by Mozilla (a browser) or Eudora by Qualcomm (an e-mail client) might mean you are less likely to be attacked.

◢ Practice and teach responsible Web surfing, such as never opening an e-mail attachment from unknown senders and never downloading from Web sites you have not carefully checked out.

◢ To make it less likely you'll launch a malicious script on your computer, set Windows to display file extensions of scripts.

◢ Create and use a less powerful account than an administrator account for most activities so that you will not unknowingly allow malicious software to use a more powerful administrator account.

◢ Back up data after about every 8 to 10 hours of data entry. For best security, store the backup media at an off-site location.

◢ Back up the system state after you have made major changes to your system, such as when you install a second hard drive or an application.

◢ For best protection, use imaging software to image your hard drive.

◢ Partitions that are huge can be difficult to back up or image. For easier maintenance, you can slice a large hard drive into two or more partitions.

>> KEY TERMS

encryption   Used to protect sensitive data, the conversion of data into code that must be translated before it can be accessed.

firewall   Software or a hardware device that protects a computer or network from unsolicited communication. A hardware firewall stands between two networks or a computer and a network. A software firewall is installed on a single computer to protect it, and is called a personal firewall.

forgotten password floppy disk   A Windows XP disk created to be used to reset a password in the event the user forgets the user account password to the system.

logical drive   A portion or all of a hard drive partition that is treated by the operating system as though it were a physical drive. Each logical drive is assigned a drive letter, such as drive C, and contains a file system. Also called a *volume*.

partition   A division of a hard drive that can be used to hold logical drives (for example, drive C).

port   A number assigned to an application or other process on a computer so that the process can be found by TCP/IP. Also called a *port address* or *port number*.

user account   The information that defines a Windows XP user, including username, password, memberships, and rights.

volume   *See* logical drive.

>> *REVIEWING THE BASICS*

1. What is the Windows Scripting Host utility used for, and what is the command line to execute it?

2. Why is using an ActiveX control considered a security risk?

3. What must you do before you can use the Windows Backup utility on a Windows XP Home Edition PC?

4. Name one browser other than Internet Explorer by Microsoft.

5. Name two e-mail clients other than Outlook or Outlook Express by Microsoft.

6. What is the best way to protect a computer or network against worms?

7. When you are traveling with your notebook computer and using a public wireless hotspot, how do you set Windows Firewall differently than you set it when working from your office network that has a hardware firewall?

8. What are five file extensions that might be used for scripts?

9. Why might someone see better security when using a browser other than Internet Explorer?

10. Name four types of media that can be used to hold backups of data.

11. What is the name of the program file of the Windows XP backup utility?

12. What two accounts are created by the Windows XP setup process?

13. What folder can you back up in order to back up e-mail messages and the address book used by Outlook Express?

14. To back up your IE favorites list, what folder do you back up?

15. What is the best way to determine if an e-mail message warning about a virus is a hoax?

>> *THINKING CRITICALLY*

1. If you have Windows Firewall set to not allow any exceptions and keep all ports closed, which of the following activities will be allowed, and which will not be allowed? Explain your answer.

   ◢ You receive e-mail.

   ◢ You receive an MSN Messenger notice that a friend wants to have a chat session with you.

   ◢ Your antivirus software informs you a new update has just been downloaded and installed.

2. You are about to install Windows XP on a new 60 GB hard drive. You plan to use the system as a file server for a small business network and you estimate the capacity required for data stored on the file server will not exceed 30 GB. How many and what size partitions should the drive have? Explain your answer.

   a. One 60 GB partition

   b. One 10 GB partition and one 50 GB partition

   c. One 30 GB partition and one 30 GB partition

>> HANDS-ON PROJECTS

PROJECT 4-1:   E-Mail Hoax

Search through your spam and junk mail for an e-mail you think might be a hoax. (Please don't click any links or open any attachments as you search.) Using the Web sites listed earlier in the chapter for debunking virus hoaxes, search for information about this potential hoax. You might need to enter the subject line in the e-mail message into a search box on the Web site.

PROJECT 4-2:   Using Firefox

Go to the Mozilla Web site (*www.mozilla.com*) and download and install Firefox. Use it to browse the Web. How does it compare to Internet Explorer? What do you like better about it? What do you not like as well? When might you recommend to someone that they use Firefox rather than IE?

PROJECT 4-3:   Researching Backup Media

You are responsible for the data on the file server of a small company. Currently, the file server hard drive is 120 GB, but only 35 GB of data is stored on the drive. You are investigating what backup media to use and have decided to compare the cost of backing up to tapes and to external USB removable storage. Research both media and answer the following questions:

1. Research tape drives and tapes. What tape drive do you recommend? How much will it cost? Print the Web page showing the drive.

2. What tapes will you use on the drive? How much will each tape cost? Print the Web page showing the tapes for sale.

3. How many tapes will it require to back up the current 35 GB of data? How many tapes will be required when the drive is full of data? If you make a backup each night and rotate tapes using the system described in Table 4-2, how much will it cost to use this tape backup system for one year?

4. Research external USB hard drives or other USB removable storage devices as your backup media. What removable storage media do you recommend? How much will it cost? Print the Web page showing the drive or other device.

5. Answer this Hands-On Project's Question 3 for the removable storage media.

6. Which storage solution is less expensive? Other than cost, what other factors should you consider when selecting a backup media?

Name of Backup	How Often Performed	Storage Location	Description
Child backup	Daily	On-site	Keep four daily backup tapes of data that has changed that day, and rotate the tapes each week. Label the four tapes Monday, Tuesday, Wednesday, and Thursday. A Friday daily (child) backup is not made, because on Friday you make the parent backup.

Table 4-2   The child, parent, grandparent backup method

Name of Backup	How Often Performed	Storage Location	Description
Parent backup	Weekly	Off-site	Perform a full backup each week on Friday. Keep five weekly backup tapes, one for each Friday of the month, and rotate them each month. Label the tapes Friday 1, Friday 2, Friday 3, and Friday 4.
Grandparent backup	Monthly	Off-site, in a fireproof vault	Perform the monthly backup on the last Friday of the month. Make a full backup of data and the system state. Keep 12 tapes, one for each month. Rotate them each year. Label the tapes January, February, and so on.

Table 4-2   The child, parent, grandparent backup method (continued)

PROJECT 4-4:   Scheduling Backups

Using Table 4-2 as your guide, set up Windows XP backup schedules to create the backups of data and the Windows XP system state. Assume all data for all users is stored in the C:\Documents and Settings folder. Print the details of each scheduled backup.

PROJECT 4-5:   Managing User Accounts

Do the following to experiment with managing user accounts:

1. Create a Limited user account and add it to the group of Backup Operators. Log on as the Backup Operator. Can you view the contents of the My Documents folder for an account with Administrator privileges?

2. As a Backup Operator, try to install a new Windows component. What error message do you receive?

3. Create a user account with Limited privileges. Log on using this account. Can you view the contents of the My Documents folder for an account with Administrator privileges?

4. What is the error message you receive if you try to create a new account while logged in under an account with Limited privileges?

>> REAL PROBLEMS, REAL SOLUTIONS

REAL PROBLEM 4-1:   Securing Your Computer

Using as many of the suggestions in the chapter as apply to your system, make your computer as secure as possible. Take notes as you work and record any problems you encounter. What other measures would you like to take to secure your computer that you don't know how to do or that cost too much?

CHAPTER 5

Wired and Wireless Made Easy

This chapter is more of a how-to chapter than others in this book. Yes, I know this book is mostly focused on fixing what's broken, but, with networking, the most common source of a problem is when things are not set up correctly to begin with. Therefore, when you're faced with a networking problem, the best way to get to the bottom of it is to check every setup and configuration detail.

We'll start by going through the step-by-step processes of connecting a single computer to the Internet and then networking two or more computers using a wired or wireless connection. At the end of the chapter, we'll talk about tools and techniques you can use when things that are set up correctly won't work. Security is always a major concern when networking, so we'll also cover how to secure both wired and wireless networks.

HOW TO CONNECT A COMPUTER TO THE INTERNET

For individual users and for small networks at home or in a small office, the entry point to the Internet is an ISP (Internet Service Provider), as shown in Figure 5-1. That ISP can provide one or more ways to connect to the Internet. The four most popular methods are DSL, cable modem, satellite, and phone lines. Phone lines are the cheapest and slowest method. Satellite might work for you if you live in a remote location where DSL or cable modem is not available. Choosing between DSL and cable modem depends on several factors, and sometimes it's a toss-up between the two.

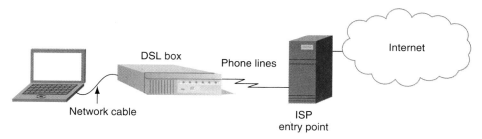

Figure 5-1 Use an ISP to connect to the Internet

The major differences and similarities between cable modem and DSL are:

▲ Cable modem uses TV cable for transmission and you can subscribe to cable modem bundled with your TV cable subscription. On the other hand, DSL uses phone lines for transmission and is bundled with your local phone service.

▲ Cable modem and DSL both can be purchased on a sliding scale depending on the bandwidth you want to buy. Also, both subscriptions offer residential and the more-expensive business plans.

▲ With cable modem, you share the TV cable infrastructure with your neighbors so that service can become degraded if many people in your neighborhood are using cable modem at the same time. I once used cable modem in a neighborhood where I found I needed to stay away from Web surfing between 5:00-7:00 p.m. when folks were just coming in from work and using the Internet. With DSL, you're using a dedicated phone line, so your neighbors' surfing habits are not important.

▲ With DSL, static over phone lines in your house can be a problem. The DSL company provides filters to install at each phone jack, but still the problem might not be fully solved. Also, some phone lines have so much static on them (called a dirty phone line) that DSL just won't work. Your phone company can test your line to see if it qualifies for DSL.

▲ Setup of cable modem and DSL works about the same way using either a cable modem or a DSL modem for the interface between the broadband jack (TV jack or phone jack) and the PC.

▲ With either installation, the cable modem or DSL provider can send you the broadband modem and you can follow the instructions to install it, or you can have the provider do the entire installation for you at an additional cost. If you pay for this installation service, a service technician comes to your home, installs all equipment, including a network card if necessary, and configures your PC to use the service.

Personally, I subscribe to two ISPs. I use Earthlink to provide dial-up connections when I travel, and I use my local cable company to provide broadband high-speed Internet access to my home office. Because I absolutely must have Internet access when I'm working, I use my Earthlink dial-up connection as my backup connection when cable is down. I used to use DSL for my broadband connection, but we had so much trouble with static and other interference on my phone lines, I switched to cable. However, I'm not criticizing DSL; I think the problem might have been with my home phone wiring job. I know others who switched from cable to DSL because cable gave them grief. What works best for you largely depends on the wiring in your house and your neighborhood and the services and infrastructure of your local providers. If you're trying to decide between going with DSL or cable modem for your high-speed Internet connection, ask several neighbors on your street which one they use and why.

Now let's turn our attention to how to connect to the Internet using cable modem, DSL, and dial-up. We begin by looking at how communication happens at three levels.

COMMUNICATION AT THREE LEVELS

Let's talk about the big picture for a moment. When your computer at home is connected to your ISP off somewhere in the distance, your computer and a computer on the Internet are communicating at three levels. The computers need a way to address each other at each level. These three levels and the addresses used at each level are diagrammed in Figure 5-2.

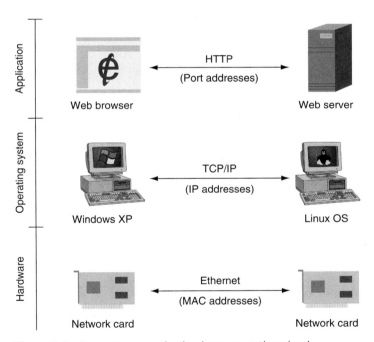

Figure 5-2 Internet communication happens at three levels

Listed next is a description of each level of communication:

▲ *Hardware level.* At the root level of communication is hardware. The hardware or physical connection might use network cables, phone lines (for DSL or dial-up), or TV cable lines (for cable modem). For local networks, DSL, or cable modem, a network adapter (also called a network card, network interface card, or NIC) inside your computer is part of this physical network. The rules for communication are predetermined and these rules are called protocols. Currently, the most common networking standard used at the hardware level is called Ethernet. So that network cards can identify each other on the network, each card contains a unique number—a 48-bit (or 6-byte) address called a MAC address. An example of a MAC address is 00-0C-6E-4E-AB-A5. Part of the MAC address refers to the manufacturer, and the rest of the address is a serial number assigned by the manufacturer. Therefore, by design, no two adapters will have the same MAC address. Most likely the MAC address is written on the adapter, as shown in Figure 5-3. At the lowest level of communication, one NIC is searching on its network for another NIC with a specific MAC address. For regular dial-up phone line connections, the physical connection is made by a modem and a phone line.

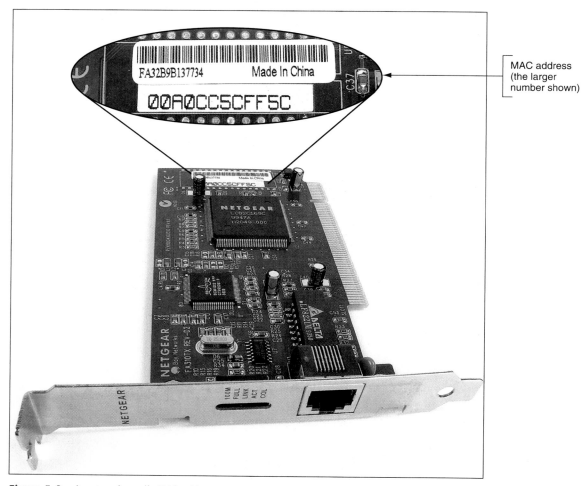

Figure 5-3 A network card's MAC address

▲ *Operating system level.* An OS is responsible for managing communication between it and another computer, using rules for communication that both OSs understand. This group, or suite, of communication protocols is collectively called TCP/IP. One OS addresses the other OS using addresses called IP addresses. IP addresses are four-digit numbers separated by periods, such as 72.56.105.12. A network can use static IP addressing, in which each computer is assigned an IP address that never changes; or dynamic IP addressing, in which each time the computer connects to the network, it gets a new IP address (called leasing the IP address).

▲ *Application level.* When you use the Internet to surf the Web or download your e-mail, you are using an application on your computer called an Internet client.

For Web surfing, that client, such as Internet Explorer or Firefox, is called a browser. The client communicates with another application somewhere on the Internet, called a server. Examples of server applications are your e-mail server at your ISP or a Web server anywhere on the Web. Recall from earlier chapters that each server is installed under the OS as a third-party service. Web browsers and servers use the HTTP protocol, and e-mail clients and servers can use POP, SMTP, and IMAP protocols. A client identifies a server by the IP address of the computer and a port number. Web servers are normally assigned port 80 and e-mail servers are assigned port 25. See Figure 5-4.

Figure 5-4   Each server running on a computer is addressed by a unique port number

Figure 5-6 shows how communication moves from a browser to the OS to the hardware on one computer and on to the hardware, OS, and Web server on a remote computer. As you set up a small network that consists of your computer

> **Notes**
>
> When you enter a domain name such as *www.microsoft.com* in a browser address box, that name is translated into an IP address followed by a port number. It's interesting to know that you can skip the translation step and enter the IP address and port number in the address box. See Figure 5-5.

connected to the ISP, keep in mind that the network must be set up at all three levels. And when things don't work right, it helps to understand that you must solve the problem at one or more levels. In other words, the problem might be with the physical equipment, with the OS, or with the application.

When you first purchase a subscription to your ISP, you might receive an installation CD from your ISP. If so, you'll want to follow the installation setup routine on this CD instead of the manual procedures outlined in this chapter. The order of doing things might differ from instructions here.

When first connecting to the Internet, the installation generally goes like this:

1. Physically connect your PC to the cable modem, DSL modem, or phone jack. (Sometimes the ISP will ask you to install software before you connect equipment.)

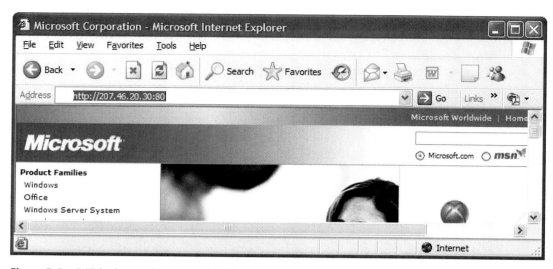

Figure 5-5   A Web site can be accessed by its IP address and port number

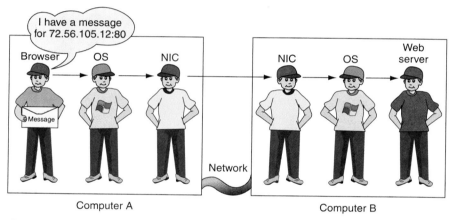

Figure 5-6   How a message gets from a browser to a Web server using three levels of communication

2. Using Windows, configure the TCP/IP settings for the connection to the ISP. To configure Windows correctly, you'll need to know these things:

   a. Your username and password to the ISP. (This username and password might be required to connect to the ISP, or it might just be used to manage your ISP account on the ISP Web site. Your ISP will let you know how to use it.)

   b. For dial-up connections, you'll need the phone number to the ISP that your modem will dial.

   c. An ISP might use static IP addressing or dynamic IP addressing. If it uses static IP addressing, you will be told the IP address to give Windows. If it uses dynamic IP addressing, you can set Windows to ask for an IP address each time it connects to the ISP.

   d. If your ISP has you set up for static IP addressing, the ISP will also tell you the subnet mask, the IP addresses of the default gateway, and the DNS servers.

3. Test the connection by using a browser to surf the Web.

Here is a quick explanation of the terms subnet mask, default gateway, and DNS server:

▲ A **subnet mask** is four numbers separated by periods that, when combined with an IP address, indicate what network a computer is on. An example of a subnet mask is 255.255.255.0.

▲ A **default gateway** is a computer on a network that acts as an access point, or gateway, to another network. Depending on the context, this can refer to the computer at the ISP that you go through to get to the Internet, or to the router on your own network that is connected to the cable modem.

▲ A **DNS (Domain Name System) server** matches up domain names with IP addresses. For example, when you enter *www.delmarlearning.com* in your browser address box, the DNS server will look up that domain name in one of its available tables and translate it into the IP address of the Delmar server.

CONNECT TO THE INTERNET USING CABLE MODEM

In most cases, cable modem and DSL use a network port or a USB port on the PC to connect to the cable modem or DSL modem. Figure 5-7 shows the setup for a cable modem connection using a network cable between the PC and the cable modem.

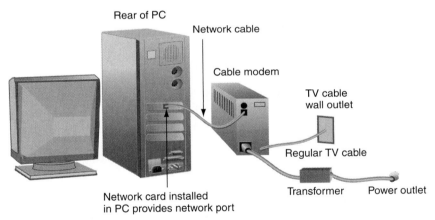

Figure 5-7 Cable modem connecting to a PC through a network card installed on the PC

Follow these instructions to connect a computer to the Internet using cable modem:

1. Select the TV wall jack that will be used to connect your cable modem. You want to use the jack that connects directly to the point where the TV cable comes into your home with no splitters between this jack and the entrance point. Later, if your cable modem connection is constantly going down, you might consider that you've chosen the wrong jack for the connection because an in-line splitter can degrade the connection. The cable company can test each jack and tell you which jack is best to use for the cable modem. (One good reason to have a technician come and hook you up for the first time.)

2. Using coaxial cable, connect the cable modem to the TV wall jack. Plug in the power cord to the cable modem.

3. When using a network port on your PC, connect one end of the network cable to the network port on the PC, and the other end to the network port on the cable modem.

4. You're now ready to configure Windows for the connection. Right-click **My Network Places** and select **Properties** from the shortcut menu. The Network Connections window opens. See Figure 5-8. Click **Create a new connection**.

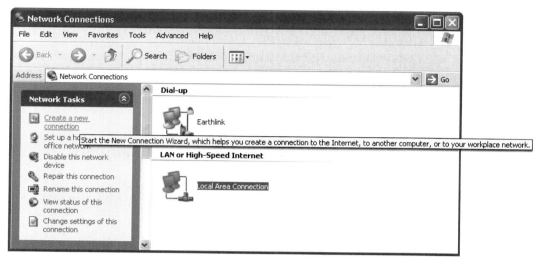

Figure 5-8 Using Windows XP, launch the New Connection Wizard

5. The New Connection Wizard opens. Click **Next** to skip the welcome screen. On the next screen, select **Connect to the Internet** and click **Next**.

6. On the next screen, select **Set up my connection manually** and click **Next**. On the following screen (see Figure 5-9), select **Connect using a broadband connection that is always on** and then click **Next**. The wizard creates the connection. Click **Finish** to close the wizard.

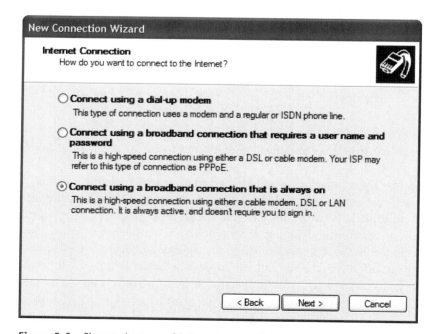

Figure 5-9 Choose the type of Internet connection

Windows XP makes assumptions about your connection. To view or change the configuration:

1. In the Network Connections window, right-click the connection icon and select **Properties** from the shortcut menu. The connection Properties window opens, as shown in Figure 5-10. Click the **General** tab to select it, if necessary.

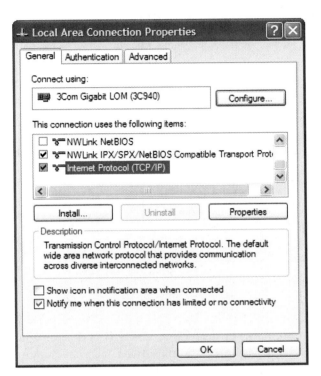

Figure 5-10 Configure an Internet connection using the Properties window of the connection icon

2. Select **Internet Protocol (TCP/IP)** and click **Properties**. The Internet Protocol (TCP/IP) Properties window opens. See Figure 5-11.

3. Most likely your ISP is using dynamic IP addressing for your connection, so you will need to select **Obtain an IP address automatically** and **Obtain DNS server address automatically**. If you are using static IP addressing (for example, if you have a business account with your ISP), select **Use the following IP address**, and enter the IP address given you by the ISP, along with the IP address of the default gateway and the IP addresses of two or more DNS servers. Click **OK** to close the window.

4. On the connection properties window, click the **Advanced** tab and then, under Windows Firewall, click **Settings** and verify the firewall is up. Click **OK** to close the window, and then click **OK** again to close the connection properties window.

Follow these directions if you are using a USB cable to connect your cable modem to your computer:

1. When using a USB port on your PC, first read the directions that came with your cable modem to find out if you install the software before or after you connect the cable modem and follow that order. For most installations, you begin with connecting the cable modem.

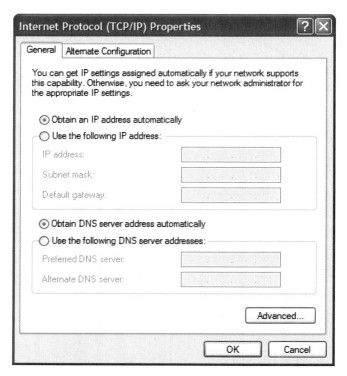

Figure 5-11   Configure TCP/IP for the connection

2. Connect a USB cable to your PC and to the cable modem. Turn on the cable modem and Windows XP will automatically detect it as a new USB device. When the Found New Hardware Wizard launches, insert the USB driver CD that came with your cable modem. The wizard searches for and installs these drivers. See Figure 5-12. Click **Finish** to close the Found New Hardware wizard. A new connection icon will be

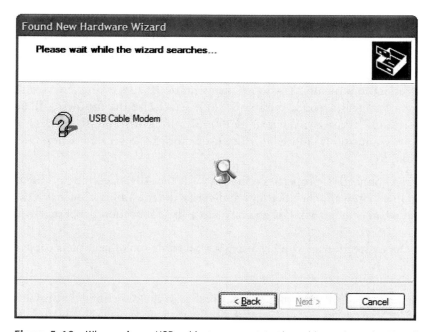

Figure 5-12   When using a USB cable to connect to the cable modem, the Found New Hardware Wizard will install the cable modem drivers

added to the Network Connections window. Check the properties of the connection to make sure TCP/IP is configured as you want it.

You are now ready to activate your service and test the connection. Do the following:

1. The cable company must know the MAC address of the cable modem you have installed. If you have received the cable modem from your cable company, they already have the MAC address listed as belonging to you and you can skip this step. If you purchased the cable modem from another source, look for the MAC address somewhere on the back or bottom of the cable modem. See Figure 5-13. Contact the cable company and tell them the new MAC address.

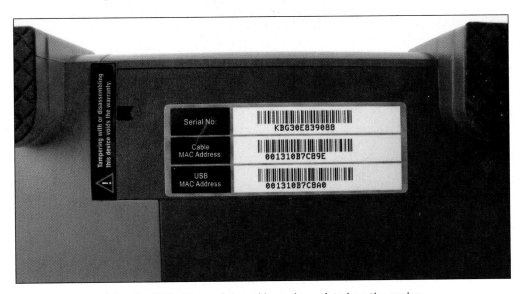

Figure 5-13   Look for the MAC address of the cable modem printed on the modem

2. Test the Internet connection using your Web browser. If you are not connected, try the following:

   a. Open the Network Connections window, right-click the connection and select **Repair** from the shortcut menu. For dynamic IP addressing, this releases and renews the IP address.

   b. If this doesn't work, turn off the PC and the cable modem. Wait a full five minutes until all connections have timed out at the cable modem company. Turn on the cable modem and wait for the lights on the front of the modem to settle in. Then turn on the PC. After the PC boots up, again check for connectivity.

   c. Try another cable TV jack in your home.

3. If this doesn't work, call the cable modem help desk. The technician there can release and restore the connection at that end, which might restore service. If this doesn't work, there may be a problem with the cable company's equipment, which they will need to repair.

CONNECT A COMPUTER TO THE INTERNET USING DSL

DSL service and the older technology, ISDN, are provided by the local telephone company. As with a cable modem, a technician from the phone company can install DSL for you, or they can send you a kit for you to install yourself. If you do the installation yourself, know that it works pretty much the same way as cable modem. Here are the steps that are different:

1. Install a telephone filter on every phone jack in your house that is being used by a telephone, fax machine, or dial-up modem. See Figure 5-14.

Figure 5-14 Filters are needed on every phone jack when DSL is used in your house

2. Connect the DSL modem as shown in Figure 5-15. If necessary, you can use a Y-splitter on the wall jack (as shown on the left in Figure 5-14) so a telephone can use the same jack. Plug the DSL modem into the DSL port on a filter or directly into a wall jack. (Don't connect the DSL modem to a telephone port on the filter; this setup would prevent DSL from working.) Plug in the power to the DSL modem. Connect a network cable between the DSL modem and the PC.

3. You're now ready to configure the network connection. If your DSL modem came with a setup CD, you can run that setup to step you through the configuration. You can also manually configure the network connection. To do that, using the Network Connections window, click **Create a new connection** and click **Next** to skip the welcome screen. Then click **Connect to the Internet** and click **Next**. Finally, click **Set up my connection manually**.

4. On the next screen, shown in Figure 5-9, you have a choice to make, based on the type of DSL subscription you have. If you subscribed to always-up DSL, click **Connect using a broadband connection that is always on.** If you have a DSL subscription that is active only when you log on with a username and password, then click **Connect using a broadband connection that requires a user name and password.** This last type of connection is managed by a protocol called PPPoE

 Notes

If your DSL subscription is not always up and requires you to enter your username and password each time you connect, using a router with auto-connecting ability can be a great help. It can automatically pass the username and password to your DSL provider without your involvement.

(Point-to-Point-Protocol Over Ethernet), which is why the connection is sometimes called a PPPoE connection. Follow the wizard through to complete the setup.

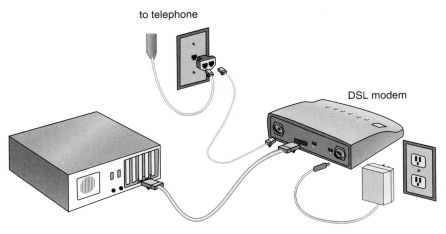

to telephone

DSL modem

Figure 5-15   Sample setup for DSL

CONNECT A COMPUTER TO THE INTERNET USING A DIAL-UP CONNECTION

Dial-up connections are painfully slow, but many times we still need them when traveling and they're good at home when our broadband connection is down or we just plain want to save money. To connect a computer to the Internet using a dial-up modem, follow these directions:

1. Plug the phone line into the modem port on your computer, if necessary.

2. To launch the New Connection Wizard in Windows XP, right-click **My Network Places** and select **Properties** from the shortcut menu. The Network Connections window appears. Click **Create a new connection**.

3. The New Connection Wizard opens. Click **Next** to skip the welcome screen. On the next screen, select **Connect to the Internet** and click **Next**.

4. On the next screen, select **Set up my connection manually** and click **Next**. On the following screen, select **Connect using a dial-up modem**. Click **Next**.

5. Enter a name to identify the connection, such as the name and city of your ISP. Click **Next**. In the following screen, enter the access phone number of your ISP. Click **Next**.

6. On the next screen (see Figure 5-16), enter your username and password at the ISP. This screen gives options to make the logon automatic and to make this the default connection to the Internet. Make your choices and click **Next**.

7. On the next screen, you can choose to add a shortcut to the connection on the desktop. Make your choice and click **Finish**. A connection icon is added to the Network Connections window; if you selected the option, a shortcut is added to the desktop.

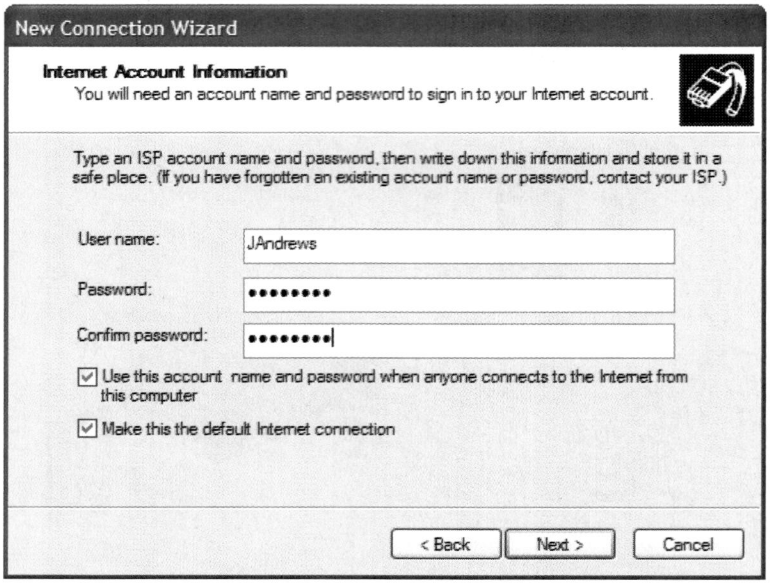

New Connection Wizard

Internet Account Information
You will need an account name and password to sign in to your Internet account.

Type an ISP account name and password, then write down this information and store it in a
safe place. (If you have forgotten an existing account name or password, contact your ISP.)

User name: JAndrews

Password: ••••••••

Confirm password: ••••••••

☑ Use this account name and password when anyone connects to the Internet from
this computer

☑ Make this the default Internet connection

[< Back]   [Next >]   [Cancel]

Figure 5-16   The New Connection Wizard asks how to configure the connection

To use the connection, double-click the connection icon. The Connect dialog box
appears (see Figure 5-17). Click **Dial**. You will hear the modem dial up the ISP and make
the connection.

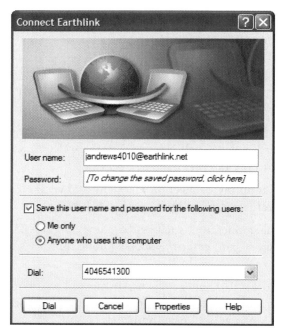

Connect Earthlink

User name: jandrews4010@earthlink.net

Password: [To change the saved password, click here]

☑ Save this user name and password for the following users:

○ Me only

● Anyone who uses this computer

Dial: 4046541300

[Dial]   [Cancel]   [Properties]   [Help]

Figure 5-17   Make a dial-up connection to your ISP

To view or change the configuration for the dial-up connection, do the following:

1. In the Network Connections window, right-click the connection and select
Properties from the shortcut menu. The connection Properties window opens, as

shown in Figure 5-18. Using the tabs on this window, you can change Windows Firewall settings (Advanced tab), configure TCP/IP (Networking tab), control the way Windows attempts to dial the ISP when the first try fails (Options tab), and change other dialing features.

Figure 5-18   Configure an Internet connection using the Properties windows of the connection icon

If the dial-up connection won't work, here are some things you can try:

- Is the phone line working? Plug in a regular phone and check for a dial tone. Is the phone cord securely connected to the computer and the wall jack?
- Check the Dial-up Networking connection icon for errors. Is the phone number correct? Does the number need to include a 9 to get an outside line? Has a 1 been added in front of the number by mistake? If you need to add a 9, you can put a comma in the field like this "9,4045661200", which causes a slight pause after the 9 is dialed.
- Try dialing the number manually from a phone. Do you hear beeps on the other end?
- Try another phone number.
- When you try to connect, do you hear the number being dialed? If so, the problem is most likely with the phone number, the phone line, or the username and password.
- Does the modem work? Check Device Manager for reported errors about the modem. Does the modem work when making a call to another phone number (not your ISP)?
- Is TCP/IP configured correctly? Most likely you need to set it to obtain an IP address automatically.
- Reboot your PC and try again.
- Try removing and reinstalling the dial-up connection. If that doesn't work, try using Device Manager to uninstall the modem and install it again. (Don't do this unless you have the modem drivers on CD or on the hard drive.)

After you have successfully connected a single computer to the Internet, you're ready to move on to the next step of connecting a second computer so the two computers can share an Internet connection.

> **Notes**
>
> If you want to disable call waiting while you're connected to the Internet, enter "*70" in front of the phone number (without the double quotes).

HOW TO SHARE AN INTERNET CONNECTION

You have just seen how you can connect a single computer to the Internet using a cable modem, DSL, or dial-up connection. Now let's look at how to connect two or more computers in a small network so they can share this one Internet connection. We're first going to build the two setups shown in Figure 5-19. In Figure 5-19a, two computers are connected with a single crossover network cable, and in Figure 5-19b, a hub or switch is used to connect three or more computers in a small network. In both setups, the host computer has the direct connection to the Internet.

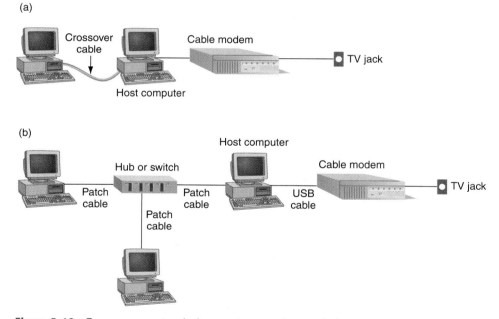

Figure 5-19 Two or more networked computers can share a single Internet connection

Windows XP **Internet Connection Sharing (ICS)** is designed to manage these types of connections. Using ICS, the host computer stands between the network and the Internet.

In the following sections, you'll learn how to physically set up the equipment and then how to configure Windows for the setup.

TWO COMPUTERS AND A CROSSOVER CABLE

Let's first look at how to set up Figure 5-19a, where a single cable connects two computers. Looking at Figure 5-19a, you can see two cables coming from the host computer. The cable on the right connecting to the cable modem can be a network cable or a USB cable. It would be best if you use a USB cable for this connection so that your one

5

network port on your host computer is free to be used to connect to the other computer. However, if you really want to use a network cable between the host computer and the cable modem, you could install a second network card to provide this port. How to install a network card is covered in Chapter 8. Know you can also use a DSL modem or phone line for this setup.

Now let's turn our attention to connecting the two computers, assuming each has a network port available for the connection. There are two types of network cables: a patch cable and a crossover cable. A **patch cable** (also called a straight-through cable) is used to connect a computer to a hub or other device. A **crossover cable** is used to connect a computer to another computer or connect a hub to a hub. The difference in a patch cable and a crossover cable is the way the read and write lines are wired in the connectors at each end of the cables. A crossover cable has the read and write lines reversed so that one computer reads off the line that the other computer writes to.

A patch cable and a crossover cable look identical and have identical connectors. The best way you can tell them apart is to look for the label imprinted on the cable, as shown in Figure 5-20. Using a crossover cable, connect each end to the network ports on your two computers.

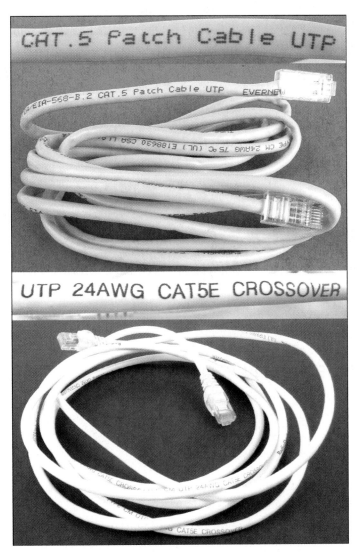

Figure 5-20 Patch cables and crossover cables look the same, but are labeled differently

THREE OR MORE COMPUTERS AND A HUB OR SWITCH

In Figure 5-19b, a hub or switch is used so you can network three or more computers. A switch costs more than a hub, but makes the network work faster because of the way it manages traffic. A switch sends incoming traffic out to only the one computer for which the data is intended, rather than to all computers it connects to. A hub, on the other hand, sends incoming traffic out to all ports. Figure 5-21 shows a hub and Figure 5-22 shows a switch. Choose, and then buy the device based on how many ports you want it to have. Most hubs or switches will also have an uplink port. An uplink port is used to connect the device directly to a router or another hub or switch for more complex networks. Connect the hub or switch to each computer in your network using patch cables.

Figure 5-21   A hub is a pass-through device to connect PCs on a network

Figure 5-22   An eight-port switch by Netgear

ASSIGN A UNIQUE NAME TO EACH COMPUTER

Each computer in your network needs to have a unique name. Also, because your computers will be sharing resources, they need to be assigned to the same workgroup. To change the computer name and workgroup name for each computer on your network, do the following:

1. Right-click **My Computer** and select **Properties**. The System Properties window opens. Click the **Computer Name** tab. See Figure 5-23.

2. Click **Change** and enter the computer name and workgroup name. Use the same workgroup name for all computers that you intend to share resources. If some computers in your network are using Windows 98/Me, make the computer name no more than 15 characters. Click **OK** in both windows to close them. Reboot your PC.

5

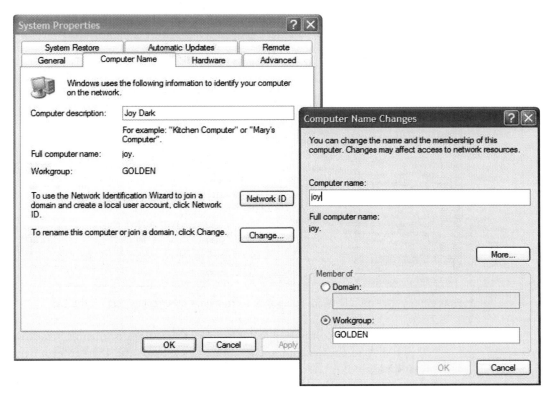

Figure 5-23   Give each computer in your workgroup a unique name

CONFIGURE WINDOWS TO SHARE AN INTERNET CONNECTION

You're now ready to configure Windows on all computers so they can share the Internet connection. Do the following:

1. On your host computer, open the Network Connections window and click the link to **Set up a home or small office network**. The Network Setup Wizard opens. Click **Next** in this window and the next.

2. Select the connection method for your host computer, which is **This computer connects directly to the Internet. The other computers on my network connect to the Internet through this computer.** Click **Next**.

3. The wizard looks at your hardware connections (USB, dial-up modem, or network port) and selects the one that it sees as a "live" connection to the Internet. Verify that the wizard selected correctly, and then follow the wizard to enter a description for your computer, your computer name, and your workgroup name.

4. The next screen of the wizard offers you the option of creating a Network Setup Disk that you can use to quickly configure every other computer on the network that is to use the Internet connection. See Figure 5-24. If the other computers in your network are not running Windows XP and they have floppy disk drives, select the option to **Create a Network Setup Disk**, insert a blank floppy disk in the drive, and click **Next**.

5. The next screen gives you the option to format the disk. If it needs formatting, click **Format Disk**. Otherwise, click **Next**.

6. The wizard tells you that to use the disk, you must insert it into the next computer on the network and run the program named Netsetup.exe from the disk. Click **Next** and then click **Finish**.

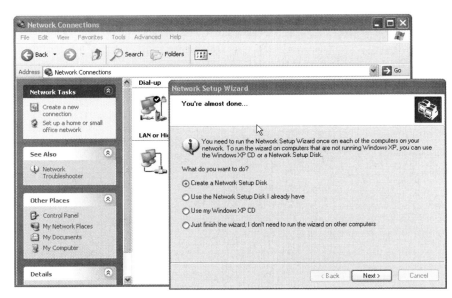

Figure 5-24   Create a Network Setup Disk to configure other computers on the LAN

7. On all the other computers in your network that are not using Windows XP, put the floppy disk in the computer, click **Start**, click **Run**, and then enter **a:netsetup.exe** in the Run dialog box. After the wizard is finished, test your connection. If a computer is not able to reach the Internet, check the TCP/IP configuration for the connection. Try rebooting the computer.

8. For the other computers in your network using Windows XP, open the Network Connections window and click the link to **Set up a home or small office network**. Follow the steps of the wizard to make the connection to the Internet. When given the opportunity, select **This computer connects to the Internet through a residential gateway or through another computer on my network**.

The disadvantage of this type of shared connection is that the host computer must always be running for another computer on the network to reach the Internet. Another disadvantage is this network is not as secure as it would be if we had a hardware firewall installed. Both these problems can be solved by using a router in our network. How to use a router in a network is covered later in the chapter.

However, before we turn our attention to routers, there's one more step we need to cover. When computers are networked together, it's nice to be able to share files, folders, printers, and other devices among all computers. So let's turn our attention to how to share resources on a network.

CONFIGURING COMPUTERS TO SHARE RESOURCES ON A NETWORK

In this section, you'll learn how to share folders, files, applications, printers, and even an entire hard drive. Remember that computers configured to share resources should each have a unique name on the network and all belong to the same workgroup.

Now let's get started with sharing resources with others in your workgroup.

SHARING FILES, FOLDERS, AND APPLICATIONS

When you open My Network Places (see Figure 5-25), you can drill down to see shared files, folders, and printers on your network. You can copy files from one computer to another, use shared applications installed on one computer from another computer, and share printers.

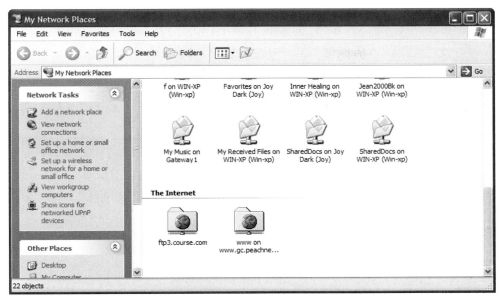

Figure 5-25 View and access shared resources on the network using My Network Places in Windows XP

Do the following to share files, folders, and applications with others on the network:

1. Two Windows components must be installed before you can share resources: Client for Microsoft Networks, and File and Printer Sharing. Client for Microsoft Networks is the Windows component that allows you to use resources on the network made available by other computers, and File and Printer Sharing allows you to share resources on your computer with others. To verify these components are installed, open the **Network Connections** window, right-click the **Local Area Connection** icon, and select **Properties** from the shortcut menu. The Local Area Connection Properties dialog box appears. See Figure 5-26.

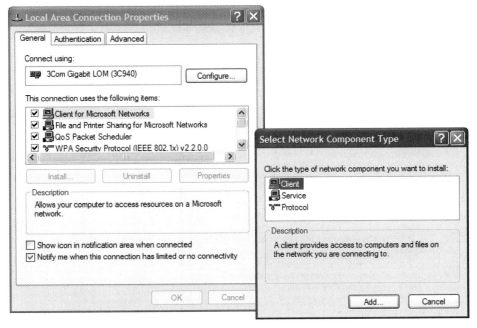

Figure 5-26 Use the Network Connections applet to install a network client, service, or protocol using Windows XP

2. Verify **Client for Microsoft Networks** and **File and Printer Sharing for Microsoft Networks** are both checked. If you don't see these items in the list, click **Install** to install them. When you're done, close all windows.

3. Using Windows Explorer, select the folder or file you want to share. In this example, we're using a folder named **C:\data**. Right-click the folder name. Select **Sharing and Security** (see Figure 5-27). The Data Properties dialog box opens, as shown in Figure 5-28.

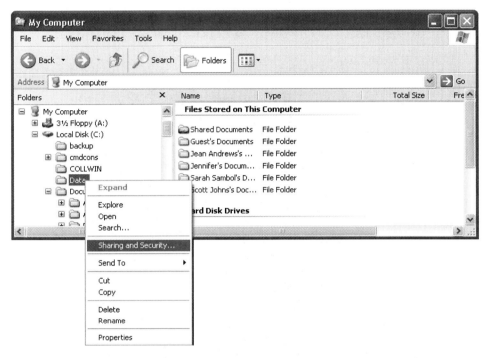

Figure 5-27 Use Windows Explorer to share a file or folder with others on a network

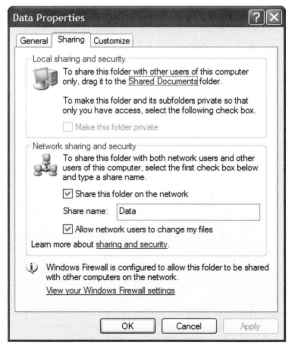

Figure 5-28 A user on a network can share a folder with others on the network

5

4. Check **Share this folder on the network**. If you want to allow others to change the contents of the folder, check **Allow network users to change my files**. Click **Apply**, and close the window. Other users on the network can now see the folder when they open My Network Places on their desktop.

> **Notes**
>
> When a window is open, you can press F5 to refresh the contents of that window. For example, press F5 to have Windows rebuild the contents of the My Network Places window.

SHARING A PRINTER

If you have a printer installed on your PC, you can share it with others on the network. Do the following:

1. Click **Start, Printers and Faxes**. Right-click the printer you want to share, and select **Sharing** from the shortcut menu. The printer's Properties dialog box opens, as shown in Figure 5-29. Select **Share this printer** and enter a name for the printer.

2. If you want to make drivers for the printer available to remote users who are using Windows 95/98/Me/NT/2000, then

> **Notes**
>
> Applications can also be shared with others in the workgroup. If you share a folder that has a program file in it, a user on another PC can double-click the program file in My Network Places and execute it remotely on his or her desktop. This is a handy way for several users to share an application that is installed on a single PC.

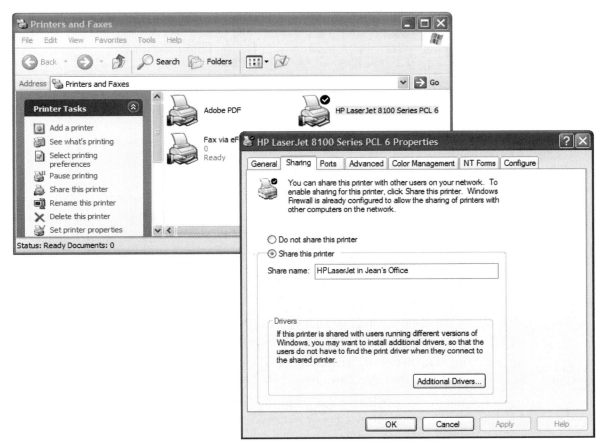

Figure 5-29 Sharing a printer on a Windows XP computer

click **Additional Drivers** and select the OS drivers you want to make available. Click **OK** twice to close both windows. You might be asked for the Windows XP setup CD or other access to the installation files. A shared printer shows a hand icon under it in the Printers window, and the printer is listed in My Network Places or Windows 9x/Me Network Neighborhood of other PCs on the network.

3. On a remote computer on the network, to use the shared printer, open **My Network Places**. Double-click the **computer** that has the shared printer. Right-click the **printer** and select **Connect**. Also, as shown in Figure 5-30, Windows Explorer can be used to locate the printer. Drill down to the printer by way of **My Network Places, Entire Network, Microsoft Windows Network**, the name of the workgroup the computer belongs in, and the name of the computer. You should then see the printer listed as a shared resource on that computer.

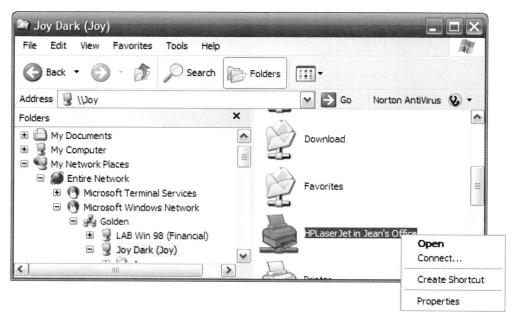

Figure 5-30   Connect to a printer shared on a remote computer on the network

MAPPING A NETWORK DRIVE

A network drive map is one of the most powerful and versatile methods of communicating over a network. By using Network File System (NFS) client/server software, the network drive map makes one PC (the client) appear to have a new hard drive, such as drive E, that is really hard drive space on another host computer (the server). To set up a network drive, follow these steps:

1. On the host computer, share the drive or folder on a drive to which you want others to have access.

2. On the remote computer that will use the network drive, open **Windows Explorer** and click the **Tools** menu. Select **Map Network Drive**.

3. The Map Network Drive dialog box appears, as shown in Figure 5-31. Select a drive letter from the drop-down list.

4. Click the **Browse** button and locate the shared folder or drive on the host computer. Click **OK** to close the Browse For Folder dialog box, and click **Finish** to map the drive. The folder on the host computer now appears as one more drive in Explorer on your computer.

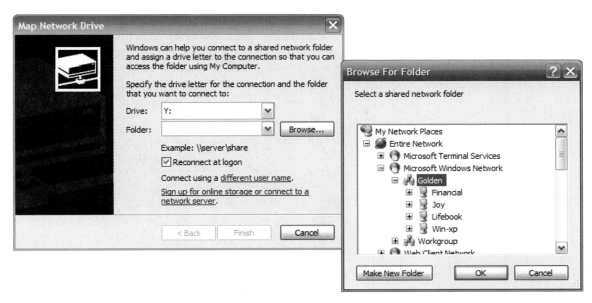

Figure 5-31 Mapping a network drive to a host computer

WHAT IF YOU DON'T WANT TO SHARE?

If you're concerned about others on your network getting to information on your computer, you can do some things to make sure your PC is secure:

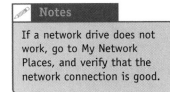

> **Notes**
>
> If a network drive does not work, go to My Network Places, and verify that the network connection is good.

- ◢ *Disable File and Printer Sharing*—In the Network Connections window, under the Local Area Connection Properties dialog box, uncheck **File and Printer Sharing for Microsoft Networks**.
- ◢ *Hide your computer from others looking at My Network Places*—In Control Panel, open the **Administrative Tools** applet and double-click **Services**. Right-click the **Computer Browser** service and select **Properties** from the shortcut menu. Under Startup type, select **Disabled** and click **Apply**. When you restart the PC, it will not be visible in My Network Places over the network.
- ◢ *Hide a shared folder*—If you want to share a folder, but don't want others to see the shared folder in their My Network Places window, add a $ to the end of the folder name. Others on the network can access the folder only when they know its name. For example, if you name a shared folder MyPrivateFolder$, in order to access the folder a user must enter \\Computername\MyPrivateFolder$ in the Run dialog box on the remote computer.

USING A ROUTER ON YOUR NETWORK

So far in the chapter, you've seen how one computer can connect to the Internet using a dial-up or broadband connection and also how this host computer can share that connection with others on a LAN. Two major disadvantages of this setup are that the host computer must always be turned on for others on the network to reach the Internet and the fact that security for your network is not as strong as it could be if you use a hardware firewall.

Also, access to the Internet for other computers might be slow because of the bottleneck caused by the host computer. Installing a router solves all these problems.

Recall from the last chapter that a router is a device that manages traffic between two networks. In Figure 5-32, you can see how a router stands between the ISP network and the local network, instead of the host computer that you learned about earlier in the chapter. The router takes the place of the host computer as the gateway to the Internet and also serves as a hardware firewall to protect your network.

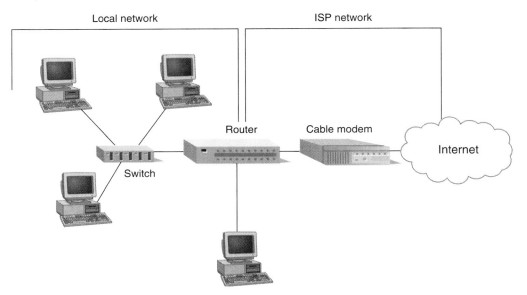

Figure 5-32 A router stands between the Internet and a local network

ADVANTAGES OF USING A ROUTER

The advantages of using a router rather than a host computer are:

◢ The host computer will not be a bottleneck to slow down performance for other computers using the Internet.
◢ Internet access is not dependent on the host computer being up and running.
◢ The router can also serve as a hardware firewall device, which provides better protection than a software firewall. In addition, a router can limit access to the Internet. This added security provided by a router is probably the most important reason to use a router for an Internet connection.
◢ The router can provide additional features—such as a DHCP server, switch, or wireless access point—not available on a host computer.

Three companies that make routers suitable for small networks are D-Link (*www.dlink.com*), Linksys (*www.linksys.com*), and NetGear (*www.netgear.com*). An example of a multifunction router is the Wireless-G Broadband Router by Linksys shown in Figure 5-33, which costs less than $60. It has one

> **Notes**
>
> A DHCP (Dynamic Host Configuration Protocol) server serves up IP addresses to computers on the network when they first connect to the network. With a DHCP server on the network, each computer can use dynamic IP addressing so you don't have to assign and keep up with unique IP addresses for each computer.

port for the broadband modem and four ports for computers on the network. The router is also an 802.11b/g wireless access point having two antennae to amplify the wireless signal and improve its range.

Figure 5-33 This Linksys router allows computers on a LAN to share a broadband Internet connection and is an access point for computers with wireless adapters

The router shown in Figure 5-33 is typical of many brands and models of routers useful in a small office or small home network to manage the Internet connection. This router is several devices in one:

- As a router, it stands between the ISP network and the local network, routing traffic between the two networks.
- As a switch, it manages four network ports that can be connected to four computers or to a hub or switch that connects to more than one computer. In the small office setting pictured in Figure 5-34, this router connects to four network jacks that are wired in the walls to four other jacks in the building. Two of these remote jacks have switches connected that accommodate two or more computers.

Figure 5-34 A router and cable modem are used to provide Internet access for a small network

> **Notes**
>
> A proxy server adds protection to a network because it stands in proxy for other computers on the network when they want to communicate with computers on the Internet. The proxy server presents its own IP address to the Internet and does not allow outside computers to know the IP addresses of computers inside the network. This substitution of IP addresses is done using the NAT (Network Address Translation) protocol.

▲ As a proxy server, all computers on the network route their Internet requests through this proxy server, which stands between the network and the Internet using NAT.

▲ As a DHCP server, all computers can receive their IP address from this server.

▲ As a wireless access point, a computer can connect to the network using a wireless device. This wireless connection can be secured using four different wireless security features.

▲ As a firewall, unwanted traffic initiated from the Internet can be blocked.

▲ As an Internet access restrictive device, the router can be set so that Internet access is limited.

INSTALLING AND CONFIGURING A ROUTER

To install the router, if your router comes with a setup CD, run the setup program on one of your computers on the network (doesn't matter which one). Follow the instructions on the setup screen to disconnect the cable modem or DSL modem from your host computer and connect it to the router. Next, connect the computers on your network to your router. A computer can connect directly to a network port on the router, or you can connect a switch or hub to the router. Plug in the router and turn it on.

You'll be required to sign in to the utility using a default password. The first thing you want to do is reset this password so others cannot change your router setup.

The setup program will step you through the process of configuring the router. After you've configured the router, you might have to turn the cable modem or DSL modem off

5

and back on so that it correctly syncs up with the router. If you don't get immediate connectivity to the Internet on all PCs, try rebooting each PC. More about how to fix networking problems is covered at the end of this chapter.

Now let's look at how this Linksys router is configured, which is typical of what you might see for several brands and models of small office

Caution

Changing the router password is especially important if the router is a wireless router. Unless you have disabled or secured the wireless access point, anyone outside your building can use your wireless network. If they guess the default password to the router, they can change the password to hijack your router. Also, your wireless network can be used for criminal activity. When you first install a router, before you do anything else, change your router password and disable the wireless network until you have time to setup and test the wireless security.

routers. Firmware on the router (which can be flashed for updates) contains a configuration program that you access using a Web browser from anywhere on the network. In your browser address box, enter the IP address of the router (for our router, it's 192.168.1.1) and press Enter. The main Setup window appears, as shown in Figure 5-35. For most situations, the default settings on this and other screens should work without any changes.

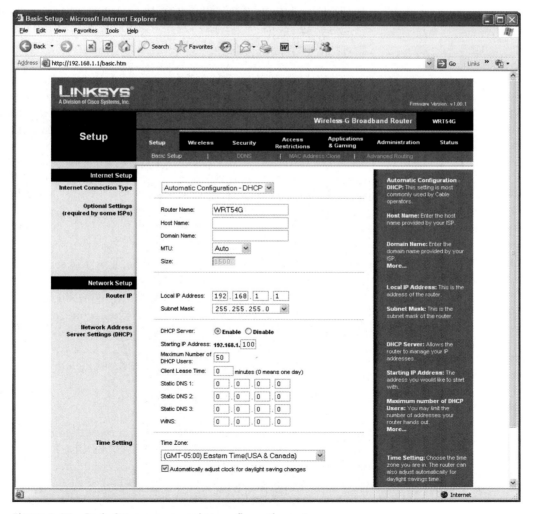

Figure 5-35 Basic Setup screen used to configure the router

Using this setup screen, under Internet Setup, you can change the host name and domain name if they are given to you by your ISP or leave them blank, which most often is the case. Under Network Setup, you can configure the DHCP server. Notice in the figure, the router can serve up to 50 leased IP addresses beginning with IP address 192.168.1.100. You can also disable the DHCP server if you want to use static IP addressing on your network or you already have another DHCP server on the network.

CONFIGURE EACH PC FOR DYNAMIC IP ADDRESSING

Configure each PC on your network to use dynamic IP addressing. At each computer, do the following:

1. In the Network Connections window, right-click the **Local Area Connection** icon and select **Properties**. The properties window opens. Select **Internet Protocol (TCP/IP)** and click **Properties**.

2. Select **Obtain an IP address automatically** and **Obtain DNS server address automatically**. Click **OK** to close each window.

3. When the windows close, Windows XP will attempt to renew its IP address. You should be able to see the new address in the lower-left corner of the Network Connections window. Also, to tell Windows to release and renew the IP address, right-click the connection and select **Repair** from the shortcut menu.

HOW TO SECURE A SMALL NETWORK

The Internet is a nasty and dangerous place infested with hackers, viruses, worms, and thieves. Knowing how to protect a single PC or a LAN is an essential skill of a PC support technician. Recall that the three most important things you can do to protect a single computer or network are to:

- ◢ Use a software or hardware firewall.
- ◢ Run antivirus software and keep it current.
- ◢ Keep Windows updates current so that security patches are installed as soon as they are available.

In earlier chapters, you learned how to use AV software, how to keep Windows updated, and how to use Windows Firewall. In this section, you will learn about hardware firewalls, how to set them for maximum security, and how to let down your shields so that if you want to allow someone on the Internet to get to your network, you can.

The best firewall solution is a hardware firewall that stands between a LAN and the Internet (see Figure 5-36). For most home and small-office LANs, a router is used as a hardware firewall. Note that some DSL devices are also routers and include embedded firewall firmware.

A hardware or software firewall can function in several ways:

- ◢ Firewalls can filter data packets, examining the destination IP address or source IP address or the type of protocol used (for example, TCP or UDP).
- ◢ Firewalls can filter ports so that outside clients cannot communicate with inside services listening at these ports. Certain ports can be opened, for example, when your network has a Web server and you want Internet users to be able to access it.

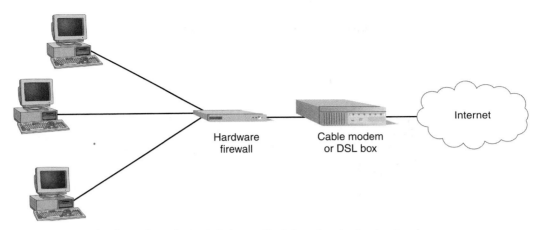

Figure 5-36 A hardware firewall stands between the Internet and a local network

◢ Firewalls can block certain activity that is initiated from inside the network—such as preventing users inside the firewall from using applications like FTP over the Internet.

◢ Some firewalls can filter information such as inappropriate Web content for children or employees, and can limit the use of the Internet to certain days or time of day.

CONFIGURING A HARDWARE FIREWALL

In this section, you'll learn how to configure the Linksys router's firewall abilities to protect the network. You can use this information as a guide to configuring another router because, although the exact steps might vary, the basic principles will be the same.

To configure security on the firewall, click the **Security** link (shown in Figure 5-35). The window shown in Figure 5-37 appears. The most important item on this window is Block Anonymous Internet Requests. Enabling this feature prevents your network from being detected or accessed from others on the Internet without an invitation.

You can set policies to determine how and when users on your network can access the Internet. To do that, click **Access Restrictions**. The window shown in Figure 5-38 appears, allowing you to set policies about the day and time of Internet access, the services on the Internet that can be used, and the URLs and keywords that are not allowed.

> **Notes**
>
> TCP is the primary TCP/IP protocol used by Internet applications such as Web servers, browsers, and e-mail servers and clients for communication. UDP is a utility protocol used to manage network traffic. TCP is like a delivery service and UDP is more like a traffic cop.

> **Caution**
>
> Remember that you should always change the password to your router's setup utility. Default passwords for routers are easily obtained on the Web or in the product documentation. This is especially important for wireless routers.

PORT FILTERING AND PORT FORWARDING

Too much security is not always a good thing. There are legitimate times you want to be able to access computers on your network from somewhere on the Internet, such as when you're hosting an Internet game or when you're traveling and want to use Remote Desktop to access your home computer. In this section, we'll look at how to drop your shields low enough so that the good guys can get in but the bad guys can't.

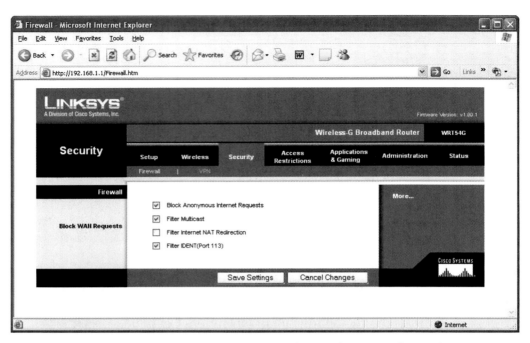

Figure 5-37   Configure the router's firewall to prevent others on the Internet from seeing or accessing your network

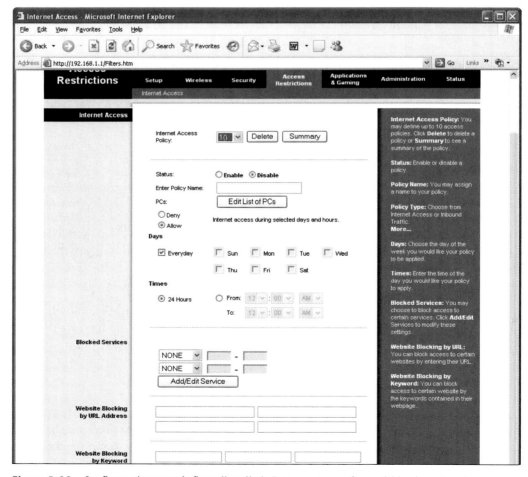

Figure 5-38   Configure the router's firewall to limit Internet access from within the network

However, know that when you drop your shields the least bit, you're compromising the security of your network, so be sure to use these methods sparingly. Here are the concepts we'll use, which are illustrated in Figure 5-39:

- Port filtering is used to open or close certain ports so they can or cannot be used. Remember that applications are assigned these ports. Therefore, in effect, you are filtering or controlling what applications can or cannot be used across the firewall.
- Port forwarding means that when the firewall receives a request for communication from the Internet, if the request is for a certain port, that request will be allowed and forwarded to a certain computer on the network. That computer is defined to the router by its IP address.
- For port forwarding to work, the local computer that is to receive this communication must have a static IP address.

Figure 5-39 With port forwarding, a router allows requests initiated outside the network

To demonstrate how to use port filtering to allow limited access to your network from the outside world, we'll use Remote Desktop as our demo application. Windows XP Professional Remote Desktop gives a user access to his or her Windows XP desktop from anywhere on the Internet. I find Remote Desktop extremely useful when I work from a remote location (my home office) and need to access a corporate network to support software on that network. Using the Internet, I can access a file server on these secured networks to make my software changes. It's easy to use and relatively safe for the corporate network. To use Remote Desktop, the computer you want to remotely access (the server) must be running Windows XP Professional, but the computer you're using to access it (the client) can be running Windows XP Home Edition or Windows XP Professional.

In this section, you'll first see how Remote Desktop can be used, and then you'll see how to set it up for first use. Then you'll learn how to configure your router (hardware firewall) to allow communication for a certain application such as Remote Desktop.

> **Notes**
>
> Many third-party applications besides Windows XP Remote Desktop exist that also allow you to remotely connect to another computer so that you can see and use the remote computer's desktop. One excellent product I've used for years is PC Anywhere by Symantec (*www.symantec.com*).

HOW TO USE REMOTE DESKTOP

To use Remote Desktop to connect to and use the desktop of your home or office computer, do the following from any Windows XP computer connected to the Internet:

1. Click **Start**, point to **All Programs**, point to **Accessories**, point to **Communications**, and then click **Remote Desktop Connection**. The Remote Desktop Connection window opens. Click **Options** and the window expands to full view, as shown in Figure 5-40.

Figure 5-40   Enter the IP address of the remote computer to which you want to connect

2. Enter the IP address of the Windows XP computer to which you want to connect and enter your user account name and password on the remote computer.

3. If you plan to transfer files from one computer to the other, click the **Local Resources** tab shown in Figure 5-41 and check **Disk drives**. If you want to print from the remote computer, also check **Printers**. Click **Connect** to make the connection.

The desktop of the remote computer appears, as shown in Figure 5-42. When you click the desktop, you can work with the remote computer just as if you were sitting in front of it, except response time is slower. To move files back and forth between computers, open Windows Explorer on your local and remote computers and drag and drop files between the two. To close the connection to the remote computer, simply close the desktop window.

HOW TO PREPARE REMOTE DESKTOP FOR FIRST USE

The first step to setting up your home or office computer for Remote Desktop or, for that matter, any server application on your computer, is to assign your computer a

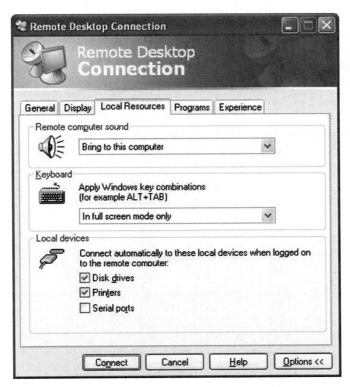

Figure 5-41 Allow files and printers to be shared using the Remote Desktop connection

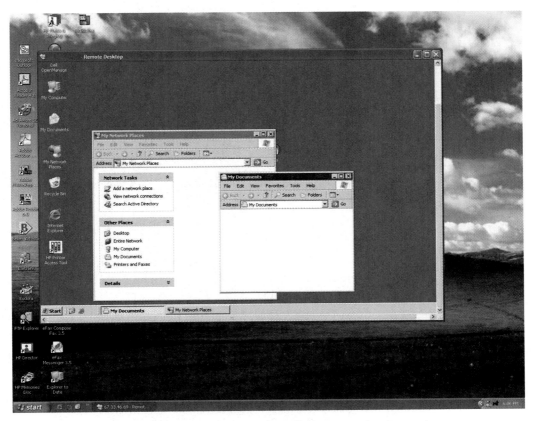

Figure 5-42 The desktop of the remote computer is available on your local computer

static IP address so that other computers can know how to address your computer. Do the following:

1. In the Network Connections window, right-click the **Local Area Connection** icon and select **Properties**. Select **Internet Protocol (TCP/IP)** and click **Properties**. The properties window opens (see Figure 5-43).

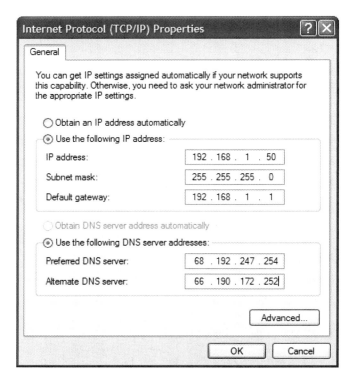

Figure 5-43   Configure your computer for static IP addressing

2. Enter the IP address you have decided to use for your computer. If the computer is connected directly to your ISP without a router, the IP address is that assigned by the ISP. If your computer is sitting behind a router, assign it a private IP address such as those that begin with 192.168. The IP address in Figure 5-43 is 192.168.1.90.

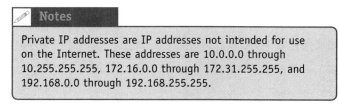

Private IP addresses are IP addresses not intended for use on the Internet. These addresses are 10.0.0.0 through 10.255.255.255, 172.16.0.0 through 172.31.255.255, and 192.168.0.0 through 192.168.255.255.

3. Enter the subnet mask. If the computer is connected directly to your ISP, the ISP will tell you the subnet mask, which will most likely be 255.255.255.0. If your computer is behind a router, use 255.255.255.0.

4. Enter the default gateway, which is the IP address of the computer or device that gives access to the Internet. For a computer connected directly to the ISP, the ISP will tell you this IP address. If you're using a router, this is the IP address of the router. In Figure 5-43, the router's IP address is 192.168.1.1.

5. Enter the IP addresses of two DNS servers, given you by your ISP. If you have more than two DNS servers, click **Advanced** and enter the other IP addresses. Click **OK** to close the window.

6. Use your browser to verify you have Internet access before you continue to the next steps. If you have a problem, first try repairing your connection and then try rebooting your PC.

You are now ready to configure Remote Desktop on your Windows XP Professional home or office computer. Do the following:

1. Right-click **My Computer** and click **Properties** to open the **System Properties** window, as shown in Figure 5-44. Click the **Remote** tab and check **Allow users to connect remotely to this computer**. Click **Select Remote Users**. In the dialog box that opens, also shown in Figure 5-44, add the users of this computer that will be using Remote Desktop. Users that have administrative privileges will be allowed to use Remote Desktop by default, but other users need to be added. Click **OK** twice to exit both windows.

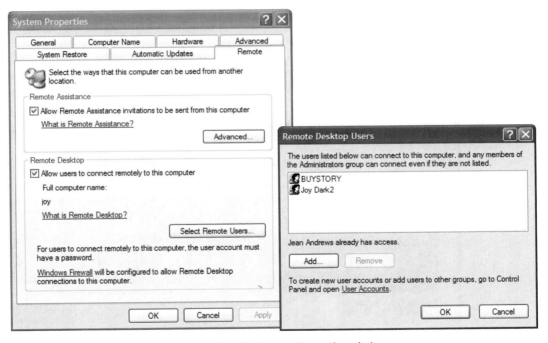

Figure 5-44 Configure Remote Desktop from the System Properties window

2. Verify that Windows Firewall is set to allow Remote Desktop activity to this computer. To do that, open the **Network Connections** window and click **Change Windows Firewall settings**. The Windows Firewall window opens. On the **General** tab, verify that Windows Firewall is turned on and that **Don't allow exceptions** is *not* selected. Then click the **Exceptions** tab and verify that **Remote Desktop** is checked so that Remote Desktop incoming activity is allowed.

3. You are now ready to test Remote Desktop using your local network. Try to use Remote Desktop from another computer somewhere on your local network. Verify you have Remote Desktop working on your local network before you move on to the next step of getting it to work from the Internet.

> **Notes**
>
> Even though Windows XP normally allows more than one user to be logged on at the same time, this is not the case with Remote Desktop. When a Remote Desktop session is opened, all local users are logged off.

HOW TO USE PORT FORWARDING TO ALLOW REMOTE DESKTOP COMMUNICATION FROM THE INTERNET

To use Remote Desktop from the Internet, you must know the IP address of the host computer at your home or office. This fact is the greatest hurdle to overcome in setting up Remote Desktop for two reasons: (a) For a home computer, most likely your ISP is using dynamic IP addressing, and (b) for a corporate computer on a LAN, most likely your office computer is using a firewall or proxy server to interface with the Internet. Either way, you won't have a public IP address on your desktop that never changes.

To overcome these obstacles, do the following:

1. If your ISP is using dynamic IP addressing, contact the ISP and request a static IP address. Most likely, the ISP will charge extra for this service. Find out the static IP address assigned to your home or business. Later, you will use this IP address to address your home or office network or computer when you want to use Remote Desktop while traveling.

2. If your office computer is sitting behind a router that is also functioning as a proxy server and firewall, first configure your router to use static IP addressing using the IP addresses provided by your ISP. For the Linksys router we're using as our example, the basic setup screen in Figure 5-45 shows how to configure the router for static IP addressing, using the subnet mask and the gateway and DNS server IP addresses provided by the ISP.

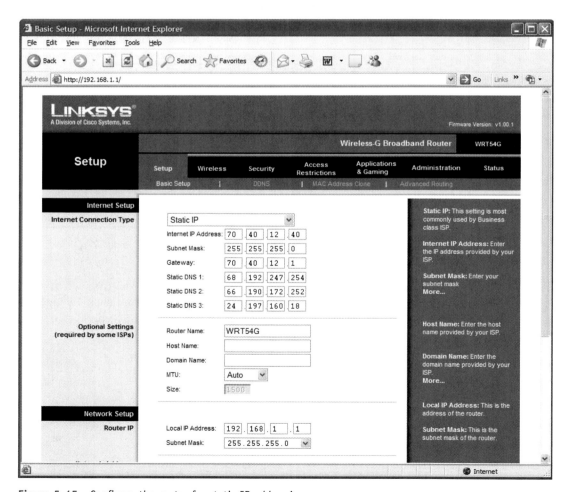

Figure 5-45 Configure the router for static IP addressing

3. Next, configure your router to use port forwarding so that it will allow Remote Desktop connections initiated from the Internet to pass through to your computer. Using your router's configuration utility, find the window that allows port forwarding, such as the one shown in Figure 5-46.

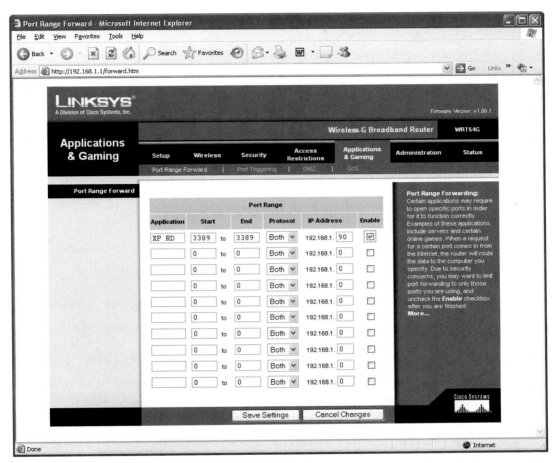

Figure 5-46 Using port forwarding, you can program your router to allow activity from the Internet to initiate a session with a computer inside the network on a certain port

4. Enter the port that Remote Desktop uses, which, by default, is port 3389, and the IP address of your desktop computer. In this example, the IP address chosen is 192.168.1.90. Check **Enable** to allow activity on this port to this computer. Save your changes.

5. On your desktop computer, verify the TCP/IP configuration is set for static IP addressing and assign the IP address 192.168.1.90 to your computer.

6. Test Remote Desktop by accessing your desktop computer from somewhere on the Internet.

Is your desktop computer now as safe as it was before you programmed the router? Actually, no, so take this into account when you decide to use Remote Desktop. In a project at the end of this chapter, you'll learn how you can take further steps to protect the security of your computer when using Remote Desktop.

HOW TO CONNECT A NOTEBOOK COMPUTER TO A WIRELESS PUBLIC HOTSPOT

Wireless LANs are becoming more and more popular and if a notebook doesn't come equipped with a wireless adapter, many people want to install and use wireless so they can surf the Net from public hotspots. This section is all about how to use a public wireless network. Wireless LANs tend to be slower than wired networks, especially when they are busy. Another problem with wireless LANs is security.

The most popular wireless technology is called WiFi, although it's official name is 802.11. Three grades of WiFi are 802.11a, 802.11b, and 802.11g. The latest, 802.11g, is the fastest and is backward compatible with 802.11b. 802.11g and 802.11b use a frequency range of 2.4 GHz in the radio band and have a distance range of about 100 meters. 802.11b/g has the disadvantage that many cordless phones use the 2.4-GHz frequency range and cause network interference. 802.11g runs at 54 Mbps and 802.11b runs at 11Mbps. To know that a wireless device supports both standards, look for 802.11b/g on the package.

Wireless connections using 802.11b/g can be made with a variety of devices, four of them shown in Figure 5-47. Notice in the figure the different types of antennae.

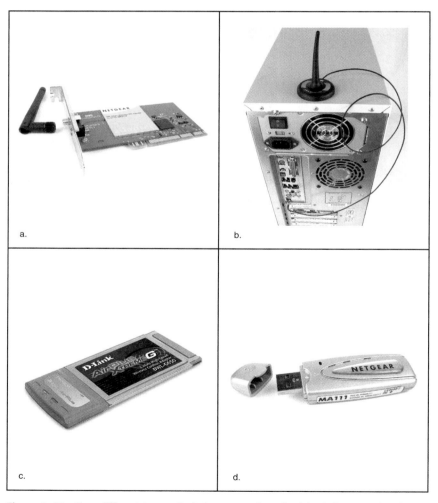

Figure 5-47   Four different types of wireless network cards: (a) wireless NIC that fits in a PCI slot; (b) onboard wireless NIC with an antenna that can be moved about; (c) PC Card wireless NIC with embedded antenna; and (d) wireless NIC that uses a USB port on a desktop or notebook computer

Wireless devices can communicate directly (such as from one PC to another, which is called Ad Hoc mode), or they can connect to a LAN by way of a wireless access point (AP), such as the one provided by the Linksys router shown earlier in the chapter in Figure 5-33. Access points are placed so that client computers can access at least one access point from anywhere in the covered area. When computers use an access point, they communicate through the access point instead of communicating directly.

Later in this section, you'll learn how to set up a wireless access point. But first, let's see how to install a wireless adapter and connect to a public hotspot.

INSTALLING A WIRELESS ADAPTER IN A NOTEBOOK

For a notebook computer, a wireless adapter will use a USB port or a PC Card slot. Most new adapters use the USB port, such as the wireless adapter shown in Figure 5-48. The adapter will come with a setup CD and some documentation and maybe an accessory or two. This adapter comes with a cradle and extender so you can move the adapter around for better reception.

Cradle and extender

Figure 5-48 This 802.11g wireless adapter by Linksys uses a USB port to connect to a notebook or desktop computer

Do the following to install the adapter:

1. Read the installation directions that come with the wireless adapter to find out if you install the software first or the adapter first. For the Linksys wireless adapter used in this example, the instructions clearly say to first install the software (see Figure 5-49).

Figure 5-49   This label makes it clear you need to install the software before installing the wireless adapter

2. Insert the CD in the CD drive. The opening screen for this adapter is shown in Figure 5-50. Click **Click Here to Start** and follow the directions onscreen to install the device drivers and the utility to configure the wireless connection.

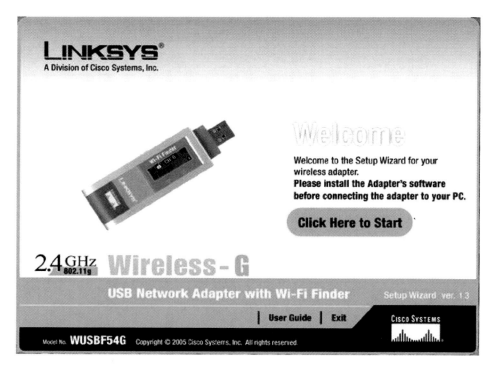

Figure 5-50   Install the wireless adapter software

3. Next, plug the wireless adapter into a USB port. See Figure 5-51. The Found New Hardware bubble appears. See Figure 5-52. Click the bubble to launch the Found New Hardware wizard. Follow the wizard to install the device.

Figure 5-51 Plug the wireless USB adapter into the USB port

Figure 5-52 Windows XP recognizes the presence of a new USB device

After the wireless adapter is installed, the next step is to configure it. Read the adapter's documentation to find out how to use the software. Most likely during installation an icon was added to your system tray. Double-click the icon to open the configuration window.

> **Notes**
>
> When a new device is being installed, if Windows recognizes the drivers were not digitally signed by Microsoft, it displays a dialog box similar to that in Figure 5-53, for a Netgear wireless adapter. Now you have a decision to make. You can stop the installation and go to the manufacturer's Web site to try to find approved drivers, or you can continue with the installations. For most devices, it is safe to continue the installation using unsigned drivers. To do that, click **Continue Anyway**.

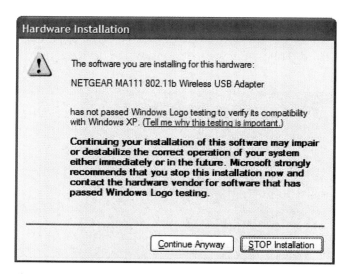

Figure 5-53 Windows asks you for a decision about using unsigned drivers

Notes

At another point in the installation, the wizard might ask if you want to disable the Windows XP Configuration Manager, which means you are choosing to use the manufacturer's utility to configure the wireless adapter (see Figure 5-54). Unless you have a good reason to do otherwise, click **Yes** to choose to use the manufacturer's utility. This utility will most likely be easier to use and allow you to better manage the wireless NIC than would the Windows XP Network Connections window. (Later, if you change your mind about which utility to use, you might need to uninstall and reinstall the device.)

Figure 5-55 shows the configuration window for the Linksys wireless adapter. Click **Manual Setup** to configure the adapter. Figure 5-56 shows the configuration window for a Netgear wireless adapter, and Figure 5-57 shows another example of the configuration window for a wireless NIC installed on another computer.

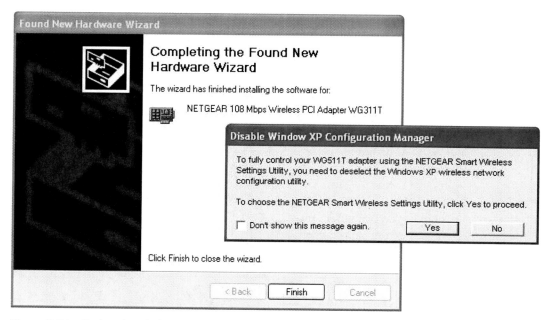

Figure 5-54 During the wireless NIC installation, you are asked which utility you want to use to configure the NIC

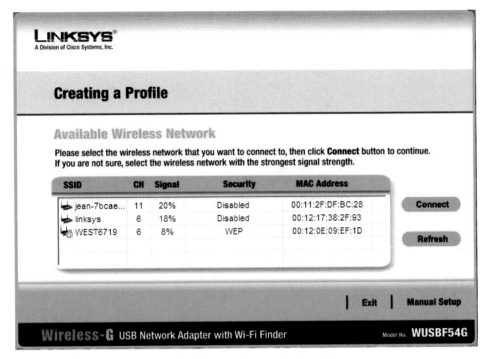

Figure 5-55 Opening screen to configure a Linksys wireless adapter

Figure 5-56 Wireless NIC configuration window allows you to view information about the wireless connection and configure the NIC

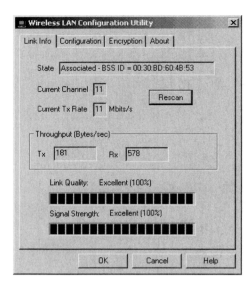

Figure 5-57 Wireless NIC configuration software reports the status of the current connection

Each manufacturer has a different configuration utility, but all utilities should allow you to view information and manage the wireless device using these parameters. Information displayed about the current connection should include:

- ◢ *The MAC address of the access point device that the adapter is currently using.*
- ◢ *The current channel the connection is using*—802.11b/g uses 14 different channels. The United States can use channels 1 through 11. The access point device is configured to use one of these 11 channels.
- ◢ *Current Tx Rate*—Current transmission rate, which is 11 Mbps in Figure 5-57.
- ◢ *Throughput, Link Quality*, and *Signal Strength*—These values indicate throughput rate and how strong the signal is. For the Netgear configuration window in Figure 5-56, this information is available in graphic form by clicking the Statistics tab. For most wireless devices, there is nothing for you to configure to get a connection. If the signal strength is poor, look for a way to scan for a new access point. For the utility shown in Figure 5-57, click the **Rescan** button, and for the utility in Figure 5-55, click the **Connect** button.

Configuration changes you can make for a wireless device include:

- ◢ *Mode or network type*—The mode indicates whether the computer is to communicate through an access point (Infrastructure mode) or directly with another wireless device (Ad Hoc mode).
- ◢ *SSID*—The SSID (service set identifier) is set to ANY by default, which means the NIC is free to connect to any access point it finds. You can enter the name of an access point to specify that this NIC should connect only to a specific access point. If you don't know the name assigned to a particular access point, ask the network administrator responsible for managing the wireless network. For public hotspots, if you don't know the SSID, try "hotspot". For some public hotspots, the access point is hidden so you must pay to know its name. Figure 5-58 shows the configuration screen for the Linksys adapter where you can choose the mode and enter an SSID.

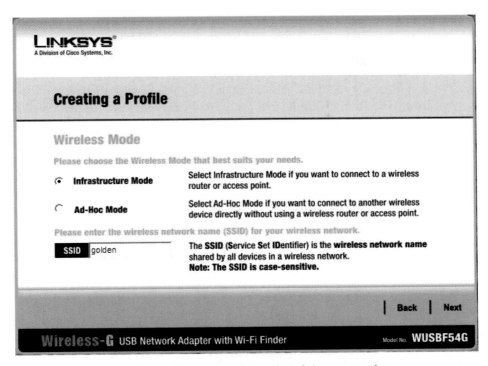

Figure 5-58   Configure the wireless mode and the SSID of the access point

▲ *WEP Encryption settings*—Most wireless devices today support encrypted wireless transmission. To enable encryption, for the utility in Figure 5-59, click the **Encryption** tab (see Figure 5-59) and select **64-bit** or **128-bit** encryption. For any wireless device, when you enable encryption, you must enter a secret passphrase or key to be used for the encryption. This passphrase is a word, such as "ourpassphrase," which generates a digital key used for encryption. (Or you can manually enter the digital key.) Every computer user on the same wireless network must enter the same passphrase or key, which can be changed at any time. For public, unsecured wireless networks, you need to disable encryption. Click **OK** to close the configuration software.

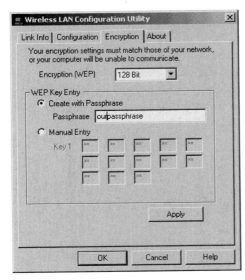

Figure 5-59   Enter a passphrase that generates a key to be used
for 128-bit encryption to secure a wireless LAN

◢ *Tx Rate*—For some adapters, you can specify the transmission rate or leave it at fully automatic so that the adapter is free to use the best transmission rate possible.

◢ *TCP/IP configuration*—Some wireless configuration utilities provide a screen to configure the TCP/IP settings to static or dynamic IP addressing. If your utility does not do that, after you configure the adapter, you'll need to use the Network Connections window to verify the TCP/IP settings. Initially, they'll be set for dynamic IP configuration.

After you have made all configuration changes, you should immediately be able to use your browser. If you can't, then try rebooting the computer. Also, try moving the computer to a better hotspot and click the button to reconnect.

Here are the steps to connect to a public hotspot for a notebook computer that has embedded wireless ability and uses Windows XP network configuration:

1. Turn on your wireless device. For some notebooks, that's done by a switch on the keyboard (see Figure 5-60).

Figure 5-60   Turn on the wireless switch on your notebook

2. Right-click **My Network Places** and select **Properties**. The Network Connections window opens. Right-click the **Wireless Network Connection** icon and select **View Available Wireless Networks** from the shortcut menu. The Wireless Network Connection window opens (see Figure 5-61).

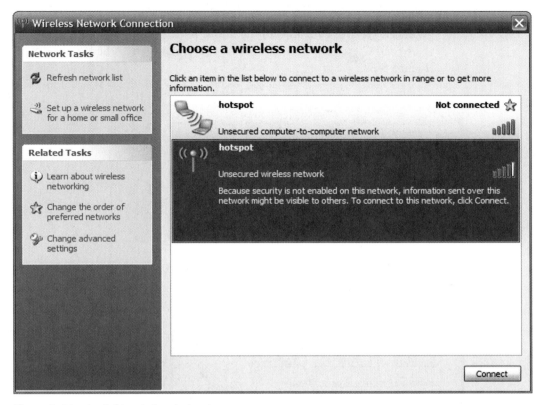

Figure 5-61 Available wireless hotspots

3. Select an unsecured network from those listed and click **Connect**. (Incidentally, if you select a secured network that is protected with an encryption key, to continue, you must enter the key, as shown in Figure 5-62)

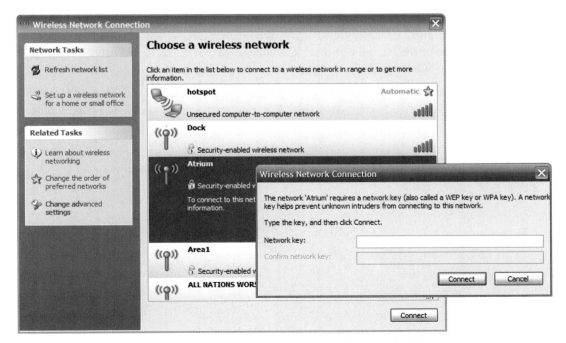

Figure 5-62 To use a secured wireless network, you must know the encryption key

4. If you have problems connecting and you know the SSID of the hotspot, on the Wireless Network Connection window, click **Change advanced settings**. The Wireless Network Connection Properties window opens. Click the **Wireless Networks** tab (see Figure 5-63).

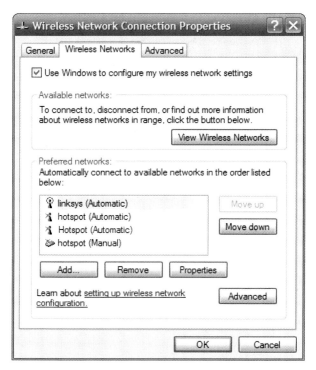

Figure 5-63 Manage wireless hotspots using the Wireless Network Connection Properties window

5. Click **Add**. The Wireless network properties window opens (see Figure 5-64). Enter the SSID of the network and make sure that Network Authentication is set to **Open** and Data encryption is disabled. Click **OK**. When a dialog box appears to warn you of the dangers of disabling encryption, click **Continue Anyway**. Click **OK** to close the Wireless Network Connection Properties window.

In the Network Connections window, right click on the **Wireless Network Connection** icon and select **View Available Wireless Networks**. You should now be able to connect to the hotspot.

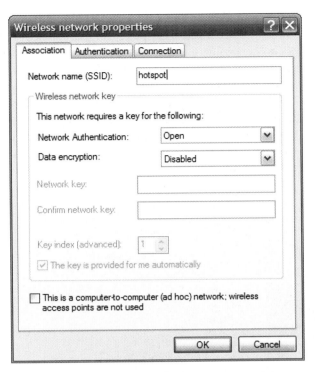

Figure 5-64   Enter the SSID of a hotspot you want to connect to

6. Open your browser to test the connection. For some hotspots, a homepage appears and you must enter a code to proceed (see Figure 5-65).

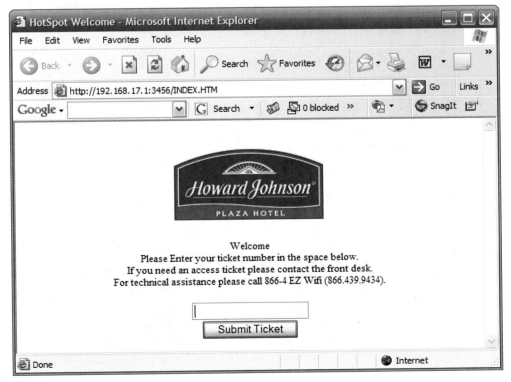

Figure 5-65   This hotspot requires a code to use the wireless network

It is possible that a private and secured wireless access point has been configured for MAC address filtering in order to control which wireless adapters can use the access point. Check with the network administrator to determine if this is the case; if necessary, give the administrator the adapter's MAC address to be entered into a table of acceptable MAC addresses.

To know the MAC address of your wireless adapter, you can look on the back of the adapter itself (see Figure 5-66) or in the adapter documentation. Also, if the adapter is installed on your computer, you can open a command prompt window and enter the command **ipconfig /all**, which displays your TCP/IP configuration for all network connections. The MAC address is called the Physical Address in the display (see Figure 5-67). By the way, if you're running Windows XP Professional, you can also display your MAC address using the Getmac command.

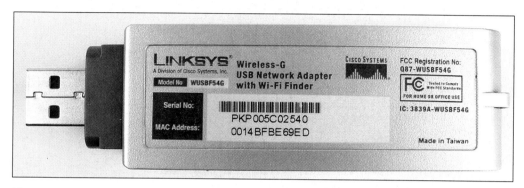

Figure 5-66 The MAC address is printed on the back of this USB wireless adapter

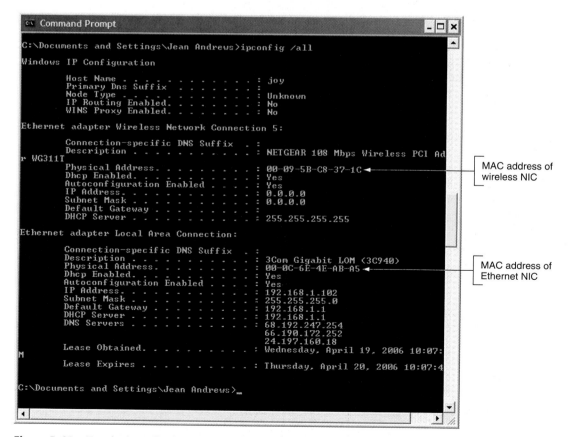

Figure 5-67 Use the ipconfig /all command to display TCP/IP configuration data

HOW TO SET UP YOUR OWN WIRELESS NETWORK

Setting up your own wireless network involves buying a wireless access point and configuring it and your wireless computers for communication. The key to successful wireless networking is good security. This section first looks at what you need to know about securing a wireless network, then shows how to choose the equipment you'll need and how to set up a wireless network.

SECURITY ON A WIRELESS LAN

Wireless LANs are so convenient for us at work and at home, but the downside of having a wireless network is that if we don't have the proper security in place, anyone with a wireless computer within range of your access point can use the network—and, if they know how, can intercept and read all the data sent across the network. They might even be able to hack into our computers by using our own wireless network against us. For all these reasons, it's terribly important to secure your wireless network.

Securing a wireless network is generally done in four ways:

▲ *Disable SSID broadcasting*—Normally, the name of the access point (called the SSID) is broadcast so that anyone with a wireless computer can see the name and use the network. If you hide the SSID, a computer can see the wireless network, but can't use it unless the SSID is entered in the wireless adapter configuration.

▲ *Filter MAC addresses*—A wireless access point can filter the MAC addresses of wireless NICs that are allowed to use the access point. This type of security prevents uninvited guests from using the wireless LAN, but does not prevent others from receiving data in the air.

▲ *Data encryption*—Data sent over a wireless connection can be encrypted. The three main methods of encryption for 802.11 wireless networks are WEP (Wired Equivalent Privacy), WPA (WiFi Protected Access), and WPA2. With either method, data is encrypted using a firmware program on the wireless device and is only encrypted while the data is wireless; the data is decrypted before placing it on the wired network. With WEP encryption, data is encrypted using either 64-bit or 128-bit encryption keys. (Because the user can configure only 40 bits of the 64 bits, 64-bit WEP encryption is sometimes called 40-bit WEP encryption.) Because the key used for encryption is static (doesn't change), a hacker who spends enough time examining data packets can eventually find enough patterns in the coding to decrypt the code and read WEP-encrypted data. WPA encryption, also called TKIP (Temporal Key Integrity Protocol) encryption, is stronger than WEP and was designed to replace it. With WPA encryption, encryption keys are changed at set intervals. The latest and best wireless encryption standard is WPA2, also called the 802.11i standard or the AES (Advanced Encryption Standard) standard. As of March, 2006, for a wireless device to be WiFi certified, it must support the WPA2 standard, which is included in Windows XP Service Pack 2. When buying wireless devices, be sure the encryption methods used are compatible!

▲ *Virtual private network (VPN)*—A VPN requires a password for entrance and encrypts data over both wired and wireless networks. The basic difference between WEP or WPA encryption and VPN encryption is that VPN encryption applies from the user's PC all the way to the host computer regardless of the type of network used. A VPN uses a technique called tunneling, in which a packet of data is encrypted as shown in Figure 5-68. The encryption methods used by VPN are stronger than WEP or WPA and are the preferred method when transmitting sensitive data over a wireless connection. How to set up a VPN is beyond the scope of this chapter.

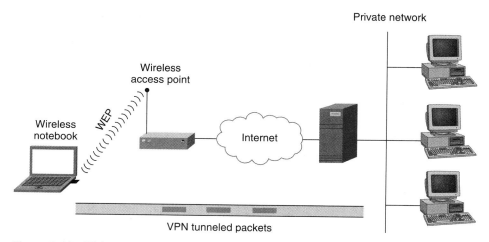

Figure 5-68 With tunneling, packets can travel over a wireless LAN and the Internet in a virtual private network (VPN), but WEP or WPA applies only to the wireless connection

CHOOSING A WIRELESS ACCESS POINT

When selecting a wireless access point, look for the ability to use all the security measures listed in the previous section. Also, be sure the access point supports 802.11 b/g. And, as always, before you buy, search the Internet to read hardware reviews about the device. Only buy a device that consistently gets good reviews. If you're also in need of a wireless adapter to use for the computers that will use your wireless networks, for best results, try to find adapters and an access point made by the same manufacturer.

Some desktop computers come equipped with a wireless adapter, such as the one in Figure 5-47b, that can be configured as a client on a wireless network or as the access point of a wireless network. A wireless access point can also be a stand-alone device such as the one in Figure 5-69 by D-Link, which supports 802.11b/g. This particular access point advertises that it can support transfer rates up to 108 Mbps, but be aware that to get this high rate, you must use a compatible D-Link wireless adapter on your notebook or desktop computer. An access point can also serve more than one purpose, such as the Linksys router shown earlier in Figure 5-33.

Figure 5-69 This wireless access point by D-Link supports 802.11b/g

CONFIGURE AND TEST YOUR WIRELESS NETWORK

To install a stand-alone access point, position it centrally located to where you want your hotspot to be and plug it in. It will have a network or USB cable that you can connect to a computer so you can configure the access point. Run the setup CD that comes with the access point and look for these items on the menus to configure it:

1. Look for a way to select the channel the access point will use, the ability to change the SSID of the access point, and the ability to disable SSID broadcasting. Figure 5-70 shows these three settings for one Linksys access point. Figure 5-71 shows how a

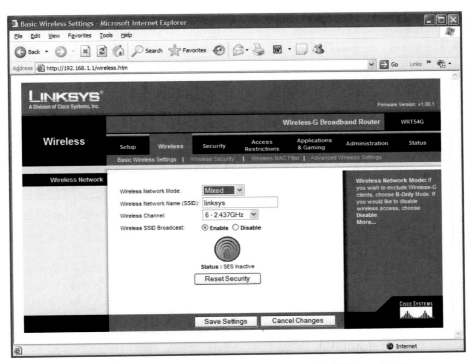

Figure 5-70 Look for the ability of the access point to disable SSID broadcasting

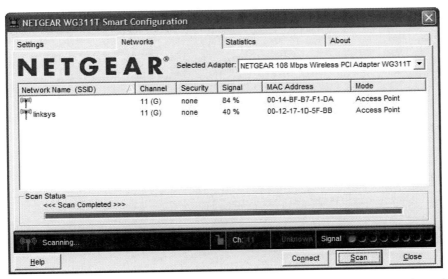

Figure 5-71 A wireless computer shows it has located two access points, but one is not broadcasting its SSID

wireless computer sees a wireless access point that is not broadcasting its SSID. This computer would not be able to use this access point until you entered the SSID in the configuration window shown in Figure 5-72.

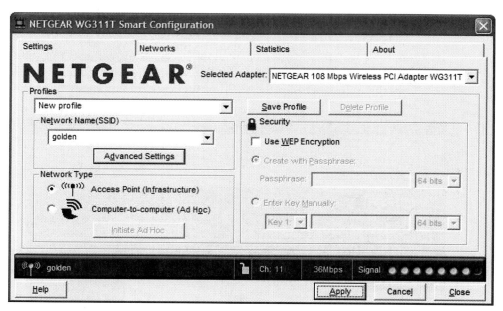

Figure 5-72   This wireless adapter configuration screen lets you enter the SSID of a hidden access point and also configure the wireless connection for WEP encryption.

2. To configure data encryption on your access point, look for a wireless security screen similar to the one in Figure 5-73 where you can choose between several WPA, WEP, or RADIUS encryption methods. (RADIUS stands for Remote Authentication Dial-In User Service and uses an authentication server to control access.) WPA Personal is the one to choose unless one of your wireless adapters doesn't support it. For example, the wireless adapter configuration screen in Figure 5-72 shows it only supports WEP encryption, so your access point is forced to use that method. Enter the same passphrase for WEP encryption on the access point screen and all your wireless adapter configuration screens.

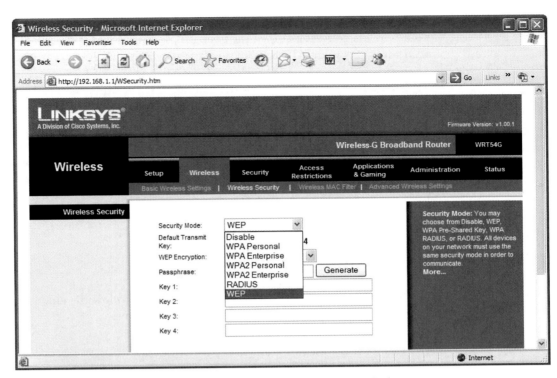

Figure 5-73   This wireless access point supports several encryption methods

3. Look for MAC filtering on your access point, similar to the screen in Figure 5-74. On this access point, you can enter a table of MAC addresses and decide if this list of MAC addresses is to be used to prevent or permit use of the access point.

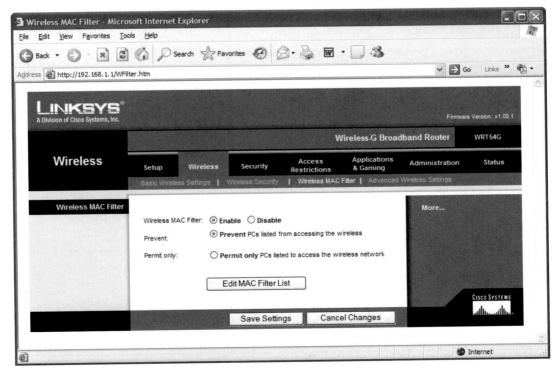

Figure 5-74   Configure how the access point will filter MAC addresses

4. Save all your settings for the access point and test the connection. To test it, on one of your wireless computers, open the configuration window for the wireless adapter and scan for access points. If the scan does not detect your access point, verify the wireless adapter is set to scan all channels or the selected channel of your access point. Try moving your access point or the computer. If you still can't get a connection, remove all security measures and try again. Then restore the security features one at a time until you discover the one causing the problem.

We've just configured your wireless access point to use several security features. Is it really necessary to use them all? Well, not really, but it can't hurt. Encryption is essential to keep others from hacking into your wireless data. For added protection, you can disable SSID broadcasting or filter MAC addresses.

FIXING NETWORK PROBLEMS

If you have problems connecting to the network, you can follow the guidelines in this section. First, here are some symptoms of network problems:

- You cannot make a connection to the network.
- My Network Places does not show any other computers on the network.
- You receive an error message while you are installing the network adapter drivers.
- Device Manager shows a yellow exclamation point or a red X beside the name of the NIC. In the Network Connections window, you see a red X over the network icon.
- There are at least two lights on a NIC: one stays on steadily to let you know there is a physical connection, and another blinks to let you know there is activity (see Figure 5-75). If you see no lights, you know there is no physical connection between the NIC and the network. This means there is a problem with the network cable; the card; or the hub, switch, or router that the PC connects to. Similar lights display on the hub, switch, or router for each network port.

Figure 5-75   Lights on the back of a NIC can be used for troubleshooting

Sometimes you might have trouble with a network connection due to a TCP/IP problem. Windows TCP/IP includes several diagnostic tools that are useful in troubleshooting problems with TCP/IP. The most useful is Ping (Packet Internet Groper), which tests connectivity by sending a signal to a remote computer. If the remote computer is online and hears the signal, it responds. Ipconfig under Windows NT/2000/XP and Winipcfg under Windows

9x/Me test the TCP/IP configuration. Try these things to test TCP/IP configuration and connectivity:

1. Try to release the current IP address and lease a new address. To do this, open the Network Connections window, right-click the network connection and click **Repair** on the shortcut menu (see Figure 5-76). Try rebooting the PC.

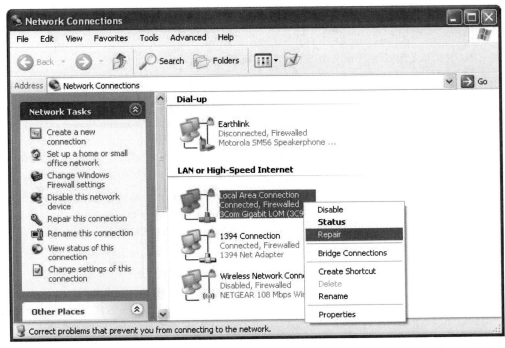

Figure 5-76   Use the Repair command to release and renew the IP address of a network connection

2. Determine whether other computers on the network are having trouble with their connections. If the entire network is down, the problem is not isolated to the PC and the NIC you are working on. Check the hub or switch controlling the network.

3. Look for problems with the TCP/IP configuration. Open a command prompt window by entering **cmd** in the Run dialog box. Then enter **ipconfig /all** at the command prompt. (Refer back to Figure 5-67.) If the TCP/IP configuration is correct and an IP address is assigned, then the IP address, subnet mask, and default gateway appear along with the adapter address. For dynamic IP addressing, if the PC cannot reach the DHCP server, then it assigns itself an IP address. This is called IP autoconfiguration and the IP address is called an Automatic Private IP Address (APIPA). The Ipconfig command shows the IP address as the IP Autoconfiguration Address, and the address begins with 169.254. In this case, suspect that the PC is not able to reach the network or the DHCP server is down.

4. Next, try the loopback address test. At a command prompt, enter the command **ping 127.0.0.1** (with no period after the final 1). This IP address always refers to your local computer. It should respond with a reply message from your computer. If this works, TCP/IP is likely to be configured correctly. If you get an error, then assume that the problem is on your PC. Check the installation and configuration of each component, such as the network card and the TCP/IP protocol suite. Remove and reinstall each component, and watch for error messages, writing them down so that

you can recognize or research them later as necessary. Compare the configuration to that of a working PC on the same network.

5. Next, Ping the IP address of your default gateway. If it does not respond, then the problem may be with the gateway or with the network to the gateway.

6. Now try to Ping the host computer you are trying to reach. If it does not respond, then the problem may be with the host computer or with the network to the computer.

7. If you have Internet access and substitute a domain name for the IP address in the Ping command, and Ping works, then you can conclude that DNS works. If an IP address works, but the domain name does not work, the problem lies with DNS. Try this command: **ping www.course.com**.

8. Make sure the NIC and its drivers are installed by checking for the NIC in Device Manager.

9. Try uninstalling and reinstalling the NIC drivers. If the drivers still install with errors, try downloading new drivers from the Web site of the network card manufacturer. Also, look on the installation CD that came bundled with the NIC for a setup program. If you find one, uninstall the NIC and run this setup program.

10. Some network cards have diagnostic programs on the installation CD. Try running the program from the CD. Look in the documentation that came with the card for instructions on how to install and run the program.

11. Check the network cable to make sure it is not damaged and that it does not exceed the recommended length for the type of network you are using.

12. Connect the network cable to a different port on the hub or switch. If that doesn't help, you may have a problem with the cable or the NIC itself. Uninstall the NIC drivers, replace the NIC, and then install new drivers.

13. Check to see whether you have the most current version of your motherboard BIOS. The motherboard manufacturer should have information on its Web site about whether an upgrade is available.

14. When a network drive map is not working, first check My Network Places and verify that you can access other resources on the remote computer. You might need to log on to the remote computer with a valid user ID and password.

>> CHAPTER SUMMARY

◢ The four most popular ways to connect to the Internet are cable modem, DSL, dial-up, and, for remote locations, satellite. Dial-up is the slowest but least expensive method.

◢ To set up a network, even as simple as one computer connecting to the Internet, it helps to know that network communication must happen at three levels: the hardware level, the OS level, and the applications level.

◢ Network addressing at the hardware level is by MAC addresses, network addressing at the OS level is by IP address, and network addressing at the application level is by port numbers. All three levels of communication and addressing are at work when you use the Internet.

◢ When connecting to the Internet using cable modem, your cable modem connects to the TV jack and uses the TV cable company broadband service. DSL uses the phone lines coming to your house. Cable modem does not interfere with your TV reception. DSL, when properly configured, does not interfere with your telephone service.

◢ TCP/IP is a suite of protocols used by the Internet and most networks. Configuring TCP/IP is done using the Properties window of your network connection in the Network Connections window.

◢ An ISP can use static or dynamic IP addressing. To use static IP addressing, you need to know the default gateway and DNS servers provided by your ISP.

◢ When a PC is connected directly to the Internet, the PC can share the Internet connection. Windows XP uses Internet Connection Sharing (ICS) to manage the connection on the host computer.

◢ The simplest of all networks is two computers connected by one crossover cable.

◢ A hub or switch is used to connect three or more computers in a network.

◢ To eliminate a host computer for your Internet connection, you can use a router that stands between the modem and the network.

◢ Use Windows Explorer to share files and folders with others on the network.

◢ A network drive is a convenient way to share a folder or entire hard drive with others on a network.

◢ A router often serves multiple purposes, for example, being a switch, firewall, proxy server, and wireless access point.

◢ To allow a computer on the network protected by a firewall to receive communication initiated by a computer on the Internet, configure the firewall for port forwarding.

◢ Remote Desktop is an example of an application that works across the Internet and requires port forwarding on your firewall so that you can access your home or office computer from the Internet.

◢ A wireless access point can secure a wireless network by using data encryption, not broadcasting its SSID, filtering MAC addresses, and supporting a virtual private network (VPN).

◢ Tools to use to solve networking problems include Ping and Ipconfig.

>> KEY TERMS

access point (AP)   A device connected to a LAN that provides wireless communication so that computers, printers, and other wireless devices can communicate with devices on the LAN.

crossover cable   A network cable used to connect two PCs into the simplest network possible. Also used to connect two hubs or switches.

default gateway   A computer or other device on a network that acts as an access point, or gateway, to another network.

DNS server   A computer that matches up domain names with IP addresses.

Internet Connection Sharing (ICS)   A Windows 98/Me and Windows XP utility that manages two or more computers connected to the Internet.

network drive map   Mounting a drive to a computer, such as drive E, that is actually hard drive space on another host computer on the network.

patch cable   A network cable that is used to connect a PC to a hub, switch, or router.

>> KEY TERMS CONTINUED

Ping (Packet Internet Groper)   A Windows and Unix command used to troubleshoot network connections. It verifies that the host can communicate with another host on the network.

protocol   A set of predetermined rules that network devices use to communicate.

subnet mask   Four numbers separated by periods (for example, 255.255.255.0) that, when combined with an IP address, indicate what network a computer is on.

WEP (Wired Equivalent Privacy)   A data encryption method used by wireless networks whereby data is encrypted using a 64-bit or 128-bit key. It is not as secure as other methods because the key never changes. Compare to WPA.

WPA (WiFi Protected Access)   A data encryption method used by wireless networks that uses the TKIP (Temporal Key Integrity Protocol) protocol. Encryption keys are changed at set intervals. Compare to WEP and WPA2.

WPA2 (WiFi Protected Access 2)   A data encryption standard compliant with the IEEE 802.11i standard that uses the AES (Advanced Encryption Standard) protocol. WPA2 is currently the strongest wireless encryption standard.

>> REVIEWING THE BASICS

1. What Windows XP component can be used to share an Internet connection with other computers on the LAN?

2. What protocol is commonly used to manage the connection between a broadband modem and a PC when the connection requires a username and password and is not always up?

3. What Windows XP Professional command can be used to display a NIC's MAC address?

4. When using a cable modem to connect to the Internet, the data transmission shares the cabling with what other technology?

5. Why is it unlikely that you will find the IP address 192.168.250.10 on the Internet?

6. What is the listening port for Windows XP Remote Desktop?

7. What are four ways a wireless network can be secured?

8. When a browser sends a request to a Web server, what port address is normally used?

9. How many bits are in a MAC address?

10. Why does your ISP need to know the MAC address of your cable modem or DSL modem?

11. What is a default gateway?

12. Does it matter which TV jack in your house should be used by your cable modem? Why or why not?

13. What two methods can an ISP use to assign your computer or router an IP address?

14. Why are no two MAC addresses the same?

15. Which data encryption is stronger, WPA or WEP?

16. Why is it important to use some type of data encryption on a wireless network?

17. Why is it necessary for your home or office computer to have a static IP address if it is to be set up for Remote Desktop?

18. What is the difference between a patch cable and a crossover cable?

19. What TCP/IP command tests for connectivity between two networked devices?

20. Give two examples of broadband technology.

>> THINKING CRITICALLY

1. You are trying to connect to the Internet using a Windows XP dial-up connection. You installed a modem card and tested it, so you know it works. Next, you create a dial-up connection icon in the Network Connections window. Then you double-click the icon and the Connect dialog box opens. You click Dial to make the connection. An error message appears saying, "There was no dial tone." What is the first thing you do?

   a. Check Device Manager for errors with the modem.

   b. Check with the ISP to verify that you have the correct phone number, username, and password.

   c. Check the phone line to see if it's connected.

   d. Check the properties of the dial-up connection icon for errors.

2. You connect to the Internet using a cable modem. When you open your browser and try to access a Web site, you get the error: "The Web page you requested is not available offline. To view this page, click Connect." What might be the problem(s) and what do you do?

   a. The browser has been set to work offline. On the File menu, verify that Work Offline is not checked.

   b. The cable modem service is down. In the Network Connections window, right-click the LAN connection and select Repair on the shortcut menu.

   c. Windows Firewall is enabled on your PC. Disable it.

   d. The cable modem is down. Go to Device Manager and check for errors with the cable modem.

3. You work in the Accounting Department and have been using a network drive to post Excel spreadsheets to your workgroup file server as you complete them. When you attempt to save a spreadsheet to the drive, you see the error message: "You do not have access to the folder 'J:\'. See your administrator for access to this folder." What should you do first? Second?

   a. Ask your network administrator to give you permission to access the folder.

   b. Check My Network Places to verify that you can connect to the network.

   c. Save the spreadsheet to your hard drive.

   d. Using Windows Explorer, remap the network drive.

   e. Reboot your PC.

>> HANDS-ON PROJECTS

PROJECT 5-1:   Networking Two Computers

Practice your networking skills by doing the following:

1. Using a crossover cable and two computers, connect them together in a network. Configure the two PCs for static IP addressing. What two IP addresses did you use?

2. Share the My Documents folder on the first PC so that the second PC can move files in and out of the folder. How did you do this?

3. Secure the My Documents folder on the second PC so that it cannot be seen by the first PC. How did you do this?

PROJECT 5-2:   Researching Switches

Find four Web pages advertising switches that meet these criteria:

1. Find two switches by different manufacturers that support Gigabit Ethernet and have at least five ports.

2. Find two switches by different manufacturers that support Fast Ethernet and have at least five ports.

3. Compare the features and prices of each switch. Which brand and type of switch would you recommend for a small network? Why?

PROJECT 5-3:   Researching a Wireless LAN

Suppose you want to set up a wireless LAN in your home. Currently, you access the Internet using a cable modem that's connected to your desktop computer. Your new notebook computer does not have wireless but it does have a USB port and a PC Card slot. You want to be able to connect your notebook to the Internet using wireless. Do the following to research the equipment you need to buy:

1. Print three Web pages showing different choices for a wireless access point.

2. Print three Web pages showing different choices for the wireless adapter for your notebook.

3. Which access point and adapter would you select for your wireless LAN? Why?

PROJECT 5-4:   Researching Routers

Research routers to find the best one to use on a small network of five computers that connect to the Internet using DSL. Do the following:

1. Print a Web page of one router that can also serve as a wireless access point.

2. Print a Web page of another router that supports Gigabit Ethernet.

3. Print a Web page of another router that has at least four ports for computers to connect to.

4. Print a Web page of another router that is a wireless access point, has at least four ports, and supports Gigabit Ethernet.

5. Compare prices. Which router is the least expensive? Which router would you recommend? Why?

>> REAL PROBLEMS, REAL SOLUTIONS

REAL PROBLEM 5-1:   Firewalling Your Home Network

At first, Santiago had only a single desktop computer, an ink-jet printer, and a dial-up phone line to connect to the Internet. Then, his wife, Maria, decided she wanted her own computer. And then they both decided it was time for a broadband connection to the Internet and chose cable modem. So now, their home network looks like that shown earlier in Figure 5-19a. Santiago chose to use a crossover cable to connect the two computers, and the cable modem connects to Santiago's computer using a USB cable.

Both computers are constantly plagued with pop-up ads and worms, so Santiago has come to you for some advice. He's heard he needs to use a firewall, but he doesn't know what a firewall is or how to buy one. You immediately show him how to turn on Windows XP Firewall on both PCs, but you know he really needs a better hardware solution. What equipment (including cables) do you recommend he buy to implement a hardware firewall? Also consider that his daughter, Sophia, has been begging for a notebook computer for her birthday, so plan for this expansion. By the way, Sophia has made it perfectly clear there's no way she'll settle for having to sit down in the same room with her parents to surf the Web, so you need to plan for a wireless connection to Sophia's bedroom.

REAL PROBLEM 5-2:   More Security for Remote Desktop

When Jacob travels on company business, he finds it's a great help to be able to access his office computer from anywhere on the road using Remote Desktop. However, he wants to make sure his office computer as well as the entire corporate network is as safe as possible. One way you can help Jacob add more security is to change the port that Remote Desktop uses. Knowledgeable hackers know that Remote Desktop uses port 3389, but if you change this port to a secret port, hackers are less likely to find the open port. Search the Microsoft Knowledge Base articles (*support.microsoft.com*) for a way to change the port that Remote Desktop uses. Practice implementing this change by doing the following:

1. Set up Remote Desktop on a computer to be the host computer. Use another computer (the client computer) to create a Remote Desktop session to the host computer. Verify the session works by transferring files in both directions.

2. Next, change the port that Remote Desktop uses on the host computer to a secret port. Print a screen shot showing how you made the change. Use the client computer to create a Remote Desktop session to the host computer using the secret port. Print a screen shot showing how you made the connection using the secret port. Verify the session works by transferring files in both directions.

3. What secret port did you use? What two Microsoft Knowledge Base Articles gave you the information you needed?

CHAPTER 6

Fixing Hardware and Application Errors

This chapter is about how to fix a problem with a hardware device or an application. It's impossible in one chapter to cover every hardware and application problem you might run across. Instead, I've attempted to show you the general approaches, tools, and strategies to use when faced with these types of problems. Then I've given an example or two of common hardware and application problems to demonstrate how these solutions can be applied.

We'll first look at some general rules for troubleshooting any computer problem, and how to solve hardware problems. Then we'll turn our attention to software problems.

> **⚄ Focus Problem**
>
> "My applications or devices give errors, won't work, won't install, or won't uninstall."

HOW TO APPROACH AND SOLVE ANY COMPUTER PROBLEM

Let's first look at some general troubleshooting guidelines, and then we'll look at some specific questions you can ask a user (including yourself) when you are first faced with helping someone solve a computer problem.

GENERAL TROUBLESHOOTING GUIDELINES

Here are some guidelines intended to help you become a good computer troubleshooter and zero in on the source of a problem in as few steps as possible:

▲ *Make backups before making changes.* Whether you are working on hardware or software, always back up important data before working on a computer. I could tell you some pretty sad stories about how not making backups resulted in a lot of pain and misery. But just take my word for it—make backups!

▲ *Approach the problem systematically.* Start at the beginning and walk through the situation in a thorough, careful way. This one rule is invaluable. Remember it and apply it every time. If you don't find the solution to the problem after one systematic walk-through, then repeat the entire process. Check and double-check to find the step you overlooked the first time. Most problems with computers are simple, such as a loose cable or circuit board. Computers are logical through and through. Whatever the problem, it's also very logical. First, try to reproduce the problem, and then try to figure out whether it is a hardware or software problem.

▲ *Divide and conquer.* This rule is the most powerful. Isolate the problem. In the overall system, remove one hardware or software component after another, until the problem is isolated to a small part of the whole system. Here are a few examples of applying this rule:

  • Boot into Safe Mode to prevent unnecessary device drivers and applications from loading.

  • If a computer won't boot, to figure out if the problem is related to the hard drive or to other vital hardware components, try to boot from the Windows XP setup CD. If that works, then you know the problem has to do with the hard drive.

  • If you're not sure whether the problem is with Windows or a hardware device such as a USB wireless adapter, try using the adapter on another computer. If the problem follows you, you know the adapter is at fault. If the adapter works on this computer, then you know the problem is with the first computer. Could be Windows or could be the USB port itself. But you're zeroing in on the culprit.

▲ *Don't overlook the obvious.* Ask simple questions. Is the computer plugged in? Is it turned on? Is the monitor plugged in? Most solutions to problems are so simple that we overlook them because we expect the problem to be difficult. Don't let the complexity of computers fool you. Most problems are easy to fix. Really, they are!

▲ *Check simple things first.* It is more effective to first check the components that are easiest to replace. For example, if the video does not work, the problem may be with the monitor or the video card. When faced with the decision of which one to exchange first, choose the easy route: Exchange the monitor before the video card.

▲ *Make no assumptions.* This rule is the hardest to follow, because there is a tendency to trust anything in writing and assume that people are telling you exactly what happened. But documentation is sometimes wrong, and people don't always describe events as they occurred, so do your own investigating. For example, if the user tells you that the system boots up with no error messages, but that his application still doesn't work, boot for yourself. You never know what the user might have overlooked.

▲ *Test all components that might affect the problem.* Be thorough in your testing. Test all hardware components related to the problem, check the Windows configuration, and use whatever testing tools are available, both hardware and software tools. Use Event Viewer and Device Manager to check for errors and for configuration problems. Many manufacturers offer diagnostic software to test their products, and Windows includes a few of its own.

▲ *Become a researcher.* Following this rule is the most fun. When a computer problem arises that you can't easily solve, be as tenacious as a bulldog. Read, search the Web, make phone calls, ask questions, and then read more, search more, make more phone calls, and ask more questions. Take advantage of every available resource, including online help, the Internet, documentation, technical support, and books such as this one. Learn to use a good search engine on the Web such as *www.google.com*. Try Googling an error message, problem, application error, or hardware device. Also, check out *groups.google.com*. There are a bunch of computer groups listed with problems, ideas, solutions, and discussions. What you learn will be yours to take to the next problem. This is the real joy of computer troubleshooting. If you're good at it, you're always learning something new.

▲ *Write things down.* Keep good notes as you're working. They'll help you think more clearly. Draw diagrams. Make lists. Clearly and precisely write down what you're learning. Later, when the entire problem gets "cold," these notes will be invaluable.

▲ *Reboot and start over.* This is an important rule. Fresh starts are good for us and uncover events or steps that we might have overlooked. Take a break; get away from the problem. Begin again.

▲ *Establish your priorities.* This rule can help make for a satisfied customer. Decide what your first priority is. For example, it might be to recover lost data, or to get the PC back up and running as soon as possible. When practical, ask the user or customer for advice about setting your priorities.

▲ *Keep your cool and don't rush.* In an emergency, protect the data and software by carefully considering your options before acting and by taking practical precautions to protect software and OS files. When a computer stops working, if unsaved data is still in memory or if data or software on the hard drive has not been backed up, look and think carefully before you leap! A wrong move can be costly. The best advice is not to hurry. Carefully plan your moves. Read the documentation if you're not sure what to do, and don't hesitate to ask for help. Don't simply try something, hoping it will work, unless you've run out of more intelligent alternatives!

▲ *Don't assume the worst.* When it's an emergency and your only copy of data is on a hard drive that is not working, don't assume that the data is lost. Much can be done to recover data. If you want to recover lost data on a hard drive, don't write anything to the drive; you might write on top of lost data, eliminating all chances of recovery.

▲ *Know your limitations and be honest.* After you've done all you know to do, you might find it necessary to pass the problem on to someone with more expertise. Also, if you make a mistake or don't know an answer to a question, be honest with the user. In fact, I've discovered one of the keys to successful help-desk support is to say, "I don't know, but I'll find out."

▲ *Know your starting point.* Before trying to solve a computer problem, know for certain that the problem is what the user says it is. If the computer does not boot, carefully note where in the boot process it fails. If the computer does boot to an OS, before changing anything or taking anything apart, verify what does and what doesn't work, preferably in the presence of the user.

◢ *Begin by asking the user to describe the problem in detail.* Don't jump right in and begin trying this or that until you first get whatever information you can from the user. One really important fact only the user can tell you is whether valuable data on the hard drive is not backed up. If that is true, you need to know that and you need to take precautions to protect the data. For some good questions to ask the user, see Chapter 1.

TOOLS FOR COMPUTER TROUBLESHOOTING

If you're serious about learning to fix computer problems, you can buy some pretty sophisticated PC repair tool kits, but what you really need are just a few simple tools such as those in Figure 6-1.

Figure 6-1 PC repair tools can be simple and not too expensive

You might want to accumulate the following tools and put them in a handy box or container of some sort:

◢ Pen and paper for taking notes
◢ Paper cups for organizing screws as you work
◢ Antistatic ground bracelet
◢ Flashlight
◢ Flat-head screwdriver and Phillips-head screwdriver
◢ Tweezers for picking pieces of paper out of printers and for picking up screws dropped in tight places
◢ Plastic ties to tie power cords together inside the case to keep cords out of the way of fans and to improve circulation. You'll also need some wire cutters to cut off long tie ends.
◢ Can of compressed air to blow dust off components. Too much dust can cause a system to overheat.
◢ Needle-nose pliers for holding objects in place while you screw them in (especially those pesky nuts on cable connectors)
◢ Diagnostic software on CD such as PartitionMagic by Symantec (*www.symantec.com*)

▲ Diagnostic card, also called a POST card

▲ USB to IDE converter

The last two items need a little explanation. Neither of them is essential for PC troubleshooting, but in some situations, they're a great help.

A **diagnostic card** costs from $25 to $100 and can be used to display error codes at startup to diagnose a startup problem with hardware. Figure 6-2 shows a diagnostic card by MSD (*www.msdus.com*). Just stick the card in an empty PCI slot, turn on the system, and read the numeric code displayed on the LED readout on the card. The code is generated by the motherboard BIOS, which can tell you which device caused the boot to halt.

Figure 6-2 A diagnostic card displays BIOS error codes at startup

A **USB to IDE converter** costs less than $30 and is extremely handy when a hard drive won't boot, but has valuable data on it. You can use the converter to install a problem drive into a working computer using a USB port. If the drive works at all, you might be able to recover the data with this little tool, which includes a power adapter and a cable (see Figure 6-3). Remove the hard drive from the computer case, and set the jumpers on the drive to the Master setting. Plug the adapter's power cord into an electrical outlet. Plug one end of the data cable into the hard drive 40-pin connector and the other end of the cable into a USB port on a working computer. Using Windows Explorer, you can browse

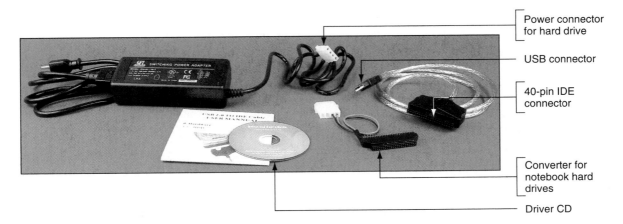

Power connector for hard drive

USB connector

40-pin IDE connector

Converter for notebook hard drives

Driver CD

Figure 6-3 Use a USB to IDE converter to recover data from a failing hard drive

the drive and copy data to another media. After you have saved the data, use Disk Management to try to repartition and reformat the drive. You can also use diagnostic software from the hard drive manufacturer to examine the drive and possibly repair it.

Some of these converters have an extra converter for small IDE hard drives used in notebook computers, such as the one shown in Figure 8-56. You can also buy a serial ATA to USB converter such as the one made by Sabrent (*www.sabrent.com*). For serial ATA drives, if you don't have a serial ATA converter, you can use a serial ATA to 40-pin IDE converter to connect to the 40-pin IDE to USB converter to make the jump from serial ATA to USB.

FIXING PROBLEMS WITH HARDWARE

Let's begin learning about how to solve hardware problems by looking at some general directions and strategies, and then we'll look at a few typical hardware problems and how to solve them.

HOW TO SOLVE A HARDWARE PROBLEM

This section addresses hardware problems that don't prevent Windows from starting. If you cannot start Windows, then move on to the next chapter, "Resurrecting the Dead."

Before we get into the how-to of problem solving, let's take a quick look at some software tools available to help you detect and manage a hardware device:

▲ *CMOS setup.* Some devices, such as motherboard ports and expansion slots, hard drives, optical drives, floppy drives, and tape drives, are detected by the startup BIOS and reported on the CMOS setup screens. On these screens, you can disable or enable some of these devices (see Figure 6-4). Know that, for ports and expansion slots, CMOS setup recognizes the port or slot, but not the device or expansion card using that slot. Any device that shows up in CMOS setup should also be listed in Device Manager.

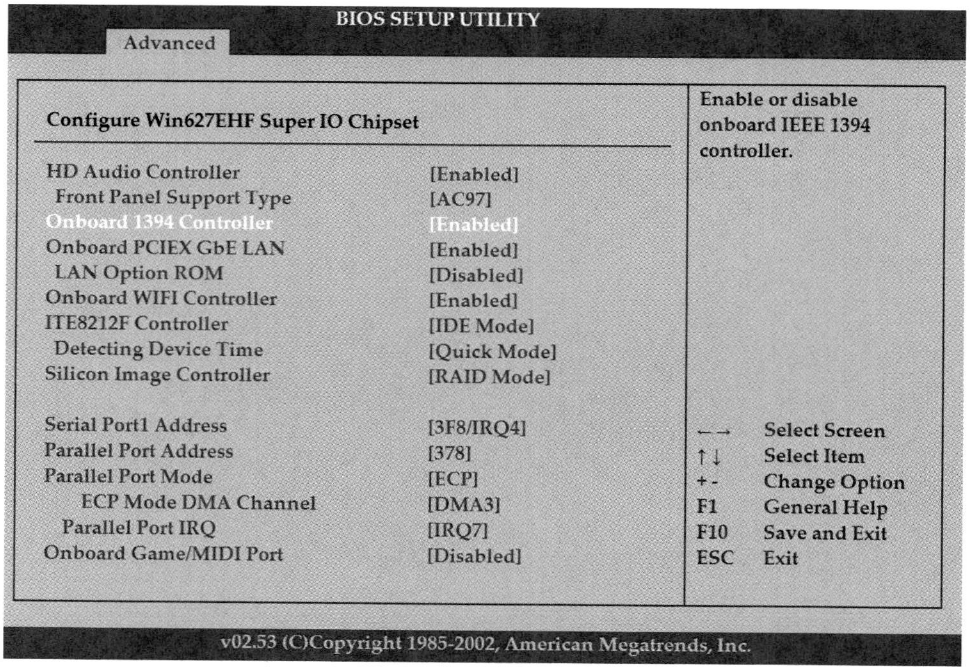

```
                        BIOS SETUP UTILITY
    Advanced

                                              Enable or disable
  Configure Win627EHF Super IO Chipset        onboard IEEE 1394
                                              controller.
  HD Audio Controller             [Enabled]
    Front Panel Support Type      [AC97]
  Onboard 1394 Controller         [Enabled]
  Onboard PCIEX GbE LAN           [Enabled]
    LAN Option ROM                [Disabled]
  Onboard WIFI Controller         [Enabled]
  ITE8212F Controller             [IDE Mode]
    Detecting Device Time         [Quick Mode]
  Silicon Image Controller        [RAID Mode]

  Serial Port1 Address            [3F8/IRQ4]     ←→    Select Screen
  Parallel Port Address           [378]          ↑↓    Select Item
  Parallel Port Mode              [ECP]          +-    Change Option
     ECP Mode DMA Channel         [DMA3]         F1    General Help
     Parallel Port IRQ            [IRQ7]         F10   Save and Exit
  Onboard Game/MIDI Port          [Disabled]     ESC   Exit

         v02.53 (C)Copyright 1985-2002, American Megatrends, Inc.
```

Figure 6-4 In CMOS setup, you can disable and enable motherboard ports and other components

▲ *Device Manager*. Device Manager is the main Windows tool for managing hardware. Using it, you can disable or enable a device, uninstall it, update its drivers, and undo a driver update (called a driver rollback). Most hardware is listed in Device Manager, but not all. Missing are printers and some USB and FireWire devices.

▲ *Event Viewer*. This tool tracks many activities about applications, security, and the system. Most of the information it provides is useless, but it can be useful in solving intermittent hardware problems (see Figure 6-5). For example, on our network, we have a file server and several people in the office update Microsoft Word documents stored on the server. For weeks people complained about these Word documents getting corrupted. We downloaded the latest patches for Windows and Microsoft Office and scanned for viruses thinking that the problem might be with Windows or the application. Then we suspected a corrupted template file for building the Word documents. But nothing we did solved our problem of corrupted Word documents. Then one day someone thought to check Event Viewer on the file server. The Event Viewer had faithfully been recording errors when writing to the hard drive. What we had suspected to be a software problem was, in fact, a failing hard drive, which was full of bad sectors. We replaced the drive and the problem went away. To access Event Viewer, in Control Panel, open the Administrative Tools applet and then open Event Viewer.

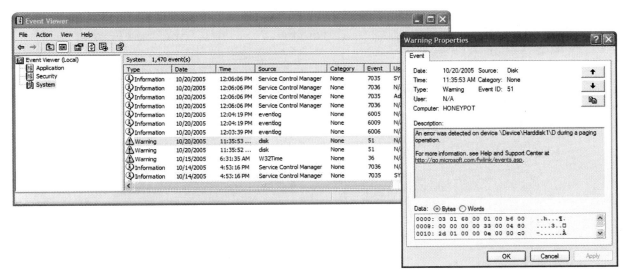

Figure 6-5 Event Viewer reporting a problem when writing to the hard drive

▲ *Printers and Faxes window*. Use this window to install and uninstall a printer, configure it, share it, and manage its print queue. For example, to install a new printer, in Figure 6-6, click **Add a printer**. If you are having problems with a document printing, one thing you can do is clear out the print queue to start fresh. To do that, double-click the printer in the Printers and Faxes window. The printer window opens, as shown in Figure 6-7, listing the print queue for this printer. To cancel all documents in the queue, click **Printer** and select **Cancel All Documents**. To cancel a single document, right-click the document and select **Cancel** from the shortcut menu. Also, when troubleshooting printer problems, if you want to find out if your PC is communicating with the printer independently of your applications, you can print a test page. To do that, in the Printers and Faxes window, right-click a printer and select **Properties** from the shortcut menu. The printer properties window opens (see Figure 6-8). Click **Print Test Page**.

Figure 6-6   Use the Printers and Faxes window to install and uninstall a printer and to manage its print queue

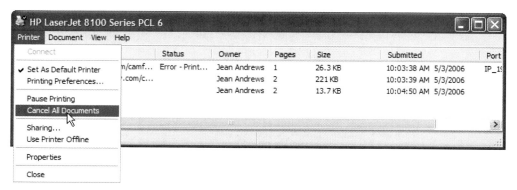

Figure 6-7   Use the printer's print queue window to clean out a print queue

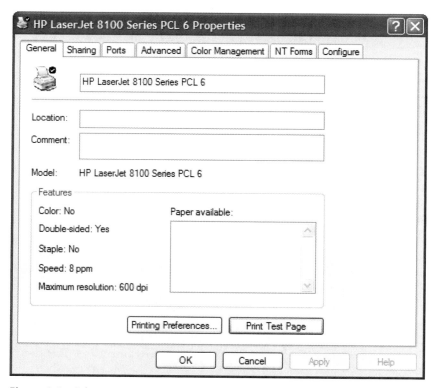

Figure 6-8   Print a test page to verify the PC can communicate with the printer

◢ *Add or Remove Programs applet.* Printers, scanners, USB or FireWire devices, and some other devices don't show up in Device Manager. For these devices, you can use the Add or Remove Programs applet to uninstall the software for the device, including its device drivers. Later in the chapter, you'll see an example of how to do this using a USB device.

◢ *Use System Restore.* If you have a problem with installing or updating a device, or if an application or a problem arises and you don't understand its source, you can use System Restore to return to a previous point in time before the problem occurred. For example, if you install a USB device that does not appear in Device Manager and now Windows gives errors when you boot, use System Restore to undo the installation. Remember from Chapter 2, to start System Restore, click **Start**, point to **All Programs**, point to **Accessories**, point to **System Tools**, and then click **System Restore**.

◢ *Utilities that come bundled with the device.* When you use a device's setup CD to install the device drivers, many times the setup also installs a utility to manage the device. When you have problems with a device, look for this utility (often on the Start, All Programs menu) and any diagnostic or testing software it might offer.

Now let's look at some general guidelines to solve a hardware problem:

◢ *Check the simple things first.* I know I'm beginning to sound repetitive on this point, but I really feel compelled to say it again. Most computer problems are simple and easy to solve. Check the simple things: Is the external device plugged in and turned on? Are the data cable connections solid at both ends? For sound, is the volume knob turned up? Is there a wall light switch controlling the power, and is it turned on? Is the power strip you're using plugged in and turned on? For expansion cards and memory modules, are they seated solidly in their slots?

◢ *Check that CMOS setup and Windows recognize the device with no errors.* For a device that should be recognized by startup BIOS, go into CMOS setup and make sure the device is correctly detected and is enabled. Also check Device Manager to verify the device is enabled and Windows thinks the device should be working. If you see errors in Device Manager, these errors must be resolved before you continue. For devices that don't appear in Device Manager—such as a scanner, printer, or some USB or FireWire devices—use the utility program that came bundled with the device to check for errors. You should find the program on the Start, All Programs menus. For printers, also use the Printers and Faxes window to check for problems.

◢ *Consider recent changes.* What hardware or software changes have you or someone else recently made? Maybe the change affected something that you have not yet considered. Once I installed a hard drive, turned on the system, and got beep code errors at POST. I opened the case and checked the drive and connections. It all looked fine, so I tried to boot again with the same results. The second time I opened the case, I discovered that I had bumped a memory module while closing the case. Reseating the module solved my problem.

◢ *Update device drivers.* A hardware device such as a network card, USB device, modem, or printer, requires device drivers to work. Device drivers are installed at the time the device is installed and these drivers can come from the device manufacturer or, for some devices, you can use the Microsoft drivers included with Windows. For best results, use the manufacturer drivers. Manufacturers often update their drivers, which can be downloaded from the manufacturer's Web site and installed on your PC. When you're having a problem with the device, try updating the drivers with the latest versions available. First, download the driver files to your hard drive. Then, in Device Manager, right-click the device and select **Properties** from the shortcut menu.

The device properties window opens. Click the **Driver** tab and then click **Update Driver**. The Hardware Update Wizard starts up, as shown in Figure 6-9. If you want to search the Microsoft Web site for Microsoft drivers (for example, if you are updating drivers for your Microsoft fingerprint reader), select **Yes, this time only**. Otherwise select **No, not this time**. On the next screen, you can point to the location of the drivers you have downloaded. If you don't like the results of the update, you can click **Roll Back Driver** (shown in Figure 6-9) to undo the update.

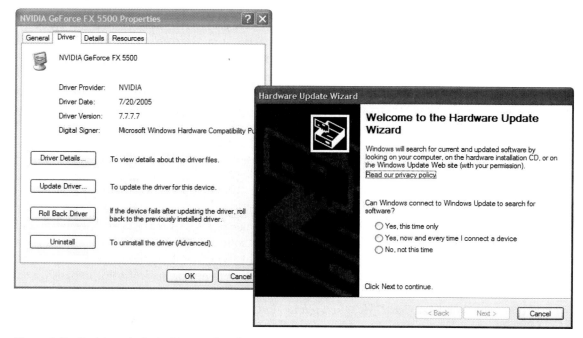

Figure 6-9   Update a device's drivers using the Hardware Update Wizard

▲ *Try reinstalling the device.* To get a clean start with a device, you can uninstall it and start over. In Device Manager, right-click the device and select **Uninstall**. Then reboot the PC. When Windows starts, it should detect a new hardware device and launch the Found New Hardware Wizard. Then you can install the device drivers again. Did the Found New Hardware Wizard launch? If not, the device might be bad or the port it is using might be bad or disabled. You'll see an example of how to deal with a bad port later in the chapter.

▲ *Check the manufacturer documentation.* When installing a device, sometimes the device will not work unless you run the setup CD for the device *before* you physically install the device. (This is sometimes true of internal modem cards, network adapters, and USB devices.) To know the right order, read the manufacturer documentation. You should also find troubleshooting guidelines there for the device and how to use any diagnostic software the manufacturer offers. Also, the manufacturer's Web site should have a support section including FAQs about the device. When all else fails, I've often found my solution there.

FIXING PROBLEMS WITH USB DEVICES

The last USB problem I encountered started when a friend plugged her USB wireless adapter into her notebook computer. The notebook paused for a moment and then her screen looked like the one in Figure 6-10. Each time she tried again, she got the same result.

If you are having a problem with a USB device, the source of the problem might be with the device or its device drivers, or the problem might be with the USB port or the USB port drivers.

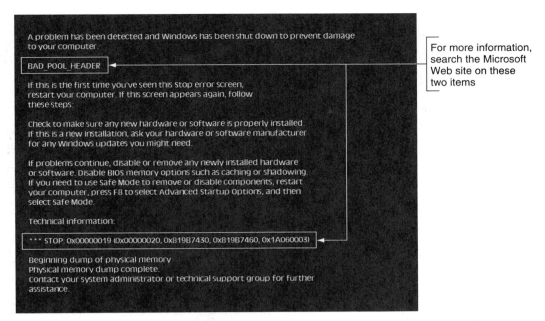

A problem has been detected and Windows has been shut down to prevent damage
to your computer.

BAD_POOL_HEADER ◄—————————— For more information,
search the Microsoft
Web site on these
two items

If this is the first time you've seen this stop error screen,
restart your computer. If this screen appears again, follow
these steps:

Check to make sure any new hardware or software is properly installed.
If this is a new installation, ask your hardware or software manufacturer
for any Windows updates you might need.

If problems continue, disable or remove any newly installed hardware
or software. Disable BIOS memory options such as caching or shadowing.
If you need to use Safe Mode to remove or disable components, restart
your computer, press F8 to select Advanced Startup Options, and then
select Safe Mode.

Technical information:

*** STOP: 0x00000019 (0x00000020, 0x819B7430, 0x819B7460, 0x1A060003) ◄——

Beginning dump of physical memory
Physical memory dump complete.
Contact your system administrator or technical support group for further
assistance.

Figure 6-10   A blue screen of death (BSOD) is definitely not a good sign; time to start troubleshooting

To isolate and fix the problem, the first step is to decide if the problem is with the USB device or the USB port. Follow these steps:

1. Try another device on the USB port. If this device works, then you know the port is good.

2. If no USB device works using this port, then turn your attention to solving the problem with the port. The port might be damaged, disabled in CMOS setup, or the port drivers might be bad. First go into CMOS setup and verify the USB port is enabled.

3. Windows might have a problem with the USB controller. Look in Device Manager for the USB controller listed (see Figure 6-11). Remember the controller shown here represents

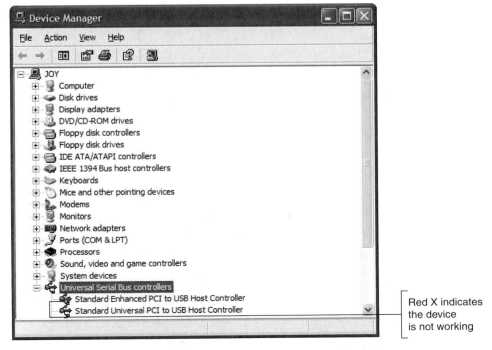

Red X indicates
the device
is not working

Figure 6-11   Device Manager uses a red X to report a problem with a device

only the USB port, not the device using the port. Make sure the USB controllers are enabled and Windows reports no errors.

4. Try updating the drivers for the USB controller. Windows has its own USB drivers, but if the USB port comes directly off your motherboard, you can try using the drivers supplied with your motherboard. Look for a drivers CD that came bundled with your motherboard and use it to update the USB controller drivers. To update these drivers, right-click the USB controller in Device Manager and select **Properties** from the shortcut menu. The controller properties window opens. Click the **Driver** tab (see Figure 6-12). Click **Update Driver** and the Hardware Update Wizard launches. On the first screen of the wizard, also shown in Figure 6-12, click **No, not this time**, and then click **Next**. Follow the directions in the wizard to point to the drivers on CD or your hard drive and complete the installation. Later, if you decide the update does not work for you, you can undo it by clicking **Roll Back Driver** on this same properties window.

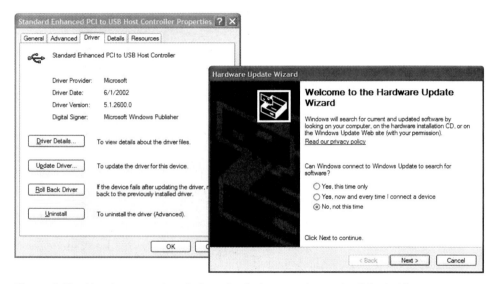

Figure 6-12 Use the properties window of a device to update and roll back drivers

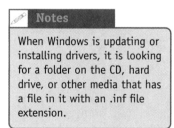

Notes

When Windows is updating or installing drivers, it is looking for a folder on the CD, hard drive, or other media that has a file in it with an .inf file extension.

5. If you still can't get the USB port to work, try flashing the BIOS on the motherboard. To do that, go to the Web site for the motherboard manufacturer to download the BIOS update and install it. However, be really careful to make sure you've got the right update. Updating your BIOS with the wrong update can make your entire system not work. Don't attempt to flash the BIOS unless you are an experienced technician or have some expert help.

6. Consider that the port might be physically damaged. To solve that problem, you can use CMOS setup to disable it and install an expansion card in a PCI slot to provide USB ports. You can also replace the motherboard, although this is more complicated and may not be worth the effort.

After you know the USB port is working, do the following to solve the problem with the USB device:

1. The USB device might be bad. To eliminate that as the problem, try installing the device on another PC. If it works, then you know the problem is not the device. If it

doesn't work, the problem might still be with the device drivers and not the device. Also, some older USB devices were picky about the order in which USB devices were installed. Try removing all other USB devices except this one.

2. To solve a problem with corrupted device drivers, first try uninstalling and reinstalling the device. To do that, find the device listed in the Add or Remove Programs applet. This might require a little doing because the software title might be a little cryptic. For example, the software listed in Figure 6-13 as MA111 Configuration Utility is driver software for a USB wireless network adapter—the title is not exactly self-explanatory. To remove the software, click **Change/Remove**. Then run the setup utility on the CD that came bundled with your device to reinstall it. Watch for errors in the installation routine.

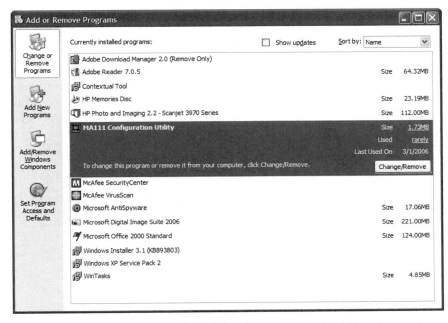

Figure 6-13   The driver software for a USB device appears in the Add or Remove Programs window

3. Check the Web site of the device manufacturer for updated drivers. Download the drivers to your hard drive. For most USB devices, to install these drivers, first uninstall the existing drivers and then double-click the downloaded file. See the Web site for specific instructions.

4. Look in your Start, All Programs menu for a utility to manage the device. It might have diagnostic software you can use. Make sure the utility has the device configured correctly.

5. The problem might be with the application that is using the device. For example, if you are trying to use a USB scanner, try scanning using a different application.

6. After you've tried all this and the problem is still not solved, I think it's time to assume your USB device is just not working. Replace it with a new one.

By the way, back to my friend and her USB wireless adapter: We tried another USB device on her notebook, and it worked fine, so we assumed the problem was not the USB port or controller. So next, we tried plugging in the wireless adapter on another computer. The Found New Hardware Wizard launched and we began installing the drivers. Partway through the installation: Poof! Blue screen of death. Just to make sure the drivers were not the problem, we downloaded new drivers from the adapter manufacturer and started fresh. When we got the same results, we decided to toss the adapter and buy her a new one.

FIXING PROBLEMS WITH APPLICATIONS

Problems with applications include errors when installing the application, loading the application, and running the application. We'll first look at some general guidelines to solving application problems and then look at an example or two of how these guidelines can be applied.

GENERAL APPROACHES TO SOLVING APPLICATION PROBLEMS

When Windows encounters a problem with an application, one thing it might do is display a message about the problem similar to the one shown in Figure 6-14. If you are connected to the Internet, you can click **Send Error Report** to get suggestions about the problem from Microsoft. Microsoft will also use the information you send to help with future Windows updates and patches.

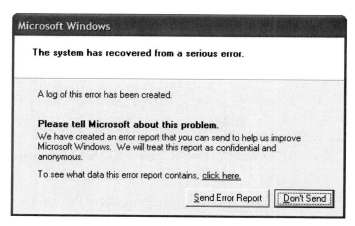

Figure 6-14   A serious Windows error sometimes generates this Microsoft Windows dialog box

After the information is sent, a dialog box similar to the one in Figure 6-15 appears. Click **More information** to see Microsoft's insights and suggestions about the problem. Your browser will open and display information from Microsoft. If the problem is caused by a Microsoft product such as Internet Explorer or Microsoft Office, sometimes the Web site will point you to a patch you can download to fix the problem. An example of an available patch is also shown in Figure 6-15.

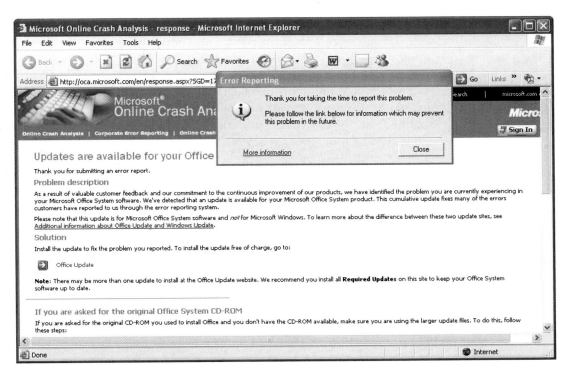

Figure 6-15 Click More information to see Microsoft's insights into a problem

Here are some other useful tips about solving problems with applications:

▲ *Try a reboot.* Reboot the system and see if that doesn't solve the problem.

▲ *Suspect a virus is causing a problem.* Scan for viruses and check Task Manager to make sure some strange process is not interfering with your applications.

▲ *Windows update might solve the problem.* When Microsoft is aware of application problems caused by Windows, it sometimes releases a patch to solve the problem. Make sure Windows updates are current.

▲ *Windows system files might be corrupted.* To have Windows verify system files and replace a bad one with a good one, use the System File Checker (sfc.exe) utility. You'll learn to use the utility later in the chapter.

▲ *You might be low on system resources.* Close all other applications. Check Task Manager to make sure you have unnecessary processes closed. If you must run more than one application at a time, you can increase the priority level for an application that is not getting its fair share of resources. To do that, on the **Processes** tab of Task Manager, right-click the application and select **Set Priority**. Then increase the priority level. This setting applies to the current session only. Also, consider that your system might be running low on memory. For good performance, Windows XP needs 512 MB of RAM. For great performance, use even more than that. How to upgrade memory is covered in Chapter 8.

▲ *Download updates or patches for the application.* Software manufacturers often publish updates or patches for their software to address known problems. You can go to the software Web site to download these updates and get information about known problems.

▲ *Uninstall and reinstall the application.* Sometimes an application gives problems because the installation gets corrupted. You can try uninstalling and reinstalling the application. However, in doing so you might lose any customized settings, macros, or scripts.

▲ *Run the application under a different user account.* The application might require that the user have privileges not assigned to the current account. Try running the application under an account with administrator privileges.

▲ *Install the application under a different account.* If an application will not install, consider the possibility that the user account you are using does not have permission to install software. Install software using an account with administrative privileges.

▲ *Consider data corruption.* It might appear that the application has a problem when the problem is really a corrupted data file. Try creating an entirely new data file. If that works, then suspect that previous errors might be caused by corrupted data. You might be able to recover part of a corrupted file by changing its file extension to .txt and importing it into the application as a text file.

▲ *Consider hard drive or file system problems.* Some older applications expect the file system used on the hard drive to be FAT32. If your drive is using the NTFS file system, problems might occur. Try installing the application and its data on a FAT32 partition.

▲ *Try restoring default settings.* Maybe a user has made one too many changes to the application settings. Try restoring all settings back to their default values. This might solve a problem with missing toolbars and other functions.

FIXING INTERNET EXPLORER

Let's take a look at some things you can do to solve problems with an application most users have on their desktop, Internet Explorer. Here are some tasks that might help with IE problems:

EMPTY THE IE CACHE

One of the first things to do when IE is giving problems is to clean out the cache by using the Internet Options window. To open the window, in Internet Explorer, click **Tools, Internet Options**. (You also can open the Internet Options applet in Control Panel.) Click **Delete Files** (see Figure 6-16). Check **Delete all offline content** and click **OK**. Emptying the cache can solve many IE problems such as not being able to save a picture to your hard drive or not being able to view Web pages.

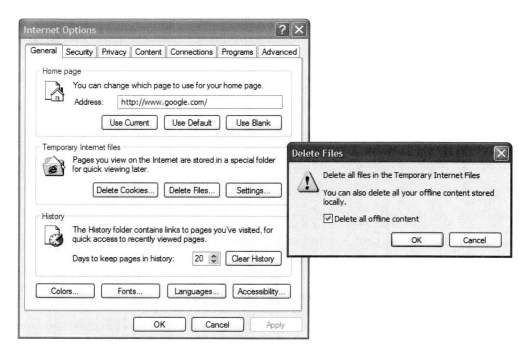

Figure 6-16   Use the Internet Options window to clean out the IE cache

REPAIR A CORRUPTED CACHE INDEX

Sometimes IE problems are caused by a corrupted index file in the cache folder. To solve the problem, you need to delete the hidden file Index.dat. The easiest way to delete the file is to delete the entire IE cache folder for the user account that has the problem. The next time the user logs on, the folder will be rebuilt. To delete the folder, first make sure you're logged onto the system using a different account that has administrative privileges. The folder you want to delete is C:\Documents and Settings*user name*\Local Settings\Temporary Internet Files. You will not be able to delete the folder if this user is logged on.

THE HOSTS FILE MIGHT HAVE AN ERROR

The Windows XP Hosts file is stored in the C:\Windows\System32\Drivers\Etc folder. It can contain domain names and their associated IP addresses. The file is usually maintained by an administrator managing the local network. A problem might arise if the IP address of a domain name changes and the change is not made in the Hosts file. Do the following to check the file for errors:

1. To view the Hosts file, you first have to unhide it. Using Windows Explorer, navigate to the C:\Windows\System32\Drivers\Etc folder. Click **Tools, Folder Options,** and, on the Folder Options window, click the **View** tab. Check **Show hidden files and folders** and uncheck **Hide protected operating system files.** Click **OK** to close the Folder Options window.

2. Now you should be able to see the Hosts file. Open it using Notepad. Figure 6-17 shows a sample Hosts file. All lines that begin with # can be ignored because they are comment lines. The last line that defines the IP address 127.0.0.1 as the localhost is standard and can be left alone. However, if you see other lines in the file, change them to comments by putting a # sign in front of them, or you can just rename the file so it will be ignored altogether.

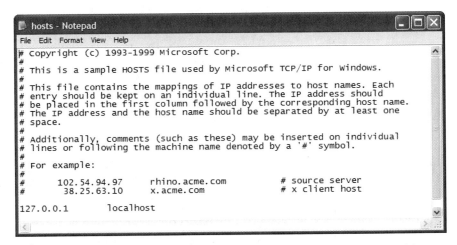

Figure 6-17 The Windows XP Hosts file is used to map domain names to IP addresses

3. Now use IE and try to access the Web site you were not able to reach earlier.

DAMAGED LAYERED SERVICE PROVIDER SOFTWARE

Windows XP has a network software component that Internet Explorer depends on to access Web pages. This software is called the Layered Service Provider (LSP) and can be damaged when some freeware that uses Internet access is installed on your PC and then uninstalled. Some poorly written uninstall routines take with them the components of the LSP layer. If your Internet access is broken after you have uninstalled software, you might want to restore the LSP software. If you have Windows XP Service Pack 2 installed, you can use this command in a command prompt window to reset the software: **netsh winsock reset**. You'll need to reboot your system for the changes to take effect (see Figure 6-18).

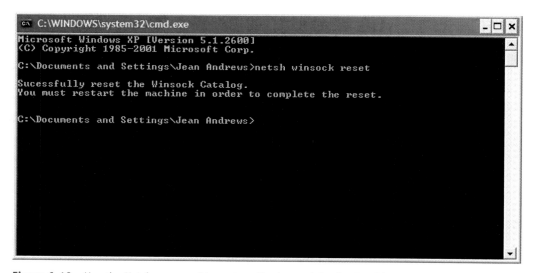

Figure 6-18   Use the Netsh command to restore the Layered Service Provider component of Windows XP

IF IE FREEZES OR CRASHES

If Internet Explorer locks up or closes unexpectedly, the problem could be caused by your video system not being able to keep up with IE. If a game or two on your computer has the same problem, it, too, might be hindered by slow video. One thing you can do is download and install updated video drivers from your video card manufacturer. If that doesn't work, you can try slowing down your video system so your video hardware can keep up. Do the following:

1. Right-click somewhere on your desktop and click **Properties**. The Display Properties window opens. Click the **Settings** tab, click **Advanced**, and then click the **Troubleshoot** tab. A window similar to the one shown in Figure 6-19 appears.

2. Move the **Hardware acceleration** meter to the left one notch. Click **Apply** and try using Internet Explorer or a game. If your system is still not stable, move it another notch to the left. Keep adjusting one notch at a time until your system becomes stable.

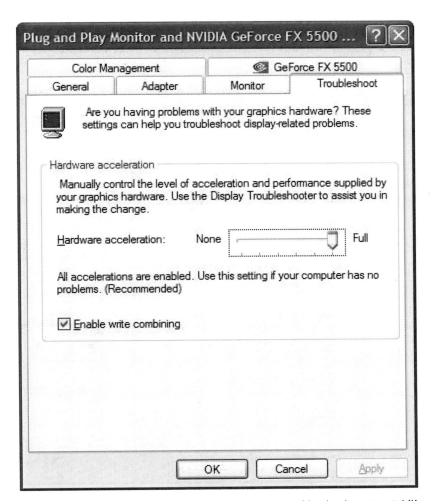

Figure 6-19   Use Hardware acceleration to adjust your video hardware to stabilize your system

REPAIR OR REINSTALL INTERNET EXPLORER

Windows XP considers Internet Explorer and Outlook Express program files to be part of the full set of Windows system files. Therefore, if you need to repair these applications, you can rely on Windows tools and methods to repair Windows system files. Next, try each of the following steps to fix your IE problem. However, know that each step is progressively more drastic than the next and you might find that, in using the method described, you change other Windows configuration settings and components. Therefore, after you try a step, check to see if your problem is fixed. Don't move on to the next step unless your problem is still present.

> **Notes**
>
> The Microsoft Web site at *http://support.microsoft.com* and many other Web sites offer solutions and tips about Internet Explorer. One site I especially like is Sandi Hardmeier's at *http://inetexplorer.mvps.org*. Look there for a bunch of other Internet Explorer and Outlook Express problems and solutions.

1. *Update Internet Explorer.* Internet Explorer 6 is included in Windows XP Service Pack 2, and normal Windows updates include updates for IE as well as other system components. To get the latest Windows XP updates, including those for IE, connect to the Internet and then click **Start**, point to **All Programs**, and click **Windows Update**.

The Web site shown in Figure 6-20 appears. Click **Express** and follow the directions onscreen to get the updates. You might have to perform the update process more than once to get them all. If your problem is not solved, move on to the next step.

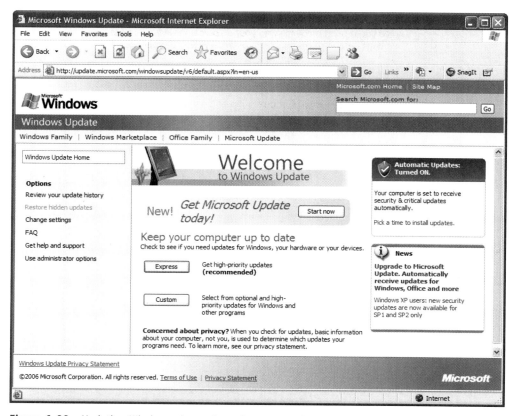

Figure 6-20 Updating Windows also updates Internet Explorer

2. *Use the Windows XP System File Checker (Sfc.exe) to verify Windows system files.* System File Checker is a Windows XP utility that protects system files and keeps a cache folder (C:\Windows\system32\dllcache) of current system files in case it needs to refresh a damaged file. To use the utility to scan all system files and verify them, first close all applications and then enter the command **sfc /scannow** in the Run dialog box. Click **OK**. The Windows File Protection window opens, as shown in Figure 6-21. Have your Windows XP setup CD handy in case it is needed during the scan, also shown in Figure 6-21. If you have problems running the utility, try the command **sfc/ scanonce**, which scans files immediately after the next reboot. If your problem is still not solved, move on to the next step.

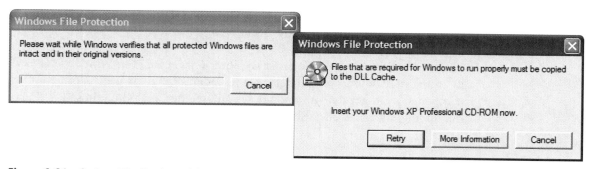

Figure 6-21 System File Checker might need the Windows XP setup CD

3. Remove and reinstall Internet Explorer 6. Internet Explorer 6 came with Windows XP Service Pack 2, so if you remove SP2, you also remove IE 6. Beware, however, that you'll change other Windows components and settings other than IE when you do this. To remove Service Pack 2, open the Add or Remove Programs applet in Control Panel. Check the check box **Show updates**, as shown in Figure 6-22. Scroll down through the list of Windows updates and select **Windows XP Service Pack 2**. Click **Remove**. Follow the directions onscreen and reboot your computer when done. To reinstall SP2, first download the service pack at this Microsoft Web page: *www.microsoft.com/athome/security/protect/windowsxp/default.mspx*. If you have problems removing or installing the service pack, see the Microsoft Knowledge Base article 875350 for additional help. If your problem is not yet solved, then move on to the next step.

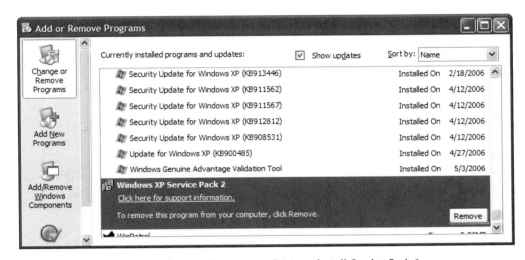

Figure 6-22   Use the Add or Remove Programs applet to uninstall Service Pack 2

4. *Repair a corrupted Windows XP installation.* At this point, if IE is still not working, most likely you have a more serious problem than just IE and you need to refresh your entire Windows installation. There are several methods and tools to do this, all discussed in the next chapter. As you read the next chapter, look for ways to repair Windows XP that require the least amount of work and make the fewest drastic changes to your system.

> **Notes**
>
> Because Internet Explorer is an integrated component of Windows XP, you cannot uninstall and install it again as you can regular applications. If IE gets corrupted and you don't want to mess with your Windows installation to fix the problem, one way you can solve the problem is to abandon IE and use Firefox by Mozilla as your Web browser. Go to the Mozilla Web site (*www.mozilla.com/firefox*) shown in Figure 6-23, download the file, and install it. If IE is not working and you can't get to the Mozilla Web site, use another computer to download the Firefox file and burn the file to a CD. Then use the CD to install Firefox on your computer.

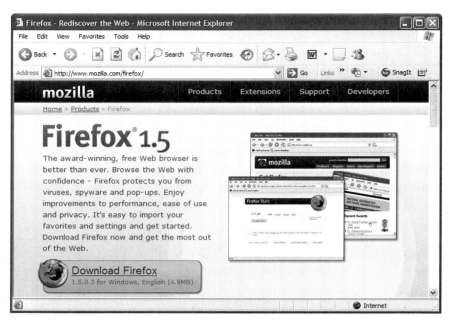

Figure 6-23 Use Firefox as your Web browser

>> CHAPTER SUMMARY

◢ Problems with computers can be divided into those that occur during the boot and those that occur after the boot.

◢ When first approaching a computer problem, always take the necessary precautions to protect any data on the hard drive that is not backed up.

◢ Approach computer problems systematically, checking the simple things first, researching all available sources of information, and establishing your priorities. Begin problem solving by asking the user questions.

◢ Learn to ask the user questions that help you understand the nature of the problem, the user's priorities, and the history behind the problem.

◢ Software tools that can help with hardware problems include CMOS setup, Device Manager, Event Viewer, the Printers and Faxes window, the Add or Remove Programs applet, System Restore, and utilities that come bundled with devices.

◢ When solving a hardware problem, check the simple things first, and check CMOS setup and Device Manager for errors. Also try updating device drivers and reinstalling the device.

◢ USB devices, FireWire devices, and printers don't show up in Device Manager and require slightly different troubleshooting strategies than other hardware devices.

◢ For devices that use ports, consider that the problem might be with the device or the port that it is using. The problem can be hardware related or related to the device drivers for the device or port.

◢ For problems with applications, you can try uninstalling and reinstalling the application, running it under a different account, downloading patches, and restoring the application to default settings.

>> KEY TERMS

diagnostic card   An expansion card that can be used to display error codes at startup to diagnose a startup problem with hardware.

Hosts file   A file stored in the C:\Windows\System32\Drivers\Etc folder that is used to map domain names to their associated IP addresses.

System File Checker   A Windows XP utility (sfc.exe) that protects system files and keeps a cache folder (C:\Windows\system32\dllcache) of current system files in case it needs to refresh a damaged file.

USB to IDE converter   An inexpensive device that allows you to connect an IDE hard drive to a USB port. It can help you recover data from an IDE drive that will not boot.

>> REVIEWING THE BASICS

1. When you have a problem with a USB device, what is the simplest way to determine that the USB port is good?

2. When you have a problem with a USB device, what is the simplest way to determine that the USB device is not causing the problem?

3. How can you determine that device drivers loaded at startup are not interfering with an application that is having problems?

4. If you cannot boot a computer, how can you determine that the problem is isolated to the hard drive and its subsystem?

5. If you are not sure which device is causing a video problem—the monitor or the video card—which one should you exchange first?

6. If a device is listed in CMOS setup, what can you assume about that device?

7. What is the term used to describe undoing a driver update?

8. What Windows tool can you use to uninstall a USB device?

9. What Windows tool can you use to uninstall a printer?

10. What Windows tool can you use to uninstall a network card?

11. What Windows tool can you use to restore the Windows system to a previous point in time before a device was installed?

12. What Windows tool can you use to update your video drivers?

13. What symbol does Device Manager use to indicate a device is not working?

14. If a USB port on your motherboard is damaged, what can you do so that your system can support USB devices?

15. What level of permission must a user account have to install software?

16. What folder holds the cache files for Internet Explorer?

17. If the index file in the IE cache folder gets corrupted, what is the easiest way to fix the problem?

18. What Windows XP file holds the associations used to manually match a domain name to an IP address?

19. What is the purpose of the "netsh winsock reset" command?

20. If your video hardware is causing errors because it is not able to keep up with games, Internet Explorer, or other applications, how can you throttle back the hardware so that your system is more stable?

>> THINKING CRITICALLY

1. As a help desk technician, list some good detective questions to ask if a user calls to say "My PC won't boot."
2. Starting with the easiest procedure, list four things to check if you plug in a USB scanner and the computer does not recognize the scanner.
3. Someone calls to say he has attempted to install a modem, but the modem does not work. List the first four questions to ask.

>> HANDS-ON PROJECTS

PROJECT 6-1:   Investigating Solutions for a Damaged USB Port

Suppose you have determined that one of your USB ports is damaged. Check CMOS setup on your computer. Is it possible to disable one port without disabling all of them? How much will it cost to buy a PCI card to provide extra USB ports? Print the Web page showing your answer.

PROJECT 6-2:   Diagnosing Notebook Computer Problems

Suppose you spend much of your day diagnosing problems with notebook computers. Newer notebooks have a mini-PCI slot that works in a similar way to PCI slots on desktop systems. Search the Internet for a diagnostic card that you can use in a mini-PCI slot that can help you diagnose hardware problems with notebooks. Print the Web pages showing your findings. Which diagnostic card would you choose to buy and why?

PROJECT 6-3:   Support for Your Installed Hardware and Software

Do the following to find out what kind of support and replacement parts are available for your computer:

1. Make a list of all the installed hardware components on your computer that are considered field replaceable components, including the motherboard, processor, power supply, optical drive, hard drive, and memory.

2. Search the Web for the device manufacturer Web pages that show what support is available for the devices, including any diagnostic software, technical support, and device driver updates.

3. Print a Web page showing a replacement part for each device that fits your system. If possible, show the exact match for a replacement part.

4. Make a list of all installed applications on your computer.

5. For each application, print a Web page showing the support available on the software manufacturer's Web site for the application.

PROJECT 6-4:   Help with Notebook Hard Drives

As a notebook computer troubleshooter, you find all too often that people bring you notebook computers that have corrupted Windows installations and hard drives containing valuable data that is not backed up. Search the Internet for a device to help you quickly recover the data. Look for a USB to IDE converter that can accommodate a 2.5" IDE notebook hard drive. Print Web pages showing your findings.

>> REAL PROBLEMS, REAL SOLUTIONS

REAL PROBLEM 6-1:   Fixing a PC Problem

This project should be fun and extremely useful. Make yourself available to family and friends who have computer problems. For the first three problems you face, keep a record that includes this information:

1. Describe the problem as the user described it to you.

2. Briefly list the things you did to discover the cause of the problem.

3. What was the final solution?

4. How long did it take you to fix the problem?

5. What would you do differently the next time you encounter this same problem?

CHAPTER 7

Resurrecting the Dead

When a computer refuses to boot or the Windows desktop refuses to load, it takes a cool head to handle the situation gracefully. What helps more than anything else is to have a good plan so you don't feel so helpless. This chapter is designed to give you just that—a plan with all the necessary details so that you can determine just what has gone wrong and what to do about it. Knowledge is power. When you know what to do, the situation doesn't seem nearly as hopeless.

In this chapter, you'll learn how to use a variety of tools to face a boot problem caused by either software or hardware. You'll also learn what to do to recover data that is lost or corrupted. Before we get into the how-to, you need to know a little about what has to be in good working order so that a computer can successfully boot. So let's start there.

> **⚒ Focus Problem**
>
> "Windows won't start up! I have data in there somewhere!"

BARE-BONES ESSENTIALS NEEDED TO BOOT A SYSTEM

A Windows XP system has successfully started when you can log onto Windows and the Windows desktop is loaded. To successfully boot, a computer needs the bare-bones minimum of hardware and software. If one of these hardware or software components is missing, corrupted, or broken, the boot fails. Here is the list of essential hardware components:

▲ CPU, motherboard, memory, keyboard, video card or onboard video
▲ A boot device, such as a CD drive with bootable CD, a floppy drive with bootable floppy, or a hard drive with an OS installed
▲ A power supply with electrical power

The motherboard contains a chip that holds the BIOS (Basic Input-Output System) or firmware embedded on the chip. This BIOS, called **startup BIOS**, is used to get the system going. It first checks all the essential hardware components to make sure they're working and displays its progress onscreen. (The computer is sometimes configured to show a manufacturer's logo or welcome screen instead.) If it has a problem and the video system is working, it displays an error message. If video is not working, BIOS might attempt to communicate an error with a serious of beeps (called beep codes) or speech (for speech-enabled BIOS). The process of BIOS checking hardware is called POST (power-on self test).

After POST, the BIOS turns to CMOS setup to find out to which device it should look to find an operating system. One of the settings stored in CMOS is the boot sequence, a list of devices such as a CD drive, floppy drive, USB device, or hard drive, arranged in order. The BIOS looks to the first item in the list for storage media that contains an OS to load and, if it doesn't find a bootable OS, moves to the next item in the list. You can change the boot sequence in CMOS setup. Usually the OS is loaded from the hard drive.

A healthy hard drive contains these elements, some shown in Figure 7-1, which all must be present for Windows to load:

▲ *The MBR.* The very first item written at the beginning of the drive is one 512-byte sector called the **master boot record (MBR)**. This sector contains the master boot program, a tiny, yet incredibly essential program that the BIOS uses to find the OS on the drive. Without this program, you can't boot from the hard drive. The sector also contains the partition table, which is a table that maps out what partitions are on the drive, where on the drive they are located, and which partition contains the OS.

▲ *The OS Boot Record.* The second 512 bytes is called the OS boot record, or boot sector, and is used to help the MBR find and load the OS, which is normally stored on drive C.

▲ *Drive C containing OS boot files.* Most often, Windows is installed on drive C. Files stored in the root directory of drive C that are needed to boot the OS include Ntldr (called the Windows XP loader), Boot.ini, Bootsect.dos (optional), Ntbootdd.sys (optional), and Ntdetect.com.

▲ *Files in the C:\Windows folder and its subfolders.* These files include Ntoskrnl.exe, Hal.dll, the registry files, and various device drivers and other system files.

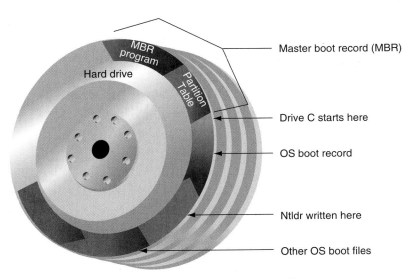

Hard drive

MBR program

Partition Table

Master boot record (MBR)

Drive C starts here

OS boot record

Ntldr written here

Other OS boot files

Figure 7-1 Components at the beginning of the hard drive necessary to boot

With this basic knowledge of the boot in hand, let's turn our attention to what to do when the boot goes sour.

WHAT TO DO WHEN WINDOWS WON'T BOOT

This section is written as step-by-step instructions for problem-solving so that you can use it to solve a boot problem by following each step, taking you from one tool to another. When you first turn on a computer and you see an error message or you see absolutely nothing, the first thing to do is determine if the problem is caused by Windows or by hardware.

We begin with problems caused by Windows. Because you want to solve the problem using the method that will make the least change to your system, we'll start with the least drastic situation. If this easier fix doesn't solve the problem, then we'll move on to the more invasive fixes. The idea is to make as few changes to your system as possible in order to solve the problem without having to do a lot of work to return the system to normal (such as having to reinstall all your applications).

> **⚡ Caution**
>
> In this chapter, I often refer to the Windows XP setup CD. If you have a notebook computer or a brand-name computer such as a Dell, IBM, Lenovo, or Gateway, be sure to use the manufacturer's recovery CD instead of a regular Windows XP setup CD. This recovery CD has drivers specific to your system, and the Windows XP build might be different from that of an off-the-shelf Windows XP setup CD. For example, Windows XP Home Edition installed on a notebook computer might have been built with all kinds of changes made to it by the notebook manufacturer so that it is different from the Windows XP Home Edition that you can buy in a retail store.

However, if you have a problem that you recognize has nothing to do with Windows, but is most likely caused by hardware, you can skip these first sections on solving Windows startup problems and move on to the section, "Problems Caused by Hardware." Examples of problems caused by hardware include a totally dead and dark system (no lights or spinning drives or noisy fans) or a message on your monitor that says no keyboard is present. These types of errors are clearly not caused by Windows.

Some of the Windows tools used in this chapter were first mentioned in Chapter 2, and are only summarized here. Here is the list of tools we'll use and the order you should use them so that you can fix the problem using the least invasive solution:

- ◢ Last Known Good Configuration on the Advanced Options menu
- ◢ Safe Mode on the Advanced Options menu
- ◢ System Restore
- ◢ Windows XP Boot Disk
- ◢ Recovery Console
- ◢ In-place upgrade of Windows XP
- ◢ Automated System Recovery
- ◢ Reformat the hard drive and reinstall Windows XP

LAST KNOWN GOOD CONFIGURATION

Recall that the registry settings collectively called the Last Known Good Configuration are saved in the registry each time the user successfully logs onto the system. If your problem is caused by a bad hardware or software installation and you get an error message the first time you restart the system after the installation, using the Last Known Good, can, in effect, undo your installation and solve your problem. Do the following:

1. While Windows is loading, press **F8**. The Advanced Options menu appears (see Figure 7-2). If the problem is so severe that this menu does not appear, then skip this section and the next and move on to the section, "Windows XP Boot Disk."

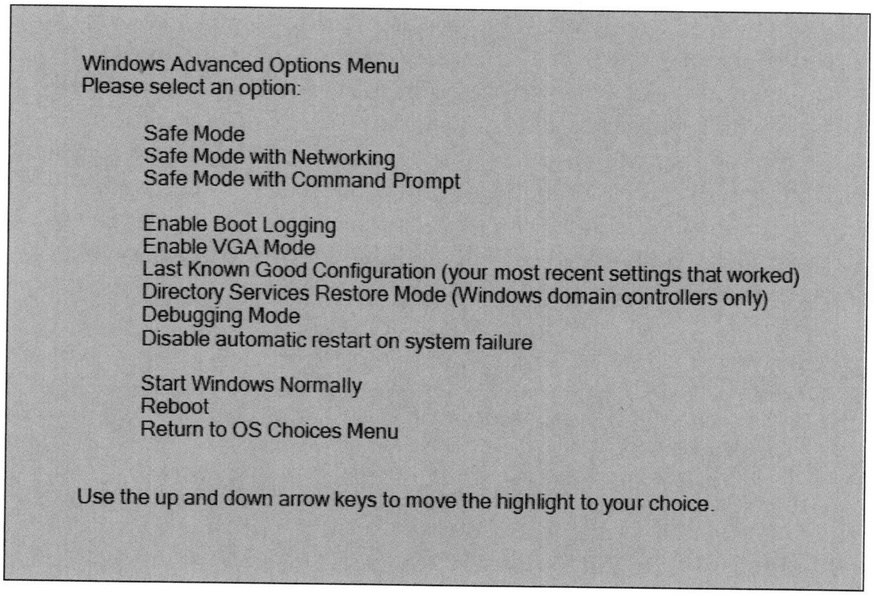

```
Windows Advanced Options Menu
Please select an option:

        Safe Mode
        Safe Mode with Networking
        Safe Mode with Command Prompt

        Enable Boot Logging
        Enable VGA Mode
        Last Known Good Configuration (your most recent settings that worked)
        Directory Services Restore Mode (Windows domain controllers only)
        Debugging Mode
        Disable automatic restart on system failure

        Start Windows Normally
        Reboot
        Return to OS Choices Menu


    Use the up and down arrow keys to move the highlight to your choice.
```

Figure 7-2   Windows Advanced Options menu

2. Select **Last Known Good Configuration (your most recent settings that worked)** and press **Enter**. The system will reboot.

Remember, the Last Known Good is taken immediately after a user logs on. Therefore, it's important to try the Last Known Good early in the troubleshooting session before it's overwritten. (However, know that if you log onto the system in Safe Mode, the Last Known Good is not taken.) If the Last Known Good doesn't work, your next option is Safe Mode.

SAFE MODE ON THE ADVANCED OPTIONS MENU

On the Advanced Options menu, before you try Safe Mode, first try Safe Mode with Networking. If that doesn't work, try Safe Mode. Here's a list of things you can do in Safe Mode to recover the system:

1. When Safe Mode first loads, if Windows senses the problem is drastic, it gives you the opportunity to go directly to System Restore. Use System Restore unless you know exactly what it is you need to do to solve your problem.

2. If you suspect a virus, scan the system for viruses. You can also use Chkdsk to fix hard drive problems. Your hard drive might be full; if so, make some free space available.

3. Use Device Manager to uninstall or disable a device with problems or to roll back a driver.

4. Use Msconfig to disable unneeded services or startup processes. Recall from Chapter 2 that you can use Msconfig to disable many services and startup processes, and then enable them one at a time until you discover the one causing the problem.

5. If you suspect a software program you have just installed, use the Add or Remove Programs applet to uninstall it.

6. You can also use System Restore from within Safe Mode to restore the system to a previous restore point.

7. If you have a recent backup of the System State, restore the system from this backup.

After you try each fix, reboot the system to see if the problem is solved before you do the next fix.

WINDOWS XP BOOT DISK

When troubleshooting a failed boot, a Windows XP boot disk can be used to solve a problem caused by corrupted or missing boot files stored in the root directory of drive C. If you boot from the disk and the Windows XP desktop loads successfully, then the problem is associated with damaged sectors or missing or damaged files in the root directory of drive C that are required to boot the OS. These sectors and files include the master boot record; the OS boot record; and the boot files—Ntldr, Ntdetect.com, Ntbootdd.sys (if it exists), Boot.ini, and perhaps a driver file used by a RAID array. (A RAID array is a group of hard drives that work in unison on a file server.) In addition, the problem can be caused by a boot sector virus. However, a boot disk won't help you if the problem is caused by unstable device drivers or any other system files stored in the \Windows folder or its subfolders.

This boot disk contains all the files that are normally found in the root directory of drive C. Therefore, when you boot from the boot disk, the beginning of drive C might be corrupted, but if the \Windows folder is intact, the boot still works.

You first create the boot disk by formatting the floppy disk using a working Windows XP computer and then copying files to the disk. These files can be copied from a Windows XP setup CD, or a Windows XP computer that is using the same version of Windows XP as the problem PC. Do the following to create the disk:

1. Using a Windows XP computer, format the floppy disk.

2. Using Explorer, copy Ntldr and Ntdetect.com from the Windows XP computer or the \i386 folder on the Windows XP setup CD to the root of the floppy disk.

3. Next, you need to put on the floppy a Boot.ini file that is identical to the one on the problem computer. Boot.ini is a small text file that contains boot settings. If the problem computer boots from the first partition on the first IDE hard drive, then the Boot.ini file in Figure 7-3 should work. Note that there is a hard return after the /NoExecute=OptIn switch.

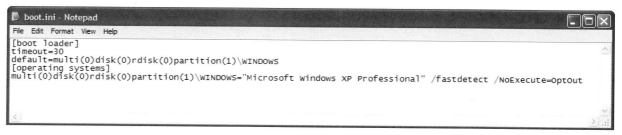

Figure 7-3   Sample Boot.ini file

4. Write-protect the floppy disk so it cannot become infected with a virus.

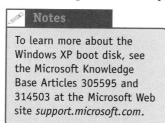

Notes

To learn more about the Windows XP boot disk, see the Microsoft Knowledge Base Articles 305595 and 314503 at the Microsoft Web site *support.microsoft.com*.

You have now created the Windows XP boot disk. Check CMOS setup to make sure the first boot device is set to the floppy disk, and then insert the boot disk and reboot your computer.

If the Windows XP desktop loads successfully, then do the following to attempt to repair the Windows XP installation:

- Load the Recovery Console and use the Fixmbr and Fixboot commands to repair the MBR and the boot sector. (How to use the Recovery Console is coming up.)
- Run antivirus software.
- Use Disk Management to verify that the hard drive partition table is correct.
- Defragment your hard drive.
- Copy Ntldr, Ntdetect.com, and Boot.ini from your floppy disk to the root of the hard drive.

If the Windows XP desktop did not load by booting from the boot disk, then the next tool to try is the Recovery Console.

Notes

SCSI (Small Computer System Interface) is a type of interface that can be used with hard drives. If your computer boots from a SCSI hard drive rather than an IDE hard drive, then obtain a device driver (*.sys) for your SCSI hard drive, rename it Ntbootdd.sys, and copy it to the root of the floppy disk. (If you used an incorrect device driver, then you will receive an error after booting from the floppy disk. The error will mention a "computer disk hardware configuration problem" and that it "could not read from the selected boot disk." If this occurs, contact your computer or hard drive manufacturer for the correct version of the SCSI hard drive device driver for your computer.) If the boot disk works, then copy the Ntbootdd.sys file from the floppy to the root of the hard drive.

RECOVERY CONSOLE

The Recovery Console is a command-line operating system that you can load from the Windows XP setup CD. You might be able to use it to fix a corrupted Windows XP installation when you cannot boot from the hard drive. Using the Recovery Console, you can:

⊿ Repair a damaged registry, system files, or file system on the hard drive.
⊿ Enable or disable a service or device driver.
⊿ Repair the master boot program in the MBR or the OS boot sector on drive C.
⊿ Repair a damaged Boot.ini file.
⊿ Copy data files from the hard drive to removable media.

To protect a hard drive from data theft, if the Recovery Console can read the Administrator password on the drive, it requires you to enter the password before you can use the Console. To use the Recovery Console, insert the Windows XP setup CD in the CD drive and restart the system. When the Windows XP Setup opening menu appears (see Figure 7-4), press **R** to load the Recovery Console.

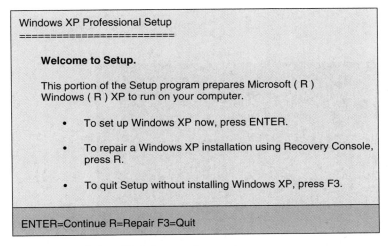

Figure 7-4 Windows XP Setup opening menu

As the Recovery Console attempts to load and give you access to the hard drive, it will display one of the following screens, depending on the severity of the problem with the drive:

⊿ If the Recovery Console cannot find the drive, the window in Figure 7-5 appears. Consider the problem hardware related. You might have a totally dead drive.
⊿ If the Console can find the hard drive, but cannot read from it, the window in Figure 7-6 appears. Notice in the window the C prompt (C:\>), which seems to indicate that the Recovery Console can access the hard drive, but the message above the C prompt says otherwise. When you try the Dir command, as shown in Figure 7-6, you find out that drive C is not available. The Fixmbr and Fixboot commands might help.

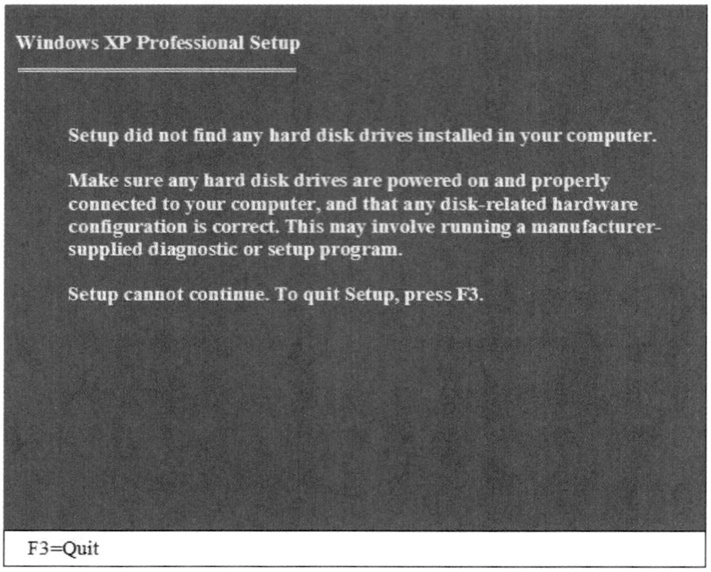

Windows XP Professional Setup

Setup did not find any hard disk drives installed in your computer.

Make sure any hard disk drives are powered on and properly connected to your computer, and that any disk-related hardware configuration is correct. This may involve running a manufacturer-supplied diagnostic or setup program.

Setup cannot continue. To quit Setup, press F3.

F3=Quit

Figure 7-5 Windows XP setup cannot find a hard drive

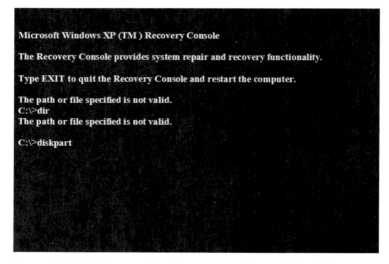

Microsoft Windows XP (TM) Recovery Console

The Recovery Console provides system repair and recovery functionality.

Type EXIT to quit the Recovery Console and restart the computer.

The path or file specified is not valid.
C:\>dir
The path or file specified is not valid.

C:\>diskpart

Figure 7-6 The Recovery Console cannot read from the hard drive

▲ If the Console is able to read drive C, but Windows is seriously corrupted, the window in Figure 7-7 appears. Use the Dir command to see what files or folders are still on the drive. Is the \Windows folder present? If not, then you might need to reformat the drive and reinstall Windows. But first try to find any important data that is not backed up.

▲ If the Console is able to determine that one or more Windows installations is on the drive, it gives you a choice of which installation you want to work with. If only one installation is shown, as in Figure 7-8, type **1** and press **Enter**. Next, you will be asked for the Administrator password. Type the password and press **Enter**. The command prompt shows that the Windows folder is the current working directory. You can now use the Recovery Console to try to find the problem and fix it. How to do that is coming up.

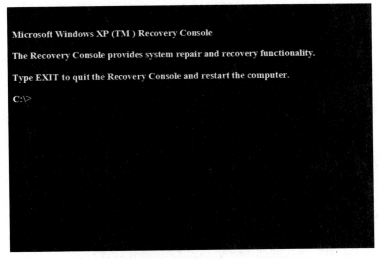

Figure 7-7 The Recovery Console can read drive C, but cannot find a Windows installation

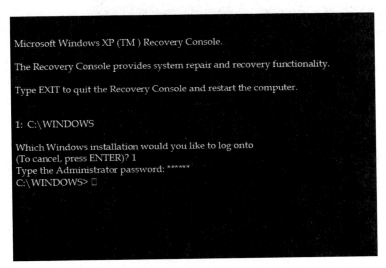

Figure 7-8 The Recovery Console has found a Windows installation

In the following sections, you'll see how you can use the Recovery Console to fix hard drive problems, restore the registry files from backup, disable a service or device driver, and restore Windows XP system files.

USE THE RECOVERY CONSOLE TO FIX HARD DRIVE PROBLEMS

Here are the commands you can use to examine the hard drive structure for errors and possibly fix them:

▲ *Fixmbr and Fixboot.* The Fixmbr command restores the master boot program in the MBR, and the Fixboot command repairs the OS boot record. As you enter each command, you're looking for clues that might indicate at what point the drive has failed. For example, Figure 7-9 shows the results of using the Fixmbr command, which appears to have worked without errors, but the Fixboot command has failed. This tells us that most likely the master boot program is healthy, but drive C is not accessible. After using these commands, if you don't see any errors, exit the Recovery Console and try to boot from the hard drive.

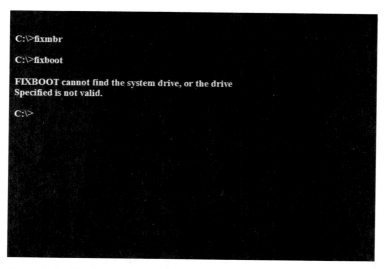

```
C:\>fixmbr

C:\>fixboot

FIXBOOT cannot find the system drive, or the drive
Specified is not valid.

C:\>
```

Figure 7-9   Results of using the Fixmbr and Fixboot commands in the Recovery Console

▲ *Diskpart*. Use the Diskpart command to view, create, and delete partitions on the drive. Type **Diskpart** and press **Enter** and a full screen appears, listing the partitions the Console sees on the drive.

▲ *Chkdsk*. Use this command to recover data from bad sectors: **Chkdsk C: /r**.

USE THE RECOVERY CONSOLE TO RESTORE THE REGISTRY

You can use the Recovery Console to restore registry files with those saved the last time the system state was backed up. The commands to do this and their descriptions are listed in Table 7-1.

USE THE RECOVERY CONSOLE TO DISABLE A SERVICE OR DEVICE DRIVER

Sometimes when Windows fails, it first displays a stop error on a blue background (called a blue screen of death, or BSOD). The stop error might give the name of a service or device driver that caused the problem. If the service or driver is critical to Windows operation, booting into Safe Mode won't help because the service or driver will be attempted in Safe Mode. The solution is to boot the system using the Recovery Console and copy a replacement program file from the Windows XP setup CD to the hard drive.

For this to work, you'll need to know the name or description of the service or driver causing the problem. If an error message doesn't give you the clue you need, you might try to boot to the Advanced Options Menu (press **F8** while booting), and then select **Enable Boot Logging**. This option logs boot events to C:\Windows\Ntbtlog.txt (see Figure 7-10). When you compare the file to one generated on a healthy system, you might be able to find the driver or service that caused the boot to halt. The log file is also generated when you boot into Safe Mode.

Notes

When you first become responsible for a computer or just after you have made major changes to it, it's a good idea to turn on the Enable Boot Logging function and boot the computer. Then save this healthy version of the Ntbtlog.txt log file so you have it to compare to one created later if the system is giving problems.

Command	Description
1. systemroot	Makes the Windows folder the current folder.
2. cd system32\config	Makes the Windows registry folder the current folder.
3. ren default default.save ren sam sam.save ren security security.save ren software software.save ren system system.save	Renames the five registry files.
4. systemroot	Returns to the Windows folder.
5. cd repair\regback	Makes the registry backup folder the current folder.
6. copy default c:\windows\system32\config copy sam c:\windows\system32\config copy security c:\windows\system32\config copy software c:\windows\system32\config copy system c:\windows\system32\config	Copies the five registry files from the backup folder to the registry folder. For hardware problems, first try copying just the System hive and reboot. For software problems, first try copying just the Software hive, and then reboot. Then try copying all five hives.

Table 7-1 Steps to restore the Windows XP registry

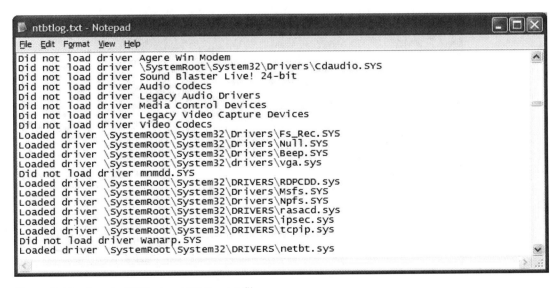

Figure 7-10 Sample C:\Windows\Ntbtlog.txt file

If you know which service is causing the problem, use these commands to list services and disable and enable a service:

▲ *Listsvc.* Enter the command Listsvc to see a list of all services currently installed, which includes device drivers. The list is really long, showing the name of the service, a brief one-line description, and its status (disabled, manual, or auto). To find the service giving the problem, you'll have to have more information than this list shows.

▲ *Disable.* Use the Disable command to disable a service. For example, to disable the service SharedAccess, which is the Windows Firewall service, use this command: **disable**

sharedaccess. When you enter the command, be sure to write down the current startup type that is displayed so you'll know how to enable the service later. For services that are auto-started like this one, the startup type is service_auto_start.

▲ *Enable*. Use the Enable command followed by the name of the service to show the current status of a service. To enable the service, use the startup type in the command line. For example, to reinstate the Firewall service, use this command: **enable sharedaccess service_auto-start**.

If you think you've found the service that is causing the problem, disable it and reboot the system. If the problem disappears, the next step is to replace the program file of the problem service with a good copy from the Windows XP setup CD.

USE THE RECOVERY CONSOLE TO RESTORE SYSTEM FILES

Based on error messages and your research about them, if you think you know which Windows system file is corrupted or missing, you can use the Recovery Console to copy system files from the Windows setup CD to the hard drive. For example, suppose you get an error message that Ntldr is corrupted or missing. The solution to this problem is shown in Figure 7-11.

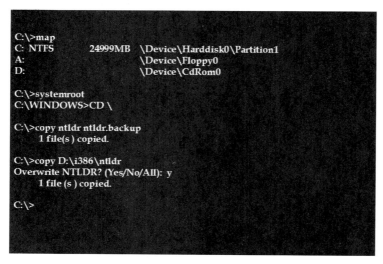

```
C:\>map
C: NTFS          24999MB    \Device\Harddisk0\Partition1
A:                          \Device\Floppy0
D:                          \Device\CdRom0

C:\>systemroot
C:\WINDOWS>CD \

C:\>copy ntldr ntldr.backup
     1 file(s) copied.

C:\>copy D:\i386\ntldr
Overwrite NTLDR? (Yes/No/All):  y
     1 file (s ) copied.

C:\>
```

Figure 7-11   Some Recovery Console commands, including those to repair Ntldr

Even though many Recovery Console commands look like Windows XP or DOS commands that you enter in a command prompt window, they don't always work exactly as these commands do. Pay close attention to command syntax and parameters when learning to use these commands. Here are commands to use to restore system files:

▲ *Map*. Displays the current drive letters. This command is useful to find your way around the system, such as when you need to know the drive letter for the CD drive.

▲ *Systemroot*. Use this command to make the Windows directory the default directory (refer back to Figure 7-11).

▲ *CD*. Change directory. For example, to make the root directory the default directory, use

```
cd \
```

▲ *Delete*. Deletes a file. For example, to delete Ntldr in the Temp directory, use this command:

```
delete C:\temp\ntldr
```

◢ *Copy.* To make a backup of the current Ntldr file, use this command:

```
copy ntldr ntldr.backup
```

To copy the Ntldr file from the Windows setup CD to the root directory of the hard drive, use this command:

```
copy D:\i386\ntldr C:\
```

Substitute the drive letter for the CD drive in the command line, as necessary. A compressed file has an underscore as the last character in the file extension; for example, Netapi32.dl_. When you use the Copy command, the file will automatically uncompress. For example, use this command to copy Netapi32.dl_ from the setup CD:

```
copy D:\i386\netapi32.dl_ netapi32.dll
```

◢ *Bootcfg.* This command lets you view and edit the Boot.ini file. Here are useful parameters:

- *Bootcfg/list.* Lists entries in Boot.ini
- *Bootcfg/copy.* Makes a copy of Boot.ini before you rebuild it
- *Bootcfg/rebuild.* Rebuilds the Boot.ini file

◢ *Expand.* When you're looking for a certain file on the Windows XP setup CD, you'll find compressed files (file extensions end with an underscore) and cabinet files (with a .cab file extension) that hold groups of compressed files. Use the Expand command to extract these files. Here are some useful parameters of the Expand command:

- To list all files in the driver.cab cabinet file:

  ```
  expand /d D:\i386\driver.cab -f:*
  ```

  To expand the file cdaudio.sys in the Driver.cab file and put the expanded file in the C:\Windows\system32\drivers folder:

  ```
  expand D:\i386\driver.cab /f:cdaudio.sys c:\windows
  \system32\drivers
  ```

- To expand the file Appwiz.cp_ and put it in the current folder:

  ```
  expand D:\i386\appwiz.cp_
  ```

  In this last command, the new file is named Appwiz.cpl.

USE THE RECOVERY CONSOLE TO RECOVER DATA

If your hard drive is corrupted, you still might be able to recover data. The problem with using the Recovery Console to do the job is that normally it will not allow you to go into folders other than the system folders or to copy data onto removable media. To do these things, you first need to use the Set command to change some Recovery Console settings.

Notes

For a complete list of all Recovery Console commands, see Appendix C.

Then you can use the Copy command to copy data from the hard drive to other media. Here are the Set commands you'll need.

▲ To allow access to all files and folders on all drives:

```
set allowallpaths = true
```

▲ To allow you to copy any file to another media such as a jump drive or floppy disk:

```
set allowremovablemedia = true
```

▲ To allow the use of wildcard characters * and ?:

```
set allowwildcards = true
```

METHODS TO REPAIR THE WINDOWS INSTALLATION

If you cannot solve your startup problem with the Recovery Console, the next step is to repair the Windows installation. Windows XP offers two ways to repair the installation. Decide between the two based on these criteria:

▲ Reinstalling Windows XP requires that you reinstall all hardware and software, but user settings and data stored on drive C might be saved.
▲ Automated System Recovery (ASR) restores the system to the last time a full backup of drive C was made. All hardware and software installed and all user data written to drive C since the backup will be lost.

Decide between the two methods, based on how recent the full backup is and what user data might be lost. Before you use either method, first copy all user data to a safe place.

If you have a notebook computer or a brand-name computer such as a Gateway, Dell, or IBM, most likely the manufacturer has set up a hidden partition on the hard drive that can be used to recover the Windows installation. During startup, you'll see a message onscreen such as "Press F2 to recover the system" or "Press F11 to start recovery." When you press the appropriate key, a menu should appear that gives you two options: one repairs the Windows installation, saving user data, and the other reformats drive C and restores your system to the way it was when purchased. First, try to save user data before you attempt the destructive recovery. If neither method works, the hidden partition might be corrupted or the hard drive might be physically damaged.

If the recovery process doesn't work, try to use the recovery CD that came bundled with your computer to repair the installation. If you don't have the recovery CD, you might be able to buy one from the computer manufacturer. For notebook computers, you really must have this recovery CD to reinstall Windows because the device drivers on the CD are specific to your notebook. If you cannot buy a recovery CD, you might be able to download the drivers from the notebook manufacturer's Web site. Download them to another computer and burn them to a CD that you can use on the notebook to install drivers.

REINSTALL WINDOWS XP

There are two ways to reinstall Windows XP: an in-place upgrade and a clean install. First try the in-place upgrade and if that doesn't work, then try a clean install.

IN-PLACE UPGRADE OF WINDOWS XP

When you do an in-place upgrade of Windows XP, all installed applications and hardware must be reinstalled, but user data should not be lost. Do the following:

1. Boot the computer from the Windows XP setup CD.

2. The Welcome to Setup screen appears, as shown back in Figure 7-4. Press **Enter** to select the option **To set up Windows XP now, press ENTER**.

3. On the next screen, press **F8** to accept the license agreement.

4. On the next screen, shown in Figure 7-12, verify that the path to your Windows XP folder (most likely C:\Windows) is selected, and then press **R** to repair Windows XP. Follow the instructions onscreen. During the installation, you'll be asked for the product key.

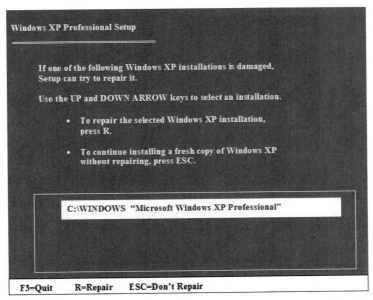

Figure 7-12   Windows XP Setup can repair the selected Windows installation

Notes

The Product Key is written on the CD cover of the Windows XP setup CD or is affixed to the back of the Windows XP documentation booklet. Technicians sometimes mount the Product Key sticker on the side of a computer. Try looking for it there (see Figure 7-13). For notebook computers, look for the Product Key sticker on the bottom of the notebook. If you have lost the Product Key and are moving this Windows XP installation from one PC to another, you can use a utility to find out the Product Key. On the PC that has the old Windows XP installation, download and run the key finder utility from Magical Jelly Bean Software at www.magicaljellybean.com/keyfinder.shtml.

If the installation gives problems or the original problem is still not solved after you finish the in-place upgrade, then try a clean installation of Windows XP.

CLEAN INSTALLATION OF WINDOWS XP

A clean installation of Windows XP gives you a fresh start with the OS. First make sure you've copied important data files to a safe place. Then do the following to reinstall Windows XP:

1. You need to completely destroy the current Windows XP installation so that the Windows XP setup process won't think it is installing Windows XP as a second OS on

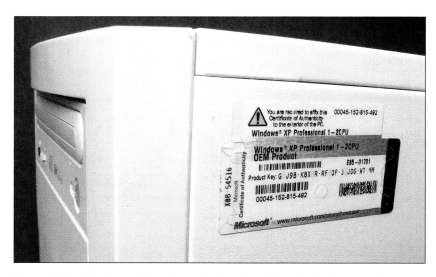

Figure 7-13 The Product Key is mounted on the side or front of a computer case

the drive (called a dual boot). One way to do that is to delete the partition used for drive C. The XP setup program will then create a new partition. A less drastic way is to delete the C:\Windows folder. Using this last method, data on the drive will be saved. Here's how to use either method:

- Boot from the Windows XP setup CD and launch the Recovery Console.
- If you decide to delete the C:\Windows folder, use this command: **del C:\windows**.
- If you decide to delete the Windows partition, use this command to launch the partition manager: **diskpart**. Then select and delete the partition for drive C:.

2. Boot again from the Windows XP setup CD.

3. The Welcome to Setup screen appears, as shown back in Figure 7-4. Press **Enter** to select the option, **To set up Windows XP now, press ENTER**.

4. Follow the directions onscreen to install the OS. You'll need the product key.

AUTOMATED SYSTEM RECOVERY

You can use the Automated System Recovery (ASR) tool to recover the system from the last time you made a full backup of drive C. Everything on drive C since the ASR backup was made is lost, including software and device drivers installed, user data, and any changes to the system configuration.

In this section, you will learn how to make the ASR backup, how to restore the system from the backup, and about best practices when using the ASR tool.

CREATING THE ASR BACKUP AND ASR DISK

The ASR backup process creates two items: a full backup of the volume on which Windows is installed and an ASR floppy disk on which information is stored that will help Windows use Automated System Recovery. The location of the backup file will be written on the floppy.

The backup file created will be just as large as the contents of the hard drive volume, so you will need a massive backup medium, such as another partition on a different hard drive, a tape drive, or a writeable CD-R or CD-RW drive.

Caution

Do not back up drive C to a folder on drive C. The ASR backup process allows you to do this, but restoring later from this backup does not work. Also, don't back up drive C to another partition on the same hard drive. When a hard drive partition fails, most likely other partitions on the drive will also be lost and so will your backup if you've put it on one of these other partitions.

Notes

By default, Windows XP Home Edition does not include the Backup utility. To install it manually, go to the \VALUEADD\ MSFT\NTBACKUP folder on your Windows XP setup CD and double-click **Ntbackup.msi.** The installation wizard will complete the installation.

Follow these directions to create the backup and the ASR floppy disk:

1. Click **Start,** point to **All Programs,** point to **Accessories,** point to **System Tools,** and then click **Backup.** The Backup or Restore Wizard appears (see Figure 7-14).

Figure 7-14   Use the Backup or Restore Wizard to back up the hard drive partition after the Windows XP installation is complete

2. Click the **Advanced Mode** link. The Backup Utility window appears. Click **Automated System Recovery Wizard.** On the following screen, click **Next.**

3. The Backup Destination window appears. Select the location of the medium to receive the backup and insert a disk into the drive. This disk will become the ASR disk. Click **Next.**

4. Click **Finish.** The backup process shows its progress, as seen in Figure 7-15.

5. When the backup is finished, label the ASR disk with the name of the disk, the date it was created, and the computer's name, and then put the disk in a safe place.

RESTORING THE SYSTEM USING AN ASR BACKUP

To restore the logical drive to the state it was in when the last ASR disk set was made, do the following:

1. Insert the Windows XP setup CD in the CD drive, and hard boot the PC (that is, shut it down until the power is off, and then turn it back on again).

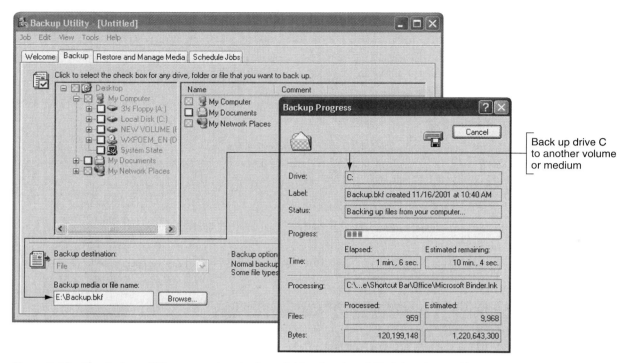

Figure 7-15   The Backup utility can create a backup of drive C and an ASR disk to be used later for the Automated System Recovery utility

2. For some computers, you might see a message that says "Press any key to boot from CD." If so, press any key.

3. A blue screen appears with the message, "Press F6 to load RAID or SCSI drivers." If you don't use RAID or SCSI, there's nothing to press. (If you do use these drivers, you'll have to press **F6** and then load your RAID or SCSI drivers from a driver floppy disk.)

4. At the bottom of the blue screen, a message says, "Press F2 to run the Automated System Recovery process." Press **F2**.

5. The screen shown in Figure 7-16 appears, instructing you to insert the ASR floppy disk. Insert the disk and then press **Enter**.

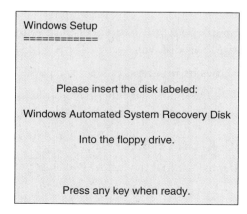

Figure 7-16   Automatic System Recovery process must have the ASR floppy disk

Windows XP Setup does the following:

- ◢ Loads files it needs to run
- ◢ Repartitions and reformats the drive
- ◢ Installs Windows from the Windows XP CD
- ◢ Launches the Automatic System Recovery Wizard to restore the Windows system state, applications, and data to what they were at the time of the last ASR backup

The ASR recovery process erases everything on the volume being restored. Figure 7-17 shows one of the previous steps in the recovery process, in which you reformat the logical drive just before the Windows XP installation process begins.

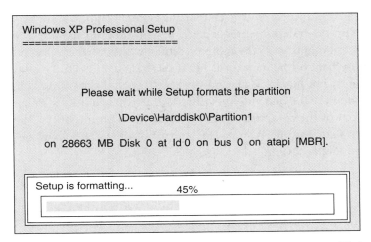

```
Windows XP Professional Setup
==============================



         Please wait while Setup formats the partition

                  \Device\Harddisk0\Partition1

      on  28663  MB  Disk 0  at  Id 0  on  bus 0  on  atapi  [MBR].


  ┌──────────────────────────────────────────────────────────┐
  │ Setup is formatting...          45%                       │
  │ ┌────────────────────────────────────────────────────┐   │
  │ │▒▒▒▒▒▒▒▒▒▒▒▒▒▒▒▒                                     │   │
  │ └────────────────────────────────────────────────────┘   │
  └──────────────────────────────────────────────────────────┘
```

Figure 7-17   As part of the Automatic System Recovery process, Windows XP Setup repartitions and reformats the volume holding Windows XP

STRATEGY FOR USING AUTOMATED SYSTEM RECOVERY

As you have seen, Automated System Recovery is a drastic step in recovering a failed Windows XP startup. All software and hardware installations, user data, and user settings on the Windows XP volume made after the backup are lost. For this reason, it's a good idea to carefully plan how best to use Automated System Recovery. Here's one suggestion if you are in a situation where you are installing Windows XP on a new hard drive: Before you install Windows XP, plan in advance how best to use Automated System Recovery. Create a partition for Windows XP that will hold Windows XP and all installed software, but not the user data. Use a second partition on the drive for user data, say drive D. After you have installed all applications and devices, make an ASR backup of drive C to a different hard drive or other media. Then use Ntbackup to schedule daily or weekly backups of the user data on drive D. In the event of a total system failure, you can recover drive C from the ASR backup media and then recover the user data from your daily or weekly backups of that data.

> **Notes**
>
> Many people find the ASR recovery process to be inconvenient and awkward to use. They prefer to use third-party backup software such as Norton Ghost (*www.symantec.com*) to keep system backups rather than ASR.

To set this plan in place, partition the hard drive so that drive C is large enough for Windows and other software, but the bulk of the hard drive space is devoted to user data. Make drive C about 5 to 15 GB in size, which should be plenty of room for Windows and other software.

When recovering from a failed boot, if the ASR process doesn't work, then try an in-place upgrade of Windows XP.

PROBLEMS CAUSED BY HARDWARE

You've just seen how you can deal with problems caused by a corrupted Windows installation, but sometimes the boot problem occurs before the OS is loaded. These problems can be caused by the failure of essential hardware devices, such as the power supply, motherboard, CPU, memory, hard drive, video, or keyboard. If any one of these devices is not working, the error is communicated using beep codes, or using onscreen or voice error messages—and then the computer halts. Following are some symptoms you might see when a hardware problem is present, and what you can do about the problem.

SYMPTOM: THE SCREEN IS BLANK

If you see absolutely nothing on the screen, check that the system is getting power and the monitor is plugged in and turned on. Check that the system is not in standby mode or hibernation: Try waking up the system by pressing any key or a special standby key on laptops, or by pressing the power-on button. Is the monitor totally without lights, or is the screen blank but the LED light on front of the monitor is lit? If the LED light is lit, try rebooting the system. If the LED light is not lit, check that power is getting to the monitor. Is it turned on?

Try trading the monitor for one you know is good. If you can hear a spinning drive and see lights on the front of the computer case and know the monitor works, the video card might be bad or not seated properly in its slot, the memory might be bad, or a component on the motherboard might have failed.

SYMPTOM: THE COMPUTER DOES NOT APPEAR TO HAVE POWER

If you can't hear the spinning drive or see lights on the front of the case, suspect the electrical system. Check power connections and switches. The power supply might be bad or connections inside the case might be loose.

SYMPTOM: AN ERROR MESSAGE APPEARS BEFORE THE OS STARTS

Recall that when you first turn on a system, system BIOS takes control, checks essential hardware devices, and searches for an OS to load. If it has a problem while doing all that and the video system is working, it displays an error message onscreen. If video is not working, it might attempt to communicate an error with a series of beeps (called beep codes) or speech (for speech-enabled BIOS).

For messages displayed onscreen that apply to nonessential hardware devices such as CD drives or floppy drives, you might be able to bypass the error by pressing a key and moving forward in the boot. But for errors with essential hardware devices such as the one shown in Figure 7-18, focus your attention on the error message, beep code, or voice message describing the problem. For example, notice in Figure 7-18 that the hard drive should have been recognized as the Primary Master device, but it is missing from the list. If you don't know what the error message or beep codes mean, you can search the Web site of the motherboard manufacturer.

SYMPTOM: THE HARD DRIVE IS NOT ACCESSIBLE

Error messages that pertain to the hard drive can be caused by a variety of things. If you have not yet seen the Windows XP splash screen, you can assume the problem has to do with BIOS finding the hard drive or reading what is on the drive. Here is a list of text error messages that indicate that BIOS could not find a hard drive:

▲ *Hard drive not found*
▲ *Fixed disk error*

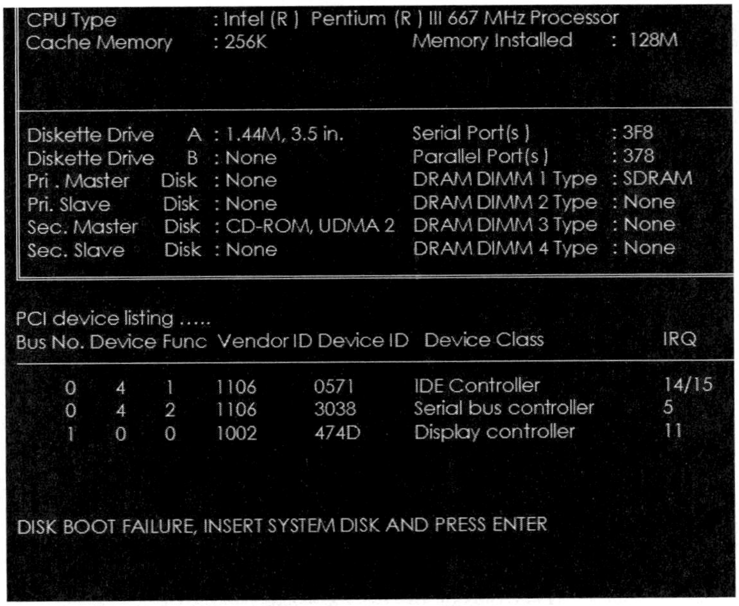

```
CPU Type          : Intel (R )  Pentium (R ) III 667 MHz Processor
Cache Memory      : 256K                  Memory Installed  : 128M


Diskette Drive    A  : 1.44M, 3.5 in.     Serial Port(s )       : 3F8
Diskette Drive    B  : None               Parallel Port(s )     : 378
Pri . Master   Disk  : None               DRAM DIMM 1 Type   : SDRAM
Pri. Slave     Disk  : None               DRAM DIMM 2 Type   : None
Sec. Master    Disk  : CD-ROM, UDMA 2     DRAM DIMM 3 Type   : None
Sec. Slave     Disk  : None               DRAM DIMM 4 Type   : None


PCI device listing .....
Bus No. Device Func  Vendor ID Device ID  Device Class           IRQ

    0     4    1     1106      0571       IDE Controller         14/15
    0     4    2     1106      3038       Serial bus controller  5
    1     0    0     1002      474D       Display controller     11


DISK BOOT FAILURE, INSERT SYSTEM DISK AND PRESS ENTER
```

Figure 7-18 This error message at POST indicates a hardware problem

▲ *Disk boot failure, insert system disk and press enter*
▲ *No boot device available*

The problem might be a physical problem with the drive, the data cable, power, or the motherboard. Start with checking CMOS setup to verify that CMOS detected the drive correctly. If the drive was not detected, check the autodetection setting. (Chapter 8 shows sample CMOS setup screens for these hard drive settings.) If autodetection is turned off, turn it on and reboot. Your problem might be solved. If startup BIOS still doesn't find the drive, power down the system, unplug it, and open the case. Physically check the hard drive power and data cable connections at both ends. Sometimes cables work their way loose.

Here is a list of error messages that indicate the BIOS was able to find the hard drive but couldn't read what was written on the drive or could not find what it was looking for:

▲ *Invalid boot disk* or *Inaccessible boot device*
▲ *Invalid drive specification*
▲ *Invalid partition table*
▲ *No operating system found, Missing operating system, Error loading operating system*
▲ *Couldn't find NTLDR* or *NTLDR is missing*

For these error messages, you need to boot from the Windows XP setup CD, but first check CMOS setup to make sure the boot sequence lists the CD drive before the hard drive.

USE CMOS SETUP TO SET THE BOOT SEQUENCE

To access CMOS setup, reboot the PC and look onscreen for a message such as "Press DEL for setup" or "Press F2 for BIOS settings" or something similar. Press that key and the CMOS setup utility loads. Find the screen, such as the one in Figure 7-19, that lets you set the boot sequence. The boot sequence is the order of devices to which BIOS

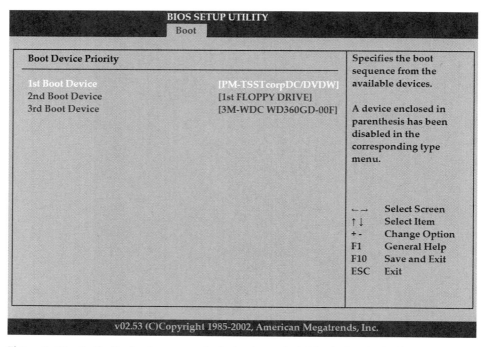

Figure 7-19 Verify the boot sequence looks to the optical drive before it checks the hard drive for an operating system

looks to find an OS to load. Make sure that the CD drive and the floppy drive are both listed before the hard drive so that you can force the system to boot from either the Windows XP setup CD or a Windows XP boot disk. Save your settings and exit CMOS setup.

The next step is to try to boot from the Windows XP setup CD.

CAN YOU BOOT FROM THE WINDOWS XP SETUP CD?

Now that you have made sure that CMOS setup is configured to boot first from the CD drive before it turns to the hard drive, you can try to boot from the Windows XP setup CD. If you cannot boot from this CD, the problem is not just the hard drive. Study the error message and solve the immediate hardware problem. If you have a DOS or Windows 9x startup floppy disk, you can try booting from the floppy. If you can boot from the floppy, then you have proven the problem is with both the hard drive and the CD drive.

If you are able to boot from the Windows XP setup CD, the main window in Figure 7-4 appears. If you see this window, you have proven that the problem is isolated to the hard drive. Now the trick is to find out exactly what is wrong with the drive and fix it.

At this point, you could try to load the Recovery Console and find out if it recognizes the hard drive. If it does not, then you could try booting from a Windows XP boot disk. If that works, then the problem has to do with the items at the very beginning of the hard drive, including the MBR, the OS boot record, or the Ntldr boot loader program.

If neither the Recovery Console nor the Windows XP boot disk is able to find the hard drive, but CMOS setup recognizes the drive, then the drive partitions and file systems are most likely toast. Third-party partition management software like PartitionMagic might be able to help.

ERROR MESSAGES AND THEIR MEANINGS

To summarize the tools and methods you can use to solve a Windows XP startup problem, Table 7-2 lists some error messages and what you can do about them. Most of these errors occur when booting.

Error Message or Condition	What It Means and What to Do About It
Invalid partition table Error loading operating system Missing operating system	The program in the MBR displays these messages when it cannot find the active partition on the hard drive or the boot sector on that partition. Use Diskpart from the Recovery Console to check the hard drive partition table for errors. Sometimes Fixmbr solves the problem. Third-party recovery software such as PartitionMagic might help. If a setup program came bundled with the hard drive (such as Data Lifeguard from Western Digital or MaxBlast from Maxtor), use it to examine the drive. Check the hard drive manufacturer's Web site for other diagnostic software.
A disk read error occurred NTLDR is missing NTLDR is compressed	A disk is probably in the floppy disk drive. Remove the disk and reboot. When booting from the hard drive, these errors occur if Ntldr is missing or corrupted, if the boot sector on the active partition is corrupted, or you have just tried to install an older version of Windows such as Windows 98 on the hard drive. First try replacing Ntldr. Then check Boot.ini settings.
An unknown stop error on a blue background is displayed, and the system halts.	Stop errors are usually caused by viruses, errors in the file system, a corrupted hard drive, or a hardware problem. Search the Microsoft Web site for information about an unidentified stop error.
Stop 0x00000024 or NTFS_File_System	The NTFS file system is corrupt. Immediately boot into the Recovery Console and copy important data files that have not been backed up to another media before attempting to recover the system.
Stop 0x00000050 or Page_Fault_in_Nonpaged_Area	Most likely RAM is defective.
Stop 0x00000077 or Kernel_Stack_Inpage_Error	Bad sectors are on the hard drive, there is a hard drive hardware problem, or RAM is defective. Try running Chkdsk from the Recovery Console.
Stop 0x0000007A or Kernel_Data_Inpage_Error	There is a bad sector on the hard drive where the paging file is stored; there is a virus or defective RAM. Try running Chkdsk.
Stop 0x0000007B or Inaccessible_Boot_Device	There is a boot sector virus or failing hardware. Try Fixmbr.

Table 7-2 Windows XP error messages and their meanings

Error Message or Condition	What It Means and What to Do About It
Black screen with no error messages	This is likely to be a corrupted MBR, partition table, boot sector, or Ntldr file. Boot the PC using a Windows XP boot disk, and then try the Fixmbr and Fixboot commands from the Recovery Console. You might have to reinstall Windows.
When you first turn on a system, it begins the boot process, but then powers down.	The CPU might be quickly overheating. Check for fans not running. Is this a new installation? If so, make sure the cooler assembly on top of the CPU is correctly installed.
When you first turn on the computer, it continually reboots.	This is most likely a hardware problem. Could be the CPU, motherboard, or RAM. First disconnect or remove all nonessential devices such as USB or FireWire devices. Inside the case, check all connections. Try reseating RAM. Check for fans that are not working, causing the CPU to quickly overheat.
You are trying to start up a computer with a power-on password that you don't know.	Most motherboards have a jumper setting on the board to clear CMOS settings to restore them to default values (see Figure 7-20). Read your motherboard documentation for the location of this jumper. Set the jumper and start your computer. After you have booted successfully, power down and undo the jumper setting.
While running Windows, a stop error appears and then the system reboots. The reboot happens so fast you can't read the error message.	Set Windows to not reboot after a stop error so you have the chance to read the message to help you understand the root problem. To change the setting, click the Advanced tab on the System Properties window, and then click Settings under Startup and Recovery. The Startup and Recovery dialog box opens (see Figure 7-21). Uncheck Automatically restart and close both windows.
	If you cannot boot to the Windows desktop to make the change, press F8 to boot to the Advanced Options menu and then select *Disable automatic restart on system failure*.

Table 7-2   Windows XP error messages and their meanings (continued)

Jumpers set for normal boot

Figure 7-20   BIOS setup configuration jumpers

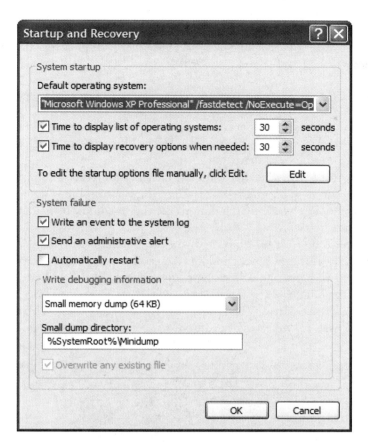

Figure 7-21 Set Windows to not reboot after displaying a stop error screen

HOW TO RECOVER LOST DATA

When data is lost or corrupted, you might be able to recover it using Windows tools, third-party software, or commercial data recovery services. This section discusses your options to recover lost data.

RECOVER A DELETED OR CORRUPTED DATA FILE

Here are some things to try to recover a deleted or corrupted data file:

- ◢ If you have accidentally deleted a data file, to get it back, look in the Recycle Bin. Drag and drop the file back to where it belongs (or right-click the file and click **Restore** on the shortcut menu).
- ◢ If a data file is corrupted, you can try to use the Recover command from a command prompt window to recover data from bad sectors on a drive. For example, use this command: **recover C:\Data\Mydata.txt**.
- ◢ If an application's data file gets corrupted, go to the Web site of the application manufacturer and search the support section for what to do to recover the file. For example, if an Excel spreadsheet gets corrupted, search the Knowledge Base at *support.microsoft.com* for solutions.
- ◢ Third-party software can help recover deleted and corrupted files. On the Internet, do a search on "data recovery" for lots of examples. One good product is GetDataBack by Runtime Software (*www.runtime.org*), which can recover data and program files

even when Windows cannot recognize the drive. It can read FAT and NTFS file systems and can solve problems with a corrupted partition table, boot record, or root directory.

RECOVER DATA FROM A COMPUTER THAT WILL NOT BOOT

If Windows is corrupted and the system will not boot, recovering your data might be your first priority. Recall that earlier in the chapter you learned how to use the Recovery Console to recover data from a failing hard drive.

Another method is to remove your hard drive from your computer and install it as a second non-booting hard drive in another system. After you boot up the system, you should be able to use Windows Explorer to copy the data to another medium. If the data is corrupted, try to use data recovery software.

Recall from Chapter 6 that for less than $30 you can purchase an IDE to USB converter kit that includes a data cable and power adapter. You can use the kit to temporarily connect an IDE hard drive to a USB port on a working computer. Set the drive beside your computer and plug one end of the data cable into the drive and the other into the USB port. The AC adapter supplies power to the drive. The setup is shown in Figure 7-22. There's also a converter kit that can be used for notebook hard drives.

Figure 7-22   To recover data, connect a failing hard drive to a PC using a USB connection

USE A DATA RECOVERY SERVICE

If your data is extremely valuable and other methods have failed, you might want to consider a professional data recovery service. They're expensive, but getting the data back might be worth it. To find a service, Google on "data recovery." Before selecting a service, be sure to read up on reviews and perhaps get a recommendation from a satisfied customer.

>> CHAPTER SUMMARY

- ◢ The hardware components required for a successful boot are the CPU, motherboard, power supply, memory, keyboard, video card or onboard video, and a boot device such as a hard drive or CD drive.

- ◢ When you first turn on a system, startup BIOS on the motherboard takes control to examine hardware components and find an operating system to load.

- ◢ If startup BIOS encounters an error, it communicates the problem by a text message onscreen, a series of beeps (called beep codes), or speech (for speech-enabled BIOS).

◢ Items on the hard drive essential for a successful boot include the MBR (master boot record), which contains the master boot program and partition table, the OS boot record, and OS boot files in the root directory and in the \Windows folder.

◢ Windows tools to use to troubleshoot a failed boot include Last Known Good Configuration, Safe Mode, System Restore, Windows XP boot disk, Recovery Console, in-place upgrade of Windows XP, and Automated System Recovery.

◢ The Windows XP boot disk contains files that are normally stored in the root directory of drive C.

◢ The Recovery Console is a command-line OS that includes a set of commands designed to recover a failed Windows installation and to recover data on the hard drive.

◢ An in-place upgrade of Windows XP restores the system to the time that Windows XP was first installed. You'll need to reinstall all hardware and software after the in-place upgrade, but user data should not be affected.

◢ To work, Automated System Recovery relies on a full backup of drive C.

◢ The boot sequence is configured in CMOS setup.

◢ If a hard drive contains valuable data, but will not boot, you might be able to recover the data by installing the drive in another system as the second non-booting hard drive in the system.

>> KEY TERMS

Automated System Recovery   A Windows XP tool that can be used to recover the system from the last time a full backup was made of drive C.

blue screen of death (BSOD)   A Windows XP stop error that appears on a blue background when Windows fails; might give the name of a service or device driver that caused the problem.

master boot record (MBR)   The first 512-byte sector on a hard drive. Contains the partition table and the master boot program, which the BIOS uses to find the OS on the drive.

OS boot record (boot sector)   The second 512 bytes on a drive, used to help the MBR find and load the OS.

Recovery Console   A command-line operating system that you can load from the Windows XP setup CD, and which can be used to recover data or fix a corrupted Windows XP installation when you cannot boot from the hard drive.

startup BIOS   Firmware embedded on the motherboard that is used to start up the system.

>> REVIEWING THE BASICS

1. What command in the Recovery Console lets you view the contents of the Boot.ini file?

2. How do you start the Automated System Recovery process to recover a Windows installation?

3. What are three methods startup BIOS might use to communicate errors?

4. What Recovery Console command is needed so that you can use wildcard characters in the Copy command line?

5. What Recovery Console command gives you permission to copy data to a floppy disk?

6. Which method does not disturb user data on drive C? Is it an in-place upgrade of Windows XP or Automated System Recovery?

7. What is the name of the log file created when you boot into Safe Mode, or boot logging is enabled from the Advanced Options startup menu?

8. What two components are created when you back up a system using the Automated System Recovery process?

9. What are the two main components of the MBR?

10. What folder on the Windows XP setup CD for the Home Edition contains the installation wizard for the Ntbackup program?

11. How do you start an in-place upgrade of Windows XP?

12. After you have backed up the system state, in what folder can you find backup copies of the registry files?

13. In the Recovery Console, if you don't know the drive letter for the CD drive, what command can you use?

14. What Recovery Console command works in a similar way to Disk Management?

15. What is the purpose of the boot file Ntbootdd.sys?

16. What Recovery Console command can be used to repair the master boot program?

17. What key do you press during the boot to load the Windows XP Advanced Options menu?

18. At what point in the boot is the Last Known Good Configuration saved?

19. What are the three files stored in the root directory of drive C that are required for Windows XP to boot when using an IDE hard drive?

20. Place these tools in the order in which you should try them when troubleshooting the boot process: Recovery Console, Advanced Options Menu, System Restore.

>> THINKING CRITICALLY

1. You have important data on your hard drive that is not backed up, and your Windows installation is so corrupted you know that you must repair the entire installation. What do you do first?

   a. Use the Automated System Recovery to repair the installation.

   b. Make every attempt to recover the data.

   c. Perform an in-place upgrade of Windows XP.

   d. Reformat the hard drive and reinstall Windows XP.

2. When you attempt to boot, you get an error message about no boot device available. List these steps in the order you should do them:

   a. Insert the Windows XP setup CD in the CD drive and reboot.

   b. Open the computer case and check cable connections.

   c. Check CMOS setup to make sure the boot sequence puts the CD drive before the hard drive.

   d. Make a Windows XP boot disk on another computer.

>> HANDS-ON PROJECTS

PROJECT 7-1: Practicing Solving Boot Problems

Unplug your computer, open the case, and disconnect the data cable to your hard drive. Turn your computer back on and boot the system. What error message did you see? Now reboot using your Windows XP setup CD. Try to load the Recovery Console. What error message did you get? Power down your computer, unplug it, and reconnect your hard drive. Reboot and verify that Windows XP loads successfully.

PROJECT 7-2: Practicing Using the Recovery Console

Boot from your Windows XP setup CD and load the Recovery Console. Do the following:

1. Get a directory listing of C:\. Are files normally hidden in Windows Explorer displayed in the list?

2. Create a folder on your hard drive named C:\Temp.

3. List the files contained in the Drivers.cab cabinet file.

4. Expand one of these files and put it in the C:\Temp folder.

5. Exit the Recovery Console and reboot.

PROJECT 7-3: Using Ntbtlog.txt

Compare an Ntbtlog.txt file created during a normal boot to one created when booting into Safe Mode. Note any differences you find.

PROJECT 7-4: Using a Windows XP Boot Disk

Create a Windows XP boot disk and use it to boot your computer. Describe how the boot worked differently than booting entirely from the hard drive.

PROJECT 7-5: More Practice with Recovery Console

Using Windows Explorer, rename the Ntldr file in the root directory of drive C. Reboot the system. What error message do you see? Now use Recovery Console to restore Ntldr without using the renamed Ntldr file on drive C. Copy the file from the Windows XP setup CD to drive C. List the commands you used to do the job.

PROJECT 7-6: Problem-Solving Using the Microsoft Knowledge Base

Your hard drive has been attacked by a malicious virus, and you have decided to restore it from the last backup made by the ASR backup process. You cannot find the ASR floppy disk required for the restore process. Search the Microsoft Knowledge Base for the steps to re-create the ASR floppy disk when the ASR backup is available. Print the Knowledge Base article.

>> *REAL PROBLEMS, REAL SOLUTIONS*

REAL PROBLEM 7-1:   Fixing a PC Boot Problem

This project should be fun, extremely useful, and give you an opportunity to find out just how much you have learned so far from this book. Make yourself available to family and friends who have problems booting their computers. For the first three problems you face, keep a record that includes this information:

1. Describe the problem as the user described it to you.

2. Briefly list the things you did to discover the cause of the problem.

3. What was the final solution?

4. How long did it take you to fix the problem?

5. What would you do differently the next time you encounter this same problem?

Upgrading Your Windows XP Computer

Have you ever asked the question or had someone ask you: "I think I need to upgrade my computer. Can you help me?" That one question can open up a whole can of worms. To help a person make upgrade decisions, you need to know the answers to lots of questions: What do you do with your computer? What kind of computer do you have? What hardware and software is installed? What does your computer *not* do that you want it to do? What are your priorities for the upgrade? How much money are you willing to spend?

In this chapter, you'll learn how to ask the right questions to make wise upgrade decisions. After you've evaluated the need and cost of an upgrade, you might decide to "Just say no." Maybe your computer is really too old to justify the expense of an upgrade and you really need to buy a new one. On the other hand, you might find that you can have your needs met by simply buying an external device and plugging it in. An upgrade can be that easy, or it might be moderately difficult such as installing memory, a second hard drive, or an expansion card. However, the upgrade might be even more difficult, such as upgrading your processor, motherboard, and power supply. The easier and moderately difficult upgrades are covered in this chapter.

"I think I might need to upgrade my computer."

EVALUATING FOR AN UPGRADE

The two big questions when evaluating for an upgrade are: "What do you want your computer to do?" and "What are your computer's limitations?" Once you know the answers to those two questions, you can investigate which components need upgrading and evaluate the cost of the upgrade. With this information in hand, you're ready to make the best possible decisions about upgrading. So let's begin by defining the user's computing needs that are not met.

DEFINE YOUR NEEDS

You might be considering an upgrade for your own computer or helping others upgrade their computers. Either way, only users (you or someone else) can say exactly what it is they want their computers to do. Maybe a user just wants to boost performance, or perhaps he needs some new functionality such as a FireWire port or a network port. To get to the specifics of what it is you're trying to accomplish, you can ask yourself or another user these questions:

- ◢ *Is performance your main concern?* If the computer is just slow, maybe there's a problem other than the need for additional hardware. In Chapters 1, 2, and 3, you learned how to clean up and tune up an old and sluggish Windows XP system. Before you decide to upgrade hardware, step through these first three chapters and make sure the problem is not something that good maintenance might solve. After you've done that, then you're ready to look at a possible need to upgrade hardware. You might need to upgrade memory, the hard drive, the processor, the network adapter, or the motherboard. Move on to the next section on benchmarking to decide which component needs upgrading.
- ◢ *Is it more software you need?* Maybe you want to add a new application such as Microsoft Office, Adobe PageMaker, or AutoCAD. For example, if you want to install AutoCAD by Autodesk (*www.autodesk.com*), you'll need a pretty powerful workstation computer with lots of hard drive space and a good video card. You'll probably also want a super-duper plotter printer. When deciding on adding new software to your system, begin by investigating the recommended system requirements of the software manufacturer. But remember, for most companies, the recommended requirements are only the bare minimum, so allow for extra computing power.
- ◢ *Is it more hardware you need?* Maybe you have a new digital camcorder that connects to the computer by way of a FireWire port, but neither your home desktop computer nor your notebook have a FireWire port. The solution might appear simple at first: Go out and buy a FireWire adapter and install it. However, before you do that, you need to evaluate whether your computer is powerful enough to support the data flow from your camcorder to your hard drive and whether you have enough hard drive space to hold that data. If you decide, yes, your computer can handle a FireWire connection and all those large video files, then the next step is to investigate all the different types of FireWire adapters available and select the best one for you. And then, because you now have video files stored on your hard drive, you might also investigate the possibility of some really neat video-editing software to make some cool self-produced videos. The point is, before you leap, investigate all your needs.

After you've clearly defined your needs, you might come to some conclusions such as in the following list. They're only sample conclusions about user needs; yours, of course, will be unique because your needs are *your* needs.

▲ My system is just slow. I've done everything I know to do to clean it up and tune it. So now I'm looking at what hardware I can install to boost performance.

▲ I want to buy Adobe PageMaker so I can publish my own newsletters. To make PageMaker work for me, I need more memory, a larger hard drive, and a really good color laser printer.

▲ I want to buy AutoCAD and use it to develop my new inventions. I have a Pentium III system with 128 MB of memory and a 10 GB hard drive. The Autodesk Web site says AutoCAD requires a Pentium III or higher CPU, 512 MB of RAM and 500 MB free hard drive space. I need to really beef up my computer, but I'm wondering if the cost of the upgrade will be so much that I should just buy a new computer.

▲ I want to network my two computers, but one of them does not have a network port. All I need is a network port.

So now, we've moved from the simple statement, "I think I need an upgrade" to "Here is specifically what I know I need." That's a good start. Now, let's move on to evaluating exactly what components need upgrading or what new components can be added.

UPGRADES TO IMPROVE OVERALL PERFORMANCE

Many times slow performance is the driving factor when considering an upgrade. Let's first look at how to benchmark the current performance of a system and then we'll look at the components that might be the bottleneck of a system that you can upgrade to improve overall performance.

BENCHMARKING

One of the best-known utilities for benchmarking a system is SiSoftware Sandra by SiSoftware (*www.sisoftware.co.uk*). The Sandra Lite version is free and is powerful enough to measure the overall performance of your system. To use it, go to the SiSoftware Web site and download and install it. Figure 8-1 shows the main window for Sandra Lite. You can use the many utilities under the tabs on this main window to burn in a new computer (test a new computer for errors), benchmark individual components, test components, and display technical information about your system.

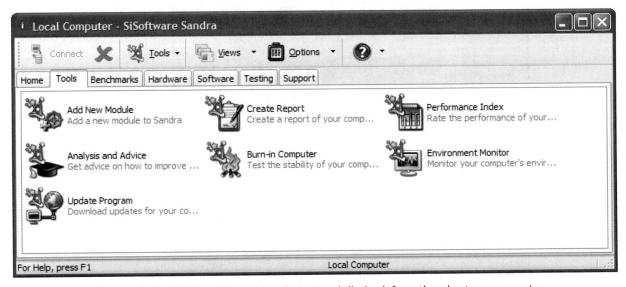

Figure 8-1 Use Sandra Lite by SiSoftware to benchmark, test, and display information about your computer

To see a summary presentation of the overall performance of your computer, click the **Tools** menu and double-click the **Performance Index** icon. Open the Combined Performance Index Wizard under the Wizard Modules section. When the wizard opens (see Figure 8-2), click the green check mark at the bottom of the window to start it up.

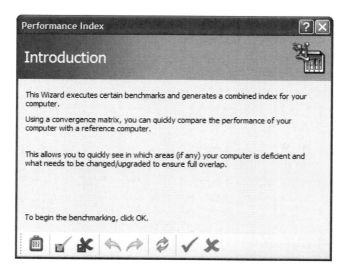

Figure 8-2 Combined Performance Index Wizard by SiSoftware Sandra

Figure 8-3 shows the results for one computer. The red shows how this computer's performance compares to the blue benchmarks. In the figure, you can see that memory performance is pretty good compared to network performance, which comes out pretty low in the overall performance of the system. Therefore, for this computer, if you wanted to improve its overall performance, begin by looking at its networking hardware. The next suspects for upgrades would be the processor and memory, in that order.

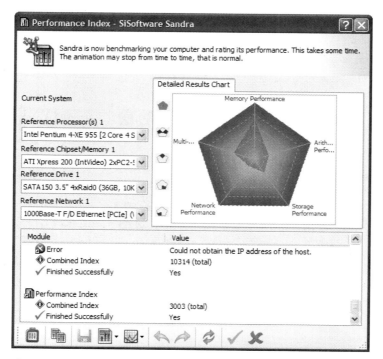

Figure 8-3 Combined performance benchmarks can help you identify bottlenecks in your computer's hardware

COMPONENTS TO UPGRADE FOR IMPROVED PERFORMANCE

When your goal is to improve the overall performance of a system, here are the primary components you need to consider for upgrade:

▲ *Memory.* Upgrading memory is one of the simplest upgrades you can do to improve performance. For good Windows XP performance, you need 256 MB or 512 MB of memory, depending on how hard you run your system. Anything over 1 GB is probably overkill unless you have special requirements. A quick way to tell how much installed memory you have is to right-click **My Computer** and select **Properties** from the shortcut menu (see Figure 8-4). Click the **General** tab if necessary. How to upgrade memory is covered later in the chapter.

Figure 8-4 Use the System Properties window to find out how much memory is installed

▲ *Hard drive.* Too little hard drive space is a common problem that results in slow performance. Recall from earlier chapters that a hard drive needs 15% or 1.5 GB of free space, whichever is larger. To know how much space you have, use Windows Explorer. Right-click each logical drive on your hard drive and select **Properties** (see Figure 8-5). If your system has room for a second drive, it's easier to install a second hard drive than to replace the existing drive. How to install a second drive is covered later in the chapter.

▲ *Network adapter.* There are three speeds of Ethernet: 10, 100, and 1000 Mbps. The 100 Mbps rating is called Fast Ethernet or 100BaseT, and the 1000 Mbps rating is called Gigabit Ethernet or 1000BaseT. Most of today's local area networks use either Fast Ethernet or Gigabit Ethernet. The reason the networking performance in Figure 8-3 is rated so slow is because this computer has a Gigabit Ethernet adapter installed, but the PC is connected to a 100BaseT switch, which means the network is running at the slower 100 Mbps rate. To improve network performance for this situation, you would have to replace the switch.

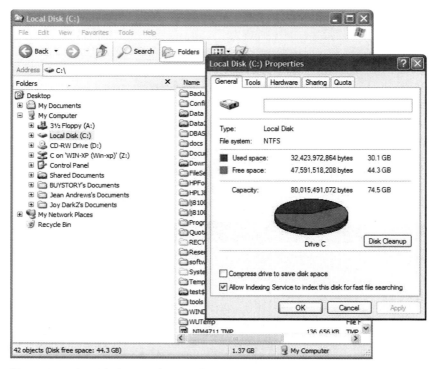

Figure 8-5   Use Windows Explorer to find out about free hard drive space

To find out the Ethernet rating of your network adapter, the easiest way is to look at the name of the adapter, which most likely includes the rating. To see the name of the adapter, open Device Manager. Figure 8-6 shows a network adapter with Gigabit in its name. Beware! When upgrading your Ethernet network to Gigabit, to get the full benefit of the upgrade, you'll need to upgrade all network devices (for example, NICs, router, switch, hub). How to upgrade a network interface card (NIC) is covered later in the chapter.

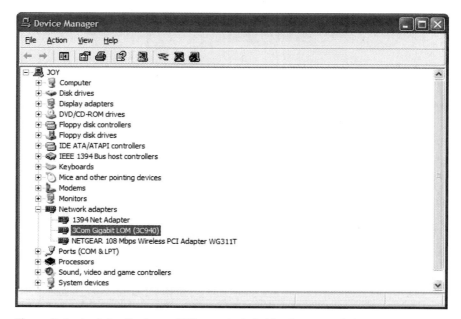

Figure 8-6   Look for the type of Ethernet included in the name of the NIC

▲ *The processor.* Your motherboard supports a fixed group of processors, and there might be room for improvement. For example, many motherboards can hold a Celeron processor or a Pentium 4. If a slow and less powerful Celeron is installed, you might see improvement if you replace it with a Pentium 4. Don't upgrade the processor unless you know what you're doing. They're delicate and easily damaged when you handle them. And if you don't install the right processor in the right slot, you can do damage. To know what processor you have, use the System Properties window. To know what processors your motherboard can support, see the motherboard user guide.

▲ *The motherboard.* Yes, you can upgrade the motherboard, which is the large board inside the computer case to which everything connects, but it's the most complicated of all upgrades, and might not be worth the effort. The two most important measures of the power of your motherboard are the processors it supports and its system bus speed (also called the front side bus or FSB speed). See the motherboard documentation to know these values. Upgrading the motherboard is a difficult upgrade that you should not tackle unless you are an experienced technician. If you upgrade the motherboard, you might be forced to upgrade the processor, memory, and maybe the power supply and case, because they must all be compatible with the motherboard. By the time you've paid for all that, you probably should just buy a new system.

▲ *Expansion cards.* If your motherboard has many onboard components, you might be able to free up some resources by installing an expansion card to replace the onboard components. For example, if a system is using a video port coming directly off the motherboard, consider disabling this port and installing a video card.

▲ *Parallel ATA configuration.* If your hard drive is sharing a parallel ATA data cable with another device, move the device to the secondary parallel ATA cable. Making the hard drive the only device on the primary parallel ATA cable can sometimes dramatically improve performance.

▲ *Operating system.* This book assumes you have Windows XP installed. However, if you're still running Windows 98, Windows Me, or Windows 2000, upgrading to Windows XP can really boost performance—assuming, of course, that your computer meets the recommended requirements for XP. Microsoft recommends a Pentium III 300 MHz or better, 128 MB of RAM or more, and 2 GB or more of free hard drive space. But, frankly, if you install XP on a system like that, don't expect it to have much power.

▲ *Planning for Windows Vista.* At the time of this writing, Windows Vista has not yet been released, but many of us will want to upgrade to Vista once it's available for consumer purchase. As you think about what to upgrade, you might want to consider making your system ready for Vista. Final system requirements for Vista have not been announced. However, Microsoft has said to expect that Windows Vista will require at least 512 MB of RAM and a modern processor (CPU), and Microsoft "strongly recommends" a video controller that has a DirectX 9 class graphics processor unit (GPU). Intel says that a "modern CPU" that can run Windows Vista is one that has Hyper-Threading Technology and uses the 945G or higher chipset. That's a pretty modern CPU. As for the video card, most likely this requirement means you'll need a high-end graphics card rather than onboard video, although Microsoft says that Vista will still work without it; you just won't see all the display features of Vista.

ADDING NEW COMPONENTS

Besides improving overall performance, another reason to upgrade is to add new functionality. Some additions are easier and less expensive than others. Here are some guidelines to keep in mind as you make decisions about adding new components to your system:

- ◢ If your computer is over five years old, it's probably too old for serious upgrading. Except for the least expensive upgrades, you're better off just starting over.
- ◢ Is the new component compatible with your system? For example, are the standards supported by your new hard drive also supported by your older motherboard? If not, the drive will not run at the higher speeds that you've paid for. Because most components connect to the motherboard, you can read your motherboard user manual to know what standards your motherboard supports. If you don't have the user manual, you can download one from the Web site of the motherboard manufacturer. How do you know what motherboard you have? One way is to use SiSoftware Sandra. In the Sandra main window, click the **Hardware** tab and then double-click **Mainboard** (see Figure 8-7).

Figure 8-7 Use SiSoftware Sandra to find out the manufacturer and model of your motherboard

Another way is to open the computer case and look for the information imprinted somewhere in the middle of the board. Look for the name of the motherboard manufacturer and the model number of the board. See Figure 8-8.

- ◢ If you plan to use a USB device, you should know that USB has two grades: original USB (also called USB 1.1) and Hi-Speed USB (also called USB 2.0). The labels that appear on products that use each standard are shown in Figure 8-9. If a device needs Hi-Speed USB, be sure your computer USB port is a Hi-Speed USB port. The ports look the same and they are interchangeable, although if you install a Hi-Speed USB device into an original USB port, the device will run at the slower speed. To know what kind of USB port your computer has, open Device Manager and expand the information on

Model

Manufacturer

Figure 8-8 Look for the manufacturer and model of a motherboard imprinted somewhere on the board

Figure 8-9 Hi-Speed and Original USB logos appear on products certified by the USB Implementer's Forum

your USB controller (see Figure 8-10). The original USB controller shows up as "Standard Universal" and the USB 2.0 controller shows up as "Standard Enhanced". If you see both types, then you have USB 2.0. If your motherboard doesn't support USB, you can add an expansion card to provide Hi-Speed and/or original USB ports.

◢ Be sure you match a FireWire device to the type of FireWire your system supports. FireWire currently has two grades, FireWire 400 (also known as 1394a) and FireWire 800 (also known as 1394b). The ports look different and they are not interchangeable unless you use special cables or converters. FireWire 400 (1394a) uses a 4-pin or 8-pin connector, and FireWire 800 (1394b) uses a 9-pin connector. FireWire 800 is a good choice for high-speed devices such as an external hard drive. Figure 8-11 shows an expansion card that you can add to a computer so that your computer has two FireWire 800 ports and one FireWire 400 port.

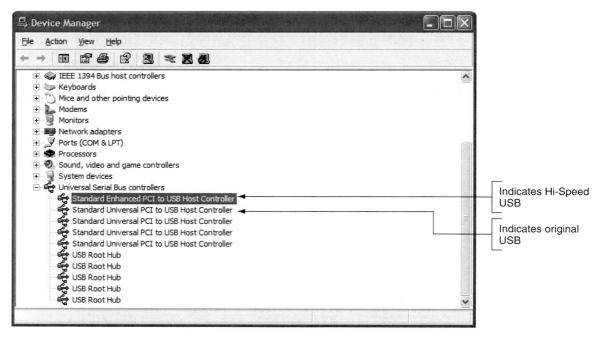

Figure 8-10 Use Device Manager to know what type of USB ports you have

Figure 8-11 This FireWire adapter card provides two FireWire 800 ports and one FireWire 400 port and uses a PCI expansion slot

▲ Before you add a component, verify the computer system has the power to handle it. Is there enough hard drive space and memory? Is the processor fast enough? Does the power supply have enough extra power for an internal component?

▲ Don't buy a component that is overly expensive for your system. For example, installing a really expensive video card into a Pentium III system with a 15-inch CRT monitor just doesn't make sense. Install a low-end video card in a low-end system to be used with a low-end monitor.

▲ Don't pay extra for standards your system does not support. For example, if your motherboard only supports AGP x4, installing an AGP x8 video card will work, but you're wasting your money on the high-end video card, because it will only run at the AGP x4 speed. The same is true when installing a hard drive that uses an expensive standard the motherboard does not support.

▲ Sometimes you have a choice between an internal component and an external one. For example, if you want to be able to watch TV on your desktop computer, you can use an external device (see Figure 8-12) that plugs into your USB port, or you can install a TV tuner card inside your case (see Figure 8-13). An external device usually costs more than an internal device, but the advantages of an external device are the installation is easier and you can easily move the device from one computer to another.

Figure 8-12   Use this USB device to watch TV on your desktop or notebook computer and capture video and stills

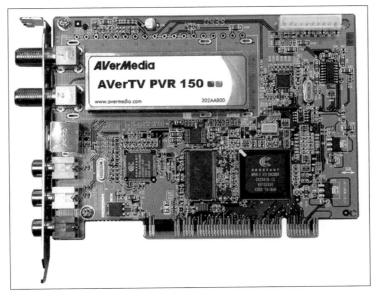

Figure 8-13   The AVerTV video capture and TV tuner card by AVerMedia uses a PCI slot and works alongside a regular video card.

◢ Don't add so many expensive internal components that you over-upgrade your system. Maybe a new computer is in order. As a rule of thumb, don't upgrade your system if the total cost of the upgrade exceeds half the value of your present system. Another rule of thumb: To determine the value of your system, multiply 0.7 by the price you paid for it one time for every year you've owned it. For example, if you paid $2,000 for a system that you've owned for three years, its current value is around $686 (calculated as 2,000 x .7 x .7 x .7).

If you've spent a little time browsing the Web for computer parts or browsing a local well-stocked computer store, you know there are a lot of variations in all the latest computer devices. Before you buy, do your homework. Shop around and also read some hardware reviews on the Web. I've found it's worth my money to pay more for a component that is made by a well-known and reputable company and gets good reviews than to save money upfront on less-expensive devices. The extra money is worth my time saved with installation problems and down time.

HOW TO WORK INSIDE A COMPUTER CASE

Before we get into how to upgrade components inside the computer case, let's take a quick look at how to work inside a computer without doing damage and how to open a computer case.

PROTECT COMPONENTS AGAINST STATIC ELECTRICITY

One of the biggest threats to components inside the case is static electricity (also called ESD for electrostatic discharge). For example, if there is a static charge between you and a memory module and you touch the module, you can fry it with even so small an amount of static electricity that you can't even feel or see the spark.

Whenever you touch a component inside a computer case, always protect your computer against static electricity. You can do that by connecting a static ground strap to your arm and the case (see Figure 8-14). If you don't have one, at least touch the side of the case

Figure 8-14 When working inside a computer case, always unplug the power cord and use a static ground bracelet between you and the computer case

before you touch anything inside the case. This causes the static electricity between you and the case to dissipate before you touch a component.

HOW TO OPEN A COMPUTER CASE

To open a computer case and work inside a computer, you'll need a Phillips-head screwdriver, a flat-head screwdriver, paper, and a pen. Do the following:

1. Power down the system and unplug the power cord. If you like, you can also unplug the monitor, mouse, keyboard, and any other peripherals or cables attached and move them out of your way.

2. Removing the cover of a computer case is different for different type cases. For newer tower cases, you first remove the panel on the front of the tower. Other cases require you remove a side panel first, and really older cases require you first remove the entire sides and top as a single unit. Study your case for the correct approach.

3. If you don't see screws on the rear edges of a tower case, you can assume the front panel is removed first. Look for a lever on the bottom of the front panel and hinges at the top. Squeeze the lever to release the front panel and lift it off the case (see Figure 8-15).

Figure 8-15   Newer cases require you to remove the front panel before removing the side panels of a computer case

Then remove any screws as necessary (in the computer shown in Figure 8-16, there is only a single screw) and slide the side panel to the front and then off the case. Also, know that some case panels don't use screws; these side panels simply pop up and out with a little prying and pulling.

4. If you're working on a tower case, lay it on its side so the motherboard is on the bottom.

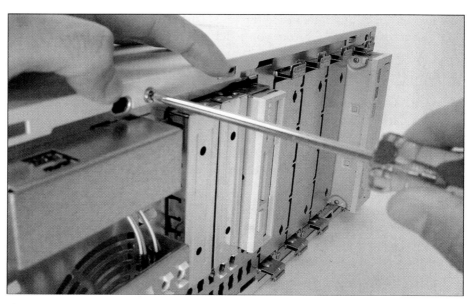

Figure 8-16 Remove any screws holding the side panel in place

5. If you find screws on the rear of the case along the edges, such as those in the desktop or tower cases in Figure 8-17, start with removing these screws. Look for the screws in each corner and down the sides. Be careful not to unscrew any screws besides these. The other screws are probably holding the power supply in place (see Figure 8-18).

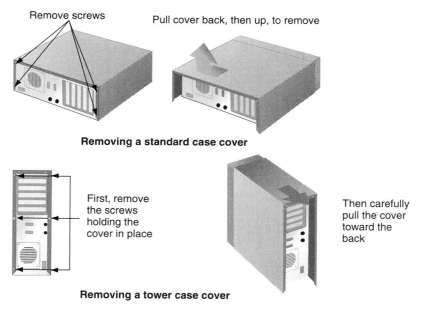

Figure 8-17 Removing the cover

6. After you remove the cover screws, slide the cover forward and up to remove it from the case, as shown in Figure 8-17. For tower cases, remove the screws and then slide the cover back slightly before lifting it up to remove it (see Figure 8-19).

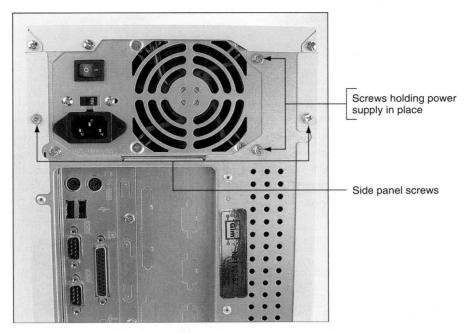

Figure 8-18 Power supply mounting screws

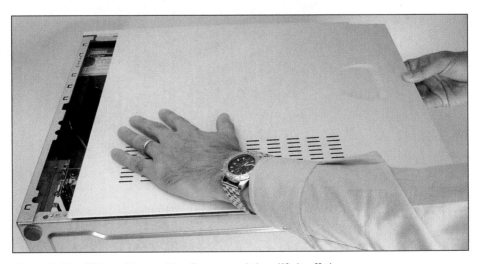

Figure 8-19 Slide a side panel to the rear and then lift it off the case

HOW TO UPGRADE MEMORY

To upgrade memory means to add more RAM to a computer. Adding more RAM might solve a problem with slow performance, applications refusing to load, or an unstable system. When Windows does not have adequate memory to perform an operation, it gives an "Insufficient memory" error.

When first purchased, many computers have empty memory slots on the motherboard, allowing you to add memory modules to increase the amount of RAM. If all memory slots are full, you can remove a memory module that has a small amount of RAM and replace it with one that has more RAM; however, in doing so, the cost of the upgrade increases.

In this section, you'll learn about memory modules, how much and what kind of memory to buy, and how to install it.

MEMORY MODULE PRIMER

Memory (also called RAM or random access memory) is installed on a motherboard on small circuit boards called memory modules. The two groups of memory modules used today are RIMMs (mostly outdated technology but occasionally you still see them) and DIMMs (most popular modules). (An older type of memory module called a SIMM is seldom used today.) Figure 8-20 shows a DIMM module installed on a motherboard. Notice in the figure, there are four DIMM slots, but only one of them is used. Plenty of room for upgrade on this motherboard.

DDR2 DIMM

Three empty
DIMM slots for
additional RAM

Figure 8-20   Memory installed on a motherboard as a DIMM module

A motherboard is designed to support a particular DIMM or RIMM technology. When upgrading memory, the trick is to buy the module that the motherboard can support and use modules that match up with modules already installed. Figure 8-21 shows the several types of DIMMs and RIMMs that might be installed in a desktop system.

RIMM MEMORY

Most likely your computer is using some type of DIMM (used in desktops) or SO-DIMM (a Small-Outline DIMM used in notebooks) memory, but just in case you have an older computer with RIMMs installed, here's the minimum of what you need to know about this technology:

- ◢ In memory ads, a RIMM module is sometimes called Rambus memory after the organization that designed the technology.
- ◢ RIMMs are more expensive than DIMMs, so expect a RIMM upgrade to cost more than a DIMM upgrade.

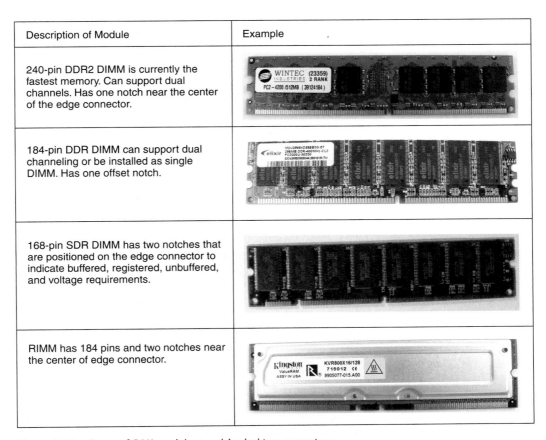

Description of Module	Example
240-pin DDR2 DIMM is currently the fastest memory. Can support dual channels. Has one notch near the center of the edge connector.	
184-pin DDR DIMM can support dual channeling or be installed as single DIMM. Has one offset notch.	
168-pin SDR DIMM has two notches that are positioned on the edge connector to indicate buffered, registered, unbuffered, and voltage requirements.	
RIMM has 184 pins and two notches near the center of edge connector.	

Figure 8-21   Types of RAM modules used in desktop computers

⊿ If a memory slot on a RIMM motherboard is not populated with a RIMM, it must have a blank module installed called a C-RIMM (see Figure 8-22). When adding new RIMMs, you remove the C-RIMM and put a RIMM in its place. RIMMs can run at internal speeds of 800 MHz to 1600 MHz.

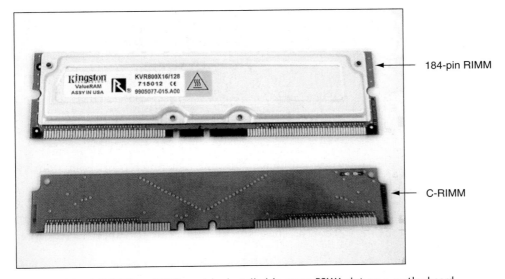

184-pin RIMM

C-RIMM

Figure 8-22   A C-RIMM or RIMM must be installed in every RIMM slot on a motherboard

Now let's turn our attention to understanding the different variations of DIMM technologies so you'll know what it is you're looking for when matching DIMMs to your motherboard.

DIMM TECHNOLOGIES

There are several variations of DIMMs. DIMMs are rated by speed, the amount of memory they hold, and whether they have memory chips on one side (single-sided) or both sides (double-sided) of the module. DIMMs have 168, 184, or 240 pins on the edge connector of the module and hold from 8 MB to 2 GB of RAM. Here are the important facts about DIMM modules that you need to know to select the right ones:

▲ *SDRAM DIMM (synchronous dynamic RAM DIMM)*. These early DIMMs, called SDRAM (pronounced "S-D-Ram"), use 168 pins and have two notches on the edge connector and run in sync with the motherboard. The two notches are placed on the module in different positions to indicate the technology the DIMM uses and to keep you from inserting the wrong module in a memory slot. Figure 8-23 shows these notch keys. The left key indicates different ways data is buffered on the module and the right key is used to indicate the voltage the module uses.

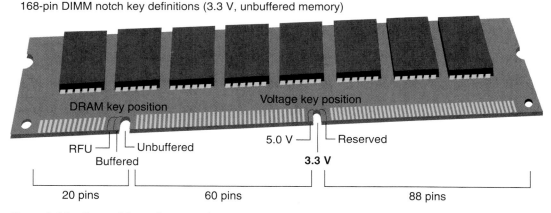

Figure 8-23 The positions of two notches on a DIMM identify the type of DIMM and the voltage requirement and also prevent the wrong type from being installed on the motherboard

▲ *DDR DIMMs (DDR stands for double data rate)*. DDR DIMMs run twice as fast as earlier DIMMs and use 184 pins. These modules have one notch offset from the center of the module.
▲ *DDR2 SDRAM*. DDR2 DIMMs are the latest type of DIMMs and run twice as fast as DDR, use less power, and have 240 pins. The notch is offset in a different position than DDR DIMMs.

When selecting DIMMs, you need to be aware of some specifications supported by the DIMM and the motherboard. These specifications can also apply to RIMMs:

▲ *Dual channeling*. A motherboard might support dual channels, which means the motherboard can communicate with two DIMMs at the same time, effectively doubling the speed of memory access. For dual channeling to work, the pair of DIMMs in a channel must be equally matched in size, speed, and features, and it is recommended they come from the same manufacturer. The motherboard shown previously in Figure 8-20 uses two dual channels. The two DIMM slots for one channel are yellow, and the two slots for the other channel are black. For dual channeling to work, matching DIMMs must be installed in the yellow slots, and, if either of the black slots is used, they, too, must have a matching pair of two DIMMs, although this pair does not have to match the first pair in size.

▲ *Error checking.* A motherboard might support error checking (also called ECC or error-correcting code) to help assure the integrity of data. Some SDRAM, DDR, DDR2, and RIMM memory modules support ECC. To use ECC, a module needs extra chips and costs more. You'll see memory advertised as ECC memory or non-ECC memory.

▲ *Registered memory.* A motherboard might support registers, which is a type of buffering. Memory modules are advertised as registered memory or unbuffered memory. Registered memory is faster and more expensive than the unbuffered kind.

▲ *CAS or RAS Latency.* Two other memory features are CAS Latency (CAS stands for "column access strobe") and RAS Latency (RAS stands for "row access strobe"), which are measures of how many clock cycles are used to read or write a column or row of data. The fewer the better. In memory ads, CAS Latency is sometimes written as CL, and RAS Latency might be written as RL. Ads for memory modules sometimes give the CL value within a series of timing numbers, such as 5-5-5-15. The first value is CL, which means the module is CL5. The second value is RL.

▲ *Tin or gold.* Module edge connectors are made of tin or gold.

▲ *Memory speed.* The speed of an SDRAM DIMM, DDR DIMM, DDR2 DIMM, or RIMM is measured in MHz. A DDR module is often described with its speed in the name, such as DDR266 for a DDR running at 266 MHz, or DDR333 for a DDR running at 333 MHz. Sometimes the DIMM or RIMM speed is measured in a PC rating. You can get a rough estimate of the speed if you divide the PC rating by eight. For example, if the PC rating is PC6400, the MHz rating is roughly 800 MHz. Current PC ratings are PC1600 (200 MHz), PC2100 (266 MHz), PC2700 (333 MHz), PC3200 (400 MHz), PC 4000 (500 MHz), PC 4200 (533 MHz), PC 5300 (667 MHz), and PC 6400 (800 MHz).

▲ *Amount of RAM.* Each memory module is rated as to the amount of memory it holds, measured in MB or GB. A motherboard is designed to support only certain amounts of memory installed in a certain set of module configurations.

NOTEBOOK MEMORY

Smaller versions of DIMMs and RIMMs, called SO-DIMMs and SO-RIMMs, are used in notebook computers. (SO stands for "small outline.") Figure 8-24 shows notebook memory modules.

Description of Module	Example
2.66" 200-pin SO-DIMM contains DDR2 SDRAM	
2.66" 200-pin SO-DIMM contains DDR SDRAM	
2.66" 144-pin SO-DIMM contains SDRAM. One notch is slightly offset from the center of the module.	
2.35" 72-pin SO-DIMMs are outdated. They have no notch on the edge connector.	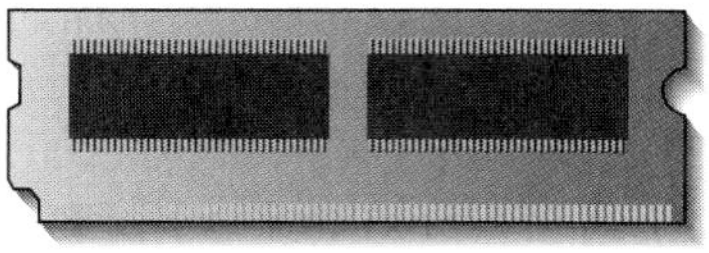 2.35" 72-pin SO-DIMM
160-pin SO-RIMM contains Rambus memory and has two notches.	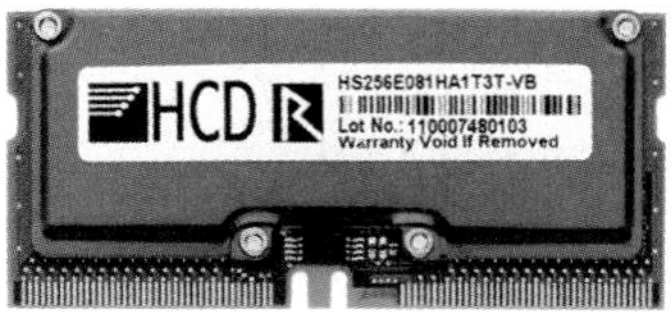

Figure 8-24 Types of RAM modules used in notebook computers

HOW MUCH AND WHAT KIND OF MEMORY TO BUY

Now that you have an understanding of the different memory technologies, you're ready to learn how to decide how much memory and what kind of memory to buy. When you add more memory to your computer, ask yourself these questions:

- ◢ How much memory do I need?
- ◢ How much RAM is currently installed in my system?
- ◢ How many and what kind of memory modules are currently installed on my motherboard?
- ◢ How much and what kind of memory can I fit on my motherboard?
- ◢ How do I select and purchase the right memory for my upgrade?

All these questions are answered in the following sections.

HOW MUCH MEMORY DO I NEED?

Because today's software places so many demands on memory, the answer is probably: "All you can get." The minimum requirement for Windows XP is 64 MB of RAM in order to install (not necessarily run) the OS. But for adequate performance, install 256 MB or more into a Windows XP system. I have 512 MB of RAM installed on my Windows XP desktop PC, which gives me good performance.

HOW MUCH MEMORY IS CURRENTLY INSTALLED?

To determine how much memory your Windows system has, you can use the Properties window of My Computer, which you saw earlier in the chapter.

HOW MANY AND WHAT KIND OF MEMORY MODULES ARE CURRENTLY INSTALLED?

The next step to upgrading memory is to determine what type of memory the motherboard is currently using and how many memory slots are used. In this section, we also take into consideration that you might be dealing with a motherboard that has no memory currently installed. If the board already has memory installed, you want to do your best to match the new memory with whatever is already installed. To learn what memory is already installed, do the following:

- Open the case and look at the memory slots. How many slots do you have? How many are filled? Remove each module from its slot and look on it for imprinted type, size, and speed. For example, a module might say "PC2-4200/512MB". The PC2 tells you the memory is DDR2; the 4200 is the PC rating and tells you the speed (533 MHz), and the 512MB is the size. This is not enough information to know exactly what memory to purchase, but it's a start.
- Examine the module for the physical size and position of the notches. Compare the notch positions to those in Figures 8-21 and 8-23.
- Read your motherboard documentation. If the documentation is not clear (and some is not) or you don't have the documentation, look on the motherboard for an imprint of its manufacturer and model. With this information, you can search a good memory Web site such as Kingston (*www.kingston.com*) or Crucial (*www.crucial.com*), which can tell you what memory this board supports.
- If you still have not identified the memory type, you can take the motherboard and the old memory modules to a good computer parts store and they should be able to match it for you.

HOW MUCH AND WHAT KIND OF MEMORY CAN FIT ON MY MOTHERBOARD?

Now that you know what memory is already installed, you're ready to decide how much and what kind of memory modules you can add to the board. Keep in mind that if all memory slots are full, sometimes you can take out small-capacity modules and replace them with larger-capacity modules, but you can only use the type, size, and speed of modules that the board is designed to support. Also, if you must discard existing modules, the price of the upgrade increases.

To know how much memory your motherboard can physically hold, read the documentation that comes with the board. For example, a Pentium motherboard might use 168-pin DIMM modules, and the documentation says to use unbuffered, 3.3V, PC100 DIMM SDRAM modules. Three DIMM sockets are on the board. Figure 8-25 shows the possible combinations of DIMMs that can be installed in these sockets.

Let's look at one more example of a DIMM installation in a desktop computer. The motherboard is the Asus P4P800 shown in Figure 8-26. The board allows you to use three different speeds of DDR DIMMs in one to four sockets on the board.

The board supports dual channeling. Looking carefully at the photo in Figure 8-26, you can see two blue memory sockets and two black sockets. The two blue sockets use one channel and the two black sockets use a different channel. For dual channeling to work, matching DIMMs must be installed in the two blue sockets. If two DIMMs are installed in the two black sockets, they must match each other.

DIMM Location	168-Pin DIMM		Total Memory
Socket 1 (Rows 0 & 1)	SDRAM 8, 16, 32, 64, 128, 256 M B	×1	
Socket 2 (Rows 2 & 3)	SDRAM 8, 16, 32, 64, 128, 256 M B	×1	
Socket 3 (Rows 4 & 5)	SDRAM 8, 16, 32, 64, 128, 256 M B	×1	
	Total System Memory (Max 768 MB)	=	

Figure 8-25 This table is part of the motherboard documentation and is used to show possible DIMM sizes and calculate total memory on the motherboard

Figure 8-26 This motherboard uses DDR DIMMs and supports dual channeling

This board supports up to 4 GB of unbuffered 184-pin non-ECC memory running at PC3200, PC2700, or PC2100. The documentation says the system bus can run at 800 MHz, 533 MHz, or 400 MHz, depending on the speed of the processor installed. Therefore, the speed of the processor determines the system bus speed, which determines the speed of memory modules you can install.

Figure 8-27 outlines the possible configurations of these DIMM modules, showing that you can install one, two, or four DIMMs, and which sockets should hold these DIMMs.

In order to take advantage of dual channeling on this motherboard, you must populate the sockets according to Figure 8-27, so that identical DIMM pairs are working together in DIMM_A1 and DIMM_B1 sockets (the blue sockets), and another pair can work together in DIMM_A2 and DIMM_B2 sockets (the black sockets).

This motherboard has two installed DDR DIMMs. The label on one of these DIMMs is shown in Figure 8-28. The important items on this label are the size (256 MB), the

> **Notes**
>
> As you can see, the motherboard documentation is essential when selecting memory. If you can't find the motherboard manual, look on the motherboard manufacturer's Web site.

Mode		Sockets			
		DIMM_A1	DIMM_A2	DIMM_B1	DIMM_B2
Single-channel	(1)	Populated	—	—	—
	(2)	—	Populated	—	—
	(3)	—	—	Populated	—
	(4)	—	—	—	Populated
Dual-channel*	(1)	Populated	—	Populated	—
	(2)	—	Populated	—	Populated
	(3)	Populated	Populated	Populated	Populated

*Use only identical DDR DIMM pairs

Figure 8-27   Motherboard documentation shows that one, two, or four DIMMs can be installed

Figure 8-28   Use the label on this DIMM to identify its features

speed (400 MHz or 3200 PC rating), and the CAS Latency (CL3). With this information and knowledge about what the board can support, we are now ready to select and buy the memory for the upgrade. For example, if you decide to upgrade the system to 1 GB of memory, you would buy two DDR, 400 MHz, CL3 DIMMs that support dual channeling. For best results, you also need to match the manufacturer and buy Elixir memory.

For most notebook computers, you can easily access the memory modules by removing a faceplate on the bottom of the notebook. First unplug the power cord and remove the battery. For the notebook shown in Figure 8-29, turn the notebook upside down and remove the screws and the panel cover to expose the modules. Look for an empty SO-DIMM slot and install in it memory that matches the SO-DIMM already installed. If both SO-DIMM slots are full, you can replace a SO-DIMM with a larger capacity one. Fortunately, replacing memory on most newer notebooks is as easy as this. But always check the notebook user guide for specific directions.

HOW DO I SELECT AND PURCHASE THE RIGHT MEMORY?

You're now ready to make the purchase. When purchasing memory from a Web site such as Crucial Technology's site (*www.crucial.com*) or Kingston Technology's site (*www.kingston.com*), look for a search utility that will match memory modules to your motherboard (see Figure 8-30). These utilities are easy to use and help you confirm you have made the right decisions about type, size, and speed to buy. They can also help if motherboard documentation is inadequate, and you're not exactly sure what memory to buy.

Figure 8-29   To access memory modules, remove a panel cover on the bottom of the notebook

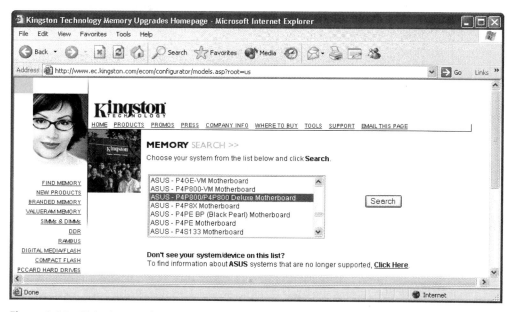

Figure 8-30   Web sites used to purchase memory, such as this Kingston site, often provide search utilities to help you select the right memory modules for your motherboard

Let's look at one example. Suppose we're looking for DDR, 400 MHz, CL3, unbuffered DIMMs for a dual channeled motherboard. We want to install 256 MB of RAM, so we need two 128 MB modules. Figure 8-31 shows the Crucial Web site where I found that match. It's the last item in the list.

> **Notes**
>
> In memory ads, if you see x64 in the ad for a DIMM or 16 in the product code for a RIMM, then the module is non-ECC memory. If you see x74 in the ad for a DIMM or 18 in the product code for a RIMM, then the module is ECC memory.

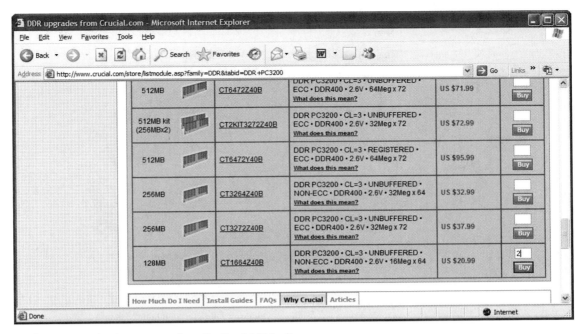

Figure 8-31 Selecting memory from the Crucial Web site

INSTALLING MEMORY

When installing RAM modules, remember to protect the chips against static electricity. Follow these precautions:

- ◢ Always use a ground bracelet as you work.
- ◢ Turn off the power and remove the cover to the case.
- ◢ Handle memory modules with care.
- ◢ Usually modules pop into place easily and are secured by spring catches on both ends. Make sure that you look for the notches on one side or in the middle of the module that orient the module in the slot.

For DIMM modules, small latches on each side of the slot hold the module in place, as shown in Figure 8-32. To install a DIMM, first pull the supporting arms on the sides of the slot outward. Look on the DIMM edge connector for the notches, which help you orient the DIMM correctly over the slot, and insert the DIMM straight down into the slot. When the DIMM is fully inserted, the supporting arms should pop back into place. Figure 8-33 shows a DIMM being inserted into a slot on a motherboard.

After you've installed the DIMMs, close the case and turn on your PC. It should boot up and recognize the new memory. You can watch it count up on the BIOS screen when you first turn on the PC. After the Windows desktop is loaded, use the System Properties window to verify the amount of installed memory. If not all memory is recognized or you get errors when you boot, don't panic! Most likely the module is not seated securely in its slot or you accidentally disconnected something as you were working inside the case. Turn off the PC, unplug it, and check your installation.

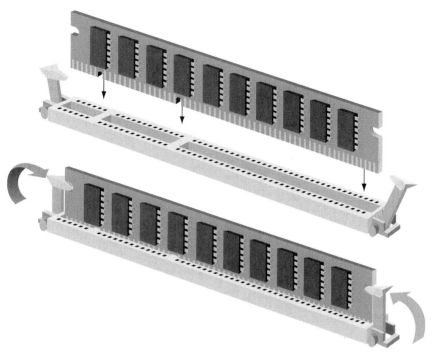

Figure 8-32   Installing a DIMM module

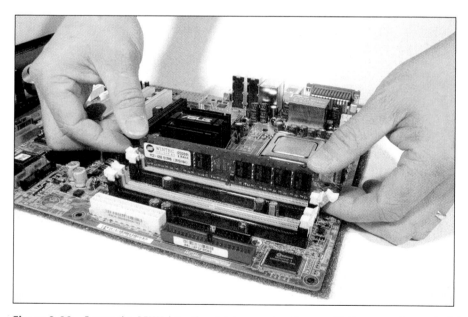

Figure 8-33   Insert the DIMM into the slot by pressing down until the support arms lock into position

HOW TO ADD A SECOND HARD DRIVE

If you find yourself running short of hard drive space, you can exchange your hard drive for a larger drive, or you can install a second hard drive. Exchanging your hard drive is a real chore because you'll have to reinstall Windows and all your software. It's a lot easier to add a second hard drive. This section discusses how to do that.

The simplest way to add a second hard drive is to use an external drive such as the one shown in Figure 8-34. Plug it in and turn it on. That's about it. External drives cost more, but then you can easily move them from one computer to another. Also, if you bring your office work home with you, it's a great way to carry large amounts of data with you.

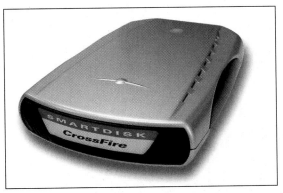

Figure 8-34 This CrossFire hard drive by SmartDisk holds 160 GB and uses a FireWire or USB connection

A less expensive solution is to install a second hard drive inside the computer case. For that to work, you'll need an empty bay and an unused parallel or serial ATA connector for the drive. This section explains how to install a second drive when your computer has the room.

DOES YOUR SYSTEM HAVE ROOM FOR A SECOND DRIVE?

Open the computer case and look for an empty bay that can hold your drive. A hard drive uses a narrow bay, but if all the narrow bays are full and a wide bay is available, you can buy a bracket assembly for a few dollars to make the narrow drive fit into the wider bay (see Figure 8-35). To prepare the drive for the large bay, screw a bracket to each side of the drive.

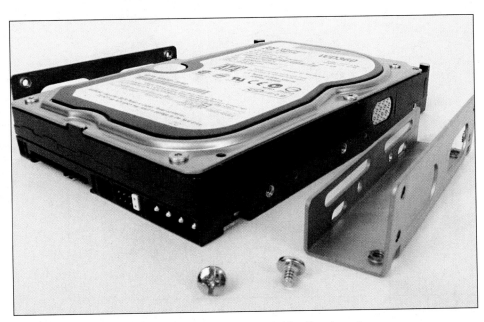

Figure 8-35 Use a universal bay kit to make a hard drive fit a large bay

Finding an available connector for your drive is a little more complicated. Hard drives can use the newer serial ATA (SATA) cable and connector like the drive in Figure 8-36, or they can use the parallel ATA (PATA) ribbon cable and connector like the drive in Figure 8-37. Serial ATA cables are small and usually red. Parallel ATA cables (also called IDE cables) are wider and have wide 40-pin connectors. The parallel ATA cable has a connector for one drive at the end of the cable and a connector for a second drive somewhere in the middle of the cable.

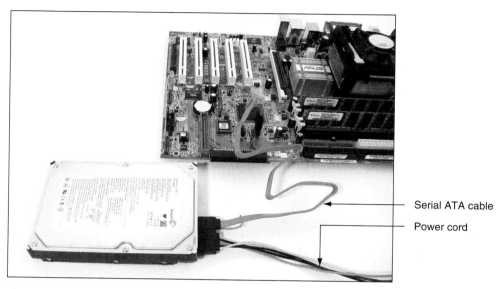

Figure 8-36   This hard drive uses a serial ATA interface to the motherboard

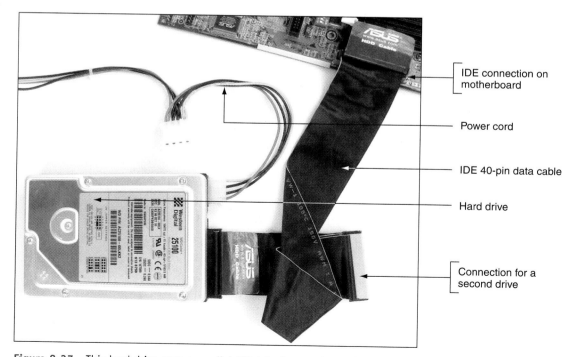

Figure 8-37   This hard drive uses a parallel ATA interface to the motherboard

To find the drive connectors on your motherboard, it helps to have a schematic of the motherboard, which will identify all the connectors on the board. The schematic like the one in Figure 8-38 is found in the motherboard user guide, on the Web site of the motherboard manufacturer, or might be pasted to the inside of the computer case cover. If you don't have that diagram, you can use the photographs in this chapter to identify the connectors.

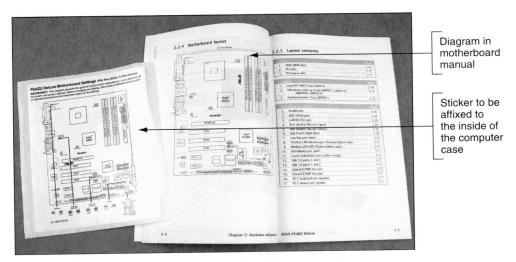

Figure 8-38 A diagram of the motherboard identifies all connectors

Using parallel ATA, an older motherboard will have two parallel ATA connectors (see Figure 8-39), and they're called the primary IDE and secondary IDE connectors. Each connector can have a ribbon cable connected to it that can hold one or two drives (see Figure 8-40). Drives that can use a parallel ATA connector are called EIDE drives and include hard drives, CD-ROM drives, DVD drives, and tape drives. For this type of setup, you can have up to four drives in the system. Verify you have one free parallel ATA connector available. Also make sure you've got a power connector available to power the drive.

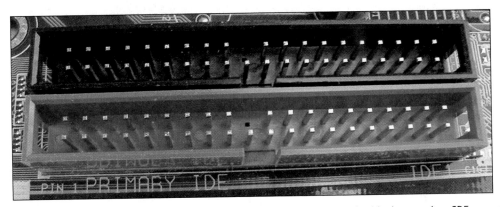

Figure 8-39 This motherboard has a blue primary IDE connector and a black secondary IDE connector

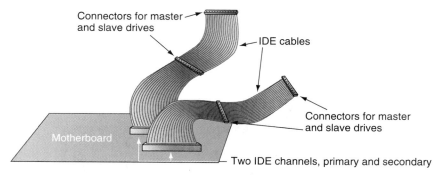

Figure 8-40 Up to four drives can be installed in a parallel ATA system

For motherboards that support serial ATA, the board will have one parallel ATA connector that can support up to two drives (hard drive or other type of drive) and two or four serial ATA connectors (see Figure 8-41). Each serial ATA connector supports a single drive (hard drive or other type of drive). Verify you have either a parallel or serial ATA connector available and a power cord to power the drive.

Figure 8-41 This motherboard has four serial ATA connectors. Use the red connectors first.

HOW TO SELECT A HARD DRIVE

When selecting a hard drive, buy one that matches the drive interface your motherboard supports. Here are the factors that affect performance, use, compatibility, and price:

- ◢ *The capacity of the drive.* Today's hard drives for desktop systems are in the range of 20 GB to more than 500 GB. The more gigabytes, the higher the price.
- ◢ *The type of interface.* Drives can use a parallel ATA ribbon cable interface or a serial ATA narrow cable interface.
- ◢ *The spindle speed.* Hard drives for desktop systems run at 5400, 7200, or 10,000 RPM. The most common are 5400 and 7200 RPM. 7200 RPM drives are faster, make more noise, put off more heat, and are more expensive than 5400 RPM drives.

8

▲ *The technology standard.* There are a bunch of hard drive ATA standards besides just parallel and serial ATA, and these standards go by a bunch of trade names that make them hard to sort out. But to keep things simple, most likely you're only going to have to choose between ATA/100 and ATA/133, which have to do with the transfer rate between the hard drive and the motherboard. Choose the one your motherboard supports.

▲ *The cache or buffer size.* Look for a 2 MB or 8 MB cache (also called a buffer). The more the better, though the cost goes up as the size increases.

▲ *The average seek time (time to fetch data).* Look for 13 to 8.5 ms (milliseconds). The lower the number, the higher the drive performance and cost.

When selecting a drive, match the drive to what your motherboard supports. To find out what hard drive standards the motherboard supports, you can check the motherboard documentation or the CMOS setup screen for information.

STEPS TO INSTALL A SECOND HARD DRIVE

To install a second hard drive, you need the drive, a serial ATA or parallel ATA data cable, and perhaps a kit to make the drive fit into a much larger bay.

> **Notes**
>
> For parallel ATA, be sure you have a newer grounded 80-conductor parallel ATA cable rather than the older 40-conductor cable. The 40-pin connectors look the same, but the 80-conductor cable has twice as many fine lines as the 40-conductor cable. For a comparison, see Figure 8-42.

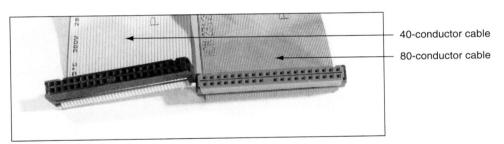

40-conductor cable
80-conductor cable

Figure 8-42   In comparing the 80-conductor cable to the 40-conductor cable, note they are about the same width, but the 80-conductor cable has many more and finer wires

Before you start the installation, do the following:

▲ Boot up the PC and verify that everything is working. Before you install a new device, it's important to know your starting point.

▲ Read the documentation that came with the drive and the section of your motherboard manual that pertains to hard drives. Make sure you've selected a compatible drive.

▲ Be sure to protect against static electricity by wearing a ground bracelet during the installation. You also need to avoid working on carpet in the winter when there's a lot of static electricity.

▲ Be sure to handle the drive carefully. It's delicate and can be damaged by bumps or static electricity.

STEP 1: SET THE JUMPERS

The rear of serial and parallel ATA drives has a set of jumpers, a connector for the power cord, and a connector for the data cable, all shown in Figure 8-43. For serial ATA drives, leave the jumpers on the rear of the drive untouched. They were set at the factory and never need to be changed. For parallel ATA drives, you must set jumpers on each drive sharing a parallel IDE ribbon cable so one drive is set to master (controls the data flow on the cable) and the other drive is set to slave (requests permission from the master drive to use the cable). If your drive is the only drive on the cable, set it to single. If your drive doesn't have that setting, set the drive to master. If it's sharing the cable, it's better to place the faster drive on the end of the cable and set it to master.

> **Notes**
>
> When a hard drive shares a parallel ATA data cable with a slower drive, hard drive performance is decreased. For best performance, install a hard drive as the only drive on a parallel ATA cable.

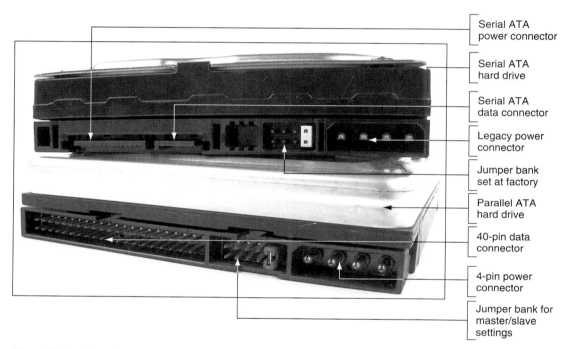

- Serial ATA power connector
- Serial ATA hard drive
- Serial ATA data connector
- Legacy power connector
- Jumper bank set at factory
- Parallel ATA hard drive
- 40-pin data connector
- 4-pin power connector
- Jumper bank for master/slave settings

Figure 8-43 Rear of a serial ATA drive and a parallel ATA drive

To know how to set the jumpers on your parallel ATA drive, look for a diagram of the jumper settings printed on the top of the hard drive housing, such as the one shown in Figure 8-44. In the key, the black rectangle represents a pair of pins with a jumper in place. Possible settings for this drive are master, slave, and single. If a drive is the only drive on a channel, set it to single. For two drives on a controller, set one to master and the other to slave.

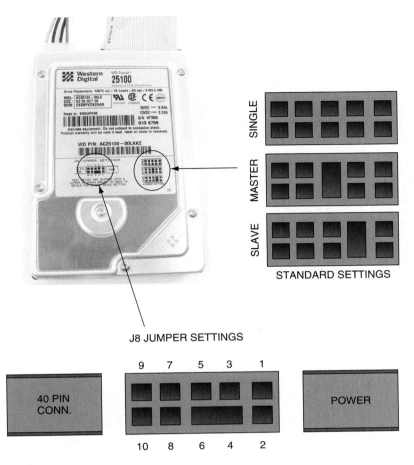

J8 JUMPER SETTINGS

MOST DRIVES ARE SHIPPED WITH A
JUMPER AS SHOWN ABOVE; NO NEED TO
REMOVE FOR SINGLE DRIVE SETTING

Figure 8-44 An ATA drive most likely will have diagrams of jumper settings for master and slave options printed on the drive housing

STEP 2: MOUNT THE DRIVE IN THE BAY

Now that you've set the jumpers, your next step is to look at the drive bay that you will use for the drive. The bay can be stationary or removable. With a removable bay, you first remove the bay from the computer case and mount the drive in the bay. Then you put the bay back into the computer case. In Figure 8-45, you can see a stationary wide bay for large drives and a removable narrow bay for small drives. One hard drive is installed in the narrow removable bay, and another hard drive is installed in a wide bay using brackets to make it fit.

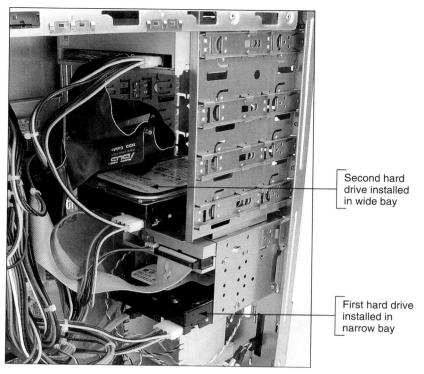

Second hard drive installed in wide bay

First hard drive installed in narrow bay

Figure 8-45 Two hard drives installed in a system

If you're using brackets so the drive will fit into a wide bay, slide the bracketed drive into the bay and secure it with two screws on both sides of the bay; for some bays, the brackets snap into place in the bay without using screws (see Figure 8-46). Make sure the drive is secure in the bay so it will not move even when the case is laid on its side.

Figure 8-46 Hard drive installed in a wide bay

If you're installing the drive in a removable bay, remove the bay, secure the drive in the bay with two screws on each side of the drive (see Figure 8-47), and reinstall the bay in the case (see Figure 8-48). A removable bay might be secured to the case with screws on the front or sides of the bay, and/or it might snap into place with a clipping mechanism.

Figure 8-47   Use four screws to secure each drive to the bay

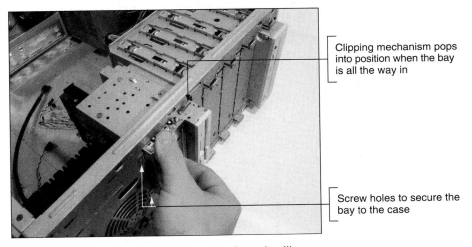

Clipping mechanism pops into position when the bay is all the way in

Screw holes to secure the bay to the case

Figure 8-48   Slide the bay into the case as far as it will go

STEP 3: CONNECT THE DATA CABLE AND POWER CORD

Next, connect the data cable. For a serial ATA drive, connect one end of the data cable to the drive and the other to the serial ATA connector. For a parallel ATA drive, the 80-conductor cable is color-coded (see Figure 8-49). Connect the blue end to the motherboard, the black connector to the single drive or master drive, and the gray connector to the second drive or slave drive. There's a missing pinhole on the connector so you can only insert it one way into a connector.

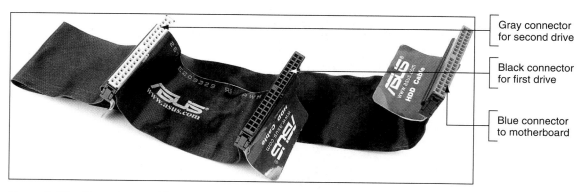

Figure 8-49 80-conductor cable connectors are color-coded

Gray connector for second drive

Black connector for first drive

Blue connector to motherboard

> ⚡ **Caution**
>
> A serial ATA drive might have two power connectors on the drive to accommodate different power connectors. Use only one power cord to the drive!

You can now install a power cord to the drive. It doesn't matter which power cord connector you use, as long as it fits. Figure 8-50 shows a power cord about to be connected to a DVD drive. A serial ATA hard drive on the right side of the photo also needs a power cord attached. Note that the power cord will only go in one way, so make sure you have it positioned correctly.

Figure 8-50 Connect a power cord to the drive

You're now finished with the physical part of the installation. Recheck all your connections, replace the cover, and turn on the PC.

STEP 4: USE CMOS SETUP TO VERIFY THE HARD DRIVE SETTINGS

When you first boot up after installing a hard drive, go to CMOS setup and verify that the drive has been recognized and that the settings are correct. CMOS setup reports and controls some basic hardware settings for the system and is independent of the OS. If CMOS setup does not recognize the new drive, then you have a hardware problem that must be solved before you move on to Windows.

To access CMOS setup, look for a message onscreen when you first turn on the PC that says "Press DEL for setup," "Press F8 for CMOS setup," "Press F2 to access setup," or something similar. When you press that key, you enter the CMOS setup utility stored on the motherboard. The menus are arranged differently for each type of BIOS utility. Look for a basic hardware screen that shows installed drives. For example, the CMOS setup screen in Figure 8-51 for one computer shows the drives listed on the Main screen. This computer has one parallel ATA connector and four serial ATA connectors. The parallel ATA connector has a CD/DVD drive connected as the Primary IDE Master. One hard drive shows up under Third IDE Master and the second drive shows as Fourth IDE Master. Both hard drives are using serial ATA connectors.

```
                          BIOS SETUP UTILITY
 Main  Advanced   Power    Boot    Exit

                                             While entering setup, BIOS
 System Time           [11:48:57]            auto detects the presence
 System Date           [Tue 03/07/2006]      of IDE devices. This
 Legacy Diskette A     [1.44M, 3.5 in.]      displays the status of
 Language              [English]             auto detection of IDE
                                             devices.

 ▶ Primary IDE Master   : [TSSTcorpCD/DVDW TS]
 ▶ Primary IDE Slave    : [Not Detected]
 ▶ Third IDE Master     : [WDC WD360GD-00FNA0]
 ▶ Third IDE Slave      : [Not Detected]
 ▶ Fourth IDE Master    : [WDC WD1200JD-00HBB]    ← →   Select Screen
 ▶ Fourth IDE Slave     : [Not Detected]          ↑ ↓   Select Item
 ▶ IDE Configuration                              Enter Go to Sub Screen
                                                  F1    General Help
 ▶ System Configuration                           F10   Save and Exit
                                                  ESC   Exit

              V02.53 (C)Copyright 1985-2002, American Megatrends, Inc.
```

Figure 8-51   CMOS setup screen shows the newly installed second hard drive

For the CMOS setup utility for another computer, the drive configuration is shown on the Advanced menu in Figure 8-52. Presently, only one hard drive is installed. This computer has two serial ATA (SATA) connectors and one parallel ATA connector. One serial connector is being used by a 40 GB hard drive. A CD-RW drive is using a parallel ATA cable connected to the parallel ATA connector. This system could accommodate a serial ATA drive that would

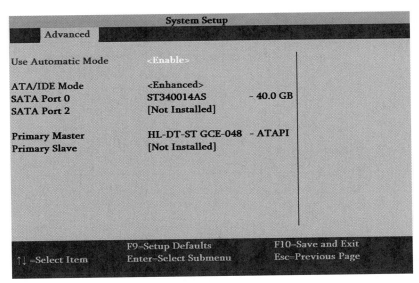

Figure 8-52   A CMOS setup screen with one hard drive and one CD-RW drive installed

use SATA Port 2 or a parallel ATA drive that would share the cable with the CD-RW drive. For best performance, it would be better to install a serial ATA drive, because a parallel ATA drive's performance is likely to be affected by having to share a parallel ATA cable with the CD-RW drive. Notice on this screen that Use Automatic Mode is enabled. This means the BIOS is set to automatically detect a new drive that is installed.

If you don't see your new drive, perhaps CMOS setup is not configured to automatically detect new drives. Look for a choice to turn on IDE HDD Auto Detection and reboot the PC. (This feature is shown in Figure 8-52 as "Automatic Mode".) The drive should then be recognized. If not, check your cable and power connections. After you verify the drive is recognized, allow it to boot to the Windows desktop and you're ready to partition and format the drive for first use.

STEP 5: USE WINDOWS XP DISK MANAGEMENT TO PARTITION AND FORMAT A NEW DRIVE

If you are installing a new hard drive in a system that is to be used for a new Windows installation, after you have physically installed the drive, boot from the Windows setup CD and follow the directions on the screen to install Windows on the new drive. The setup process partitions and formats the new drive before it begins the Windows installation. If you are installing a second hard drive in a system that already has Windows XP installed on the first hard drive, use Windows Disk Management to partition and format the second drive.

After you have reached the Windows desktop, do the following to partition and format your new drive:

1. In Control Panel, open the **Administrative Tools** applet. In that window, open the **Computer Management** console. In that console, click the **Disk Management** utility. (A shortcut to Disk Management is to enter **diskmgmt.msc** in the Run dialog box.) The Disk Management window is shown in Figure 8-53. In this window, the first hard drive shows up as Disk 0 and has one partition, logical drive C. The new drive is Disk 1.

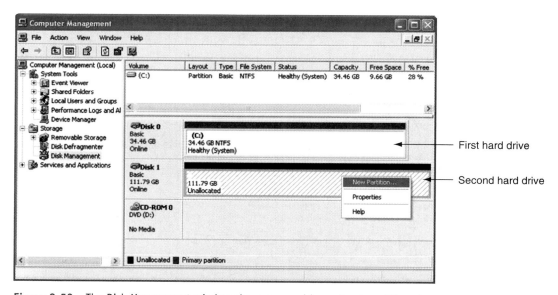

Figure 8-53 The Disk Management window shows a new drive not yet partitioned

2. Right-click the new drive and select **New Partition** from the shortcut menu. The New Partition Wizard launches. Click **Next**.

3. On the next screen, chose **Primary partition** and click **Next** (see Figure 8-54). A primary partition has only a single logical drive.

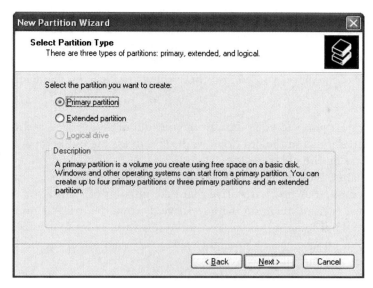

Figure 8-54   The first partition on a hard drive should be the primary partition

4. On the next screen, you can decide to include all the available space on the drive in this one partition or leave some for other partitions. Enter the amount of available space for this partition and click **Next**. On the next screens, you must decide the drive letter to be assigned to the logical drive, the file system (**NTFS** is the best choice), and the volume name. When the wizard finishes partitioning and formatting the drive, it will look similar to the drive shown in Figure 8-55.

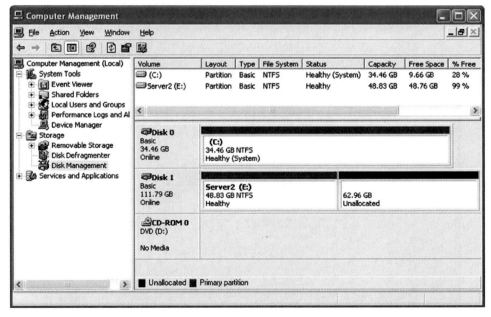

Figure 8-55   One partition created and formatted on the new hard drive

5. Make sure you can use the drive space by creating a folder in the new partition and copying some files to it.

Notes

A hard drive can have up to three primary partitions and one extended partition. Each primary partition can have only a single logical drive, but the extended partition can have several logical drives.

MAKING THE BEST USE OF A SECOND HARD DRIVE

If your new hard drive is faster than your current drive, consider reinstalling Windows on the faster drive for an overall performance increase. If you decide to leave Windows on your older drive, you can do these things to clear up some space on the Windows drive:

- Use Windows Explorer to copy data from your old drive to the new drive. After you've copied data from the old drive, verify it's accessible on the new drive and then delete the data on the old drive.
- In Control Panel, look in the Add or Remove Programs applet for software applications installed on your first hard drive that take up a lot of space. You can uninstall them and then reinstall them on the new drive. During the installation routine, you will be asked what folder to use to install the software. Point to a folder on the second hard drive. For convenience, you might want to create a folder on this drive called Program Files and put all software there.
- Windows XP uses a hidden file called Pagefile.sys for virtual memory. (Virtual memory is used by Windows in addition to RAM in order to have more memory available.) This file can be quite large and normally it is stored as a hidden file in the root directory of the drive on which Windows is installed. You can move the file to the largest partition on your second hard drive that has the most free space. (Pagefile.sys needs plenty of room so you don't choke off the virtual memory manager.) However, don't move the file if your second hard drive is sharing a parallel ATA cable with a slower CD drive—doing so could actually slow down your system. To change the location of Pagefile.sys, do the following:

1. Right-click **My Computer** and select **Properties** on the shortcut menu. The System Properties dialog box opens (see Figure 8-56). Click the **Advanced** tab. Under Performance, click **Settings**. The Performance Options dialog box opens.

2. Click the **Advanced** tab and then click the **Change** button. The Virtual Memory dialog box opens. In this dialog box, select the drive for the file. If you select more than one drive, the file will be spread over these drives.

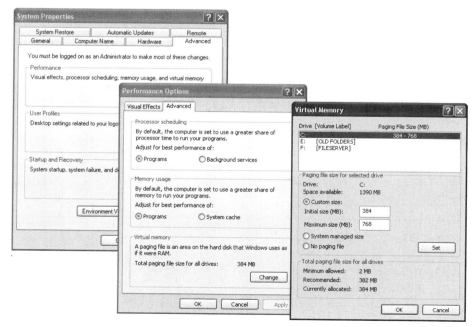

Figure 8-56 Use the System Properties dialog box to change page file settings

3. You can also move your Internet Explorer cache folder to the second hard drive. To do that, in Internet Explorer, click **Tools, Internet Options**. In the Internet Options window, click **Settings**. Then click **Move Folder** and point to your second drive.

HOW TO UPGRADE A HARD DRIVE ON A NOTEBOOK COMPUTER

Using a notebook computer, you don't have the space to add a second hard drive inside the notebook, but you can add an external drive using a USB or FireWire port. And, with newer notebook computers, you can easily replace a small drive with a larger drive. For example, to remove the IBM (now Lenovo) ThinkPad X20 hard drive, first power down the system and remove the battery pack. Then remove a coin screw that holds the drive in place (see Figure 8-57). Pull the drive out of its bay, and replace it with a new drive. Next, replace the screw and power up the system.

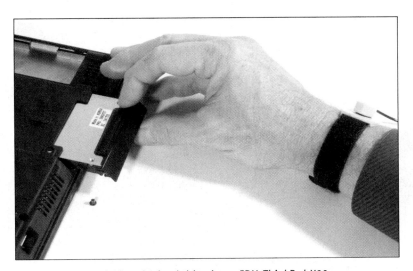

Figure 8-57   Replacing the hard drive in an IBM ThinkPad X20

When the system boots up, if CMOS setup is set to autodetect hard drives, BIOS recognizes the new drive and searches for an operating system. If the drive is new, boot from the Windows recovery CD that came from the notebook manufacturer and install the OS.

> **Notes**
>
> Here's a tip that can help you recover data when Windows will not boot: Install your hard drive as a second drive in a working computer and use Windows Explorer to copy data from your drive to the system's primary drive. This should work if your drive is not physically damaged and the partition table is intact. Recall that in Chapter 6, you saw a USB to ATA converter that you can use to connect the failing drive to the working computer using a USB port.

HOW TO INSTALL AN EXPANSION CARD

Expansion cards can be added to a system to provide extra ports on the rear of the computer case or internal ports inside the case so you can use a new technology not already supported by your system. In this section, you'll learn how to match expansion cards to the slots you have available on your motherboard and how to install an expansion card. We'll install a sound card and a video card as our two examples of installing expansion cards.

IDENTIFYING EXPANSION SLOTS

An expansion card is installed in an expansion slot on a motherboard, and the card must match the slot. The major groups of expansion slots used on today's motherboards are conventional PCI, PCI Express, and AGP. In this section, you'll see examples of all the slots and the cards that use them for today's desktop computers. (Two other types of slots are PCI-X and ISA, but ISA is out of date and PCI-X is mostly used on servers.)

CONVENTIONAL PCI

The first PCI slots had a 32-bit data path, supplied 5V of power to an expansion card, and operated at 33 MHz. Then PCI Version 2.x introduced the 64-bit, 3.3V PCI slot, doubling data throughput of the bus. Because a card can be damaged if installed in the wrong voltage slot, a notch in a PCI slot distinguishes between a 5V slot and a 3.3V slot. A Universal PCI card can use either a 3.3V or 5V slot and contains both notches (see Figure 8-58).

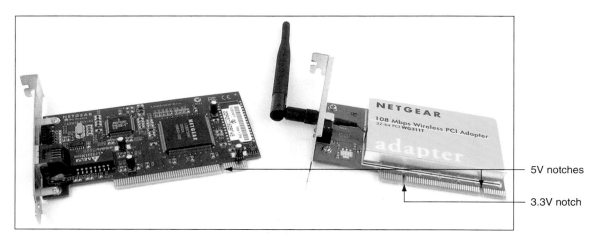

Figure 8-58 A 32-bit, 5V PCI network card and a 32-bit, universal PCI wireless card show the difference in PCI notches set to distinguish voltages in a PCI slot

Conventional PCI now has four types of slots and six possible PCI card configurations to use these slots (see Figure 8-59).

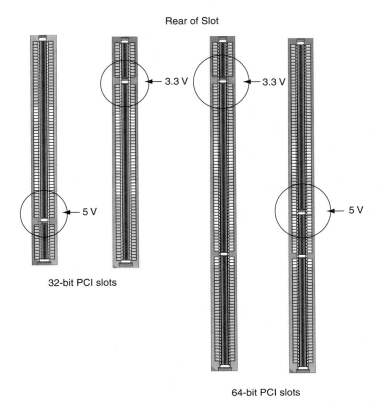

Rear of Slot

3.3 V   3.3 V

5 V   5 V

32-bit PCI slots

64-bit PCI slots

Figure 8-59   With PCI Version 2.x, there are four possible types of expansion slots and six differently configured PCI expansion cards to use these slots

PCI EXPRESS

PCI Express (PCIe) is the latest and fastest expansion slot, and PCI Express slots are not backward compatible with PCI. Motherboards that have PCI Express slots usually also have some PCI slots (see Figure 8-60). Whereas PCI uses a 32-bit or 64-bit parallel bus, PCI Express uses a serial bus, which is faster than a parallel bus and transmits data in packets, similar to Ethernet networks. All desktop motherboards today will have either a PCI Express slot or an AGP slot to be used by the video card. The fastest PCI Express slot is about twice as fast as the fastest AGP slot.

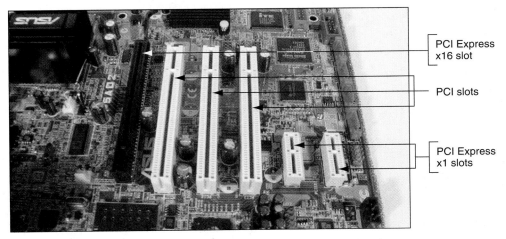

PCI Express x16 slot

PCI slots

PCI Express x1 slots

Figure 8-60   Three PCI Express slots and three PCI slots on a motherboard

PCI Express currently comes in four different slot sizes called PCI Express x1 (pronounced "by one"), x4, x8, and x16 (see Figure 8-61). PCI Express x16 is the fastest and is used for the video card slot. A shorter PCI Express card (such as a x1 card) can be installed in a longer PCI Express slot (such as a x4 slot).

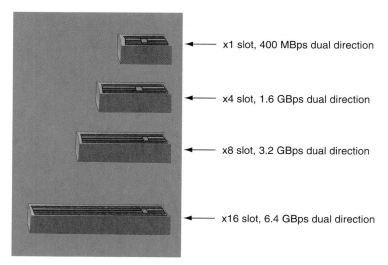

x1 slot, 400 MBps dual direction

x4 slot, 1.6 GBps dual direction

x8 slot, 3.2 GBps dual direction

x16 slot, 6.4 GBps dual direction

Figure 8-61 Current PCI Express slots

Figure 8-62 shows a PCI Express video card. Notice the tab next to the card's connectors that fits into a retention mechanism on the motherboard to help stabilize the card.

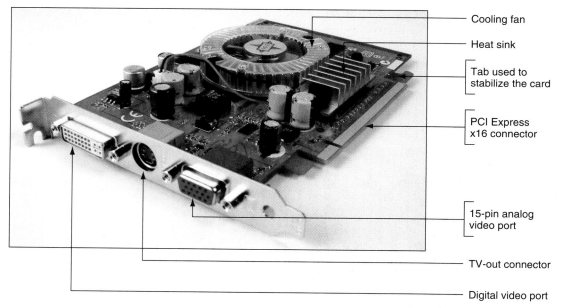

Cooling fan

Heat sink

Tab used to stabilize the card

PCI Express x16 connector

15-pin analog video port

TV-out connector

Digital video port

Figure 8-62 This PCX 5750 graphics card by MSI Computer Corporation uses a PCI Express x16 slot

AGP

AGP has evolved over the years, and the different AGP standards can be confusing. The major releases of AGP are AGP 1.0, 2.0, 3.0, and AGP Pro. Without getting into the details about these standards, here are the six different types of AGP slots, which you can see in Figure 8-63:

- ◢ *AGP 3.3V.* The notch in the slot is near the rear of the case. This is the oldest type of AGP slot used by 3.3V video cards, which you seldom see today.
- ◢ *AGP 1.5V.* The notch on this slot is near the center of the case. Only video cards that need 1.5 V will fit in this slot.
- ◢ *AGP Universal.* This slot has no notch and 1.5V or 3.3V video cards can use the slot. Notice in Figure 8-63, the AGP Universal slot is the same size as the two earlier slots.
- ◢ *AGP Pro Universal.* All the AGP Pro slots are wide slots with extra pins to provide extra voltage for high-end AGP video cards. The AGP Pro Universal slot can accommodate 1.5V or 3.3V video cards. When using a video card that requires high voltage, to prevent overheating, try to keep the slot next to the video card open for ventilation.
- ◢ *AGP Pro 3.3V.* This AGP Pro slot can only be used by 3.3V video cards.
- ◢ *APG Pro 1.5V.* This AGP Pro slot can only accommodate 1.5V cards.

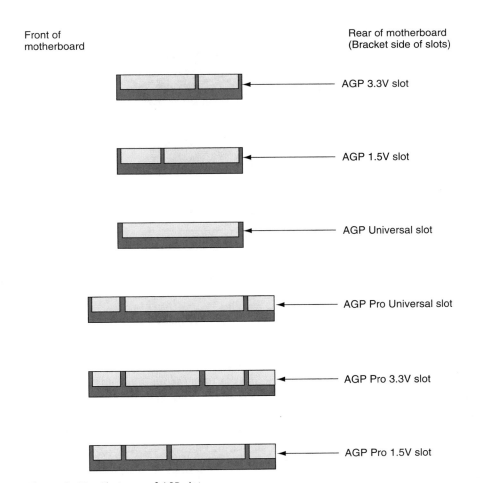

Figure 8-63 Six types of AGP slots

> **Notes**
>
> If you're trying to buy an AGP video card to match a motherboard slot, you have to be really careful. When reading an AGP ad, it's easy to not distinguish between AGP 3.3V and AGP 3.0, but there's a big difference in these standards, and they are not interchangeable. AGP 3.0 is the latest AGP standard and all these video cards use 1.5V.

> **Notes**
>
> When comparing AGP video cards, look for the speed rating advertised as 2x, 4x, or 8x. Buy the fastest rating you can afford as long as the card fits the AGP slot on your motherboard.

An AGP video card will be keyed to 1.5V or 3.3V, or a universal AGP video card has both keys so that it can fit into either a 1.5V keyed slot or a 3.3V keyed slot. A Universal AGP video card also fits into a Universal AGP slot. If an AGP video card does not use the extra pins provided by the AGP Pro slot, it can still be inserted into the AGP Pro slot if it has a registration tab that fits into the end of the Pro slot near the center of the motherboard. The video card shown in Figure 8-64 is a Universal AGP card that is keyed for 3.3V or 1.5V slots and has a registration tab that allows it to also fit into an AGP Pro slot.

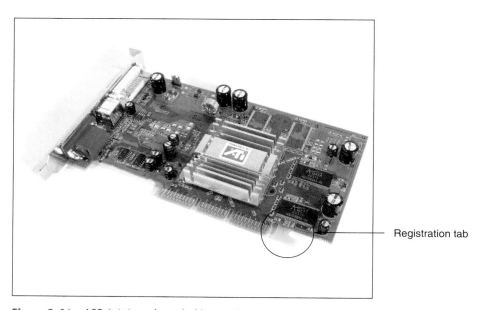

Registration tab

Figure 8-64 AGP 3.0 8x universal video card

Now let's turn our attention to how to install an expansion card. We'll use a sound card as our first example.

INSTALLING A SOUND CARD

When you purchase an expansion card, it comes bundled with its drivers on CD. You can also expect to find some basic instructions, a user manual, and maybe some application software to use the card. However, you don't have to use the application software, so installing that is optional. Also, Windows XP has its own drivers available for many devices and will attempt to use those drivers instead of the ones on the device's setup CD.

The sound card we're installing is shown in Figure 8-65. It's a 24-bit Creative Labs Sound Blaster card that has a universal PCI connector and works under Windows NT/2000/XP, Windows 9x/Me, and DOS. The card comes with a user manual, drivers, and application software all on a CD.

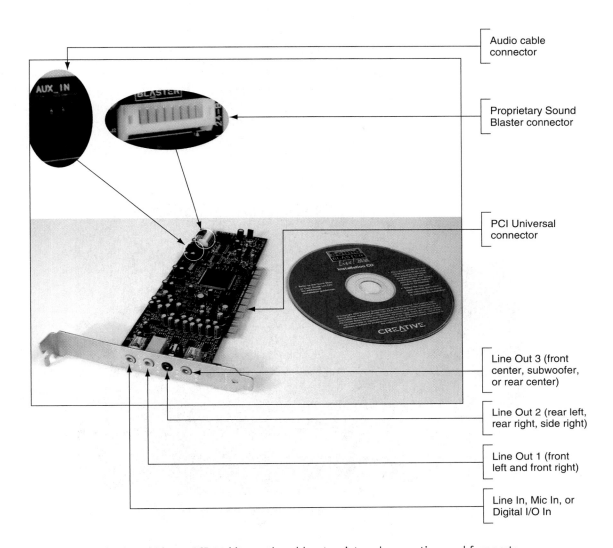

Audio cable connector

Proprietary Sound Blaster connector

PCI Universal connector

Line Out 3 (front center, subwoofer, or rear center)

Line Out 2 (rear left, rear right, side right)

Line Out 1 (front left and front right)

Line In, Mic In, or Digital I/O In

Figure 8-65   The Sound Blaster PCI 24-bit sound card has two internal connections and four ports

Generally, the main steps to install an expansion card are to install the card in an empty slot on the motherboard and install the drivers on the CD that comes with the sound card. (Know that a device manufacturer might instruct you to first install the setup CD drivers before you install the card.) Also, on the CD you might find optional applications to install.

INSTALL THE CARD INSIDE THE CASE

Follow these steps to install the sound card:

1. If you are planning to use the sound card in place of sound on your motherboard, go into CMOS setup and disable sound on your motherboard so there will be no conflicts.

2. Read the instructions that came with the sound card to make sure you understand the installation process.

3. Make sure that you are properly grounded. Wear a ground bracelet to protect against static electricity.

4. Turn off the PC, remove the cover, and locate an empty expansion slot for the card. Because we need to connect a cable from the sound card to the CD drive (the cable

comes with the sound card), place the sound card near enough to the CD drive so that the cable can reach between them.

5. Attach the cable to the sound card (see Figure 8-66) and to the CD drive. This cable is used to feed audio data from the CD or DVD drive directly to the sound card.

DVD drive

Audio cord and connector to optical drive

Figure 8-66 Connect the cable to the sound card that will make the direct audio connection from the DVD drive

6. Remove the cover from the slot opening at the rear of the PC case, and place the card into the PCI slot, making sure that the card is seated firmly. Use the screw taken from the slot cover to secure the card to the back of the PC case.

7. Check again that both ends of the wire are still securely connected and that the wire is not in the way of the CPU fan, and then replace the case cover.

8. Plug in the speakers to the ports at the back of the sound card, and turn on the PC. The speakers may or may not require their own power source. Check the product documentation or manufacturer's Web site for more information.

In this installation, we connected the audio cable from the sound card to a DVD drive. However, sometimes you might connect the audio cable to a CD drive or TV Tuner card.

Notes

Some high-end sound cards have a power connector to provide extra power to the card. For this type of card, connect a power cable with a miniature 4-pin connector to the card. Be careful! Know for certain the purpose of the connector is for power. Don't make the mistake of attaching a miniature power cord designed for a $3\frac{1}{2}$-inch disk drive coming from the power supply to the audio input connector on the sound card. The connections appear to fit, but you'll probably destroy the card by making this connection.

8

INSTALL THE SOUND CARD DRIVERS

After the card is installed, the device drivers must be installed. Follow these steps using Windows XP to install the sound card drivers:

1. After physically installing the card, turn on the system. When Windows XP starts, it detects that new audio hardware is present. A bubble message appears on the system tray (see Figure 8-67) and the Found New Hardware Wizard opens (see Figure 8-68).

Figure 8-67   Windows XP detects new hardware is present

Figure 8-68   The Windows XP Found New Hardware Wizard steps you through a hardware installation

2. In order to use the drivers on CD that came with the sound card, select **Install from a list or specific location (Advanced)** and click **Next**.

3. The next window in the wizard appears (see Figure 8-69). Select **Search for the best driver in these locations**, and check **Search removable media**. Also check **Include this location in the search** and verify the CD drive letter is showing. In our example, that drive is D:\. Click **Next**.

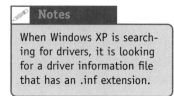

Notes

When Windows XP is searching for drivers, it is looking for a driver information file that has an .inf extension.

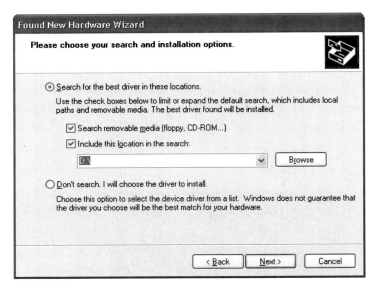

Figure 8-69 The Found New Hardware Wizard asks for direction in locating driver files

4. Windows XP locates the driver files and loads them. On the final screen of the wizard shown in Figure 8-70, click **Finish**. You're now ready to test the sound card.

Figure 8-70 Found New Hardware Wizard has successfully finished the installation

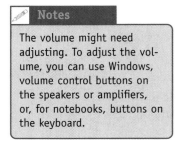

Notes

The volume might need adjusting. To adjust the volume, you can use Windows, volume control buttons on the speakers or amplifiers, or, for notebooks, buttons on the keyboard.

5. To test the sound card, insert a music CD in the optical drive. Depending on how Windows XP is configured, the CD automatically plays; nothing happens; or, if this is the first time a music CD has been used with the system, the Audio CD window appears, as shown in Figure 8-71.

6. Select **Play Audio CD using Windows Media Player** and click **OK**. Windows Media Player launches to play the CD (see Figure 8-72).

Figure 8-71 Windows XP asks what to do with the detected music CD

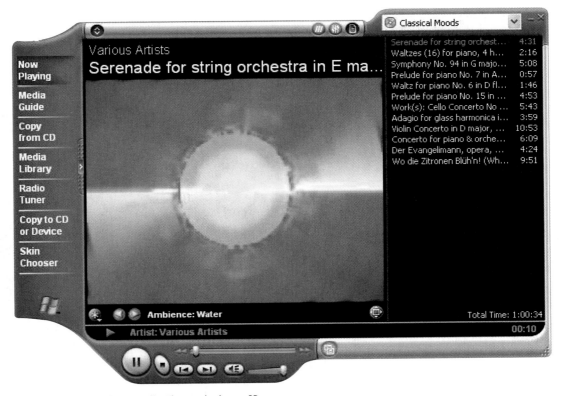

Figure 8-72 Windows Media Player playing a CD

UPGRADING THE VIDEO CARD

The video card we're installing, shown in Figure 8-64, is a universal AGP card that is keyed for 3.3V or 1.5V slots and has a registration tab that allows it to also fit into an AGP Pro slot.

Do the following to install the video card:

1. An AGP slot might require a retention mechanism around it that helps hold the card securely in the slot. Some motherboards require that you install this retention mechanism on the slot before you install the card, as shown in Figure 8-73. Check your motherboard documentation for specific instructions.

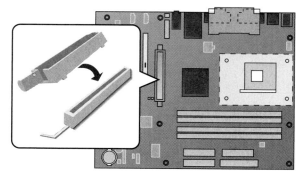

Figure 8-73 Some motherboard installations require you to install a retention mechanism around the AGP slot before installing the video card

2. Remove the faceplate for the slot from the computer case, and slide back the retention mechanism on the slot. Insert the card in the slot and slide the retention mechanism back in position. The retention mechanism slides over the registration tab at the end of the AGP slot to secure the card in the slot. Use a single screw to secure the card to the computer case (see Figure 8-74).

Figure 8-74 Secure the video card to the case with a single screw

3. Replace the computer case cover, plug in the video cable, and turn on the system. When Windows starts up, it will launch the Found New Hardware Wizard. Follow instructions onscreen to install the drivers. Windows will most likely install its own generic video drivers.

4. To take full advantage of the features of your video card, rather than using Windows generic drivers, you need to use the video card drivers provided by the manufacturer. To do that, right-click anywhere on the desktop and select **Properties** from the short-cut menu. The Display Properties window opens, as shown in Figure 8-75.

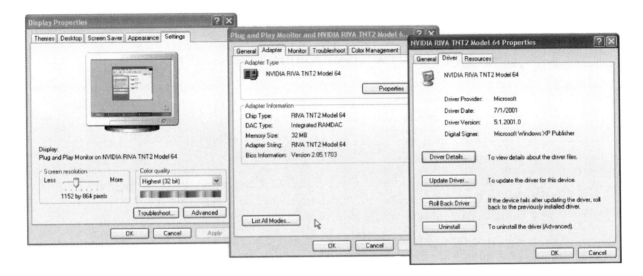

Figure 8-75 Updating the video card drivers in Windows XP

5. Select the **Settings** tab and click **Advanced**. On the next window, click the **Adapter** tab, also shown in Figure 8-75. The adapter's Properties window appears.

6. Insert the CD that came with the video card and click **Update Drivers**. Follow the directions onscreen to install the new drivers.

7. After the drivers are installed, use the Display Properties window to check the resolution and refresh rate for the monitor.

>> CHAPTER SUMMARY

◢ When evaluating for an upgrade, first decide exactly what are the user needs and determine the limitations of the current computer.

◢ When installing new applications, verify that your computer hardware can handle the application. Check the processor, memory requirements, and hard drive space.

◢ When you need more hardware, verify that the current system can support the needs of the new hardware device.

◢ If you need better performance, you can benchmark your system and then evaluate the processor, the memory, the network hardware, the hard drive, the motherboard, and the OS.

◢ Generally, you should not put money into an upgrade if your computer is five years old or older or if the cost of the upgrade exceeds half the value of the present system.

◢ USB has two standards, original USB and Hi-Speed USB. Hi-Speed USB is backward compatible with the earlier standard.

◢ FireWire has two current standards, FireWire 400 (1394a) and FireWire 800 (1394b). FireWire 800 is not compatible with FireWire 400.

◢ External components cost more, but installing them is easier than installing internal components.

◢ Protect a system against static electricity when you are working inside a computer case.

◢ Current memory modules are RIMMs and DIMMs, which both come in several speeds and standards. You must match the standards to those which the motherboard supports and to already-installed modules.

◢ Three major types of DIMMs are SDRAM, DDR, and DDR2.

◢ Memory specifications include dual channeling, error checking, registered or buffered memory, CAS or RAS latency, tin or gold connectors, speed, and amount of RAM contained on the module.

◢ Notebook computers use SO-DIMMs or SO-RIMMS that are smaller than regular DIMMs and RIMMs.

◢ A motherboard might have two parallel ATA connectors that can support up to four drives in a system, or use a combination of parallel ATA and serial ATA connectors. Each serial ATA connector supports a single drive.

◢ When selecting an internal hard drive, consider the capacity of the drive, the type of interface (parallel or serial), the spindle speed, the ATA standards supported, the cache size, and the average seek time of the drive. Buy a drive that your motherboard can support.

◢ A parallel ATA hard drive must have its jumpers set to the single, master, or slave setting. Use an 80-conductor parallel ATA cable for the connection.

◢ Use Windows XP Disk Management to partition and format a second hard drive for first use.

◢ The three types of expansion slots used in desktop computers are PCI, PCI Express (PCIe), and AGP. AGP is used strictly for video, and some systems use PCI Express for the video slot instead of AGP.

◢ Conventional PCI now has four types of slots and six possible PCI card configurations to use these slots.

◢ PCI Express currently comes in four different slot sizes called PCI Express x1, x4, x8, and x16.

◢ There are six kinds of AGP slots, using these AGP standards: AGP 1.0, 2.0, 3.0, and AGP Pro.

◢ When installing an expansion card in an expansion slot, sometimes you install the drivers before you install the card and at other times you install the card first. Follow the manufacturer's directions to know the right order.

>> KEY TERMS

CAS Latency   A feature of memory that reflects the number of clock cycles that pass while data is written to memory.

dual channel   A motherboard feature that improves memory performance by providing two 64-bit channels between memory and the chipset. DDR and DDR2 memory can use dual channels.

electrostatic discharge (ESD)   Another term for static electricity. It can destroy sensitive computer components, such as memory modules, if proper precautions are not taken.

FireWire 400 (1394a)   A version of the FireWire external bus standard that supports data rates up to 400 Mbps; uses a 4- or 8-pin connector.

FireWire 800 (1394b)   A version of the FireWire external bus standard that supports data rates up to 800 Mbps; uses a 9-pin connector.

front side bus (FSB) speed   The speed of a PC's system bus.

Hi-Speed USB (USB 2.0)   A version of USB that supports data rates up to 480 Mbps. USB 2.0 is backward-compatible with USB 1.1.

RAS Latency   A feature of memory that reflects the number of clock cycles that pass while data is written to memory.

>> **REVIEWING THE BASICS**

1. How many pins are on a SDRAM DIMM? On a DDR DIMM? On a DDR2 DIMM?

2. Which is likely to be more expensive, a 512-MB DIMM or a 512-MB RIMM?

3. How many notches are on a DDR DIMM?

4. What prevents a DDR DIMM from being installed in a DDR2 DIMM slot on a motherboard?

5. Looking at an SDRAM DIMM, how can you know for certain the voltage needed by the module?

6. What is the name of the Windows XP virtual memory file?

7. Name two current ATA standards that pertain to the transfer rates of hard drives.

8. Name two ATA standards that pertain to the data cables used by hard drives.

9. What are the two most popular spindle speeds (measured in RPMs) currently used for hard drives?

10. If a motherboard has two parallel ATA connections, how many EIDE devices can the system support?

11. If a hard drive is too small to physically fit snugly into the drive bay, what can you do?

12. Describe how you can access the CMOS setup program.

13. What Windows XP utility is used to partition and format a second hard drive?

14. What are two data bus widths used by conventional PCI slots?

15. Which is faster, a PCI Express x16 slot or the latest AGP slot?

16. When examining a PCI expansion card, how can you tell what voltage(s) the card can use?

17. What is the purpose of a wire that connects a sound card to the optical drive?

18. What Windows XP wizard is used to install a new hardware device?

19. What does the AGP Pro slot offer over other AGP slots?

20. Can a PCI Express x4 card be used in a PCI slot? In a PCI Express x16 slot?

>> THINKING CRITICALLY

1. Why does a motherboard sometimes support more than one system bus speed?

2. If your motherboard supports DIMM memory, will RIMM memory still work on the board?

3. When troubleshooting a motherboard that is no longer under warranty, you discover the modem port no longer works. What is the least expensive solution to this problem? What additional questions might you ask a user about the situation before you are ready to make a recommendation as to which solution is best for the user?

    a. Replace the motherboard.

    b. Disable the modem port, and buy and install a modem card in an expansion slot.

    c. Buy an external modem that connects to the serial or USB port.

    d. Return the motherboard to the factory for repair.

4. You have just upgraded memory on a computer from 64 MB to 128 MB by adding one DIMM. When you first turn on the PC, the memory count shows only 64 MB. Which of the following is most likely the source of the problem? What can you do to fix it?

    a. Windows is giving an error because it likely became corrupted while the PC was disassembled.

    b. The new DIMM you installed is faulty.

    c. The new DIMM is not properly seated.

    d. The DIMM is installed in the wrong slot.

5. You install a hard drive and then turn on the PC for the first time. You access CMOS setup and see that the drive is not recognized. Which of the following do you do next?

    a. Turn off the PC, open the case, and verify that memory modules on the motherboard have not become loose.

    b. Turn off the PC, open the case, and verify that the data cable and power cable are connected correctly and jumpers on the drive are set correctly.

    c. Verify that BIOS hard drive autodetection is enabled.

    d. Reboot the PC and enter CMOS setup again to see if it now recognizes the drive.

>> HANDS-ON PROJECTS

PROJECT 8-1:   Reading Motherboard Documentation

Obtain the manual for the motherboard for your PC. (If you cannot find the manual, try downloading it from the motherboard manufacturer's Web site.) List the processors that the board supports. List at least three types of connectors on the board that are not currently used. In what situations might you find it useful to use each connector?

PROJECT 8-2:   Planning and Pricing Memory

You need the documentation for your motherboard for this project. If you don't have it, download it from the Web site of the motherboard manufacturer. Use this documentation and the motherboard to answer the following:

1. What is the maximum amount of memory the banks on your motherboard can accommodate?

2. What type of memory does the board support?

3. How many modules are installed, and how much memory does each hold?

4. Look in a computer catalog, such as *Computer Shopper*, or use a retail Web site such as Kingston Technology (*www.kingston.com*) or Crucial Technology (*www.crucial.com*) to determine how much it costs to fill the banks to full capacity. Don't forget to match the speed of the modules already installed, and plan to use only the size modules your computer can accommodate. How much will the upgrade cost?

PROJECT 8-3:   Helping with Upgrade Decisions

Upgrading an existing system can sometimes be a wise thing to do, but sometimes the upgrade costs more than the system is worth. Also, if existing components are old, they might not be compatible with components you want to use for the upgrade. A friend, Renata, asks your advice about several upgrades she is considering. Answer these questions:

1. Renata has a Windows XP notebook that does not have a FireWire port. She wants to use a camcorder that has a FireWire 400 interface with her notebook. How can she perform the upgrade and what is the cost? Print Web pages to support your answers.

2. Renata has a Windows XP desktop computer that has one USB port, but she wants to use her USB printer at the same time she uses her USB scanner. How can she do this, and how much will it cost? Print Web pages to support your answers.

3. Renata uses her Windows XP computer for gaming. The computer has an AGP 2.0 1.5V video slot. What is the fastest and best graphics card she can buy to install in this slot? How much does it cost? Print Web pages to support your answer.

>> REAL PROBLEMS, REAL SOLUTIONS

REAL PROBLEM 8-1:   Upgrading Your Computer

What do you want your own computer to do that it currently does not do? Describe your needs and your computer's limitations in detail. Then do your research and print the Web pages showing the hardware and software you will need to install to perform the upgrade. How much will the total upgrade cost? Do you think your computer is powerful enough and valuable enough to merit this upgrade? Why or why not?

Useful Web Sites and Other Resources

Tables A-1 through A-6 list important URLs alphabetically within each table.

BIOS MANUFACTURERS AND SUPPLIERS OF BIOS UPDATES

When looking for a BIOS upgrade for your desktop or notebook computer, the most reliable source is the Web site of the motherboard or notebook manufacturer.

Company	URL
Abit	www.abit-usa.com
American Megatrends, Inc. (AMI)	www.megatrends.com or www.ami.com
Asus	www.asus.com
Dell	www.dell.com
Driver Guide (database of firmware, drivers, and documentation)	www.driverguide.com
Driverzone by Barry Fanion	www.driverzone.com
eSupport.com (BIOS upgrades)	www.esupport.com
Gateway	www.gateway.com
Hewlett-Packard and Compaq	thenew.hp.com
IBM	www.ibm.com
Lenovo (includes IBM ThinkPads)	www.lenovo.com, www.pc.ibm.com/us
Marco Volpe	www.mrdriver.com
NEC	www.nec-computers.com
Packard Bell	www.packardbell.com
Phoenix Technologies (First BIOS, Phoenix, and Award)	www.phoenix.com
Toshiba	www.toshiba.com
Unicore (BIOS upgrades)	www.unicore.com
VIA Technologies	www.viatech.com
Wim's BIOS	www.wimsbios.com

Table A-1 BIOS manufacturers and suppliers of BIOS updates

MOTHERBOARD MANUFACTURERS, REVIEWERS, AND SUPPLIERS

Company	URL
Abit	www.abit.com.tw
American Megatrends, Inc. (AMI)	www.megatrends.com or www.ami.com
Amptron	www.amptron.com
ASUS	www.asus.com
A-Trend	www.atrend.com
Chaintech	www.chaintech.com.tw
Dell	www.dell.com
DFI	www.dfiweb.com
ECS	www.ecs.com.tw
EpoX	www.epox.com
Famous Tech	www.magic-pro.com.hk
First International Computer of America, Inc.	www.fica.com or www.fic.com.tw
FreeTech	www.freetech.com
Gateway	www.gateway.com
Gigabyte Technology Co., Ltd.	us.giga-byte.com
IBM	www.ibm.com
Intel Corporation	www.intel.com
Iwill Corporation	www.iwill.net
Lenovo (includes IBM ThinkPad notebooks)	www.lenovo.com
MicroStar	www.msicomputer.com
Motherboards.com	www.motherboards.com
Motherboards.org	www.motherboards.org
NEC	www.nec-computers.com
Panasonic	www.panasonic.com
PC Chips	www.pcchips.com.tw
QDI	www.qdigrp.com
Shuttle	www.spacewalker.com
Soyo	www.soyo.com
Supermicro	www.supermicro.com
Tyan	www.tyan.com

Table A-2   Motherboard manufacturers, reviewers, and suppliers

HARD DRIVE MANUFACTURERS

Company	URL
Fujitsu America, Inc.	www.fujitsu.com
IBM	www.ibm.com
Iomega (removable drives)	www.iomega.com
Maxell Corporation	www.maxell.com
Maxtor Corporation	www.maxtor.com
Quantum Corporation	www.quantum.com
Seagate Technology	www.seagate.com
Sony	www.sony.com
Western Digital	www.wdc.com

Table A-3   Hard drive manufacturers

TROUBLESHOOTING PCs AND TECHNICAL INFORMATION, INCLUDING HARDWARE REVIEWS

Company	Description	URL
Administrator's Pak by Winternals	Diagnostics, repair, and data recovery for hard drive, network, and more; includes ERD Commander to deal with corrupted Windows XP system	www.winternals.com
CNET, Inc.	Technical information and product reviews	www.cnet.com
Computing.NET	Technical information	www.computing.net
EdScope, LLC	Technical information and hardware reviews	www.basichardware.com
GetDataBack by Runtime Software	Data recovery software	www.runtime.org
Hardware Central by Jupitermedia	Technical information and hardware reviews	www.hardwarecentral.com
How Stuff Works	Explanations of how computer hardware and software work	www.howstuffworks.com
Inboost.com	Performance information	www.inboost.com
Jupitermedia	Hardware reviews	www.earthwebhardware.com/computers
Microsoft	Windows support and Microsoft applications support	support.microsoft.com
MicroSystems Development Technologies	POST diagnostic cards, port test software, loop-back plugs, floppy drive diagnostic tools	www.msdus.com
MK Data	Tons of technical information	www.karbosguide.com

Table A-4   Troubleshooting PCs and technical information, including hardware reviews

Company	Description	URL
Motherboards.com	Aggregate site on motherboards; includes hardware reviews	www.motherboards.com
Motherboards.org	Aggregate site on motherboards; includes hardware reviews	www.motherboards.org
Norton SystemWorks by Symantec	PC maintenance and troubleshooting software suite includes Norton AntiVirus, Norton Utilities, Norton GoBack, CheckIt Diagnostics, and System Optimizer	www.symantec.com
PartitionMagic by Symantec	Manages a hard drive, including resizing and copying partitions	www.symantec.com
PC Guide	Technical information and troubleshooting	www.pcguide.com
PC World	Technical information and hardware reviews	www.pcworld.com
SiSoftware Sandra	Benchmarking, diagnostic, and tune-up software	www.sisoftware.co.uk
SpinRite by Gibson Research	Data-recovery software	www.grc.com
Sysinternals	Tons of technical information about Windows and utilities to download	www.sysinternals.com
The Elder Geek	Solutions for Windows, hardware, network, Internet, and system problems; includes downloads	www.theeldergeek.com
Tom's Hardware Guide	In-depth technical information	www.tomshardware.com
Uniblue	Utility software to solve Windows problems	www.liutilities.com
Unicore	POST diagnostic cards and BIOS upgrades	www.unicore.com
Webopedia by Jupitermedia	Encyclopedia of computing terms	www.webopedia.com
ZD Net Help	Technical information and downloads	www.zdnet.com

Table A-4   Troubleshooting PCs and technical information, including hardware reviews (continued)

VIRUS DETECTION, REMOVAL, AND INFORMATION

Product or Site	Description	URL
AVG Anti-Virus by Grisoft	Antivirus software	www.grisoft.com
Command Antivirus	Antivirus software and virus information	www.authentium.com
Dr. Solomon's Software	Antivirus software	www.drsolomon.com
ESafe by Aladdin Knowledge Systems, Ltd.	Antivirus software	www.esafe.com
F-Prot by Frisk Software International	Antivirus software available as shareware	www.f-prot.com
F-Secure Anti-Virus	Virus information and antivirus software	www.f-secure.com
NeatSuite by Trend Micro (for networks)	Antivirus software for networks	www.trendmicro.com
Norman Virus Control	Sophisticated antivirus software	www.norman.com
Norton AntiVirus	Antivirus software	www.symantec.com
PC-cillin by Trend Micro (for home use)	Anitvirus software for home use	www.trendmicro.com
Virus Bulletin	Virus information	www.virusbtn.com
VirusScan by McAfee	Antivirus software	www.mcafee.com

Table A-5   Virus detection, removal, and information

HELP WITH WINDOWS TROUBLESHOOTING AND WINDOWS DRIVERS

Site	URL
Computing.NET	www.computing.net
DriverUpdate.com	www.driverupdate.com
Driverzone by Barry Fanion	www.driverzone.com
HelpWithWindows.com	www.helpwithwindows.com
Hermanson, LLC	www.windrivers.com
Marco Volpe	www.mrdriver.com
Microsoft Support	support.microsoft.com
PC Pitstop	www.pcpitstop.com
Sysinternals	www.sysinternals.com
The Driver Guide	www.driverguide.com
Windows IT Library	www.windowsitlibrary.com
Windows User Group Network	www.wugnet.com

Table A-6   Help with Windows troubleshooting and Windows drivers

NOTEBOOK COMPUTER MANUFACTURERS

Manufacturer	URL
Acer America	global.acer.com
Apple Computer	www.apple.com
Dell Computer	www.dell.com
eMachines by Gateway	www.emachines.com
Fujitsu/Fuji	www.fujitsu.com
Gateway	www.gateway.com
Hewlett-Packard and Compaq	www.hp.com
Lenovo (includes IBM ThinkPads)	www.lenovo.com
Micron Electronics	www.micronpc.com
NEC	www.nec.com
PC Notebook	www.pcnotebook.com
Sony (VAIO)	www.sonystyle.com
Toshiba America	www.csd.toshiba.com
WinBook	www.winbook.com

Table A-7   Notebook computer manufacturers

APPENDIX B

Entry Points for Startup Processes

This appendix contains a summary of the entry points that can affect Windows startup. The entry points include startup folders, Group Policy folders, the Scheduled Tasks folder, initialization files, and registry keys. For an explanation of each entry point, see Chapter 2. Entry points are listed here.

Programs and shortcuts to programs stored in these startup folders:

- ◢ C:\Documents and Settings*username*\Start Menu\Programs\Startup
- ◢ C:\Documents and Settings\All Users\Start Menu\Programs\Startup
- ◢ C:\Windows\Profiles\All Users\Start Menu\Programs\Startup
- ◢ C:\Windows\Profiles*username*\Start Menu\Programs\Startup

Scripts used by Group Policy that can be stored in these folders:

- ◢ C:\WINDOWS\System32\GroupPolicy\Machine\Scripts\Startup
- ◢ C:\WINDOWS\System32\GroupPolicy\Machine\Scripts\Shutdown
- ◢ C:\WINDOWS\System32\GroupPolicy\User\Scripts\Logon
- ◢ C:\WINDOWS\System32\GroupPolicy\User\Scripts\Logoff

Scheduled tasks stored in this folder:

- ◢ C:\Windows\Tasks

Entries in these legacy initialization files:

- ◢ System.ini
- ◢ Win.ini

Registry keys known to affect startup:

- ◢ HKCU\Software\Microsoft\Windows\CurrentVersion\RunOnce
- ◢ HKCU\Software\Microsoft\Windows\CurrentVersion\RunOnceEx

- ◢ HKLM\Software\Microsoft\Windows\CurrentVersion\RunOnce
- ◢ HKLM\Software\Microsoft\Windows\CurrentVersion\RunOnceEx
- ◢ HKCU\Software\Microsoft\Windows\CurrentVersion\Policies\Explorer\Run
- ◢ HKLM\Software\Microsoft\Windows\CurrentVersion\Policies\Explorer\Run
- ◢ HKLM\Software\Microsoft\Windows\CurrentVersion\ShellServiceObjectDelayLoad
- ◢ HKLM\Software\Microsoft\Windows NT\CurrentVersion\Winlogon\Userinit
- ◢ HKLM\Software\Microsoft\Windows NT\CurrentVersion\Winlogon\Shell
- ◢ HKCU\Software\Microsoft\Windows NT\CurrentVersion\Windows
- ◢ HKCU\Software\Microsoft\Windows NT\CurrentVersion\Windows\Run
- ◢ HKLM\Software\Microsoft\Windows\CurrentVersion\Run
- ◢ HKCU\Software\Microsoft\Windows\CurrentVersion\Run
- ◢ HKLM\System\CurrentControlSet\Control\Services
- ◢ HKLM\System\CurrentControlSet\Control\Session Manager
- ◢ HKCU\Software\Microsoft\Command
- ◢ HKCU\Software\Microsoft\Command Processor\AutoRun
- ◢ HKCU\Software\Microsoft\Windows\CurrentVersion\RunOnce\Setup\
- ◢ HKCU\Software\Microsoft\Windows NT\CurrentVersion\Windows\load
- ◢ HKLM\Software\Microsoft\Windows NT\CurrentVersion\Windows\AppInit_DLLs
- ◢ HKLM\Software\Microsoft\Windows NT\CurrentVersion\Winlogon\System
- ◢ HKLM\Software\Microsoft\Windows NT\CurrentVersion\Winlogon\Us
- ◢ HKEY_CLASSES_ROOT\batfile\shell\open\command\
- ◢ HKEY_CLASSES_ROOT\comfile\shell\open\command\
- ◢ HKEY_CLASSES_ROOT\exefile\shell\open\command\
- ◢ HKEY_CLASSES_ROOT\htafile\shell\open\command\
- ◢ HKEY_CLASSES_ROOT\piffile\shell\open\command\
- ◢ HKEY_CLASSES_ROOT\scrfile\shell\open\command\

Other ways processes can be launched at startup:

- ◢ Services can be set to launch at startup. To manage services, use the Services Console (services.msc).
- ◢ Device drivers are launched at startup. For a listing of installed devices, use Device Manager.

Recovery Console Commands

Table C-1 lists Recovery Console commands. How to use the Recovery Console is covered in Chapter 7. For extensive information about all the Recovery Console commands, go to the Microsoft Web site at *support.microsoft.com* and search on "Recovery Console commands." When using the Recovery Console, to retrieve the last command, press F3 at the command prompt. To retrieve the command one character at a time, press the F1 key.

RECOVERY CONSOLE COMMANDS

Command	Description
Attrib	Changes the attributes of a file or folder. For example, this command removes the read, hidden, and system attributes from file1.ext: **attrib -r -h −s file1.ext**
Batch	Carries out commands stored in a batch file: **batch file1.bat file2.txt** The commands stored in file1.bat are executed, and the results written to file2.txt. If no file2.txt is specified, results are written to the screen.
Bootcfg	Displays, edits, and rebuilds the Boot.ini file. For example, this command lists the contents of Boot.ini: **bootcfg/list**
Cd	Displays or changes the current directory: **cd C:\Windows**
Chkdsk	Checks a disk and repairs or recovers the data.
Cls	Clears the screen.
Copy	Copies a file. For example, **copy D:\file1 C:\windows\file2** copies the file named file1 on the CD drive (drive D) to the hard drive's Windows folder, naming the file file2. Use the command to copy data from the hard drive to another media or to replace corrupted system files.
Delete or Del	Deletes a file: **del file1**
Dir	Lists files and folders.
Disable	Used when a service or driver starts and prevents the system from booting properly: **disable *servicename***

Command	Description
Diskpart	Creates and deletes partitions on the hard drive. Enter the command with no arguments to display a user interface.
Enable	Enables a Windows XP system service or driver. For example, to assign the startup status of automatic to the service Service1, use the command: **enable service1 service_auto-start**
Exit	Quits the Recovery Console and restarts the computer.
Expand	Extracts a file from a cabinet file or expands a compressed file and copies it to the destination folder; for example: **expand D:\file1 C:\Windows** Expands the file and copies it to the hard drive.
Fixboot	Rewrites the OS boot sector on the hard drive. If a drive letter is not specified, the system drive is assumed. Type the **fixboot C:** command when the boot sector is damaged.
Fixmbr	Rewrites the Master Boot Record boot program. Use this command when you suspect the Master Boot Record is damaged.
Format	Formats a logical drive. If no file system is specified, NTFS is assumed. Type **format C: /fs:FAT32** to use the FAT32 file system. Type **format C: /fs:FAT** to use the FAT16 file system.
Help	Help utility appears for the given command: **help fixboot**
Listsvc	Lists all available services.
Logon	Allows you to log on to an installation with the Administrator password.
Map	Lists all drive letters and file system types.
Md or Mkdir	Creates a directory: **md C:\temp**
More or Type	Displays contents of a text file on screen: **type *filename.txt***
Rd or Rmdir	Deletes a directory: **rd C:\TEMP**
Rename or Ren	Renames a file: **rename file1.txt file2.txt**
Set	Displays or sets Recovery Console environmental variables.
Systemroot	Sets the current directory to the directory where Windows XP is installed.

Table C-1   Recovery Console commands

How Windows XP Works

In this appendix, we're going to the back rooms of Windows operation so you can understand how Windows works on the inside. With that understanding comes tremendous power! Once you understand a problem, solving it becomes easy and even fun. In fact, problems with Windows can become a game of mastering mind over matter. You truly can become a master Windows fixer-upper.

So let's begin by walking through a door labeled, "Not for the normal user," and into the heart of Windows operations. In this first section, we'll go behind the scenes and see how Windows is put together and how it works.

THE WINDOWS XP STRUCTURE

Windows XP is the most refined, secure, and stable desktop operating system Microsoft has ever created. Unlike Windows 98, you can install numerous applications without affecting the stability of the operating system, and hardware installations are more carefree. In this section, you'll learn how Windows XP is structured and how it is designed to create this stability.

Figure D-1 shows the layout of the many components and subsystems of Windows XP. Each of the boxes in the figure represents a group of program files assigned to that task. In this appendix, as you learn about system files, services, processes, and threads, this figure can serve as your map to how they all interrelate.

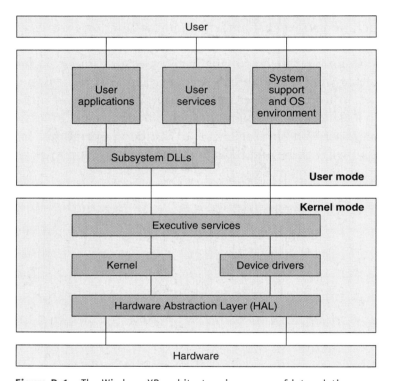

Figure D-1 The Windows XP architecture is a group of interrelating components that form the interface between the hardware and the user and application software

WHAT THE USER SEES

In this section, I want you to view what the user sees, not as a user, but as a Windows expert. Let's look at the Windows desktop with a new awareness of why and how things appear and work as they do.

VIEWING THE WINDOWS DESKTOP

On the surface, the Windows desktop (see Figure D-2) is the interface from which a user can store a document or photograph or launch a program to create and manage files, play a game, or surf the Web. To the user, the Windows desktop is similar to the desktop of a physical desk; it's a place to put things you're working on or are saving for easy access. A user can place files and shortcuts to programs on the desktop for easy access.

The horizontal bar along the bottom of the screen, called the taskbar, can be used to easily switch between open or running programs. The system tray, located on the right corner of the taskbar, displays the clock and icons that represent some of the programs that are running in the background.

Figure D-2 The Windows XP desktop

The Start button, located on the left side of the taskbar, provides access to a menu that contains a variety of applications, utilities, and system settings (see Figure D-3). Applications at the top of the Start menu are said to be "pinned" to the menu—in other words, permanently listed there until you change them in a Start menu setting. Applications that are often used are listed below the pinned applications and can change from time to time. The programs in the white column on the left side of the Start menu are user-oriented applications; the programs in the lower part of the dark column on the right side of the menu are OS-oriented and most likely to be used by an administrator or technician responsible for the system.

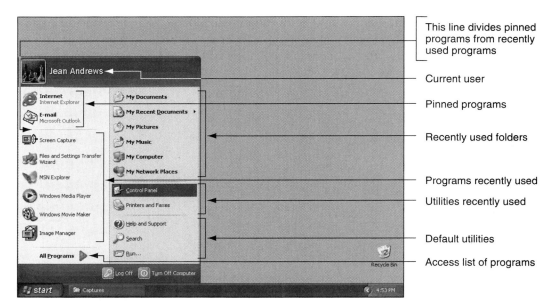

Figure D-3   The Windows XP desktop and Start menu

UNDERSTANDING THE WINDOWS DESKTOP

On the surface, the Windows desktop is made up of shortcuts, a taskbar, the Start button, and the system tray. All of these items make up the dynamic user interface. Now let's look behind the scenes.

The Windows desktop is created and managed by a single program, Explorer.exe. Explorer.exe is a system file located in the C:\Windows folder; we commonly know it as Windows Explorer. Explorer.exe is launched at startup and opens as the Windows desktop. For this reason, Explorer.exe is always being used by Windows and cannot be deleted.

Explorer.exe provides the graphical user interface and can be unloaded and loaded very easily. To unload the Windows desktop, you must stop Explorer.exe, which causes the desktop and taskbar to disappear. Once this occurs, you can start Explorer.exe again, which reloads the Windows desktop. Do the following to unload and load the Windows desktop:

1. Press and hold the **Ctrl-Alt-Delete** keys. If you are on a Windows domain, the Windows Security dialog box opens and you need to click the **Task Manager** button. If you are in a Windows workgroup or not connected to a network, instead of the Windows Security dialog box, you'll see the Task Manager window. Regardless of how you got there, when you see the Task Manager window, click the **Processes** tab (see Figure D-4).

2. Click the **explorer.exe** process and then click the **End Process** button. A warning dialog box appears. Click **Yes** to say you really want to do this. All icons on the desktop and the taskbar disappear. You should still see the Task Manager window and the desktop wallpaper.

3. Click the **Applications** tab and then click the **New Task** button. The Create New Task dialog box appears.

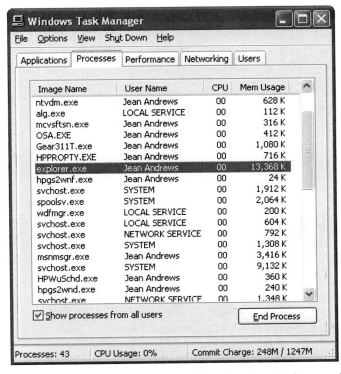

Figure D-4 Windows Task Manager dialog box shows Explorer.exe is running

4. Type **Explorer.exe**, as shown in Figure D-5, and then click **OK**. The Windows desktop reappears.

5. Click **File** and then click **Exit Task Manager** to close the Task Manager window.

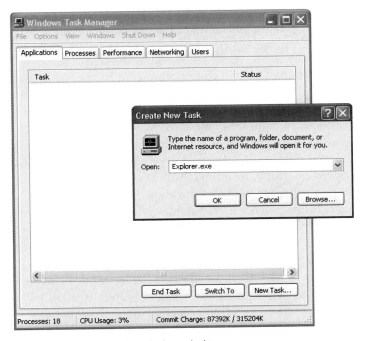

Figure D-5 Loading the Windows desktop

> **Notes**
>
> If an application locks up or does not close properly, sometimes you can solve the problem by using Task Manager to stop the program. If this doesn't work, try stopping the Explorer.exe program to unload the Windows desktop. Then use Task Manager to reload the desktop. If you still have a problem, then reboot the PC.

In summary, you can think of the Windows desktop, along with its icons and taskbar, as a type of visual presentation of Windows Explorer that is different from the normal Explorer window we're all accustomed to using. Anything you can do on the Windows desktop, such as save a file or open an application, can be done using the Windows Explorer window shown in Figure D-6.

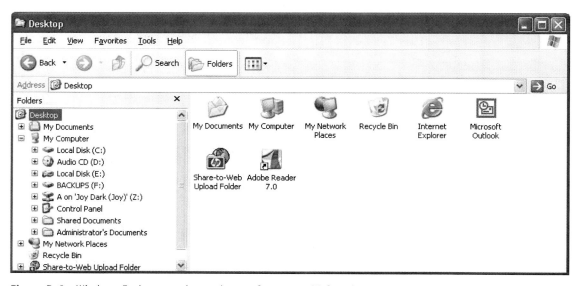

Figure D-6   Windows Explorer can be used to perform most OS functions

UNDERSTANDING WINDOWS COMPONENTS

An operating system is a group of related components used to manage a computer. An OS is responsible for managing hardware, running applications, providing an interface for the user, and managing files and folders. A system file is a file that is part of the OS that is used to (1) boot the OS; (2) hold configuration information about the OS, software, hardware, and user preferences; or (3) perform one of the many functions of the OS, such as managing the printing process or interfacing with the hard drive. A system file might have an .exe, .dll, .drv, .sys, or .ocx file extension, or it might not have a file extension at all (for example, Ntldr). Many system files are never used and some are used only occasionally. Others run all the time Windows is running and are essential for Windows operations. For example, Explorer.exe is a core system file used to display the Windows XP desktop and is constantly in use. Another example of a system file is Spoolsv.exe, which is responsible for managing the printing process to a printer.

To understand the many functions of the OS is to understand the purpose of groups of system files and how they relate to other groups of system files. In fact, the system files *are* Windows. In this section, you'll learn about these groups of system files and how they work to boot the OS, hold configuration information, and perform the different OS functions.

D

SYSTEM FILES USED TO LOAD THE OS

The system files that are used to load the operating system are called boot files. Boot files are loaded each time you power up your computer or perform a Windows restart. They begin to load after POST, just before the Windows XP logo screen is displayed. As the Windows XP logo screen is displayed, other boot files are loading, which helps Windows initialize and prepare itself for a user. Loading these boot files often requires a bit of time, which is why the Windows XP logo screen is displayed for several seconds. After all the boot files have been loaded, Windows will load the desktop or prompt the user to enter a password. If a boot file is missing or corrupted, the Windows XP logo screen may not be displayed or the computer may automatically restart. Files that boot the OS are listed in Table D-1.

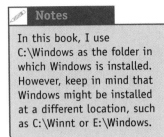

Notes

In this book, I use C:\Windows as the folder in which Windows is installed. However, keep in mind that Windows might be installed at a different location, such as C:\Winnt or E:\Windows.

File	Location and Description
Ntldr	The bootstrap loader program located in the root folder of the system partition (usually C:\)
Boot.ini	Text file located in the root folder of the system partition (usually C:\); contains boot parameters
Bootsect.dos	Located in the root folder of the system partition (usually C:\) and used to manage a dual boot system
Ntdetect.com	Located in the root folder of the system partition (usually C:\); detects hardware devices and their requirements
Ntbootdd.sys	Used to boot from a SCSI boot device and located in the root folder of the system partition (usually C:\)
Ntoskrnl.exe	Located in C:\Windows\system32 and used to load the Windows desktop and other Windows components
Hal.dll	Located in C:\Windows\system32; the core Windows kernel component
System	Located in C:\Windows\system32\config; this registry hive contains hardware information used during the boot
Device drivers	The C:\Windows\system32\drivers folder contains device drivers

Table D-1 Files that boot Windows XP

Next, let's look at the boot process. As you read, you'll learn about the boot files and what they do:

▲ When startup BIOS turns to the hard drive to find an OS, it first reads the MBR, the first sector on the hard drive that contains the partition table and Master Boot Program. This program and partition table are created when the hard drive is partitioned for first use. Startup BIOS loads the MBR program and turns control over to it.

▲ The MBR program looks in the partition table for the location of the logical drive or volume that is designated as the active partition. It reads the first sector of this partition and the loader program stored there. This loader program searches for and loads Ntldr, the bootstrap loader program for Windows XP. Ntldr is put in control.

◢ Ntldr creates a file system environment, reads the contents of Boot.ini, and, if Boot.ini requires it, displays the boot menu.

◢ Ntldr runs Ntdetect.com, which gathers information about hardware.

◢ Ntldr turns to the folder where Windows is installed (most likely C:\Windows) to find and load Ntoskrnl.exe and Hal.dll from the C:\Windows\system32 folder.

◢ Ntldr reads the registry file, System, and loads device drivers specified in the registry. Control is now given to Ntoskrnl.exe.

◢ Ntoskrnl.exe runs Winlogon.exe, which runs Lsass.exe. Lsass.exe displays the welcome screen or the Windows logon dialog box. Lsass.exe and Ntoskrnl.exe continue the startup process and remain running in the background after the Windows desktop is loaded. You'll learn more about these and other Windows background programs necessary for Windows operation later in this appendix.

SYSTEM FILES THAT HOLD INFORMATION

Most system files are program files that contain programming code, but some system files are used only to hold information. Of those files that hold information, some of them are plain text files and others are database files. Some types of system files that hold information are the following:

◢ Initialization files are text files with an .ini file extension. An example of an .ini file is Boot.ini, a text file that holds startup settings.

◢ Log files are text files that have a .txt file extension used to record errors or progress made during some Windows event or process. For example, modemlog.txt is a log file that Windows XP uses to record a dialog with a modem.

◢ Pagefile.sys is a database file used as virtual memory. Pagefile.sys is a hidden system file stored in the root directory of the drive used for the Windows installation (most likely drive C).

◢ The five registry files are database files. Their names are Sam, Security, System, Software, and Default. The registry holds configuration information for Windows, hardware, applications, and user preferences.

◢ Database files other than the registry files usually end with a .dat file extension. Two important database files that hold user settings and information about file extensions are Ntuser.dat and Usrclass.dat.

The most important Windows component that holds information for Windows is the registry. The registry is a hierarchical database that contains configuration information for Windows, users, software applications, and installed hardware devices. Windows builds the registry from the five registry hives, the current hardware configuration, and the Ntuser.dat and Usrclass.dat database files. The registry is built in memory and remains there until Windows shuts down. During startup, Windows builds the registry and then reads from it to obtain information about the startup process. After Windows is loaded, it continually reads from many of the subkeys in the registry.

The registry is divided into six keys; each key serves a specific purpose for the normal functioning of the operating system. Five of these six keys are discussed in detail in Chapter 2 and all six are listed here:

◢ HKEY_CURRENT_USER—Contains information about the current user

◢ HKEY_USERS—Information about all users

◢ HKEY_LOCAL_MACHINE—Hardware, software, and security data

▲ HKEY_CLASSES_ROOT—Information about applications and associated file extensions
▲ HKEY_CURRENT_CONFIG—Hardware configuration data, including Plug and Play information
▲ HKEY_PERFORMANCE_DATA—A pass-through placeholder for performance data. This key is used only as a reference point for Windows processes, does not contain data, and, therefore, is not displayed by the registry editor.

Figure D-7 shows the way the five subtrees that hold data are built from the five hives stored in the C:\Windows\System32\config folder. Also take into consideration that the registry pulls information from locations other than these five hives.

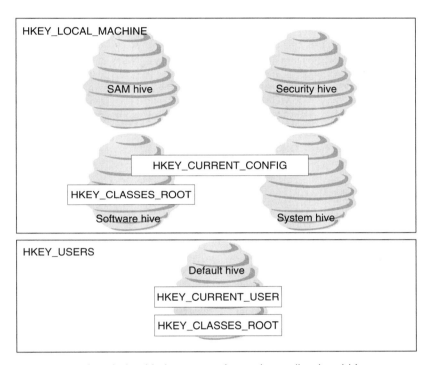

Figure D-7   The relationship between registry subtrees (keys) and hives

Here is the breakdown:

▲ HKEY_LOCAL_MACHINE (abbreviated HKLM) data is taken from four hives: the SAM hive, the Security hive, the Software hive, and the System hive. In addition, the HARDWARE key of HKLM is built when the registry is first loaded, based on data collected about the current hardware configuration.
▲ HKEY_CURRENT_CONFIG (abbreviated HKCC) data is gathered when the registry is first loaded into memory. Data is taken from the HKLM keys, which are kept in the Software hive and the System hive.
▲ HKEY_CLASSES_ROOT (abbreviated HKCR) data is gathered when the registry is built into memory. It gathers data from these locations:

  • HKLM keys that contain systemwide data stored in the Software hive

  • For the currently logged-on user, data is taken from the HKCU keys, which gather current user data from the file \Documents and Settings*username*\Local Settings\Application Data\Microsoft\Windows\Usrclass.dat.

◢ HKEY_USERS (abbreviated HKU) data is partly kept in the Default hive and partly gathered from these two files:

- \Documents and Settings\username\Ntuser.dat

- \Documents and Settings*username*\Local Settings\Application Data\Microsoft\Windows\Usrclass.dat

◢ HKEY_CURRENT_USER (abbreviated HKCU) data is built at the time the registry is loaded into memory when a user logs on from HKEY_USERS data kept in the Default hive and data kept in the Ntuser.dat and Usrclass.dat files of the current user.

As you can see, only two root keys have associated hives, HKEY_LOCAL_MACHINE (four hives) and HKEY_USERS (the default hive). Using the registry editor, you can expand HKEY_LOCAL_MACHINE to see its five subkeys, as shown in Figure D-8. The HARD-WARE subkey is built from the hardware configuration at the time the registry is loaded into memory, but the other four subkeys come from the hives they are named after (Sam, Security, Software, and System).

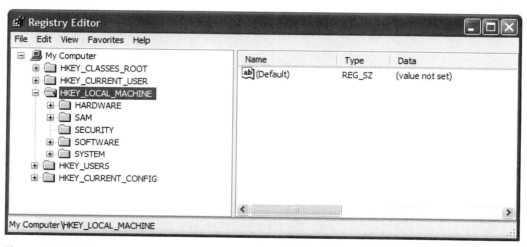

Figure D-8   Windows Registry Editor shows the five subkeys of the HKEY_LOCAL_MACHINE subtree

Notes

Device Manager reads data from the HKLM\HARDWARE key to build the information it displays about hardware configurations. You can consider Device Manager to be an easy-to-view presentation of this HARDWARE key data.

Now let's look at Windows system files that perform the many ongoing and as-needed operations for Windows. We'll first look at Windows components that run in user mode, and then we'll look at components that run in kernel mode.

USER-MODE SYSTEM SUPPORT AND ENVIRONMENT COMPONENTS

Looking back at Figure D-1, you can see that some system files run in user mode and some run in kernel mode. The three main categories of system programs that run in user mode are system support programs, services, and the subsystem DLLs. User applications also run in user mode.

Many of the programs that support the system and create the Windows environment are started as soon as a user logs on and remain running as long as the user session is active. Key components are listed here (the list is by no means complete):

- The Session Manager (C:\Windows\system32\smss.exe). This program performs many of the first steps in starting Windows, including opening the page file, starting core Windows processes, and starting the Windows logon program. If errors occur during these key events, Smss.exe will terminate the startup, crashing the system.
- The Winlogon program (C:\Windows\System32\Winlogon.exe). The Windows logon program oversees the logon process, calling other programs as needed. One program it calls is Lsass.exe.
- The Local Security Authority program (C:\Windows\System32\Lsass.exe) is responsible for authenticating a password the user keys in to log onto the system. Lsass.exe also calls Userinit.exe, which performs whatever instructions are stored in the registry for this user at logon.
- The Service Control Manager (C:\Windows\system32\Services.exe) starts up the services component of Windows. A service is a program that runs in the background to serve or support other programs. Services.exe starts up child services such as the generic service host process (Svchost.exe). An example of a service is the print spooler, Spoolsv.exe.
- The Windows subsystem program (C:\Windows\system32\Csrss.exe) provides an interface for Windows applications. It provides text windows, creates and deletes processes and threads, and creates and maintains a 16-bit virtual DOS machine for DOS programs.

DLL SUBSYSTEM

The DLL (dynamic link library) subsystem is a group of subroutines (also called routines, programs, or subprograms) that serve other programs. Several subroutines are linked or grouped together in a file to form a library of subroutines available to a program. When a program requires one of these subroutines, it is loaded into memory and used. Then, when the subroutine is no longer needed, it is unloaded from memory. A DLL subroutine is said to be dynamic because it is loaded and unloaded in and out of memory as needed.

The library of DLL subroutines provides the interface between the kernel-mode programs that relate to hardware and the user-mode programs that relate to the user and applications and provide the Windows environment. For example, if Microsoft Word needs to print a file, it doesn't have the programming knowledge or access to the printer to do the job. Microsoft Word must ask the OS for help and cannot communicate directly with the printer drivers. Instead it calls a DLL subroutine. This subroutine belongs to the OS, and it can communicate with the kernel mode printer drivers. See Figure D-9.

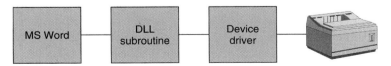

Figure D-9 An application depends on the DLL subroutines to request access to hardware

The DLL subsystem, including the core programs Kernel32.dll, Advapi32.dll, User32.dll, and Gdi32.dll, is responsible for receiving requests from user applications and other Windows components that run in user mode and for translating these requests into system service calls to programs running in kernel mode such as Ntoskrnl.exe and Win32k.sys.

The granddaddy of all DLL programs is Ntdll.dll (see Figure D-10). This program is really a library of programs all lumped together into one system file. It contains over 200 DLL components and most of these components communicate with the granddaddy program of Executive Services, which is Ntoskrnl.exe, running in kernel mode.

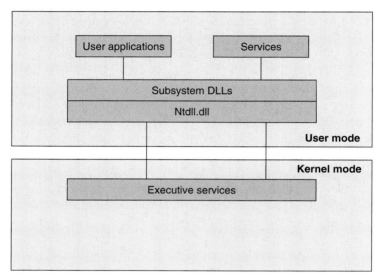

Figure D-10   Ntdll.dll runs in user mode and is a core component of the DLL subsystem that relates to the OS kernel

To fully understand exactly how a DLL works, you need to be a software engineer. However, it might help to see a DLL call from the point of view of a programmer. Suppose you're writing a Visual Basic program and you're working your way through several lines of code to calculate some numbers. You come to the point where you want to display your calculation onscreen in a dialog box. Because your Visual Basic program can't relate directly with the video card and monitor, you must make a DLL call to ask the OS to do the job for you. Here's a sample line of programming code that will display a dialog box onscreen with your message in it:

```
MsgBox "The value calculated is:" & MyValue.LastValue
```

The programmer knows the MsgBox command to be an API call (application programming interface call). To the programmer, she is just using a tool that allows her to communicate with the outside world. But behind the scenes, a DLL routine is managing this API call. When her program is compiled by the Visual Basic compiler, it will automatically insert a DLL call in the place of the programmer's MsgBox command line.

When applications are installed, many times the installation program is aware that the application will not run correctly unless a certain version of a DLL program is present. Therefore, the installation program compares the version of a DLL program already installed on the hard drive to a version stored on the setup CD. If the installation program finds the version number already installed to be incorrect, it might replace this DLL with one from the setup CD. Problems can arise if the "new" version is actually an older version or is incompatible with other applications already installed. When an application begins to give errors after a new application has been installed, most likely the root of the problem lies in a replaced Windows DLL program.

Earlier Windows operating systems allowed their DLL programs to be replaced by application installation programs, but Windows XP prevents this from happening, or at least takes some measures to prevent a conflict. We'll talk more about how Windows protects its system files later in this appendix.

SERVICES

Recall that a service is a program that runs in the background to support other programs. Many services start before the logon event when the Windows XP startup logo is displayed, and they remain running until Windows is shut down. Some are started as needed. Other services can be started when a software application is executed or a hardware device (such as a USB device) is plugged into a running computer.

Let's look at one example of a service that we're all familiar with: a Web server, which serves up Web pages over the Internet. A Web server is installed on a computer as a service, and this computer is then called the Web host. Another program, called a Web client or browser, can request information from the server. The Web server waits until it's called on to go to work. In the same fashion, all services run in the background waiting for a request from another program.

Services can be turned on or off. Therefore, a user can control which services are run when Windows loads. Be careful, though, because some services are required in order for Windows XP to run properly. Other services are optional and provide added functionality for Windows XP.

All services that run under Windows can be viewed and managed using the Services console (Services.msc). To launch the Services console, enter **services.msc** in the Run dialog box, or open the Services applet in the Control Panel. Either way, the Services console appears, as shown in Figure D-11.

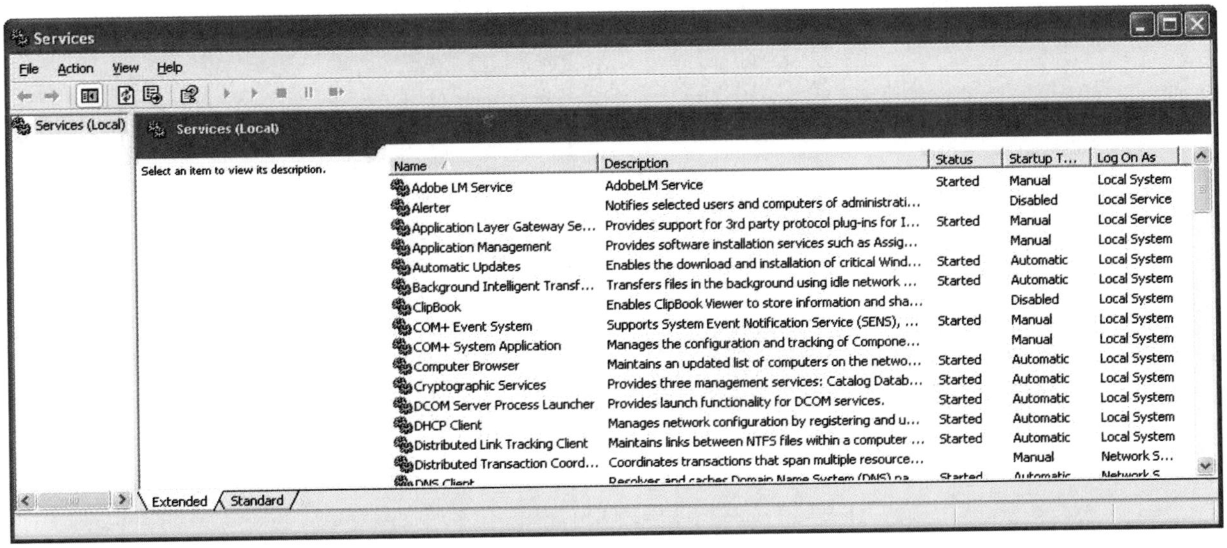

Figure D-11 Manage services using the Services console window

In the right pane, a list of most services that are installed on a PC is displayed. The list of installed services will vary depending on the hardware and software installed in your PC. Services can be set to three different startup types: Automatic, Manual, and Disabled.

The services that are set to Automatic should show a status set to Started. These services are running right now on your PC and are configured to start each time Windows starts. They usually begin loading when the Windows XP logo screen is displayed. Most of the services that are set to Automatic are required for Windows XP to function properly. In other words, these services run system files that control basic functions required to use your PC, such as services to use hardware and access a network.

Some services are set to Manual. These services will only start if a user runs a program or hardware device that requires the services. A small collection of services may be set to Disabled. These are most likely services that are no longer needed by Windows XP, hardware devices, or other software that is installed on your PC.

Most installed services have a brief description of how they're used on your PC. To view this description, do the following:

1. Click the **Automatic Updates** service. The following description of this service appears to the left of the services list: "Enables the download and installation of Windows updates. If this service is disabled, this computer will not be able to use the Automatic Updates feature or the Windows Update Web site." In other words, this service is used to download Windows XP-related security patches from the Microsoft Web site.

2. Double-click the **Automatic Updates** service. The Automatic Updates Properties window appears, as shown in Figure D-12.

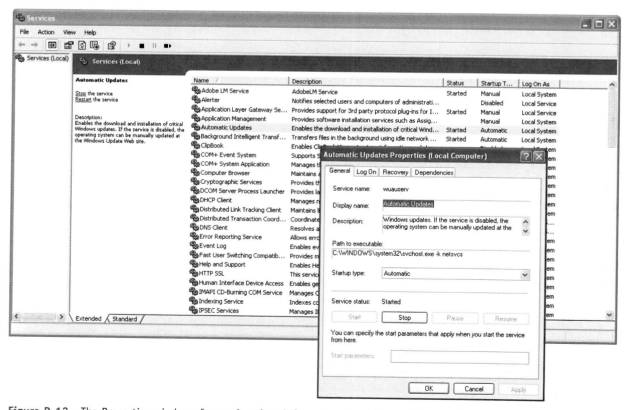

Figure D-12 The Properties window of a service gives information about the service and allows you to control it

3. Click the **Stop** button to stop this service. Now your PC will no longer check the Microsoft Web site for Windows XP security patches. Of course, when your PC is rebooted, the Automatic Updates service will start again because it's set to Automatic.

If you really wanted to stop this service from running again, you could set the start type to Disabled. Then, the Automatic Updates service would not start when your PC is rebooted. This is not recommended because Windows XP security patches are required in order to protect your PC. Also, it's best to control a program from the window designed for that purpose. Windows Updates are normally controlled using the Automatic Updates tab on the System Properties window. (If you're following along at your computer trying out each step as it's discussed, make sure Automatic Updates is enabled before you close your Services console.) Notice that the path to the Automatic Updates executable is C:\WINDOWS\system32\svchost.exe -k netsvcs. Notice Svchost.exe in the path. Svchost.exe is a generic service program that can be used to start many services. The parameters in the command line "-k netsvcs" point to a location in the registry where the actual program file for the Automatic Updates service is named. Svchost.exe can be used to launch many Internet or network-related services.

For a service that does not use Svchost.exe to start, the path to the program file will be listed in the Properties window for the service. For example, the Properties window for the McAfee Task Scheduler service is shown in Figure D-13. You can see that the service program file and path are C:\Program Files\mcAfee.com\agent\mctskshd.exe.

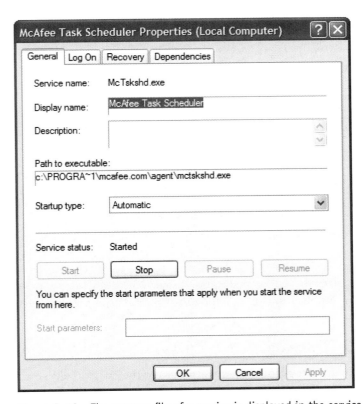

Figure D-13 The program file of a service is displayed in the service Properties window

Looking back at Figure D-11, you can see that, when started, most services register themselves as belonging to the Local System account, which is sometimes displayed as the System account. You can also view the account a service runs under using Task Manager. For example, the Task Manager window shown in Figure D-14 shows services running under the current user (Jean Andrews), System, Local Service, or Network Service accounts. The Network Service and Local Service accounts are new to Windows XP. Both these accounts have lower privileges than the System account. Core Windows services running in user mode run under the System account. Services that run under the System, Local Service, or

Network Service accounts can't display a dialog box onscreen or interact with the user. To do that, the service must be running under a user account.

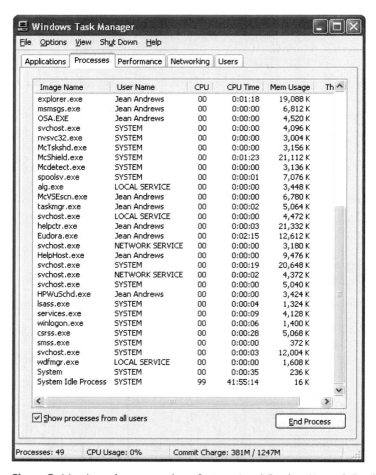

Figure D-14 A service runs under a System, Local Service, Network Service, or user account

Now let's turn our attention to understanding how Windows works with processes and threads to manage applications and Windows programs running in user mode.

PROCESSES AND THREADS

Put simply, a process is a program that is running together with the resources the running program needs (see Figure D-15). When a program is started up, such as when you double-click a program file in Windows Explorer or select a program from the Start menu, the program is copied from the hard drive or other secondary storage media and loaded into memory. It's then executed. A program often starts by telling the OS what other programs or subroutines it needs and what system resources it requires to run. These other programs are also launched, and the system resources (such as memory addresses for the program's data) are assigned to the process. Sometimes a process requires a DLL subprogram after the process has already started. These DLL processes are loaded and unloaded as needed. Also, a program might be running with duplicate processes such as when you open two instances of Microsoft Word so you can work on two documents at the same time.

D

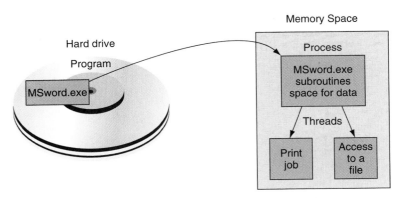

Figure D-15 A process is a running program and its resources

When a process asks the OS to perform a certain task, a thread is created. A **thread** is a task that a process has requested of the OS. For example, a process might request that the OS print a file and then immediately request that another file on the hard drive be opened. In this case, two threads are in progress as shown in Figure D-15.

When a process starts another process, the two processes are called a process tree. Let's demonstrate what a process tree looks like by using Task Manager. For example, do the following to show how a process tree works under Windows:

1. Enter **cmd** in the Run dialog box and click **OK** to open a Command Prompt window.

2. In the Command Prompt window, type **mspaint.exe** and press **Enter**. This opens a Paint window.

3. Click **Start**, point to **All Programs**, point to **Accessories**, and then click **Paint**. Another Paint window opens.

4. The first Paint window was opened by the Cmd process, which becomes its parent process. The second Paint window does not have a parent process. Now press **Ctrl-Shift-Esc**, which causes Task Manager to open.

5. On the Applications tab of Task Manager, you should see three applications running (see Figure D-16).

6. Right-click the **Cmd** process and select **Go To Process** from the shortcut menu. The Processes tab window appears, and the cmd.exe process is selected (see Figure D-17).

7. Right-click the **cmd.exe** process and select **End Process Tree** from the shortcut menu. When the Task Manager Warning message box appears, click **Yes** to continue. The Command Prompt window and one of the Paint windows close. The Paint window that is not part of the Cmd process tree remains open.

We've just used Task Manager to demonstrate that processes are often related to parent processes and Windows keeps track of which process is related to which. We've also demonstrated that Task Manager can be a powerful tool when trying to weed through several process trees.

Based on what you've learned so far about Windows and the information presented in the Task Manager window in Figure D-17, it should be apparent that more processes are running in the Windows background than are running in the Windows foreground. Most of these background processes are required in order for Windows XP to function properly. Some of the programs were started by services that are configured to automatically run when Windows XP loads. Other programs have created icons in the system tray to let the

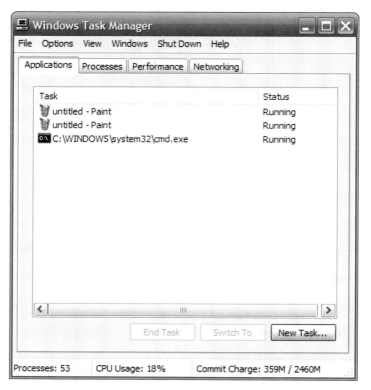

Figure D-16   Use Task Manager to view and manage running processes

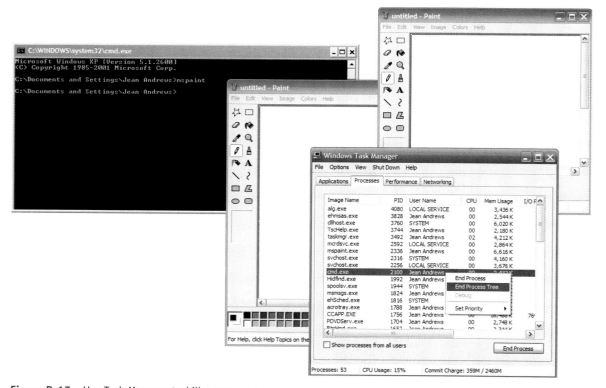

Figure D-17   Use Task Manager to kill a process tree

user know they're running and to provide an interface for configuration. Still other programs are launched at startup from other locations.

In order to troubleshoot Windows XP problems, you must have a strong understanding of what's running and what is really required to run for Windows XP to function properly. So how can you tell what user mode processes are running on your computer? Use Task Manager. Task Manager can be used to determine the executables that are running and what percentage of system resources they're using. In Chapter 2, you use Task Manager to examine each process that is launched at startup for a clean Windows XP installation.

KERNEL MODE SYSTEM FILES

Let's take a more detailed look at what's running in kernel mode. When a process is running in kernel mode, it has access to all CPU instructions and all of memory. In Figure D-18, you can see five categories of programs that run in kernel mode:

▲ Executive services are a group of programs that form the core of the Windows operating system. They include programs to manage memory and to manage network, security, and I/O operations.
▲ The kernel is a group of lower-level programs that also manage hardware.
▲ Device drivers are programs that make the interface between the OS and a hardware device. Each command from the OS is translated into the exact command and parameters a device can understand and obey. Some device drivers are supplied when a new device is installed, and some come preinstalled on Windows. An example of a core device driver preinstalled with Windows is the file system device driver, Srv.sys.
▲ The hardware abstraction layer (HAL) is a group of programs that take into account the differences between core hardware components, such as the processor or motherboard, installed on this system. The HAL isolates these differences from the other components operating in kernel mode.
▲ Windows allows certain graphics programs that interface with the video card and run in kernel mode to interact directly with the video card rather than going through the HAL.

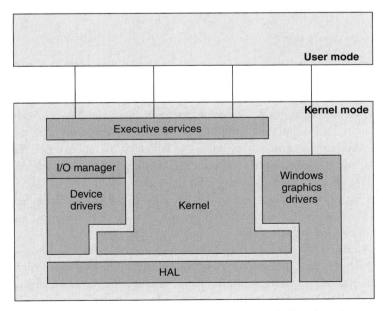

Figure D-18 Windows XP core components running in kernel mode

The core programs that make up the kernel mode of the OS include Ntoskrnl.exe, Ntkrnlpa.exe, Hal.dll, Win32k.sys, Ntdll.dll, Kernel32.dll, Advapi32.dll, User32.dll, and Gdi32.dll. Notice that Ntdll.dll is listed as running in both kernel mode and user mode. Several system programs do this because they are go-between programs responsible for communicating with components running in each mode. Also, a program can be part of Executive Services and also part of the kernel core component.

SYSTEM FILES AND WINDOWS UPDATING

It's important to understand how system files are managed when Windows is updated. First let's look at why and how we need to update Windows, and then we'll look at how the update process works so that system files are safely updated.

USING WINDOWS UPDATE

When you're responsible for a Windows system or you are trying to fix a Windows problem, one thing you want to do is make sure all the latest Windows updates and patches are installed. Many applications and Windows problems are solved simply by downloading the latest Windows patch.

Here are some situations when updating Windows can be especially useful:

◢ Microsoft releases a service patch or fix to solve some problem with Windows or include a new feature. The vast majority of security patches are designed to replace system files with a version of the file that solves some sort of security flaw.
◢ The user installs a new application or device, which requires a newer version of a system file in order to function properly.
◢ New device drivers are available and can be installed to solve hardware compatibility issues. For example, new video adapter drivers can be installed to solve problems with freezing programs.

Part of learning to protect and fix Windows is to make it a habit to keep Windows updates current. The easiest way to do that is to set Windows to automatically check for and apply updates without your help. How to make this setting is covered in Chapter 1.

UPDATING SYSTEM FILES

You need to understand how a system file is replaced when you apply a Windows update or patch. When the patch is applied, Windows needs to overwrite a system file with a new version. If the file that needs updating is currently being used (said to be open) by Windows, an application, or some other program, Windows will not allow the file to be overwritten. So how can a system file be replaced when it's being used by Windows? Suppose, for example, the Windows update has a new version of the Winsock.dll system file. When the security patch is installed, it copies the new Winsock.dll system file to the hard drive with a different name, say, for example, Seta.tmp. The security patch then tells Windows to replace Winsock.dll with Seta.tmp during the next reboot, before Winsock.dll has been loaded. For this method to work, Windows must reboot, which explains why most security patches require the user to reboot the computer.

So how does Windows keep up with system files that are constantly being replaced by security patches? Each system file is given a version number. Windows confirms the signatures of system files and records each system file's version number in a catalog database called Catdb. Multiple Catdb files make up the Windows catalog database and exist throughout subfolders in the \Windows\system32\CatRoot2 directory.

As you work through the book and are solving Windows problems, you might need to know the version number of a system file or program file. This knowledge can help you decide if an older system file is causing a problem or if a patch has been successfully applied. To find out the version number, right-click the filename and select **Properties** from the shortcut menu. For example, the Properties window for the Winsock.dll system file is shown in Figure D-19. Click the **Version** tab. Notice the version number near the top of the window.

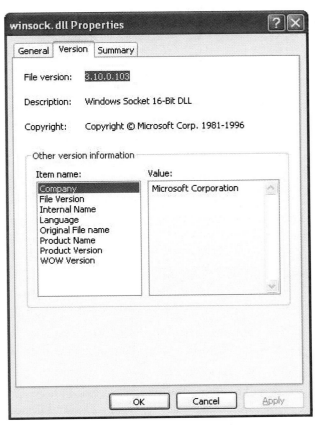

Figure D-19 System files and program files have a Version tab on their Properties window with a version number

The basic rule that Windows follows is that a system file can always be replaced with a higher version number. This process is called upgrading a system file. If a system file is replaced with another system file with a lower version number, Windows most likely will not operate correctly.

WINDOWS FILE PROTECTION

As was mentioned earlier in this appendix, when using older versions of Windows, an application installation program can accidentally replace a system file with an older version. Many applications use the same system files as Windows 98 uses. After the application is installed, when Windows 98 tries to use the downgraded system file, an error can occur because the older system file doesn't work as expected. As a result, Windows 98 can crash. As an application developer, I can remember the terrible frustration of searching through hundreds of system files on a Windows 98 system looking for the one file with the outdated version number. We came to call the mess DLL hell.

Notes

While we're talking about Windows File Protection, don't forget System File Checker (SFC), which verifies and restores system files. To use it, enter **sfc.exe** at a command prompt.

But help was on the way! In Windows XP, Microsoft implemented a system file protection method called Windows File Protection (WFP). WFP is always running and can detect when an attempt to downgrade a system file has occurred. WFP automatically restores the file using an extra copy it keeps in the \Windows\System32\dllcache folder, or WFP requests you insert the Windows XP setup CD so it can retrieve the file from there. If an attempt is made to downgrade a system file, WFP also puts an extra copy of the file in the \Windows\System32\dllcache folder for safekeeping.

>> APPENDIX SUMMARY

◢ The Windows XP architecture is a group of interrelated components that form the interface between the hardware, the user, and applications software.

◢ The system tray holds icons that represent running programs and services.

◢ The Windows desktop is a presentation made by Windows Explorer that is used to manage files, folders, and programs.

◢ System files stored in the root folder of the system partition are used to load the OS and then are no longer needed. These files are Ntldr, Boot.ini, Bootsect.dos, Ntdetect.com, and Ntbootdd.sys.

◢ Other system files needed to complete the boot are stored in the C:\Windows\system32 folder and subfolders. They are Ntoskrnl.exe, Hal.dll, System, and various device drivers.

◢ A few system files are used to hold information. The registry is made up of five files. Initialization files, such as Boot.ini, hold text data. Pagefile.sys is used for virtual memory.

◢ Key system files used to create and maintain the Windows environment, services, and subsystems include Smss.exe, Winlogon.exe, Lsass.exe, Services.exe, and Csrss.exe.

◢ The DLL subsystem is a group of library files that contain subroutines used by applications and by Windows. These subroutines act as the go-between for programs running in user mode and programs running in kernel mode.

◢ A program that runs in the background to support other programs is called a service. The Service Control Manager is Services.exe. The console, Services.msc, can be used to interact with the Service Control Manager.

◢ A process is a running program together with its resources. A process must have at least one thread.

◢ Use Task Manager to view current processes and how they relate to each other. You can start and stop a process using Task Manager.

◢ The core programs that make up the kernel mode of Windows XP include Ntoskrnl.exe, Ntkrnlpa.exe, Hal.dll, Win32k.sys, Ntdll.dll, Kernel32.dll, Advapi32.dll, User32.dll, and Gdi32.dll.

>> KEY TERMS

boot files   System files that are used to load the operating system.

process   A program that is running, together with the resources needed by the running program.

service   A program running in the background that provides support to Windows, an application, or a device.

system file   A file that is part of the OS that is used to: boot the OS; hold configuration information about the OS, software, hardware, and user preferences; or perform one of the many functions of the OS, such as managing the printing process or interfacing with the hard drive.

thread   A task that a process has requested of the OS.

>> REVIEWING THE BASICS

1. What is the main function of the Windows taskbar?

2. How can you tell that an antivirus program is running in the background by looking at the desktop?

3. What system file loads and manages the Windows desktop?

4. What is the function of the Windows desktop?

5. Which registry key contains Plug and Play information?

6. What is the bootstrap loader program for Windows XP?

7. What are the five Windows XP registry files?

8. Why are DLL subroutines said to be dynamic?

9. Why does Windows XP prevent applications from downgrading DLL programs?

10. Name the three different startup types for services.

11. What is the difference between a process and a thread?

12. What are the five categories of programs that run in kernel mode?

13. Why do some DLL programs run in both kernel and user mode?

14. How do you find the version number of a system file or program file?

15. What is the difference between WFP and SFC?

>> THINKING CRITICALLY

1. Why do user-mode processes run at a lower priority than kernel-mode processes? What could happen if this were reversed?

2. Why does Windows allow some graphics programs to bypass the HAL and interact directly with the video card? What is the advantage of having a hardware abstraction layer?

>> *HANDS-ON PROJECTS*

<u>**PROJECT D-1:**</u>   CPU Time Used by Processes

Open Task Manager to view the processes currently running. On the menu bar, click **View** and then click **Select Columns**. Check **CPU Time** and click **OK**. Which process has used the greatest amount of CPU time? Why?

<u>**PROJECT D-2:**</u>   Using Task Manager to View Processes

Reboot your Windows XP system and open Task Manager. Under the Processes tab, write down the list of processes or take a screen shot and print it so that you have a printed record of the running processes. Now boot Windows XP into Safe Mode. Again, write down or print a list of running processes. Did the list of running processes change when you booted into Safe Mode?

<u>**PROJECT D-3:**</u>   Process Management with the Task Manager

Configure Task Manager to display a Thread Count column. How many threads are being used by Explorer.exe? Now open My Computer. How many threads are now being used by Explorer.exe? Why does the thread count change when you open My Computer?

<u>**PROJECT D-4:**</u>   Task Management at the Command Prompt

Task Manager in Windows XP Professional offers some commands that can be used at the command prompt. If you are using Windows XP Professional, do the following to use Task Manager commands at a command prompt:

1. Open a Command Prompt window. Enter the command **tasklist** and press **Enter**.

2. Enter the command **tasklist /svc** and press **Enter**.

3. What is the difference in the output of the two command lines?

4. What services are running under the Lsass.exe process?

5. Enter the command **calc.exe** and press **Enter**. The Calculator opens on the desktop.

6. Enter the command **taskkill /f/im calc.exe** to end the Calculator process.

7. Try to end the **winlogon.exe** process. What happens?

8. Search the Windows XP Help and Support Center for the Taskkill command. What is the purpose of the /f parameter in the command line in Step 6? What is the purpose of the /im parameter?

9. Launch the Calculator again. What is the PID assigned to the process?

10. Now kill the process using the PID. What command did you use?

<u>**PROJECT D-5:**</u>   Loaded Device Drivers

You can use the System Information utility to view a list of system and signed device drivers currently running. To open System Information, enter **Msinfo32.exe** in the Run dialog box and click **OK**. Then expand **Software Environment** and click **System Drivers**. Answer the following questions:

1. What are the two types of system drivers?

2. In what folder are most system drivers stored?

3. What is the filename of the CD-ROM driver?

PROJECT D-6: Just How Lean Can Windows Get?

Using Task Manager, how many processes can you kill before Windows locks up? Do the following:

1. Make sure no one else is logged onto the system and you've closed important applications, saving any work.

2. Open Task Manager.

3. End all the processes you can. List the processes that refuse to end. Which process reappears after you end it?

4. Ending which process caused the system to begin the shutdown event? (When you end this process, the system shuts down. Restart the system and don't attempt to end this process again. Begin at Step 1 again.)

5. Shut down the system. In this stripped-down state, does Windows XP shut down with no errors? How did you perform the shutdown?

>> REAL PROBLEMS, REAL SOLUTIONS

REAL PROBLEM D-1: Researching How Windows XP Works

This appendix gives you background information on how Windows XP works, but it's only a good start. So much more information is available on the Microsoft Web site and on other sites. Pose one good question about the material in this appendix that will take your understanding deeper into the internals of Windows XP. Research the Internet to find your answer. In a classroom environment, report your question and your findings to the class.

GLOSSARY

This glossary defines the key terms listed at the end of each chapter and other terms related to fixing Windows XP.

access point (AP)   A device connected to a LAN that provides wireless communication so that computers, printers, and other wireless devices can communicate with devices on the LAN.

adware   Software installed on a computer that produces pop-up ads using your browser; the ads are often based on your browsing habits.

API (application program interface)   A predefined Windows procedure that allows a program to access hardware or other software.

API call   A request made by software to the OS to use an API procedure to access hardware or other software.

Automated System Recovery   A Windows XP tool that can be used to recover the system from the last time a full backup was made of drive C.

blue screen of death (BSOD)   A Windows XP stop error that appears on a blue background when Windows fails; might give the name of a service or device driver that caused the problem.

boot files   System files that are used to load the operating system.

boot sector virus   A virus that hides in one or both of the small programs at the beginning of the hard drive used to initiate the boot of the operating system.

browser hijacker   A malicious program that infects your Web browser and can change your home page or browser settings. It can also redirect your browser to unwanted sites, produce pop-up ads, and set unwanted bookmarks.

CAS Latency   A feature of memory that reflects the number of clock cycles that pass while data is written to memory.

crossover cable   A network cable used to connect two PCs into the simplest network possible; also used to connect two hubs or switches.

default gateway   A computer or other device on a network that acts as an access point, or gateway, to another network.

device driver   A program stored on the hard drive that tells the computer how to communicate with a hardware device such as a printer or modem (for more explanation, see Appendix D).

diagnostic card   An expansion card that can be used to display error codes at startup to diagnose a startup problem with hardware.

dialer   Malicious software that can disconnect your phone line from your ISP and dial an expensive pay-per-minute phone number without your knowledge.

DLL (dynamic link library)   A group or library of programs packaged into a single program file that can be called on by a Windows application. A DLL file can have a .dll, .fon, .ocx, .drv, .nls, .evt, or .exe file extension.

DNS server   A computer that matches up domain names with IP addresses.

dual channel   A motherboard feature that improves memory performance by providing two 64-bit channels between memory and the chipset. DDR and DDR2 memory can use dual channels.

electrostatic discharge (ESD)   Another term for static electricity. It can destroy sensitive computer components, such as memory modules, if proper precautions are not taken.

encrypting virus   A type of virus that can continually transform itself so that it is not detected by AV software.

encryption   Used to protect sensitive data, the conversion of data into code that must be translated before it can be accessed.

file virus   A virus that hides in an executable (.exe, .com, or .sys) program or in a word-processing document that contains a macro.

firewall   Software or a hardware device that protects a computer or network from unsolicited communication. A hardware firewall stands between two networks or a computer and a network. A software firewall is installed on a single computer to protect it, and is called a personal firewall.

FireWire 400 (1394a) A version of the FireWire external bus standard that supports data rates up to 400 Mbps; uses a 4- or 8-pin connector.

FireWire 800 (1394b) A version of the FireWire external bus standard that supports data rates up to 800 Mbps; uses a 9-pin connector.

forgotten password floppy disk A Windows XP disk created to be used to reset a password in the event the user forgets the user account password to the system.

freeware Software you can download for free or with a donation.

front side bus (FSB) speed The speed of a PC's system bus.

handle A relationship between a process and a resource it has called into action.

Hi-Speed USB (USB 2.0) A version of USB that supports data rates up to 480 Mbps. USB 2.0 is backward-compatible with USB 1.1.

honeypot A computer exposed to the Internet with the intent of attracting malicious software, and which is sometimes used by security professionals as traps to catch computer attackers, study their habits, and identify security weaknesses in protected networks.

Hosts file A file stored in the C:\Windows\System32\Drivers\Etc folder that is used to map domain names to their associated IP addresses.

infestation *See* malicious software.

Internet Connection Sharing (ICS) A Windows 98/Me and Windows XP utility that manages two or more computers connected to the Internet.

kernel mode The Windows privileged processing mode that has access to hardware components.

keylogger A type of spyware that tracks your keystrokes, including passwords, chat room sessions, e-mail messages, documents, online purchases, and anything else you type on your PC. Text is logged to a text file and transmitted over the Internet without your knowledge.

logic bomb A type of malicious software that is dormant code added to software and triggered at a predetermined time or by a predetermined event.

logical drive A portion or all of a hard drive partition that is treated by the operating system as though it were a physical drive. Each logical drive is assigned a drive letter, such as drive C, and contains a file system. Also called a *volume*.

macro A small sequence of commands, contained within a document, that can be automatically executed when the document is loaded, or executed later by using a predetermined keystroke.

macro virus A virus that can hide in the macros of a document file.

malicious software Any unwanted program that is transmitted to a computer without the user's knowledge and that is designed to do varying degrees of damage to data and software. Types of infestations include viruses, Trojan horses, worms, adware, spyware, keyloggers, browser hijackers, dialers, and downloaders. Also called *malware* or an *infestation*.

malware *See* malicious software.

master boot record (MBR) The first 512-byte sector on a hard drive. Contains the partition table and the master boot program, which the BIOS uses to find the OS on the drive.

multipartite virus A combination of a boot sector virus and a file virus. It can hide in either type of program.

network drive map Mounting a drive to a computer, such as drive E, that is actually hard drive space on another host computer on the network.

open handle A handle that is still in progress.

OS boot record (boot sector) The second 512 bytes on a drive, used to help the MBR find and load the OS.

partition A division of a hard drive that can be used to hold logical drives (for example, drive C).

patch cable A network cable that is used to connect a PC to a hub, switch, or router.

phishing Sending an e-mail message with the intent of getting the user to reveal private information that can be used for identify theft.

Ping (Packet Internet Groper) A Windows and Unix command used to troubleshoot network connections. It verifies that the host can communicate with another host on the network.

polymorphic virus A type of virus that changes its distinguishing characteristics as it replicates itself. Mutating in this way makes it more difficult for AV software to recognize the presence of the virus.

port A number assigned to an application or other process on a computer so that the process can be found by TCP/IP. Also called a *port address* or *port number*.

process A program that is running together with the resources needed by the running program.

protocol   A set of predetermined rules that network devices use to communicate.

RAS Latency   A feature of memory that reflects the number of clock cycles that pass while data is written to memory.

Recovery Console   A command-line operating system that you can load from the Windows XP setup CD, and which can be used to recover data or fix a corrupted Windows XP installation when you cannot boot from the hard drive.

restore point   A snapshot of the Windows XP system state, usually made before installation of new hardware or applications. *Also see* System Restore.

rootkit   A type of malicious software that loads itself before the OS boot is complete and can hijack internal Windows components so that it masks information Windows provides to user-mode utilities such as Windows Explorer or Task Manager.

scam e-mail   E-mail sent by a scam artist intended to lure you into a scheme.

script virus   A type of virus that hides in a script which might execute when you click a link on a Web page or in an HTML e-mail message, or when you attempt to open an e-mail attachment.

service   A program running in the background that provides support to Windows, an application, or a device (for more explanation, see Appendix D).

shareware   Software you can download and try before you buy.

spam   Junk e-mail you don't ask for, don't want, and which gets in your way.

spyware   Malicious software that installs itself on your computer to spy on you. It collects personal information about you that it transmits over the Internet to Web-hosting sites that intend to use your personal data for harm.

startup BIOS   Firmware embedded on the motherboard that is used to start up the system.

stealth virus   A virus that actively conceals itself by temporarily removing itself from an infected file that is about to be examined, and then hiding a copy of itself elsewhere on the drive.

subnet mask   Four numbers separated by periods (for example, 255.255.255.0) that, when combined with an IP address, indicate what network a computer is on.

system file   A file that is part of the OS that is used to boot the OS; hold configuration information about the OS, software, hardware, and user preferences; or perform one of the many functions of the OS, such as managing the printing process or interfacing with the hard drive.

System File Checker   A Windows XP utility (sfc.exe) that protects system files and keeps a cache folder (C:\Windows\system32\dllcache) of current system files in case it needs to refresh a damaged file.

System Restore   A Windows XP utility that is used to create a restore point and then restore the system to a restore point.

third-party utility   Software not written by Microsoft that you can download from the Web and install on your system to help solve a Windows problem.

thread   A task that a process has requested of the OS.

Trojan horse   A type of malicious software that hides or disguises itself as a useful program, yet is designed to cause damage at a later time.

USB to IDE converter   An inexpensive device that allows you to connect an IDE hard drive to a USB port; can help you diagnose problems and recover data from an IDE drive that won't boot.

user account   The information that defines a Windows XP user, including username, password, memberships, and rights.

user mode   In Windows XP, a processing mode that provides an interface between an application and the OS, and only has access to hardware resources through the code running in kernel mode

virus   A malicious program that often has an incubation period, is infectious, and is intended to cause damage. A virus program might destroy data and programs or damage a hard drive's boot sector.

virus hoax   E-mail that does damage by tempting you to forward it to everyone in your e-mail address book with the intent of clogging up e-mail systems or by persuading you to delete a critical Windows system file by convincing you the file is malicious.

virus signature   The distinguishing characteristics of malicious software that are used by AV software to identify a program as malicious.

volume   *See* logical drive.

WEP (Wired Equivalent Privacy)   A data encryption method used by wireless networks whereby data is encrypted using a 64-bit or 128-bit key. It is not as secure as other methods because the key never changes. Compare to WPA.

worm   Malicious software designed to copy itself repeatedly to memory, on drive space, or on a network, until little memory or disk space remains.

WPA (WiFi Protected Access)   A data encryption method used by wireless networks that uses the TKIP (Temporal Key Integrity Protocol) protocol. Encryption keys are changed at set intervals. Compare to WEP and WPA2.

WPA2 (WiFi Protected Access 2)   A data encryption standard compliant with the IEEE 802.11i standard that uses the AES (Advanced Encryption Standard) protocol. WPA2 is currently the strongest wireless encryption standard.

INDEX

errors
  hardware, during
    boot, 3
  responding to startup,
    104–105
ESD (electrostatic
    discharge), 331
Ethernet rating, 282
Eudora (Qualcomm),
    126, 146
Event Monitor, using,
    227
events
  See also specific event
  login and logout, 49
exceptions, Windows
    Firewall settings,
    122–123
.exe files and viruses, 94
expansion cards, 283,
    317–322
expansion slots, identifying,
    318–322
Explorer.exe, 49, 348–349

F

FAT32 file system, 141
File and Printer Sharing,
    Windows Firewall
    settings, 123
file encryption, 133–134
file extensions, Windows
    handling of, 131–132
file viruses, 111
files
  boot, 367
  recovering deleted,
    corrupted, 271–272
  registry, 352–354
  sharing, 174–177
  system. *See* system files
filtering, port, 185–187
Firefox (Mozilla), 125,
    241–242

firewalls
  configuring hardware, 185
  described, 151
  how they work, 119–121
  personal, 118–121
  using on small networks,
    184–185
FireWire 400, 800, 278,
    285, 286, 331
fixing problems. *See*
    troubleshooting
floppy disks, forgotten
    password, 151
folders
  encryption, 133–134
  fonts, 62–63
  hidden shared network,
    134–135
  sharing, 174–177
  startup, 55–56
fonts, uninstalling unused,
    62–63
forgotten password floppy
    disk, creating, 137–138
forwarding, port, 185–187,
    192–193
free space
  checking hard drive's,
    5–7
  freeing up additional,
    16–19
  verifying in Safe Mode, 40
freeware, 34

G

gateways, default, 215
GetDataBack (Runtime
    Software), 271
Gpedit.msc, 60
grayware, 101
Group Policy, launching
    scripts at startup, 60–62
groups, user, 135–138
Guest user accounts, 135

H

hard drives
  adding second, 303–317
  as backup media,
    140–142
  checking free space, 5–7
  cleaning up, 13–19
  connectors for, 304–306
  defragmenting, 14–15
  essentials needed for
    Windows to load, 248
  freeing up additional
    space, 16–19
  imaging, 147–150
  manufacturers (table), 337
  partitioning, 7, 150,
    151, 265
  quick check of, 3
  Recovery Console
    fixes, 255–258
  scanning for startup
    errors, 40–41
  SCSI (Small Computer
    System Interface), 252
  selecting, installing,
    306–315
  upgrading notebook
    computer's, 317
hardware
  device reviews, 141,
    337–338
  devices, disabling, 54
  evaluating your need
    for, 278
  firewalls, configuring,
    185
  Internet communication
    and, 157–158
  protecting, 139
  reviews, 141, 337–338
  troubleshooting,
    224–230, 249, 266–268
Hi-Speed USB, 331
hidden files
  shared folders, 134–135